BUDDHAHOOD WITHOUT MEDITATION

Düdjom Lingpa's Visions of the Great Perfection

This three-volume series presents English translations of Düdjom Lingpa's five visionary teachings on *Dzokchen*, the Great Perfection, along with three essential commentaries by his disciples.

Volume 1. Heart of the Great Perfection

The Sharp Vajra of Conscious Awareness Tantra, Düdjom Lingpa

Essence of Clear Meaning, Pema Tashi

The Foolish Dharma of an Idiot Clothed in Mud and Feathers, Düdjom Lingpa

The Enlightened View of Samantabhadra, Düdjom Lingpa

Volume 2. Buddhahood Without Meditation

Buddhahood Without Meditation, Düdjom Lingpa

The Fine Path to Liberation, Sera Khandro

Garland for the Delight of the Fortunate, Sera Khandro

Volume 3. The Vajra Essence

The Vajra Essence, Düdjom Lingpa

Buddhahood Without Meditation

Düdjom Lingpa's Visions of the Great Perfection, Volume 2

Foreword by Sogyal Rinpoche

Translated by B. Alan Wallace

Edited by Dion Blundell

Wisdom

Wisdom Publications
199 Elm Street
Somerville, MA 02144 USA
wisdompubs.org

Library of Congress Cataloging-in-Publication Data
Bdud-'joms-glin-pa, Gter-ston, 1835–1904.
[Works. Selections. English]
Dudjom Lingpa's visions of the Great Perfection / Translated by B. Alan Wallace ; Edited by Dion Blundell.
volumes cm
Includes bibliographical references and index.
Contents: Volume 1. Heart of the Great Perfection — volume 2. Buddhahood without meditation — volume 3. The Vajra essence.
ISBN 1-61429-260-4 (pbk. : alk. paper)
1. Rdzogs-chen. I. Wallace, B. Alan. II. Title.
BQ942.D777A25 2016
294.3'420423—dc23
2014048350

ISBN 978-1-61429-346-0 ebook ISBN 978-1-61429-275-3

19 18 17 16 4 3 2 1

Cover and interior design by Gopa & Ted2, Inc.
Set in Garamond Premier Pro 10.6/13.16.
Hūṃ syllable calligraphy by Lama Chönam.

Wisdom Publications' books are printed on acid-free paper and meet the guidelines for permanence and durability of the Production Guidelines for Book Longevity of the Council on Library Resources.

This book was produced with environmental mindfulness.
For more information, please visit wisdompubs.org/wisdom-environment.

Printed in the United States of America.

MIX
Paper from responsible sources
FSC www.fsc.org FSC® C011935

Please visit fscus.org.

Contents

TASHI CHOLING

CENTER FOR BUDDHIST STUDIES

TASHICHOLING.ORG

P.O BOX 64
ASHLAND, OR 97520

VEN. GYATRUL RINPOCHE
SPIRITUAL DIRECTOR

The revelations of the great treasure revealer, enlightened master, and fearless conduct yogi from eastern Tibet Heruka Düdjom Lingpa are treasure troves of teaching, advice, and insights into the human mind's true nature of wisdom awareness. For those who connect to the lineage through empowerment, transmission, and instruction under the guidance of qualified lineage masters, these teachings hold the key to understanding the true meaning of permanent happiness and benefit. Having known Alan for many years and observed his enthusiastic devotion and passion for Dharma in general and especially for the teachings of the Great Perfection as transmitted through Heruka Düdjom Lingpa's revelations, I am certain that he has done his very best to make these translations as accurate as possible and I rejoice in this effort from the bottom of my heart. This trilogy of English translations is a wondrous gift for disciples of the tradition. May there be great waves of benefit for countless sentient beings!

Gyatrul Rinpoché
Tashi Choling

Dhomang Gyatrul

Foreword

TWELVE HUNDRED YEARS AGO, one of the most dramatic and daring spiritual undertakings in history took place in Central Asia. The entire teaching of the Buddha, as it existed at the time in India and the Himalayan region, was imported and transplanted in Tibet. Sometimes I try to imagine what it must have been like to be there at that spectacular moment. To see the unforgettable, awe-inspiring figure of Guru Rinpoché, Padmasambhava, whose protection and inspiration enabled this whole revolutionary endeavor to unfold. To witness the great Madhyamaka scholar and abbot Śāntarakṣita, who brought with him the vast heritage of Nālandā Monastery, and the Tibetan king Trisong Detsen, the thirty-seventh in his line, who sponsored this massive and imaginative program. Or to gaze in wonder as Guru Rinpoché stood atop Mount Hepori and bound the spirits of Tibet under his command, and to watch the first monastic university, called Samyé "The Inconceivable," gradually take shape. If you had been there, you would have caught sight of scores of realized and learned paṇḍitas, who had made the arduous journey across the Himalayas and were working with translators to render the sutras, tantras, and treatises into Tibetan. Transmissions of various kinds were taking place, the first seven Tibetan monastics were being ordained, and Guru Padmasambhava was opening the maṇḍala of the Secret Mantrayāna teachings at Chimpu for his twenty-five disciples. They were the first saints and siddhas of Tibet, headed by Guru Rinpoché's closest disciple and consort, Yeshé Tsogyal, the king himself, and the virtuoso translator Vairocana. What a glorious and momentous time this must have been! And although history tells us that this did not happen without opposition and resistance, both human and nonhuman, as Kyapjé Düdjom Rinpoché explains, "Because the kingdom was protected by the true Dharma, Tibet is known to have enjoyed the happiness of paradise."

For about fifty-five years, it is said, the Great Guru stayed in Tibet and the Himalayan regions, sowing his blessings into the environment and the psyche of the Tibetan people. Foreseeing the needs of future generations and the limits of people's understanding at the time, Padmasambhava concealed countless *terma* treasure teachings in the landscape and in the unchanging pure awareness of his realized disciples. The terma teachings remain concealed until the precise moment in time when they will be of maximum benefit and relevance, and they are then revealed by a continuing series of incarnations of the same twenty-five disciples whom Padmasambhava had entrusted with his teachings and his blessings. As a result, the ancient Nyingma tradition of early translations that follows Padmasambhava's vision comprises both the long, unbroken *kama* lineage of canonical teachings and the close lineage of terma treasures. And at the heart of the Nyingma tradition flows the deepest current of wisdom within the Buddhist teachings of Tibet, the pinnacle of all spiritual vehicles—the Great Perfection, *Dzokpachenpo*, with its living lineage of realization stretching from the Primordial Buddha Samantabhadra down to the present day.

One of Guru Rinpoché's twenty-five disciples showed remarkable aptitude at a very early age. He learned Sanskrit with ease and was quickly chosen to be part of the group of Tibetan translators. Drokpen Khyeuchung Lotsawa lived as a *ngakpa*, a lay mantric practitioner, wearing his hair long and dressing in white. He mastered all the secret Mantrayāna teachings Padmasambhava conferred on him and became a great siddha. His realization and power were such that he could summon birds from the sky through his mere gaze or a gesture of his hand, and then, it is said, give them teachings. Like others among the twenty-five disciples, Khyeuchung Lotsawa reincarnated over the centuries as a series of realized masters who spread and deepened the teachings of the Buddha and brought enormous benefit to beings. In the nineteenth century he appeared as the great treasure revealer, visionary, and powerful mystic Düdjom Lingpa.

I first came to learn about this amazing master after meeting his incarnation, Kyapjé Düdjom Rinpoché, who became one of my most beloved teachers. I discovered that everything about Düdjom Lingpa was extraordinary: his birth in 1835 in the Serta Valley of the Golok region on Guru Rinpoché's day, the tenth day of the waxing moon; his amazing life story, which was a continuous stream of visions, dreams, and prophecies starting at the age of three; the way in which he received visionary teachings of the greatest depth and clarity directly from enlightened beings of every kind; his mastery of earth termas, mind termas, and pure visions; the sheer profundity of his revelations, such as those contained in these volumes; his visits to pure lands, including Sukhāvatī and the Copper Colored Mountain paradise of Guru Rinpoché—a visit that spanned one human day but for him lasted twelve years; and his continuous perception of enlightened beings and pure realms.

No less astounding was the way in which he predicted his own incarnation, Düdjom Rinpoché Jikdral Yeshé Dorjé. Having spent most of his life in eastern Tibet and the Golok area, Düdjom Lingpa received a number of visionary instructions that he should go to Pemakö, perhaps the most famous of the "hidden lands" of Padmasambhava and one that had been opened by Düdjom Lingpa's earlier incarnation, Rikzin Düdul Dorjé (1615–72). It lay far to the southeast and was a region of legendary, majestic beauty and sacred significance. There, Guru Rinpoché said, "All the mountains open like blossoming flowers, all the rivers naturally resound mantras and flow with nectar, and rainbows arch across the trees and bushes." During his lifetime, Düdjom Lingpa was unable to travel to Pemakö. Yet he knew of the devastation that within decades would ravage Tibet, and not long before he passed away in 1904, he called his disciples together and told them to pack up and leave for Pemakö: "Now in this final age of degeneration, it's time to go to the hidden land of Pemakö. Anyone who puts his or her trust in me should go there as well. But this old man will get there before you youngsters arrive!"

Just as he predicted, when his disciples eventually made their way to Pemakö, they discovered a three-year-old child who called them by name, spoke not in the local language but in the Golok dialect, and had already asked his parents to prepare for a party of guests. The young boy was Düdjom Lingpa's reincarnation. It is said that Düdjom Rinpoché was conceived while Düdjom Lingpa was still alive, for there are no limits that can possibly impede the enlightened mind.

As I pay homage here to Düdjom Lingpa, I would like to take this opportunity to share a few of my memories of Kyapjé Düdjom Rinpoché, whom I had the privilege and blessing of knowing personally. I first met him thanks to my master Jamyang Khyentsé Chökyi Lodrö. He always used to talk about what a wonderful and realized master Düdjom Rinpoché was, and how he was the living representative of Guru Padmasambhava. They held each other in the highest esteem. In Lhasa, where they met in the 1950s, Düdjom Rinpoché confided to Trulshik Rinpoché that he considered Jamyang Khyentsé the holiest master they could ever hope to find. Düdjom Rinpoché moved to Kalimpong in India in around 1957, and my master took me to meet him and receive his blessing. Jamyang Khyentsé told him he had never had the privilege of receiving the entire transmission of his terma revelations and asked him for a special blessing. Düdjom Rinpoché gave him the "seal of authorization" for all of his own terma treasures. He also conferred on Jamyang Khyentsé the empowerments and instructions for his mind treasure of Dorjé Drolö, the wild, wrathful aspect of Guru Padmasambhava. They wrote long-life prayers for each other. My master spoke of Düdjom Rinpoché as "the authentic great Sovereign Lord of the extraordinary and profound secret terma treasures." Düdjom Rinpoché called him "the sole champion in our time of the great and supreme path of the Vajra Heart Essence, the magical wisdom manifestation of the lotus-born lord Padmasambhava and Vimalamitra."

Some years later, I went to visit Düdjom Rinpoché in Kalimpong and by coincidence found myself translating for one of his American disciples. It was then that I realized just how extraordinary he was. By the end of his teaching, a pointing-out instruction on the nature of mind, tears were running down my face, and I understood what Jamyang Khyentsé had meant when he said this was an exceptional master. I instantly felt enormous faith in him, and there and then I requested Düdjom Rinpoché to be my master and grant me teachings.

Düdjom Lingpa's revelations and Düdjom Rinpoché's terma cycles are together known as the *Düdjom Tersar*, the "New Treasures of Düdjom," which are new in the sense that they are still fresh with the warm breath of the ḍākinīs, and because there is only one master in the lineage between Guru Rinpoché and the practitioners of the treasures. Although I see these two great masters as one and the same, their outward characters were quite different. Düdjom Lingpa was a commanding and unpredictable figure, well known for his wrathful demeanor and behavior. Düdjom Rinpoché describes how to visualize him: "His body is red in color, his beard reaching as far as his heart, and his eyes are open wide, staring steadily straight ahead. His long hair is mostly tied up in a knot on top of his head with a small sacred book, while the rest tumbles loosely over his shoulders. He wears a gown of reddish brown silk, a shawl of white cotton, and conch-shell earrings, with a sword of wisdom thrust through his belt. His right hand wields a vajra in the sky, and his left hand rolls a *purba* dagger of meteoric iron. He sits with his left leg stretched out slightly in the posture of royal play."

In marked contrast, Düdjom Rinpoché had about him an air of captivating kindness, gentleness, and serenity. In fact, he used to tell a story about his predecessor that always brought a twinkle to his eye. When Düdjom Lingpa was about to pass away and leave this world, some of his disciples approached him timidly and begged him to return in a more peaceful form. He chuckled and said, "Well, all right. But don't complain if I am *too* peaceful."

Like his previous incarnation, Düdjom Rinpoché was a very great Dzokchen master. It is said of him that he was the body emanation of Khyeuchung Lotsawa, the speech emanation of Yeshé Tsogyal, and the mind emanation of Guru Padmasambhava. In *The Tibetan Book of Living and Dying*, I tried to sum up some of his characteristics: "He was small, with a beautiful and gentle face, exquisite hands, and a delicate, almost feminine presence. Like a yogin, he wore his hair long and tied up in a knot; his eyes always glittered with secret amusement. His voice seemed the voice of compassion itself, soft and a little hoarse." One of Padmasambhava's terma prophecies captured his qualities with remarkable prescience: "In a noble family there will appear an emanation of Khyeuchung Lotsawa bearing the name Jñāna, keeping the yogic discipline of a master of mantras, his appearance not fixed in any way, his behavior spontaneous like a child, and endowed with piercing wisdom. He will reveal new termas and safeguard the ancient ones, and he will guide whoever has a connection with him to the Glorious Copper Colored Mountain in Ngayab Ling."

Düdjom Rinpoché, I learned, began receiving termas when he was a young boy, and he met Guru Rinpoché and Yeshé Tsogyal in a vision when he was only thirteen. Although he revealed his own powerful terma treasures, he decided to prioritize maintaining, protecting, and spreading the older termas as well as the kama tradition of the Nyingmapas. While still quite young, he was regarded as a supreme master of the Great Perfection, and by the time he was in his thirties he had already accomplished an enormous amount. When other lamas saw his famous prayer *Calling the Lama from Afar*, which he composed at the age of thirty and which captured completely his profound realization, they immediately recognized him as a great tertön and Dzokchen master. Chökyi Nyima Rinpoché told me that his father, Tulku Urgyen Rinpoché, one of the greatest teachers of Dzokchen and Mahāmudrā in recent times, used to say that if anyone ever wondered what a true Dzokchen master and practitioner was like, they only had to look at Düdjom Rinpoché. His eyes always sparkled with a kind of freshness and vibrant clarity. Unencumbered by opinions of good or bad, and ever carefree, spacious, and relaxed, Düdjom Rinpoché had about him a child-like innocence—you could call it an enlightened purity.

His work in compiling the Nyingma kama, which he began at the age of seventy-four, paralleled the achievement of Jamgön Kongtrul in compiling the treasure teachings in the *Precious Treasury of Termas*. He saved many precious texts and sacred relics from loss, and with meticulous care, he compiled, preserved, emended, and annotated the older texts and practices, to the extent that there seems hardly anything he did not have a hand in perfecting. In fact Düdjom Rinpoché's achievements for the Nyingma tradition as a whole were monumental. He gave the transmission of the *Precious Treasury of Termas* ten times, and he transmitted the kama and *The Hundred Thousand Tantras of the Nyingmapas* as well as countless treasure cycles and priceless teachings. Unanimously requested to become the supreme head of the Nyingma tradition, his own revelations and writings fill twenty-five volumes, among which his *History of the Nyingmapas* and *Fundamentals of the Nyingmapas* are classics. His compositions were amazing, his scholarship famous, his calligraphy much copied, his poetry lucid yet profound, and his detailed knowledge of every aspect of Vajrayāna practice and ritual truly phenomenal.

Düdjom Rinpoché also played a huge part in reestablishing Tibetan culture and education in exile, and he composed his *History of Tibet* at the request of His Holiness the Dalai Lama. On occasion, His Holiness has expressed his regret at not having been able to receive transmissions directly from Düdjom Rinpoché, although when he embarked on a retreat on the Kagyé—Eight Great Practice Maṇḍalas—according to the *sangwa gyachen* pure visions of the Great Fifth Dalai Lama, Düdjom Rinpoché wrote a practice guide for him that he found outstanding. Among Düdjom Rinpoché's countless disciples were the most eminent lamas of the last century, including the most senior masters of Mindröling and Dorjé Drak monasteries, and he had innumerable followers all over Tibet and the Himalayas, Europe, America, Taiwan, and Hong Kong. When he gave the transmission of the *New Treasures of Düdjom* at Boudhanath in Nepal in 1977–78, thousands upon thousands flocked to attend.

After my master Jamyang Khyentsé passed away, Düdjom Rinpoché held me with all his care and compassion, and I had the great privilege of serving as his translator for a number of years. I quickly discovered that he had a unique way of inspiring the realization of the innermost nature of mind. It was through the very way he spoke. The words he used were simple and down to earth, and yet they had a way of penetrating right into your heart. As the instructions on the nature of mind flowed effortlessly from his wisdom mind, it seemed as if he became the teaching of Dzokpachenpo itself, and his words served to gather you into the actual experience. Through his presence, and through his gaze, he created a subtle but electrifying atmosphere, enveloping you in his wisdom mind, so that you could not help but feel the pure awareness that he was pointing out. I can only compare it to sitting in front of a blazing, open fire—you cannot help but feel warm. It was as simple as that.

Düdjom Rinpoché demonstrated, again and again, that when a great master directs the blessing of his wisdom mind, something extraordinary and very powerful can take place. All your ordinary thoughts and thinking are disarmed, and you arrive face to face with the deeper nature—the original face—of your own mind. In Düdjom Rinpoché's words, "all the stirrings of discursive thoughts melt, dissolve, and slip into the expanse of *rigpa*, your pure awareness, which is like a cloudless sky. All their power and strength is lost to the rigpa awareness." At that moment everything drops, a completely different dimension opens up, and you glimpse the sky-like nature of mind. With Düdjom Rinpoché I came to understand that what the master does, through the power and blessing of his realization, is to make the naked truth of the teaching come alive in you, connecting you to your buddha nature. And you? You recognize, in a blaze of gratitude, that there is not, and could never be, any separation between the master's wisdom mind and the nature of your own mind. Düdjom Rinpoché said just this in his *Calling the Lama from Afar*:

> Since pure awareness of nowness is the real buddha,
> in openness and contentment I found the lama in my heart.
> When we realize this unending natural mind is the very nature of the lama,
> then there is no need for attached, grasping, or weeping prayers or artificial complaints.
> By simply relaxing in this uncontrived, open, and natural state,
> we obtain the blessing of aimless self-liberation of whatever arises.

At the same time, Düdjom Rinpoché wore his realization and learning with such simplicity and ease. I sometimes felt that his outward appearance was so subtle and understated that it would have been easy for a newcomer to miss who he really was. Once in 1976 I traveled with him from France to the United States. I shall never forget that flight for as long as I live. Düdjom Rinpoché was always very humble, but now and then he would say something that betrayed what an incredible master he was. At one point I was sitting next to him and he was gazing out the window at the Atlantic Ocean when he said quietly, "May I bless all those I fly over, all the beings living in the ocean down below." It was the way he said it that struck me and sent a shiver down my spine. I could feel that there was simply no question: He actually did possess the power to bless and relieve the suffering of countless living beings. And beyond any shadow of doubt, there and then, they were receiving his blessing. In that moment I realized what a great master he was—and not just a master, but a buddha.

To tell the truth, even now, thirty years or so since he left this world, Düdjom Rinpoché's greatness still continues to dawn on me, day after day. The gratitude I feel toward him is boundless, and not a day goes by when I do not think of his words:

> Having purified the great delusion, the heart's darkness,
> the radiant light of the unobscured sun continuously rises.
> This good fortune is the kindness of the lama, our only father and mother;
> Lama of unrepayable kindness, I only remember you.

I must also mark my gratitude to Düdjom Rinpoché's spiritual wife, Sangyum

Kushok Rikzin Wangmo, who was one of the greatest ḍākinīs I have ever known. She played a unique and crucial role in Rinpoché's life. With her extraordinary love, care, and magnetic charm, she provided the perfect environment for Rinpoché, so that the teachings and revelations could pour from his wisdom mind. She lengthened his life and enabled him to stay among us for as long as he did, longer in fact than had been predicted by his masters, so as to teach, guide, and bless so many disciples and benefit countless sentient beings. Not only do I have the greatest devotion and respect for her but also a deep feeling of love, and I feel honored that both she and Rinpoché made me truly feel like part of their family.

How impossible it seems to try to measure in words the qualities and realization of masters like Düdjom Lingpa and Düdjom Rinpoché! Even their contributions to the future of the Dharma, I feel, are fathomless and not widely known. The longer I live, the more convinced I am that the Dzokchen teachings have enormous potential at this time to touch and awaken people *all over the world*, people from any country and any kind of background. I have heard a number of prophecies about these teachings and how powerful, transformative, and relevant they are at critical points in our history—at times such as this. One prophecy says, "In this dark age, the heart essence of Samantabhadra will blaze like fire." If these predictions are to come true, I know it will have a lot to do with the two great masters Düdjom Lingpa and Düdjom Rinpoché and their epic contributions to the Dharma, to sentient beings, and to the world.

Just look at the impact of their work: Düdjom Lingpa's prolific treasures have spread all over Tibet, east and west, the Himalayan lands like Bhutan, and now the Western world as well. His revelations, edited by Düdjom Rinpoché himself, fill twenty large volumes. Then, Düdjom Lingpa's eight sons were all incarnations of great masters, perhaps the most renowned being Jikmé Tenpé Nyima, the Third Dodrupchen Rinpoché, who was my master Jamyang Khyentsé's root lama, and whose writings on Dzokchen are treasured by H. H. the Dalai Lama. Düdjom Lingpa's daughters were considered to be ḍākinīs. It was not only his children who were exceptional but his students as well. In the prayer that Düdjom Rinpoché composed celebrating Düdjom Lingpa's extraordinary life story, there is this verse:

> Your eight sons, holders of the family line, were the eight great bodhisattvas,
> thirteen supreme disciples accomplished the body of light,
> and one thousand attained the stage of vidyādhara—
> to you, who established this victorious line of realized beings, I pray.

Thirteen of Düdjom Lingpa's disciples attained the rainbow body, and in his prophecies Düdjom Lingpa was told that a hundred might even attain the great transference rainbow body. As Düdjom Rinpoché wrote, "In this precious lineage of ours, this is not just ancient history. For today, just as in the past, there are those who through the paths of *trekchö* and *tögal* have attained the final realization and have dissolved their gross material bodies into rainbow bodies of radiant light." In his *History*, he wrote, "It is impossible to estimate the number of those who passed into the rainbow body by following the paths of the profound treasures of the Great Perfection..." and he lists a number of those who attained the rainbow body, including the father of my own tutor Lama Gyurdrak, a simple man called Sönam Namgyal whose body dissolved into light, leaving nothing behind but his nails and hair. These were offered to Jamyang Khyentsé, who verified it as an actual case of a rainbow body. Even today we continue to hear of instances of the rainbow body, for example the well-known case of Khenpo Achö in eastern Tibet in 1998.

There is a story about Düdjom Lingpa that I find fascinating. In the mid 1850s he had a dream in which he was given a conch shell and asked to blow it in each of the four directions. The loudest sound was in the west, and he was told in the dream that this was a sign that disciples particularly suited to him were to be found in the western regions, where his renown would spread and where he would have countless followers in the future.

Something uncannily similar happened to Düdjom Rinpoché, and he told us the story many years later, in France. One of the lamas who had traveled to Pemakö to find Düdjom Lingpa's incarnation was Ling Lama Orgyen Chöjor Gyatso, an accomplished Dzokchen master who had been a disciple of Patrul Rinpoché before becoming a close student of Düdjom Lingpa. He was one of Düdjom Rinpoché's first teachers. He told Düdjom Rinpoché that Patrul Rinpoché had asked Düdjom Lingpa's son Jikmé Tenpé Nyima, the Third Dodrupchen, to give a teaching on the *Guide to the Bodhisattva Way of Life* at the age of eight. Orgyen Chöjor Gyatso reasoned that if the son could do so at eight, then the father—in other words Düdjom Lingpa's reincarnation—should do so by the age of seven and a half at the latest. So he requested Düdjom Rinpoché to teach from the first chapters of Śāntideva's great work. When the teaching had finished, Orgyen Chöjor Gyatso was overjoyed, and he invited Düdjom Rinpoché to go outside and sound a conch in each of the four directions. In the south there was a beautiful tone, but in the west an even louder and sweeter sound rang out. Orgyen Chöjor Gyatso told him that his work would be of immeasurable benefit in the south and in the west.

Thinking of this, how meaningful it is that Düdjom Rinpoché came and taught and blessed so many people in the West. And how moving it is that he chose to pass away in Europe, in France, thereby blessing the Western world with the power of his enlightenment and confirming the arrival of these teachings in lands that had not known them before. The fact that Sangyum Kushok Rikzin Wangmo also chose to leave this world in the United States points to the same truth. It is as if they were placing their seal on Düdjom Rinpoché's celebrated aspiration:

> May the living tradition of Guru Padmasambhava, Bodhisattva Śāntarakṣita, and the Dharma-king Trisong Detsen
> spread throughout the world in all directions.
> May the Buddha, Dharma, and Saṅgha be present in the minds of all,
> inseparably, at all times, bringing peace, happiness, and well-being.

Just as Düdjom Rinpoché's life covered most of the twentieth century, Düdjom Lingpa's spanned the nineteenth century, a time when a number of great masters were pioneering a far-reaching renewal of Buddhism in Tibet, in the open-minded, ecumenical spirit of *Rimé*. They included masters such as Jamyang Khyentsé Wangpo, Jamgön Kongtrul Lodrö Thayé, Chokgyur Dechen Lingpa, and Jamgön Mipam Rinpoché. Interestingly, it was Jamyang Khyentsé Wangpo who sent his own close disciple, the incarnate lama Gyurmé Ngedön Wangpo, to Düdjom Lingpa. He told him: "You have a karmic link with Düdjom Lingpa from past lives, so meeting him will be enormously useful to the teachings and to beings." Gyurmé Ngedön Wangpo became the great treasure revealer's heart son and custodian of his treasures, and he stayed with him until he passed away. He then traveled to Pemakö, where he recognized Kyapjé Düdjom Rinpoché as the reincarnation of Düdjom Lingpa, became his root lama, and gave him many of the most important transmissions, including Düdjom Lingpa's revelations.

My own predecessor, the treasure revealer Lerab Lingpa, who was born in 1856, was somewhat younger than Düdjom Lingpa, and I know of no record of their having met. And yet their lives were mysteriously entwined. Lerab Lingpa was a very close confidant, student, and teacher of Dodrupchen Jikmé Tenpé Nyima, Düdjom Lingpa's eldest son, and he was also the master of Düdjom Lingpa's youngest son, Dorjé Dradul, as well as three of Düdjom Lingpa's grandsons, Terchen Kunzang Nyima, Sönam Deutsen, and Tenzin Nyima. In fact, Lerab Lingpa composed and gave to Dorjé Dradul a guru yoga practice that focuses on the lama as embodying the Primordial Buddha Samantabhadra, Guru Padmasambhava, Dorjé Drolö, Düdul Dorjé, Düdjom Lingpa, Jikmé Tenpé Nyima and himself. On another occasion, one day in 1923, Lerab Lingpa experienced a vision of Guru Rinpoché and a throng of ḍākinīs, who gave him a five-part *ladrup*—a sādhana practice for accomplishing the lama—in which Düdjom Lingpa, Khanyam Lingpa, Jamyang Khyentsé Wangpo, Kusum Lingpa, and Jamgön Kongtrul each appear in the form of a deity. Düdjom Lingpa manifests as Dorjé Drolö. In the vision, Lerab Lingpa was told how urgent it was that he accomplish this practice.

The more we look, the more it seems that Düdjom Lingpa's impact on the spread of the Buddha's teachings is endless, and we can detect his traces everywhere. There is one more intriguing link between Düdjom Lingpa and Terchen Lerab Lingpa, one that had a momentous significance for the flourishing of the Dharma. In 1980, the great Khenchen Jigmé Phuntsok Rinpoché (1933–2004), one of the incarnations of Lerab Lingpa, founded his Buddhist Academy in the Larung Valley in Serta. He built his own residence on the very same site as Düdjom Lingpa's hermitage, a place also associated with the thirteen disciples who attained the rainbow body. One of Düdjom Lingpa's prophecies had in fact predicted that after a hundred years, when only the name of the Buddhadharma remained, in this very place a master would come to fan the flames of the embers and make the Nyingma teachings blaze once more. It was there that the truly remarkable Larung Gar Five Sciences Buddhist Academy developed, a center of excellence setting the highest standards of study and practice, seeing six hundred fully trained khenpos graduate in the first twenty years, and putting in motion a renaissance of Buddhist teaching and practice in eastern Tibet.

I am deeply touched to be asked to write this foreword to a collection of translations of Düdjom Lingpa's Dzokchen teachings, and I do so out of my deep and undying devotion to Kyapjé Düdjom Rinpoché and Sangyum Rikzin Wangmo, to his lineage, and to all the masters who hold it. This is a major achievement, as these teachings are legendary because of their profundity and completeness. As Düdjom Rinpoché wrote: "Even if you were to actually meet Samantabhadra, I swear that he would not say a single word other than these." Alan Wallace has made a great contribution in translating these precious teachings, and I am moved by the fact that he is not simply a very experienced translator but also someone who is a deeply conscientious and dedicated practitioner, one who has a knowledge of many Buddhist traditions but has found his home in these extraordinary treasures of the lineage of Düdjom Lingpa. How wonderful as well that he has translated the brilliant clarifications provided by the great Sera Khandro and Pema Tashi.

The profound teachings in these volumes speak for themselves, and there is no need to elaborate on their contents. But to highlight a few crucial points, I believe that the teachings of Dzokpachenpo need to be approached with great care, reverence, and maturity. First, we need to recognize just how rare, how precious, and how deep they are, as they actually possess the capacity to bring realization and even liberation in one lifetime. As Düdjom Rinpoché wrote, "Don't throw away such a precious jewel as this and then look around for semiprecious stones. Now that you have had such great good fortune as to have met this profound teaching, the very heart blood of the ḍākinīs, your mind should be uplifted and you should practice with tremendous inspiration and joy."

As we can see, Düdjom Lingpa's revelations explicitly spell out the qualities we need in order to embrace this path and practice these teachings. They include devotion and pure perception, trust and faith, a keen understanding of impermanence and cause and effect, contentment and disenchantment with mundane distractions, compassion and bodhicitta motivation, honesty and courage, commitment and single-minded enthusiasm, and the ability to see the appearances of this life as dreamlike and integrate the practice into everyday life.

Düdjom Rinpoché would always encourage students to embrace the *ngöndro* practice, saying how profound and important it is: "A full understanding and realization of the true essence of Dzokpachenpo depends *entirely* on these preliminary practices. In particular it is vital to put all your energy into the practice of guru yoga, holding on to it as the life and the heart of the practice." In these remarkable teachings, Düdjom Lingpa gives direct instructions about how to consider the master as Guru Padmasambhava in person, see him as the nature of our own clear-light rigpa awareness, and through the practice of guru yoga, unite our mind with his wisdom mind. "By merging your mind with his," he says, "you will experience the nonconceptual primordial consciousness of ultimate reality, and extraordinary realizations will arise in your mindstream."

And so I encourage you from the bottom of my heart, if you have not already done so, to seek out qualified lamas of this lineage and receive the necessary empowerments, oral transmissions, and instructions for these sacred and profound teachings so that you can put them into practice and proceed along the sublime path of Dzokpachenpo. It is our great good fortune that the New Treasure lineage of Düdjom Lingpa and Düdjom Rinpoché thrives today, thanks to the kindness and enlightened vision of their own incarnations, their family lineages, and the masters who hold these precious teachings, allowing them to resound all over the world. The prophecy of the conch shell is playing out before our very eyes.

Finally, let me take this opportunity to pray that this great Nyingma lineage and the tradition of the two extraordinary masters Düdjom Lingpa and Düdjom Rinpoché may continue in the future, going from strength to strength, touching countless sentient beings, and awakening them to their own enlightened nature—the indestructible heart essence. May all the visions and aspirations of Düdjom Lingpa and Düdjom Rinpoché be accomplished, as fully and as quickly as possible. I believe that these two great masters continue to bless the whole world. Freed from physical form, they abide in the unconditioned timeless splendor of the dharmakāya, benefitting all beings beyond the limitations of time and space, and I know that if we call upon them now with all our hearts, we will find them with us instantly. So I pray that with their blessings the lives of all the great masters may be safe and strong, and that the precious teachings of the Buddha may flourish and spread, to pacify conflict, suffering, and negativity all over the world, to bring peace and tranquility, and to ensure the welfare and happiness of living beings everywhere. And may all of us who are striving to follow and practice the sublime teachings of the clear-light Dzokpachenpo progress in our realization, overcome all obstacles, and finally seize the stronghold of Samantabhadra!

Sogyal Rinpoche

Publisher's Acknowledgment

THE PUBLISHER gratefully acknowledges the generous contribution of the Hershey Family Foundation toward the publication of this book.

Preface

HERUKA DÜDJOM LINGPA (1835–1904) was one of the foremost tantric masters of nineteenth-century Tibet. His written works include five visionary texts describing the path to perfect enlightenment from the unexcelled perspective of the Great Perfection, or Dzokchen. This series includes these five seminal texts, along with three essential commentaries by his disciples. They all reveal the same path to realizing the rainbow body in this very lifetime, but each one offers different degrees of detail and highlights different aspects of the path. Dzokchen's essential terminology and practices are clearly explained while potential misunderstandings and errors are systematically eliminated. Together they constitute a vast wealth of practical guidance and pith instructions concerning the view, meditation, and conduct of Dzokchen, the pinnacle of the Nyingma school of Tibetan Buddhism. These revered teachings have inspired generations of Tibetans, yet only one has become well known to English speakers, thanks to Richard Barron's popular translation of *Buddhahood Without Meditation*.[1]

These translations were developed and refined over many years. I served as interpreter for Venerable Gyatrul Rinpoché and translated several Dzokchen texts under his guidance beginning in 1990. In 1995, while living with him in the hills above Half Moon Bay, California, I asked whether he would like me to translate any other text. "How about the *Vajra Essence*?" he replied. "Sure!" I said, without knowing anything about these teachings received by Düdjom Lingpa in pure visions (Tib. *dag snang*) of the "Lake-Born Vajra" manifestation of Padmasambhava. Reading the text for the first time, I knew that I had found my heart's desire: a presentation of the entire path to enlightenment that was coherent, integrated, and richly informative. I was profoundly inspired—I felt that if I were marooned alone on a proverbial desert island with only one book to read, this would be it!

1. Dudjom Lingpa, *Buddhahood Without Meditation: A Visionary Account Known as Refining One's Perception (Nang-jang)*, trans. Richard Barron and Susanne Fairclough (Junction City, CA: Padma Publishing, 2006).

Between 1995 and 1998, I translated it under his guidance. Then I served as his interpreter as he explained the text line by line to a hand-picked group of his close disciples, enabling me to correct errors in my translation and clear up points of lingering uncertainty in my comprehension.[2]

In 1972, Gyatrul Rinpoché was chosen by His Holiness the Dalai Lama and His Holiness Düdjom Rinpoché, Jikdral Yeshé Dorjé (1904–87), to be the Nyingmapa representative accompanying the first group of Tibetans resettling in Canada. In 1976, Düdjom Rinpoché appointed him as his spiritual representative for America and as director of Pacific Region Yeshe Nyingpo, his network of Dharma centers. For decades Gyatrul Rinpoché has taught students, established Dharma centers, and trained teachers and translators according to traditional methods and with deep understanding of the needs of his Western disciples. Gyatrul Rinpoché received the oral transmission of the *Vajra Essence* three times from three of Düdjom Lingpa's emanations: In Tibet he received it from his root guru, Jamyang Natsok Rangdröl (1904–58), recognized as the enlightened activity emanation of Düdjom Lingpa, and from Dzongter Kunzang Nyima (1904–58), Düdjom Lingpa's enlightened speech emanation and grandson. Later in Nepal he received it from Düdjom Rinpoché, the enlightened mind emanation of Düdjom Lingpa.

In 1998 I served as Rinpoché's interpreter as he gave the oral transmission and his commentary to the *Foolish Dharma of an Idiot Clothed in Mud and Feathers* to a small group of his close disciples. He asked that this be translated and made available to sincere, qualified Dharma students.[3] Rinpoché authorized me to teach all the texts he taught me, and several years later I taught the opening section of the *Vajra Essence* to a small group of students in Wales. Between teaching sessions, I began reading the text immediately following the *Vajra Essence* in Düdjom Lingpa's collected works, his *Enlightened View of Samantabhadra*. I had already concluded from the *Vajra Essence* that among the wide range of meditations explained in that text, only four were absolutely indispensable on the Dzokchen path: śamatha, vipaśyanā, cutting through, and direct crossing over. The *Enlightened View of Samantabhadra*,

2. This resulted in the publication of the first edition of the *Vajra Essence* a few years later: Düdjom Lingpa, *The Vajra Essence: From the Matrix of Pure Appearances and Primordial Consciousness, a Tantra on the Self-Originating Nature of Existence*, trans. B. Alan Wallace (Alameda, CA: Mirror of Wisdom, 2004).

3. This was published as the first text in Dudjom Rinpoche and Dudjom Lingpa, *Sublime Dharma: A Compilation of Two Texts on the Great Perfection*, trans. Chandra Easton and B. Alan Wallace (Ashland, OR: Vimala Publishing, 2012), 17–52.

presenting the entire path to enlightenment in one lifetime, focused on just those four practices, which reaffirmed my conclusion from the *Vajra Essence*.

Not long afterward, while teaching the opening section of the *Enlightened View of Samantabhadra* to a small group of students gathered for a retreat in the high desert of eastern California, I described how I had been deeply moved by my first encounter with this text—the very heart of the *Vajra Essence* presented with great clarity and brevity. A student then asked, "What comes next in that volume?" When I checked, I discovered the *Sharp Vajra of Conscious Awareness Tantra* and its commentary. This is the most quintessential and concise of Düdjom Lingpa's visionary texts, summarizing each of the four essential stages of the path with breathtaking clarity. I felt I had no choice but to translate the *Enlightened View of Samantabhadra* and the *Sharp Vajra of Conscious Awareness Tantra* and its commentary, and with Rinpoché's encouragement I did so.

In the summer of 2005, in Ojai, California, Gyatrul Rinpoché gave the oral transmission and a brief commentary on *Buddhahood Without Meditation*, for which I served as interpreter. With his encouragement I translated the text along with Sera Khandro's commentary, enabled by a generous grant from Dzongsar Khyentse Rinpoché, the son of Thinley Norbu Rinpoché and grandson of Düdjom Rinpoché.

Acknowledgments

The mission of transmitting the authentic Buddhadharma to the modern world has been led by H. H. the Dalai Lama, and the dissemination of the Nyingma tradition in particular was the lifelong work of Düdjom Lingpa's incarnation His Holiness Düdjom Rinpoché, who blessed us with his scholarship and wisdom, established Dharma centers, and taught many of today's lamas. The present translations were inspired by Venerable Gyatrul Rinpoché, who transmitted and explicated these peerless teachings. Lama Tharchin Rinpoché kindly granted me permission to listen to his oral commentary on the *Sharp Vajra of Conscious Awareness Tantra* given during his 2013 retreat on the practice of cutting through at Pema Osel Ling in California. I gratefully received the oral transmissions of the *Sharp Vajra of Conscious Awareness Tantra* and the *Enlightened View of Samantabhadra* from Tulku Orgyen Phuntsok.

I have received much help and guidance from many Dharma friends and mentors as I prepared these translations, and I have done my best to render these sacred texts in English. I am deeply grateful to Dion Blundell, who has tirelessly devoted himself with sincere faith and altruism to editing my translations. His assistance has been invaluable. However, flaws in the translation may well remain, and I ask that scholars, translators, and contemplatives who identify any errors bring them to my attention so that they can be corrected in any future editions of these works.

Technical Notes

My goal in translating these sublime treasure teachings has been to render them as accurately and clearly as possible, without omitting or adding anything. In discussing the profound nature of reality, the Great Perfection literature presents significant challenges for the translator. It employs its own special vocabulary in addition to the highly developed general lexicon of Buddhism. Because these are early days in the translating of the Dharma into English, many terms have not yet become standardized. I have noted the Tibetan and Sanskrit equivalents of key terms to assist readers familiar with other translation choices. Many Sanskrit terms that were translated into Tibetan have become well known, and I have used these original terms where their English equivalents are unsettled or awkward: for example, *kāya* instead of "enlightened body" to refer to embodiments of enlightenment.

As a further challenge, it is not uncommon for a single Tibetan term to refer to both the ultimate and the relative natures of its referent—ultimate truth and relative truth—depending on the context. One example is the Tibetan term *rigpa* (*rig pa*, Skt. *vidyā*), which sometimes refers to ordinary awareness, or cognizance. In other contexts it refers to pristine awareness, which is none other than the *primordial consciousness* (Tib. *ye shes*, Skt. *jñāna*) that is transcendently present in the ground of being. The Sanskrit term *jñāna*, in turn, also has ultimate and relative meanings, depending on the context. On the ultimate level, *jñāna* is primordial consciousness, but at the level of relative truth it simply means "knowledge," as in the two accumulations of merit and knowledge. In Buddhist psychology it simply refers to the basic knowing function of the mind.

Similarly, the Sanskrit term *dhātu* carries multiple meanings, with both ultimate and relative senses. It can mean "space" (Tib. *dbyings*) or "domain" (Tib. *khams*), but more typically in these works it is an abbreviation of *dharmadhātu*, translated as the *absolute space of phenomena*, the ground of being that is inseparable from primordial consciousness. In other cases, however, *dharmadhātu* has a more mundane meaning as the relative *space of awareness*, which is synonymous with "element of phenomena" throughout these translations. This dharmadhātu is the range of phenomena that can be perceived by mental consciousness and is one of the eighteen elements (Tib. *khams*, Skt. *dhātu*) commonly cited in Buddhist phenomenology.

Definitions of key terms are embedded throughout these texts as *contextual etymologies* (Tib. *nges tshig*), which gloss each component of the Tibetan term, unlike the linguistic etymologies commonly found in dictionaries. The term being etymologized is given in a footnote because it manifests in Tibetan only as a sequence of marked components, whose English equivalents are italicized in the text. The results in English may not be as elegant as the Tibetan constructions, but the core vocabulary of Dzokchen is defined succinctly and powerfully, in a variety of ways, throughout our texts.

Tibetan compositions are often endowed with brief or extensive outlines (Tib. *sa bcad*), but they don't always appear explicitly. Topics are simply listed as they come up. Lacking the typographical features English readers expect, a Tibetan text can be very difficult to peruse without first understanding its outline. The *Sharp Vajra of Conscious Awareness Tantra* may be considered the root text of these revealed teachings not only for its brevity and profundity but also for its outline, consisting of eight progressive *phases* (Tib. *skabs*) in the unsurpassed path of the Great Perfection. Pema Tashi's commentary includes a detailed outline built around these eight phases. But the longer explanations in the *Enlightened View of Samantabhadra* and the more elaborate *Vajra Essence* have come to us as transcripts with no divisions whatsoever. As an aid to navigation, we have indicated the phase headings of the root text in these two longer texts, where they are implicit. In the *Vajra Essence*, additional headings were suggested by the text itself or taken from *Essence of Clear Meaning*. Furthermore, many of that commentary's key passages clearly derive from the *Enlightened View of Samantabhadra* and the *Vajra Essence*; such quotations are not cited in the Tibetan, but many have been noted here. Comparisons between the parallel sections and passages in our texts will clarify understanding and drive home the essential points.

Our texts are found in the *Collected Works of the Emanated Great Treasures, the Secret Profound Treasures of Düdjom Lingpa.*[4] My translations are based on the computer-input edition of that collection published in 2004 by Lama Kuenzang Wangdue of Bhutan, known as Lopon Nikula, who was Düdjom Rinpoché's senior disciple and personal secretary for many years. The colophons of several of our texts show that Düdjom Rinpoché himself edited them for publishing. The process of converting texts from woodblock prints into digital form is critical for the accurate preservation of the vast and profound literature of Tibetan Buddhism. We are fortunate beneficiaries of the many lamas, monks, and laypeople who are engaged in this mission. In particular, Gene Smith, who founded the Tibetan Buddhist Resource Center, established an extensive library of scanned and computer-input editions

4. The Tibetan Buddhist Resource Center (www.tbrc.org) identifies this as W28732.

of Tibetan Buddhist works, making them available online to current and future generations of scholars and practitioners.

Tibetan names and terms are spelled phonetically in the body of the texts, with Wylie transliteration given in parentheses. Sanskrit terms include diacritics to give readers an appreciation for the correct pronunciation of this beautiful language, whose roots are often visible in English. Foreign terms are italicized on first appearance in each volume; most can be found in the glossary, which appears at the end of volume 1. Tibetan readers may consult the source texts via the folio references to Kuenzang Wangdue's edition in square brackets. Source notes, appearing as smaller characters in the original Tibetan, have been included here in parentheses, whereas my own clarifications appear in brackets. Cross-references between our texts are given using the following abbreviations followed by the folio references:

SV	The Sharp Vajra of Conscious Awareness Tantra
CM	Essence of Clear Meaning
MF	The Foolish Dharma of an Idiot Clothed in Mud and Feathers
VS	The Enlightened View of Samantabhadra
BM	Buddhahood Without Meditation
FP	The Fine Path to Liberation
GD	Garland for the Delight of the Fortunate
VE	The Vajra Essence

Requirements

These texts clearly reveal the most sublime of all Dharmas—secret mantra, Vajrayāna, or the Vajra Vehicle. The Sanskrit term *vajra* signifies the nature of ultimate reality, with its seven attributes of invulnerability, indestructibility, reality, incorruptibility, stability, unobstructability, and invincibility; and *yāna* means a vehicle for spiritual practice. Such profound instructions are guarded as secrets due to their potential for being dangerously misunderstood and to protect the teachings from disparagement. However, these texts also maintain their own secrecy, as Düdjom Lingpa states:

> Only those who have stored vast collections of merit in many ways, over incalculable eons, will encounter this path. They will have aspired repeatedly and extensively to reach the state of perfect enlightenment, and they will have previously sought the path through other yānas, establishing propensities to reach this path. No others will encounter it.

> Why not? Although people lacking such fortune may be present where this yāna is being explained and heard, because they are under the influence of their negative deeds and the strength of the powerful, devious *māras*[5] of mental afflictions, their minds will be in a wilderness five hundred *yojanas*[6] away.

If you wish to put the meaning of these sacred texts into practice, you must seek out a qualified guru to guide you in your understanding and practice. Düdjom Lingpa continues by stating that you must have "belief in the Dharma and your guru; unwavering trust in the path; earnest mindfulness of death and the conviction that all composite phenomena are impermanent, so that you have little attraction to mundane activities; contentment with respect to food, wealth, and enjoyments; insatiability for the Dharma due to great zeal and determination; and integration of your life and spiritual practice, without complaining." Rather than merely striving to accumulate virtues that might benefit you in some future lifetime, you should seize this precious opportunity—a human life in which you can practice the sublime Dharma—and generate the aspiration to achieve enlightenment in this present lifetime. He continues:

> If you arrive with that aspiration at the gateway of secret mantra—and you have firm faith and belief in it and strong, unflagging enthusiasm—the time has come to practice. . . . Once you have obtained a human life and encountered a guru and the secret-mantra Dharma, if this is not the time to practice the Great Perfection, then there will never be a better time than this in another life—this is certain.[7]

Gyatrul Rinpoché has authorized the publication of these translations with the stipulation that they should be restricted to suitable readers, specifically those who earnestly aspire to achieve liberation and enlightenment. Such people will not be fixated on material success, but due to understanding the first noble truth of suffering, they will have turned away from the allures of saṃsāra. Suitable readers will honor the fundamental Buddhist teachings

5. Tib. *bdud.* A demonic force or being that manifests as all kinds of grasping involving hopes and fears.

6. A *yojana* is an ancient Indian measure of a day's range for an ox cart, about five miles.

7. VE 14–18.

included in the Śrāvakayāna, and they will revere the Mahāyāna as well, including the cultivation of the four immeasurables, the six perfections, and the insights presented in the Yogācāra and Madhyamaka views. In addition, they will value all the outer, inner, and secret classes of the tantras and have a genuine desire to practice the cutting through and direct crossing over stages of the Great Perfection. Finally, suitable readers will treat these volumes with reverence and care. This is Gyatrul Rinpoché's sincere request for those interested in *Düdjom Lingpa's Visions of the Great Perfection.*

While those who devote themselves to the practice of these Dzokchen teachings should receive the appropriate empowerments, oral transmissions, and explanations of the lineage masters, the texts themselves do not restrict their readership to those who have completed certain preliminary practices, such as a hundred thousand recitations of the Vajrasattva mantra and so on. So I do not feel that it is appropriate for me as the translator of these texts to impose such restrictions. This is a decision to be made by individual qualified lamas of this lineage. The teachings translated in this series describe in detail the qualities needed on the part of disciples following the path of the Great Perfection, without mentioning empowerments. In fact, the *Vajra Essence* states that ultimately, through the realization of emptiness and pristine awareness, one spontaneously receives all four empowerments:

> Establishing saṃsāra and nirvāṇa as great emptiness is the *vase empowerment*. Recognizing precious spontaneous actualization as the self-emergent kāyas and facets of primordial consciousness is the *secret empowerment*. The revelation of pristine awareness, the nonconceptual primordial consciousness of ultimate reality, is the *wisdom empowerment*. Mastering the fruition in yourself is called the *word empowerment*. These are the actual four empowerments, devoid of a bestower and a recipient.[8]

May these translations be of great benefit to all those who study and practice them, resulting in their swift realization of śamatha, vipaśyanā, cutting through, and direct crossing over!

B. Alan Wallace
Santa Barbara, California
April 17, 2015

8. VE 248–49.

Introduction

PLEASE REFER TO the volume 1 introduction for brief overviews of the life of Düdjom Lingpa, the author of our first text, *Buddhahood Without Meditation*, and of the path of the Great Perfection. Sera Khandro's life was centered on upholding Düdjom Lingpa's lineage, and her commentary to this text is considered essential to its study and practice. We are fortunate that even as this volume was being polished, another fine English translation by Ngawang Zangpo of the root text and commentary was published.[9] Furthermore, a great deal of interest in Sera Khandro has led to the recent publishing of her autobiographies translated by Sarah Jacoby, based on her doctorate research.[10] These sources should be consulted to further illuminate this important teacher in the Great Perfection tradition of Düdjom Lingpa.

Sera Khandro

The dramatic life story of Sera Khandro Dechen Dewé Dorjé (1892–1940) would be inspiring in any context, but in twentieth-century Tibet, where women were rarely accepted as teachers, her example highlights how gender need not prevent spiritual practice and realization. She is called the "ḍākinī of Sera" after the nonsectarian Sera Monastery in Serta, where she spent the

9. Sera Khandro, *Refining Our Perception of Reality: Sera Khandro's Commentary on Dudjom Lingpa's Account of His Visionary Journey*, trans. Ngawang Zangpo (Boston: Snow Lion, 2013).

10. Sera Khandro, *Love and Liberation: Autobiographical Writings of the Tibetan Buddhist Visionary*, trans. Sarah H. Jacoby (New York: Columbia University Press, 2014). The short autobiography is published as Sarah H. Jacoby, "The Excellent Path of Devotion: An Annotated Translation of Sera Khandro's Short Autobiography," in *Himalayan Passages: Tibetan and Newar Studies in Honor of Hubert Decleer*, eds. Benjamin Bogin and Andrew Quintman (Boston: Wisdom Publications, 2014). See also the unpublished PhD thesis of Sarah Hieatt Jacoby, entitled "Consorts and Revelations in Eastern Tibet: The Auto/Biographical Writings of the Treasure Revealer Sera Khandro (1892–1940)." (PhD dissertation, Department of Religious Studies, University of Virginia, January 2007).

latter part of her life. Born to a Mongolian father and Tibetan mother in a noble Lhasa family, Sera Khandro fled an arranged marriage at the age of fifteen to pursue a prophesied religious calling. Abandoning her privileged life, she joined a group of pilgrims headed for Düdjom Lingpa's religious encampment at Dartsang in the eastern wildlands of Golok. She was devoted to the group's leader, Drimé Özer (1881–1924), and despite many hardships and obstacles, she eventually became his consort. He was Düdjom Lingpa's fifth son and a treasure revealer (Tib. *gter ston*) in his own right. After his untimely death, Sera Khandro dedicated her life to the preservation of the teachings of Düdjom Lingpa and Drimé Özer, and she herself revealed many treasure teachings. Although she had no formal religious education, this most prolific female writer in Tibetan history left us a detailed biography of Drimé Özer along with her autobiography and more than two thousand folio pages of treasure teachings in four volumes.

Unfortunately, most of Drimé Özer's corpus has not been found, with the notable exception of his commentary to his father's Tröma mind treasure, called *Stainless Luminous Expanse*.[11] His commentarial teachings on his father's most famous treasure text, *Buddhahood Without Meditation*, were recorded by Sera Khandro, who first received this teaching from him at the age of sixteen. The colophon mentions that these notes were edited by Drimé Özer himself and that she clarified them by drawing from his oral teachings. Known in Tibet simply as Sera Khandro's "Notes," the commentary is entitled *Garland for the Delight of the Fortunate.* We are blessed that Düdjom Lingpa's lineage was maintained by Sera Khadro's disciple Chatral Sangyé Dorjé Rinpoché (1913–2015), who also received these transmissions from Düdjom Lingpa's eighth son, Sangdak Tulku Dorjé Dradul.[12]

11. This is translated in part 2 of Lama Chönam and Sangye Khandro, trans., *The Sole Essence of Clear Light: Tröma Tögal Practice, The Terma Revelations of Heruka Dudjom Lingpa and Commentary by One of His Foremost Disciples, Tülku Drimed Ödzer* (Boulder: Kama Terma Publications, 2011).

12. Traktung Dudjom Lingpa, *A Clear Mirror: The Visionary Autobiography of a Tibetan Master*, trans. Chönyi Drolma (Hong Kong: Rangjung Yeshe Publications, 2011), 297.

Buddhahood Without Meditation

If there are a few individuals who have accrued vast accumulations [of merit and knowledge] over the course of countless eons, conjoined them with fine prayers, and established a karmic connection with the ultimate Dharma, I have bestowed this as their inheritance.
—Düdjom Lingpa, BM 293

Known by Tibetans as the *Nangjang*, which can be translated as "refining one's perception," this is Düdjom Lingpa's most widely taught visionary text. Subtitled "Advice for Revealing One's Own Face As the Nature of Reality, the Great Perfection," it has become widely known by the title of the first English translation, *Buddhahood Without Meditation*.[13] In a series of fourteen visionary encounters with wisdom beings and historical figures in the Great Perfection lineage, Düdjom Lingpa's transcendent teachers emphasize the view of cutting through (Tib. *khregs chod*) to the original purity of pristine awareness. This view is developed via four themes: nonexistence, oneness, uniform pervasiveness, and spontaneous actualization, which are known as the four special *samaya*s, or pledges, of the Great Perfection.

At each stage of his spiritual progress, Düdjom Lingpa's doubts are dispelled and his realizations enhanced by pithy advice. Most of these teachings concern the view: Avalokiteśvara, the bodhisattva of compassion, demonstrates nonexistence, the emptiness of all phenomena; Padmasambhava, the Lake-Born Vajra of Orgyen, shows how all appearances manifest from the empty ground due to grasping; the omniscient Longchenpa explains the nature of the wisdom that realizes emptiness; Dorjé Drolö, the wrathful emanation of Guru Rinpoché, synthesizes all phenomena of saṃsāra and nirvāṇa as displays of one ground of being, ultimate reality; the vidyādhara Hūṃchenkāra reveals the uniform pervasiveness of the sugatagarbha, or buddha-nature; and Mañjuśrī, the Lion of Speech, presents the definitive meaning of spontaneous actualization and then describes how relative meanings are skillfully used to lead us to the ultimate truth.

Meditation and conduct are taught by Śrī Siṃha, the Indian vidyādhara who transmitted the Great Perfection lineage to Padmasambhava. He bestows the pith instructions for meditation practice that is naturally free and intellect-transcending, explains the vital points of conduct, and warns

13. Dudjom Lingpa, *Buddhahood Without Meditation: A Visionary Account Known as Refining One's Perception (Nang-jang)*, trans. Richard Barron and Susanne Fairclough (Junction City, CA: Padma Publishing, 2006).

against the pitfalls of becoming fixated on mundane meditative experiences. Finally Zurchung Sherap Drakpa, the famous eleventh-century Nyingma adept, summarizes the vital points for achieving buddhahood and the key distinctions to be made in reaching the ultimate truth.

The Fine Path to Liberation

The contributing condition for all Dharmas
dwells on the summit of your aspirations.
— Sera Khandro, FP 5

Sera Khandro's short composition *Fine Path to Liberation* establishes the necessary motivation and conduct for receiving teachings such as *Buddhahood Without Meditation*. This sublime Dharma is to be seen in the context of the five perfections of the *saṃbhogakāya*: the teacher, place, time, disciples, and Dharma are fully perfected and must not be reified as ordinary. She urges us to bring our practice to its culmination by developing the motivation of the awakening mind, *bodhicitta*; avoiding faulty comprehension; cultivating reverence for the guru, love for our spiritual companions, compassion for all sentient beings, and renunciation for saṃsāra; and meditating upon the impermanence of all composite phenomena. These preliminaries are equally essential for receiving and practicing all the teachings in this series.

Garland for the Delight of the Fortunate

This is without meditation, for pristine awareness identifies itself within
itself as the nature of existence of suchness, it is decisively determined,
the ground is sustained by itself, indwelling confidence and liberation
flow forth directly from it, and you are manifestly united with your true
nature without even the slightest bit of meditation on anything else.
— Sera Khandro, GD 25

The wisdom beings who emanate from the sphere of ultimate reality in *Buddhahood Without Meditation* are responding to the queries of a Dharma prodigy. Following in his footsteps can be challenging for us, as the root text moves quickly from one crucial point to the next, with little elaboration. Happily, *Garland for the Delight of the Fortunate* fills in the gaps, explains the metaphors, and spells out the implications of the root text's highly condensed verses. This extensive commentary is liberally supported with quotations from seminal sūtras, tantras, and commentaries.

Augmenting the teachings of the root text, Sera Khandro's commentary provides detailed discussions of many Dharma practices, visualizations, and ritual activities. In each case, she begins by describing their ultimate meaning and then offers the ordinary, conventional interpretation. We are continually challenged to maintain the Great Perfection's view of original purity without falling into the trap of reification. Like many Tibetan compositions, this text includes a detailed structural outline that reveals the implicit organization of Düdjom Lingpa's visionary teaching. The outline is a valuable tool for understanding the context and significance of each visionary encounter. We have also indicated the root text's fourteen encounters with chapter breaks in the commentary. Unless one has already reached a very high level of realization, this commentary is an essential key for unlocking the profound wisdom contained in *Buddhahood Without Meditation*.

Buddhahood Without Meditation

Advice for Revealing Your Own Face
as the Nature of Reality, the Great Perfection

by
Düdjom Lingpa

"BUDDHAHOOD WITHOUT MEDITATION: Advice for Revealing Your Own Face as the Nature of Reality, the Great Perfection," Is Presented Here.

[292] With unshakable faith I pay homage to the Omnipresent Lord and Primordial Protector, the display of the supreme cities of apparitions of primordial consciousness.

Nowadays, when the five kinds of degeneration are on the rise, due to the uncouth nature of sentient beings and their powerful, negative karma, every one of them clings to this life—which is no more than an episode in a dream—makes long-term plans for living indefinitely, and shows no concern for meaningful pursuits pertaining to future lifetimes. Therefore, those who strive for the states of liberation and omniscience appear no more often than stars in the daytime.

Although some people bear death in mind and enthusiastically practice Dharma [293], they let their lives pass while engaging in mere verbal and physical spiritual practices and striving for higher rebirths as gods and humans.

Some, while lacking even the faintest understanding of the view of emptiness, ascertain their own minds as empty, merely identify the nature of discursive thoughts or inactive consciousness, and then passively remain in that state. As a result, they are simply propelled into rebirths as gods in the desire and form realms, without coming even a hair's breadth closer to the path to omniscience.

Therefore, if there are a few individuals who have accrued vast accumulations [of merit and knowledge] over the course of countless eons, conjoined them with fine prayers, and established a karmic connection with the ultimate [294] Dharma, I have bestowed this as their inheritance. Those who have no karmic connection with me and who lack the particular fortune of mastering the Dharma of the Great Perfection will engage in either projection or denial regarding this teaching and will thereby banish their own minds into the wilderness. You people who are not like that and whose fortune is equal to my own, attend to this advice—and by investigation, analysis, and familiarization, recognize saṃsāra and nirvāṇa as great emptiness, and realize its nature.

Among the three divisions—the division of the mind, the division of the expanse, and the division of pith instructions—of [the teachings on] the nature of reality, the Great Perfection, this is called the category of secret pith instructions. [295] In this regard there are three sections: view, meditation, and conduct. First, the view is determined and authentically realized by way of four themes: nonexistence, oneness, uniform pervasiveness, and spontaneous actualization. This is a sublime, essential point.

Teachings of Avalokiteśvara

First, to determine the manner of nonexistence, there are the determination of personal identity and the determination of phenomenal identity. First, as for so-called personal identity, the mere appearance of the existence of a self during waking experience, dreaming experience, the intermediate period, and future lifetimes [296] is called *personal identity*. As soon as this appearance occurs, there is a latent consciousness that takes it to be "I," and this is called *subsequent consciousness* or *discursive thinking*. This consciousness clarifies [the appearance of the self] and then stabilizes and fortifies it.

Investigating the source from which the so-called "I" first arises leads to the conclusion that no such source exists.

This is how to investigate whether or not the so-called "I" has a location and is an agent bearing real characteristics that can be individually identified in the interim period [between its origin and cessation].

The head is called the *head*; it is not the "I." Likewise, the scalp is called *skin*; it is not the "I." The bones are called *bones*; they are not the "I." Likewise, the eyes are *eyes* and not the "I." The ears are *ears* and not the "I." The nose is the *nose* and not the "I." The tongue is the *tongue* and not the "I." The teeth are *teeth* and not the "I." The brain, too, is not the "I." Moreover, regarding the flesh, blood, lymph, channels, and tendons, each has its own name and is not the "I." This is revealing.

Moreover, the arms are *arms* and not the "I." The shoulders are likewise not the "I," nor are the upper arms, the forearms, or the fingers. The spine is the *spine* and not the "I." [297] The ribs are not the "I," nor are the chest, lungs, heart, diaphragm, liver, or spleen. The intestines and kidneys are not the "I," nor are urine or feces. Furthermore, the word "I" is not attributed to the legs. The thighs are called *thighs* and not "I," and the hips are similarly not the "I," nor are the calves, the soles of the feet, or the toes.

In short, the outer skin is not called "I"; the intervening flesh and fat are called *flesh* and *fat*, not "I"; the inner bones are called *bones* and not "I"; and the innermost marrow is called *marrow* and not "I." Consciousness, too, is so called and is not named "I." Therefore, emptiness as the nonexistence of a location and agent during the interim [between the origination and cessation of the self] is certain.

Finally, you should likewise come to a decisive understanding that this transcends all destinations and the agents who go to them. The apparent existence of something that in fact does not exist is like a hallucination. Uttering the names [of such things] is like talking about the horns of a hare.

Second, to determine the identitylessness of phenomena, there are (A') searching for the bases of designation of names, (B') dissolving grasping at the permanence of things [298], (C') counteracting the flaws of benefit and harm, and (D') collapsing the false cave of hope and fear.

First, if you seek out the referents of all names, you will see that they do not exist and are nothing more than imputations upon the merely natural displays of thoughts; for it is impossible for any phenomenon to be established as self-sustaining upon its own basis of designation. For instance, upon what is the so-called head designated and why? Is it so designated because it is the first part of the fetus to develop, or because it is round, or because it appears above? In fact, the head does not arise as the first part of the fetus; everything that is round is not called a *head*; and if you examine *above* and *below*, you will find that they do not exist in space. Likewise, hair is not the *head*. Skin is only skin and is not called a *head*. Bones are called *bones* and not a *head*. The brain is not the *head*, nor are the eyes, ears, nose, or tongue.

If you think that none of these individually is the *head*, but their collective assembly is called a *head*, consider: If you severed a creature's head, pulverized it into its constituent molecules and atoms, and showed this to anyone in the world, no one would call it a *head*. Even if you reconstituted these molecules and atoms with water, it would not be called a *head*. Therefore, know how the so-called head is nothing more than a verbal expression, with no objective basis for this utterance. [299]

Likewise, regarding the *eyes*—that name is not attributed to all pairs of spheres. The sclera is not an *eye*, nor are tears, veins, or blood. An *eye* is none of these individually, nor is it the assembly of their particles, or the lump of them reconstituted with water. That which sees forms is consciousness, not the eyeballs, which is evidenced by the fact that visual perception takes place in dreams and in the intermediate period.

Likewise, regarding the *ears*—neither the auditory canals nor the skin are the ears, and the flesh, channels, ligaments, blood, and lymph all have their own names, so they are not the *ears*. The powder that would result from reducing them to tiny particles is not the *ears*, nor is the lump that would be formed by reconstituting them with water. If you think that the name *ear* is attributed to that which hears sounds, check out what hears sounds in a dream, the waking state, and the intermediate period. It is only the primordially present consciousness of your mind and not the ears.

Likewise, regarding the *nose*—the nostrils, skin, cartilage, flesh, channels, and ligaments all have their own names, so they are not called a *nose*. Moreover, that which smells odors is consciousness itself, so you should investigate what smells odors in a dream and in the intermediate period.

Likewise, regarding the *tongue*— [300] its flesh, skin, blood, veins, and nerves all have their own names, so they are not called a *tongue*. If they were pulverized into a powder, this would not be called a *tongue*, and if it were reconstituted into a lump, it would still not be called a *tongue*. This applies to all the following instances as well.

Likewise, regarding the *arms*—the shoulders are not the *arms*, nor are the upper arms, forearms, fingers, knuckles, flesh, skin, bones, or marrow. Likewise, regarding the *shoulders*—the skin is not the *shoulders*, nor are flesh, bones, their assembled particles, or the lump reconstituted with water. The basis of designation of the name *shoulder* is empty in that it has no objective existence. Likewise, by investigating the upper arms and forearms, it becomes apparent that each component has its own name, with flesh being called *flesh*, bones called *bones*, skin called *skin*, and marrow called *marrow*. Not even an atom can be established as their basis of designation.

By investigating the bases of designation of the *body* and the *aggregates*, it becomes apparent that the *body* does not refer to the spine or ribs, or to the chest, flesh, skin, or bones. The heart, lungs, liver, diaphragm, spleen, kidneys, and intestines are all called by their own names, so the bases of designation of the *body* and *aggregates* [301] are empty in that they have no objective existence: they are emptiness.

Likewise, by investigating the *legs*, it becomes apparent that the hips are not the *legs*, nor are the thighs, calves, or ankles. Similarly, the name *hips* does not refer to flesh, skin, bones, channels, or ligaments. Regarding the *thighs* as well, this name does not refer to any of the skin, flesh, bones, channels, or ligaments. This goes for the *calves*, too. These names would not be applied if they were pulverized into powder, nor would they refer to the lump formed from that powder mixed with water.

If you seek the basis of designation of a *mountain* externally, it becomes apparent that earth is not a *mountain*, nor are shrubs, trees, stones, boulders, or water.

If you seek the basis of designation of a *building*, it becomes apparent that neither mortar, nor stones, nor lumber is a *building*. Moreover, just as walls are called *walls* and not a *building*, likewise there is nothing in the exterior or interior that is established as a *building*.

Although you may seek the bases of designation of a *human being*, a *horse*, a *dog*, and so on, it becomes apparent that their eyes, ears, noses, tongues, flesh, blood, bones, marrow, channels, and ligaments, together with their consciousnesses, all have their own names, so the bases of designation of a *human being*, a *horse*, and a *dog* have no objective existence. [302] These [names] are indicative of everything else.

Furthermore, among material objects, the name *drum* is not attributed to the wood, leather, exterior, or interior. Moreover, the term *knife* is not attributed to the metal, blade, back of the blade, tip, or haft. None of these is established as the object designated *knife*. Names and their referents change. For example, when a knife is formed into an awl, its name changes, and when this is made into a needle, all its previous names disappear.

In dependence upon the teachings I have received during a dream from my guru, the supreme ārya, the Great Compassionate One (Avalokiteśvara), I have thoroughly realized both the so-called "personal identity" [as identityless] and this search for the bases of designation of names.

Teachings of the Lake-Born Vajra of Orgyen

On one occasion when I encountered the illusory body of the primordial consciousness of the Lake-Born Vajra of Orgyen, he granted me these instructions on perceiving appearances as illusory: "In order to be introduced to the dependent origination of the confluence of causes and conditions, consider this: Lucid, luminous absolute space, as the ground, having the potential to manifest any kind of appearance, serves as the cause; and consciousness that grasps at the 'I' serves as the contributing condition. In dependence upon the confluence of these two, all appearances manifest like illusions. Thus, absolute space, as the ground, the mind that arises from its creative power, and all the outer and inner phenomena that are appearances of this mind are called *dependently related events*, for they are interrelated as a sequence of events, like the sun and its rays. [303]

"This is like the appearance of an illusion that arises in dependence upon the interaction of transparent, clear space, the primary cause, with the magical substances, mantras, and mind that views the object, the contributing conditions.

"In this way, all appearing phenomena manifest due to the power of grasping at the 'I,' even though they don't exist. This is like the appearance of a mirage due to the confluence of a lucid clear sky, warmth, and moisture.

"All waking appearances, dream appearances, and appearances during the intermediate period and thereafter appear, even though they don't exist, and confusion arises due to reifying them. As an analogy, during a dream, instead of thinking, 'This is a dream' and recognizing it as delusive, you apprehend it as an enduring, objective world and fixate on it.

"The appearances of various phenomena as something 'other' due to the dominant condition of inwardly grasping at the 'I' are like the appearances of reflections arising from the interaction of your face and a mirror.

"Due to being completely ensnared by the reification of the self, the worlds of the six cities appear to arise one after another. These are like the appearances of a city of gandharvas manifesting in an area such as a plain at sunset, which occur as visions grasped by the mind.

"While the appearances to the physical senses have never been established as real, your own diverse experiences of seeing, hearing, experiencing, and feeling appear as something 'other,' like echoes.

"All appearances are not other than the ground, [304] and they are of one taste with the ground itself, just as all the planets and stars reflected in the ocean are not other than the ocean and are of one taste with the water itself.

"Due to grasping at the 'I,' 'self' and 'other' appear as if truly existent in the panoramic sweep of the expansive, all-pervasive absolute space of the ground. These appearances are like bubbles emerging from water.

"The lucid luminosity of the empty absolute space of the ground is crystallized into self-appearances to mental consciousness. Due to this becoming reinforced, various delusive appearances manifest, which are like hallucinations caused by pressure on the nerves of the eyes or by disturbances in the channels due to the vital energies.

"Although various appearances from the ground manifest to a consciousness that grasps at the 'I,' they do not waver from or occur outside of that ground. As an analogy, when someone who has mastered the samādhi of emanation and transformation settles in meditative equipoise in such samādhi, various emanations appear, even though they have no ground or root and do not exist as real objects.

"O my incredible child, gradually meditate in this way, and you will become an illusory yogin by realizing the illusory nature of appearances."

So saying, he disappeared.

Teachings of Vidyādhara Düdul Dorjé

On one occasion Vidyādhara Düdul Dorjé spoke these words to me:

> The vajra is the eternal vajra;
> for its meaning, look to space itself!

Elaborating on this point, [305] he said, "Behold! This empty space is the ground of the appearances of all physical worlds and their sentient inhabitants. To provide analogies, the ground of the appearances of reflections is a mirror, for reflections are not established as anything other than the mirror. The ground of the appearances of images of the moon in water is water, for these images are not established as anything other than the water. The ground of the appearances of rainbows is space, for rainbows are not established as anything other than space.

"This space cannot be injured, so it is invulnerable. Space cannot be conquered or destroyed, so it is indestructible. Space abides as the ground of the appearances of the phenomenal world, so it is real. Space cannot be affected by good or bad qualities, so it is incorruptible. Space is unmoving and unfluctuating, so it is stable. Space can penetrate even the minutest particles, so it is unobstructable. Space cannot be harmed by anything whatsoever, so it is completely invincible.

"Since all other substances can be injured by weapons, they are vulnerable. Since they can be conquered and destroyed by circumstances, they are destructible. Since they can change into one thing or many, they are unreal. Since they can be affected by other things, they are corruptible. Since they move and fluctuate, with no enduring stillness, [306] they are unstable. They can be obstructed by certain things, and since they can be nullified by other influences, they are vincible. Such things, having the characteristic of not being established as truly existent, are empty.

"Moreover, by pulverizing coarse materials, they are reduced to particles. Decomposing these particles by a factor of seven results in molecules. The empty, partless atoms that result from decomposing these molecules by a factor of seven are characterized by not being established as real.

"If you think they existed at first but were then reduced to nothing due to being acted upon, take heed of the appearances of dreams, which are not established as real from the very moment they manifest, regardless of whether or not they have been acted upon, either by observation or by physical contact.

"Observe how appearances emerge and cease due merely to opening and closing your eyes or lowering and raising your feet. If you think it is not that the previous appearances cease and vanish as the subsequent ones emerge, but rather that the earlier ones go elsewhere, with all the former and later appearances being truly existent, look at the appearances of a dream. In particular, it is impossible for some substantial nature to exist except as something designated as a relative [truth] upon the interrelations of causes and effects. So consider this issue well.

"Well then, these accounts of space having the seven vajra qualities are presented using metaphors to show how space is devoid of movement and change due to its insubstantiality. They demonstrate how ultimate reality [307] is present as the essential nature, which is inexpressible by speech or thought and is devoid of change. It is worthwhile to apply these accounts to explanations of the distinctions between substantiality and insubstantiality and between reality and unreality. So when the moon is symbolically pointed out with a finger, you should look at the moon and not be satisfied with looking merely at the tip of the finger. If you do not decisively recognize appearances as empty by repeatedly familiarizing yourself with these points, you will not come the slightest bit closer to the path of omniscience.

"My child, endowed with the pinnacle of conscious awareness, carefully attend to this point, and by realizing all appearances as space itself, become a yogin of the uniform pervasiveness of space!"

With these words, he disappeared.

Teachings of Longchenpa, Drimé Özer: An Introduction in the Form of a Question-and-Answer Session for the Sake of Developing Certainty

By gaining a strong conviction about the above points, I understood all appearances to be empty from their own side. Nevertheless, regarding the outer appearances of the physical world, its inner, animate sentient inhabitants, and all the intervening appearances of the five kinds of sensory objects, I still thought they would be left behind when I departed for other realms, and that all sentient beings existed with their own individual mindstreams. During that period my guru, Drimé Özer, appeared to me in a dream and gave me the following introduction in the form of a question-and-answer session. [308]

He said, "O son of the family, the outer appearances of the physical world, its inner, animate sentient inhabitants, and the intervening appearances of the five kinds of sensory objects are like illusory apparitions that dissolve into the space of awareness. Accordingly, once they have disappeared into the vacuous space of the substrate, eventually, due to the projections resulting from the movements of karmic energies, there is an appearance of your own body, giving rise to a physical world, its sentient inhabitants, and all sensory appearances. As fixation arises toward them, delusion sets in. Finally, this appearing world once again disappears into the vacuous space of the substrate, like a rainbow dissolving into the sky. Then waking appearances emerge like before."

I responded, "I think this body of mine is not a mere appearance but definitely arose from the causes and conditions of a father and mother."

He replied, "If you think your body arose from a father and mother like that, tell me: What are the beginnings and ends of your fathers and mothers, and what are their origins, locations, and destinations?"

I answered, "I believe they exist, but I can't remember them. I think it's impossible for there to be a body without parents."

He countered, "Check to see who are the parents of a body in a dream, the intermediate period, a hell realm, and so on."

Consequently, I gained a decisive understanding that this body is not established as anything other than a mere appearance. [309]

I commented, "O guru, I think that when my body is in bed covered with bedclothes and dream appearances arise, my body and the human environment remain unchanged."

The guru replied, "Examine the dream appearances of the vast outer physical world, its numerous inner sentient inhabitants, and the well-displayed intervening appearances of the five senses to see whether they are located in the head, the limbs, or the upper or lower parts of your body."

Consequently, I became certain that such was not the case.

Nevertheless, I persisted, "Guru, perhaps dream appearances arise when consciousness goes elsewhere. Then, when it reenters the body, waking appearances arise."

The guru replied, "Well, if that were so, this body would be like a hotel, in which case, identify and report to me what is the door to this hotel, as it were, by which consciousness comes and goes. In addition, you must identify where the mind is located. If the mind is located in the upper part of the body, why is pain experienced when the lower part is pricked with a thorn? Likewise, if it resides in the lower part, there would be no reason for pain to be experienced in the upper part. It doesn't make sense for it to fluctuate in size, such that a tiny consciousness enters the body through an orifice, [310] increases in size until it pervades the body, and then shrinks again as it departs through that orifice. If that were so, once awareness is separated from the material body, why wouldn't consciousness reenter the corpse after death?

"Where do dream appearances go? Do they go above, below, or in one of the cardinal or intermediate directions? Do you believe they are the same as the waking appearances of the physical world and its sentient inhabitants or different? If you believe they are the same, does sleep define their boundaries or not? If it does, then they are not waking appearances; and if it doesn't, they are not dream appearances. On the other hand, it is invalid to believe that these appearances exist, while imagining that they are above or below, outside or inside."

I replied, "Guru, then how is this to be decided? Where should I stand? Sublime guru, please show me."

The guru replied, "Throughout beginningless lifetimes you have never been born; there have been only appearances of birth. You have never died; there have been only appearances of a change of place, like dream appearances and waking appearances. Regarding the eyes, ears, nose, tongue, and body, all things that are seen as forms, heard as sounds, smelled as odors, experienced as tastes, and felt as tactile sensations are simply your own appearances arising to yourself, [311] without their ever existing, even in the slightest way, as something else.

"If you think that things exist autonomously as something else since you can directly see them with your eyes, really hold them in your hands, and experience them through your senses, consider: All the forms, sounds, odors, tastes, and tactile sensations in a dream appear at the time to be truly existent. But from the next day onward, they have no objective existence. This should tell you something.

"Throughout your beginningless succession of lifetimes, you have never moved from one place to another, and you have never lived anywhere else. This condition is equivalent to appearances in a dream. If you think there is a difference in the reality or unreality of dream appearances and waking appearances, observe for yourself: From the time you were born until now, are all the dream and waking appearances of working, farming, striving, saving, and planning the same or not? If you carefully examine them without regard for their duration and quantity, you will definitely recognize that they are alike.

"Moreover, if dream appearances were unreal and waking appearances were real, this would mean that dream appearances are delusive and waking appearances are not delusive. In that case, you would have to believe that you are a sentient being while dreaming and a buddha during the waking state! If both are delusive appearances, it is pointless to distinguish one as being real and the other as unreal, [312] for something is called a delusive appearance if it appears and is apprehended as something it is not.

"Until now you have eaten enough food to fill Mount Meru and drunk an ocean of liquid, but still you are not full. You have worn a galaxy of clothing, but still you are not warm. Know that this indicates that these are mere appearances and are not established as real.

"It is a great mistake not to recognize that what appears as your body is empty and to cling to it as real. This is a consuming demon, since the efforts you make for the sake of your body eat away at the fruit of omniscience. It is a murderous executioner, since it links one cycle of existence to the next, displaying the appearances of birth and death. It cuts your life force, since, for the sake of your body, you seek happiness from clothing and so on, and you are imprisoned by clinging to attachments and aversions that perpetuate hopes and fears; thus, your lifeline to liberation is cut. And it asphyxiates you, for it robs you of the breath of eternal bliss. Therefore, all those who cling to the objective appearances of the six kinds of consciousness are like deer that mistake a mirage for water and run to it. There is not even an iota of an essence that is established as real.

"Even though you know appearances to be empty in this way, they might remain as before, as if they were truly existent, without turning into nothing. So if you wonder why it is necessary to know this, consider: If you do not know that the essential nature of the object of meditation is emptiness, all your meditations [313] will certainly turn out to be ethically neutral.

"Furthermore, you may wonder why the mere realization of emptiness should reveal the nature of nonexistence, given that mere understanding and mere realization resulting from all other visualizations and meditations are not liberating. Moreover, if everything is primordially empty, you may think that it makes no difference whether or not you know everything to be empty. If so, consider this: Know that saṃsāra and nirvāṇa and liberation and delusion come about due to the differences between awareness and unawareness and between knowing and not knowing. Realize that awareness is essential.

"Some people may think that if you can't understand this on your own, then hearing teachings and contemplating them will be of no use. But since beginningless time you have failed to realize this on your own and have wandered in saṃsāra. Know that through studying and training you will realize emptiness, thereby gaining the view that accords with all the tantras, oral transmissions, and pith instructions.

"Furthermore, whether you realize emptiness after undergoing great hardships in studying, training, and so on, or you realize emptiness without experiencing the slightest difficulty, there is no difference in the quality of your realization. For example, whether you discover gold after undergoing great hardships or you find it under your bed without the slightest difficulty, there is no difference in the quality of the gold. [314]

"The consciousness that analytically ascertains all appearances as emptiness is called *discerning wisdom*. The continuum of subsequent consciousness that definitely ascertains saṃsāra and nirvāṇa as great emptiness is called the *wisdom that realizes identitylessness*. Once these two types of wisdom have been generated in your mindstream, there is first realization, then experience, and finally acquiring indwelling confidence. This is a crucial point.

"Moreover, if you say that it is incorrect to assert that the body and so forth are not established except as mere appearances, because if the body of someone who has realized them as empty is touched by fire or water or struck by an arrow, a spear, or a club, then pain arises, consider: Until you reach absolute space, in which phenomena are extinguished in ultimate reality, dualistic appearances do not subside; and until they vanish, appearances of benefit and harm will uninterruptedly arise. But in reality, even the fires of hell do not burn."

With these words, he disappeared.

Teachings of Saraha

On another occasion when I had a vision of Mahāsiddha Saraha, I asked the great lord of siddhas, "By what means are obscurations purified? How are deities to be realized? By what means can one be freed of demons and obstructive beings? Please explain!"

He replied, "O great being, [315] you must counteract the faults of benefit and harm. As for so-called obscurations, ignorance of the essential nature of the ground as emptiness is called an *obscuration* and *ignorance*, and the entrenchment of such ignorance is called a *habitual propensity*. These cannot be purified by ordinary efforts, such as striving at physical and verbal spiritual practices. Rather, obscurations are naturally purified as a result of ascertaining ultimate reality by means of discerning wisdom.

"Where are all beneficial virtues of the body and speech located? Where is the storehouse in which they are accumulated? By investigating and analyzing the origin from which they arise, their location, and the destination to which they go, if you find that none of them have any objective existence, then what do they benefit? By investigating what it could mean to benefit the empty ultimate nature of mind—in terms of its exterior, interior, middle, top, or bottom—you will become certain that such benefit has no objective existence. Then you will see that there is nothing more than an accumulation of merit within saṃsāra.

"Likewise, in what cardinal or intermediate direction are the heaps of accumulated vices located? Where is their storehouse? Investigate how they harm the exterior, interior, in between, top, or bottom of the empty mind. Now if you carefully examine the streams of consciousness of people who have constantly applied themselves to physical and verbal virtues [316] and those of others who have devoted their whole lives to perpetrating evil, you will find that there is not one iota of difference between them in terms of the perpetuation of all their attachment and hostility, hope and fear. If they are liberated, they are freed due to their streams of consciousness being freed; and if they are deluded, they are bewildered due to their streams of consciousness being bewildered. There is not even the slightest difference in terms of their streams of consciousness wandering in saṃsāra without being liberated. Therefore, virtue and vice are different merely insofar as they generate temporary happiness and suffering, but other than this, they do nothing more than perpetuate saṃsāra.

"If you do not determine the nature of virtue in this way, you will confuse the virtue of accumulating temporary merit with the path to liberation, so you will not achieve the fruition of omniscience. If you fail to determine the nature of vice, you will not know that ignorance of your own essential nature is an obscuration and the basis of delusion, so you will not recognize the cause of delusion. Consequently, you will have no alternative but to remain endlessly deluded in saṃsāra. So recognize the crucial importance of determining this.

"By investigating the initial origin, interim location, and final destination of so-called benevolent and protective gods, you will see that they have no objective existence. In which of the objects of form, sound, smell, taste, and tactile sensations appearing as sensory objects is their existence established? If you think they exist in the domain of one of the elements of the physical world and its sentient inhabitants, [317] investigate within molecules and atoms, examine the individual names and constitutions of the elements, and see how these gods could be of benefit.

"By investigating malevolent demons in the same way, you will see that they have no objective existence either. All joys and sorrows are dreamlike mental appearances, so no benefit or harm by gods or demons occurs from their bases of designation. If you think demons inflict harm, consider: Since they lie outside the domains of form, sound, smell, taste, and tactile sensations, that which is called a *demon* is nothing more than a mere name. By investigating how it can inflict harm, you will see it as not anything existent—nothing other than nonobjective and empty.

"Out of delusion, people view the upper and lower portions of the body as good and bad respectively. Since the upper body appears to be clean, they regard it as if it were a god, and since the lower body appears unclean, they regard it as if it were a demon. This results in a continuous stream of hope and fear, and due to the tight bondage of self-grasping, a continuous stream of joyful and miserable experiences arises. All these consist of nothing more than experiential appearances of saṃsāra, without even an iota of true existence as anything else. This is simply illustrated with the metaphor of a dream.

"The essential point of all this is knowing the way things exist, [318] which dispels obstacles to meditation. After this has cleared away all obstacles of lack of conviction and distrust toward meditation, you will acquire indwelling confidence and be filled with conviction and freedom from doubt regarding the meaning of ultimate reality. Freed of the obscuration of ignorance, this will provide you with mastery over the great, continuous displays of pristine awareness.

"This is also the root of the profound practices of pacification and the severance of māras. Do not seek any divinity other than your own pristine awareness. You will come to the decisive recognition that there are no demons other than discursive thoughts. And this recognition is indispensable for all sādhanas and rituals for dispelling obstacles. If you have such knowledge, you are certainly a great, illusory yogin who realizes all phenomena as being like illusions.

"O little one whose pristine awareness transcends the mind, teach this to your disciples and they may all become Mahāyāna yogins of this great mystery."

Saying this, he vanished from sight.

Teachings of Vajrapāṇi

On one occasion when I encountered the glorious Vajrapāṇi in a pure vision of clear light, I asked him, "O Jina, great Vajradhara, is so-called buddhahood something I awaken to within myself, or do I need to go elsewhere to become enlightened?"

He replied, "Behold! [319] Fortunate son of the family, if you think that so-called buddhas are people who live in a vast realm, noble individuals of fine and flawless countenance, peaceful and cooling, clear and free of blemishes, handsome and attractive, consider: Who are their parents? If they were born from mothers, they would fall to the extreme of birth. If they dwell somewhere, they would fall to the extreme of having a permanent location. If they were to cease to exist, they would fall to the nihilistic extreme of disappearing. In short, nothing that has a self-sustaining, truly existent nature of arising, ceasing, and remaining has a mode of existence free of the two extremes. These appearances that seem to arise and cease are nothing more than imputations.

"Moreover, if you reify that which is authentically enlightened, you will bind yourself. If there is a real difference between the ultimate natures of saṃsāra and nirvāṇa, then references to the equal mode of existence of mundane existence and the peace [of nirvāṇa] are nothing more than empty words. Many people, clinging to nirvāṇa as substantially existent, fall into the trap of hope and fear. There are many accounts of the enjoyments in the pure realms, but if you think of their vast qualities and reify them, that still constitutes grasping at the identities of phenomena. [320] However you name them, in reality, viewing the tathāgatas as being eternal and truly existent is nothing more than viewing them as identities of persons.

"If you think a buddha has eyes, he would also have visual consciousness. As soon as visual consciousness is established, the emergence of visual appearances is inevitable. They are known as the objects apprehended by the eyes. Once such objects are established, subtle conceptual states of mind that closely hold to forms inevitably arise. These are the mental states of visual apprehension. The dualistic conceptualization of the apprehender and the apprehended is called *mind*, and anyone who has a mind is known as a *sentient being*.

"Likewise, if you think a buddha has ears, he must have auditory consciousness as well as sounds. If you think he has a nose, he must have olfactory consciousness as well as smells. If you think he has a tongue, he must have gustatory consciousness as well as tastes. If you think he has a body, he must have tactile consciousness as well as tactile sensations. And all these would be their apprehended objects. The assemblies of concepts closely holding these objects are the mental states that apprehend them. As before, whoever has a mind is called a *sentient being*.

"Regarding so-called buddhas, if it were possible for there to be buddhas who did not transcend dualistic grasping, [321] their qualities could also be transferred to sentient beings, just like the qualities of one human being can be transferred to another. If you think buddhas teach Dharma to others, then the teachers would appear as selves, the Dharma would appear as the teaching, and those who are taught would appear as sentient beings; and if buddhas were apprehended as such, they would not have even a sesame seed's worth of qualities superior to those of sentient beings. So they would all be sentient beings.

"If you think a buddha has a pleasant environment, a beautiful form, fine companions, great enjoyments and pleasures, and no anger or attachment, and that these are the exceptional qualities of a buddha, then a buddha would be no better than a god of the form realm. So such a buddha would not be anything more than a sentient being either.

"In terms of the definitive meaning, your own ground, Samantabhadra, is called the *sugatas of the three times*. Ultimately, a buddha has never come into the world or taught Dharma. Many of the tantras, oral transmissions, and pith instructions clearly explain how the self-appearing teacher manifests to disciples themselves. Observe and realize this point.

"Furthermore, it is incorrect to think that there are other kinds of realms of saṃsāra that are established as existent, and that many sentient beings migrate from one of those places to another and successively experience joys and sorrows. If the appearance of your previous body [322] being discarded were true, whence would you obtain your body in the intermediate period? If sentient beings these days can die merely from wounds, from burns on their arms and legs, or from cold wind on a single winter's day, then when a body is formed that experiences the heat and cold of hell realms, why doesn't it die even though it has been boiled and burned for a long time?

"Likewise, if death can occur nowadays due to starvation for only a few months or even days, why don't sentient beings in the preta realms perish due to being starved for eons?

"Therefore, all sentient beings in the six states of existence, as well as those in the intermediate period, manifest merely like appearances in a dream; but apart from that, they are empty and are not established as real. They are deluded due to obsessively grasping at the true existence of things that have no objective existence.

"If you determine the nature of delusive appearances in that way and realize them as not truly existent, as empty, and as having no objective existence, you have dredged saṃsāra from its depths. If you decisively understand that buddhas do not exist apart from your own ground and you acquire confidence within yourself, you will actually attain what is called the *natural liberation of a multitude of buddhas*.

"O Lord of Space, Omnipresent Vajra, determine that all the phenomena of saṃsāra and nirvāṇa are nonexistent and empty, and realize their nature of nonexistence."

Saying this, he disappeared. [323]

Teachings of Dorjé Drolö

After considering it for a long time, a decisive understanding of nonexistence arose, so that I knew that all the appearances of the physical world and its sentient inhabitants are empty from their own side. Nevertheless, many kinds of emptiness seemed to be ethically neutral. At that point I had a vision of the supreme Dorjé Drolö chanting the melody of *Hūṃ*, which reveals saṃsāra and nirvāṇa as displays of emptiness.

On that occasion I asked, "O great and supreme special deity, although I understand saṃsāra and nirvāṇa to be empty, this emptiness seems to be without benefit or harm. Why is that?"

He replied, "O my child, Lord of Space, reduce all of saṃsāra and nirvāṇa to emptiness; reduce emptiness to the essential nature of reality; reduce this essential nature to the ground of being; reduce saṃsāra and nirvāṇa to displays of this ground; and reduce the entirety of saṃsāra and nirvāṇa to this very ground.

"The reflections of the planets and stars in the ocean are none other than the ocean. The physical world and its sentient inhabitants are none other than space. Saṃsāra and nirvāṇa are none other than displays of ultimate reality. This unifying principle and ultimate reality are all-pervasive and all-encompassing. Understand these metaphors and what they exemplify. [324] Thus you will become a yogin who embraces saṃsāra and nirvāṇa."

So saying, he disappeared.

Teachings of Vajradhara

Seven years later, when the dharmakāya teacher Vajradhara appeared to me in a pure dream, I asked him, "O Teacher, Bhagavān, how is one freed on the path of liberation and omniscience, and how is one deluded on the impure path of saṃsāra? May the Teacher explain!"

He replied, "O great being, listen! The distinction between the emergence of buddhas and sentient beings is the difference between knowledge and ignorance. The fundamental primordial protector, Samantabhadra, is of the nature of the four kāyas and five facets of primordial consciousness. His empty essential nature is the dharmakāya, his luminous nature is the saṃbhogakāya, his self-liberating compassion is the nirmāṇakāya, and his pervasive and encompassing nature throughout all of saṃsāra and nirvāṇa is the svabhāvikakāya.

"The *primordial consciousness of absolute space* is so called because it accommodates all phenomena; *mirror-like primordial consciousness* is so called because it is lucid, luminous, and free of contamination; the *primordial consciousness of equality* is so called because saṃsāra and nirvāṇa are displays of purity and equality; *discerning primordial consciousness* is so called because of the unimpeded nature of the primordial consciousness that knows and perceives; and the *primordial consciousness of accomplishment* is so called because it accomplishes its tasks by way of purification and liberation.

"The path pristine awareness that liberates you as a self-emergent buddha manifests [325] in the nature of the four kāyas and five facets of primordial consciousness. The display of the essential nature of pristine awareness—all-pervasive, extending to the limits of space, without objective existence, a great uniform pervasiveness with no ground or root—is free of conceptual elaboration, and is therefore the dharmakāya. Regarding its nature as self-illuminating, it is the saṃbhogakāya; regarding its unimpeded luminosity of primordial consciousness, it is the nirmāṇakāya; and regarding its being the common ground of saṃsāra and nirvāṇa, it is the svabhāvikakāya.

"Having determined the nature of the ground, the realization of the one taste of saṃsāra and nirvāṇa in the absolute space of ultimate reality is the primordial consciousness of the absolute space of phenomena. Without reducing emptiness to a mere immateriality, lucidity and luminosity free of contamination, like a stainless mirror in which anything can appear, is mirror-like primordial consciousness. The awareness of the equal purity of saṃsāra and nirvāṇa in great emptiness is the primordial consciousness of equality. The unimpeded luminosity of primordial consciousness that discerns the displays of pristine awareness is discerning primordial consciousness. By gaining mastery over pristine awareness, activities of purification and liberation are naturally accomplished, so this is the primordial consciousness of accomplishment.

"Without knowing this mode of being, many people take as their path a passive state of consciousness that does not distinguish between the mind and pristine awareness. They grasp at outer appearances as ethically neutral entities bearing their own intrinsic characteristics. [326] Inwardly, they are tightly bound by the chains of reifying their own bodies as ethically neutral and permanent. In between these two [the outer and inner], as it were, they gain stability in a mere unimpeded, luminous, and cognizant state of consciousness. However, while it is possible that this may constitute a virtue that propels them to the two higher realms of existence, they will not achieve the states of liberation and enlightenment. So this is a flawed approach.

"Authentically knowing how all the phenomena included in saṃsāra and nirvāṇa are of one taste in the nature of suchness, ultimate reality, is the *wisdom that knows reality as it is*. Even while dwelling in the essential nature of pristine awareness, the self-emergence of unimpeded consciousness that is all-knowing and all-cognizing is the *wisdom that perceives the full range of phenomena*. Although such wisdom is unimpeded, it does not merge with objects, like a drop of mercury [does not merge with soil] when it falls on the ground.

"The mind views saṃsāra and nirvāṇa as autonomous, reifies appearances, and is unaware of the nature of existence of the ground. From this mind emerge thoughts that arise and pass, merging with their objects, like drops of water falling on dry ground.

"As a result of ignorance obscuring your own face of buddhahood of the pure ground, which has mastery over the ground of being, all the kāyas and facets of primordial consciousness of the natural inner glow of the ground subside into that inner glow. [327] The outer radiance is projected externally, with the aspects of the five lights manifesting as displays of the five elements.

"Here is how this occurs: Due to the primordial consciousness of the absolute space of phenomena being obscured by ignorance, its outer radiance appears as indigo light. This is called the *inner element*, *great element*, and *quintessence of space*. Due to reifying and clinging to this light, it appears as space, and this is called the appearance of the *outer element*, *derivative element*, and *residue*.

"Due to mirror-like primordial consciousness being obscured by ignorance, its inner glow subsides, resulting in its outer radiance appearing as white-colored light. This is the quintessence of water, its great element, and its inner element. Due to reifying and clinging to this light, it appears as water, and this is its residue, derivative element, and outer element.

"Due to the primordial consciousness of equality being obscured by ignorance, its inner glow subsides, resulting in its outer radiance appearing as yellow-colored light. This is the quintessence of earth, its inner element, and its major element. Due to reifying and clinging to this light, it appears as earth, and this is its residue, derivative element, and outer element.

"Due to discerning primordial consciousness being obscured by ignorance, its inner glow subsides, resulting in its outer radiance appearing as red-colored light. This is the quintessence of fire, its inner element, and its major element. Due to reifying and clinging to this light, it appears as fire, and this is its residue, [328] derivative element, and outer element.

"Due to the primordial consciousness of accomplishment being obscured by ignorance, its inner glow subsides, resulting in its outer radiance appearing as green-colored light. This is the quintessence of air, its inner element, and its major element. Due to reifying and clinging to this light, it appears as air, and this is called its residue, derivative element, and outer element.

"Due to the condition of these lights and radiances remaining within, the various colors and appearances of the five elements manifest uninterruptedly.

"The creative power of these five bases of delusion manifests in the following ways. Due to the obscuration of the ground by ignorance, the actual substrate, which is space-like and immaterial, devoid of thoughts and appearances, is like deep sleep and fainting. Immersion in this state is of the essential nature of delusion, a vast field of ignorance.

"The arousal of the karmic energies of an eon from that state is the essential nature of envy. Due to its activity, luminosity emerges from emptiness, and this is the substrate consciousness, which is present in the essential nature of hatred. The ego-grasping that arises from it with respect to the mere appearance of the self is afflictive mentation, which is present in the essential nature of pride. Mentation arises from this, and it establishes the potential for appearances to emerge from immaterial emptiness, thus bringing forth luminosity; and this is present in the essential nature of attachment. [329] These constitute the five essential natures arising as outer creative expressions of the inner glow.

"The essential nature of the five poisons is like fire, from which afflictive thought formations emerge like sparks.

"In this way, objects unimpededly emerge as appearances in the uniformly pervasive emptiness and luminosity of the substrate and mentation. Consequently, due to the simultaneous confluence of the movements of karmic energies as the contributing conditions and the potential of the ground for manifesting appearances as the primary cause, the appearances of various forms emerge in dependence upon the ground and without relation to anything other than the ground.

"Whatever objects emerge as appearances of form are called by mere convention *visual consciousness*. Therefore, appearing objects, which may be likened to the ocean, are called *objects*, and the appearances of forms, which may be likened to [reflections of] planets and stars, are said to be *that which is apprehended.*

"Consequently, a subtle, apprehending mental consciousness attributes names to these forms, invests them with meaning, and reifies them. Thoughts arise that cling to forms as pleasant, unpleasant, and neutral, and they are called the *mind of visual apprehension.*

"Likewise, the unimpeded objects that emerge as sounds are called *objects*, the appearances that emerge as sounds are said to be *that which is apprehended*, and the mental consciousness that adheres to them is called the *apprehending mind.* [330] As described above, these are dependently related events arising from the assembly of causes and conditions.

"Likewise, the appearances that emerge as smells are merely conventionally named *olfactory consciousness*, the appearances that emerge as tastes are merely named *gustatory consciousness*, and the appearances that emerge as tactile sensations are merely named *tactile consciousness*. But they do not actually appear to those various orifices, which is made clear by the appearances in dreams and the intermediate period.

"Some people take appearances to be the mind, and they may think that all outer appearances are discursive thoughts and really their own minds, but it is not so. This is demonstrated by the fact that appearances change from the very moment they arise, with former moments sequentially passing away and giving rise to later ones, while the mind does not take on the nature of any of these moments, which would render it nonexistent. Thus, as appearances to the eight types of consciousness sequentially emerge in their natural order, saṃsāra fully manifests. As they reabsorb back into the substrate consciousness, they subside into the peak of mundane existence.

"In this way the whole world of appearances of saṃsāra and nirvāṇa is none other than the ground of being, and it is of one taste in that very ground. As an analogy, you must understand that even though various reflections of the planets and stars appear in the ocean, in reality they are of one taste in the water. The revelation of all phenomena to be your own appearances [331] is the essential teaching of Vajradhara."

Saying this, he disappeared from view.

Teachings of Hūṃchenkāra

On yet another occasion when I met the great vidyādhara Hūṃchenkāra, I asked him, "What is this array of appearances like?"

He replied, "O great being, the five kinds of sensory consciousness are like space, in which anything may emerge. Discursive thoughts are like substances and mantras used by an illusionist, such that illusion-like arrays of appearances arise due to their simultaneous conjunction. Consciousness that closely attends to them is like a spectator.

"Thus, all substances that are offered and donated are like illusory substances. The approach of the illusion-like yoga is to dissolve them into emptiness with purifying mantras, and then use enriching mantras to immeasurably increase the appearances of these offerings to the six senses of the objects of worship, so that they are well pleased. Further, by means of the illusion-like yoga, you generate appearances like a city of gandharvas to emanation-like sentient beings; and by transforming these dream-like appearances, you liberate and guide them and so forth, and by so doing you gain mastery over the great yoga of illusion.

"No matter how many planets and stars are reflected in a lake, [332] the reflections are encompassed within the water itself. No matter how many physical worlds and their sentient inhabitants there are, they are encompassed within a single space. And no matter how vast and numerous are the appearances of saṃsāra and nirvāṇa, they are encompassed within the single ultimate nature of mind. Observe how this is so!

"The ultimate nature of mind, which is called the *sugatagarbha*, is a uniform pervasiveness uncontaminated by faults. For example, even if it were possible for space to be filled with buddhas, there is uniform pervasiveness in that there is no object that could be benefited by their primordial consciousness and sublime qualities. And even if there were autonomous sentient beings throughout the whole of space, there is uniform pervasiveness in that there is no object that can be harmed by them.

"The ground dharmakāya, the sugatagarbha, has no place, object, or agent of origination, so it is free of the extreme of origination. Since it transcends any time of cessation and any agent that ceases to exist, it is free of the extreme of cessation. Since it is invisible even to the eyes of the jinas due to not falling to the extreme of real existence, it is free of the extreme of permanence. Since it is the universal basis of saṃsāra and nirvāṇa, without being totally nonexistent, it is free of the extreme of nihilism. Because it is beyond all locations, objects, and agents of going, [333] it is free of the extreme of going. Since no location, object, or agent of coming is established as real, it is free of the extreme of coming.

"In the expanse of the ground sugatagarbha, all phenomena of saṃsāra and nirvāṇa appear distinctly and individually; like [reflections of] planets and stars in the ocean, they are free of the extreme of unity. However the modes of saṃsāra and nirvāṇa arise, they are of one taste in the ground sugatagarbha; just as the planets and stars reflected in the ocean are not other than the ocean, this is free of the extreme of diversity. Since it does not fall to any of the eight extremes of conceptual elaboration, its uniform pervasiveness is unsullied by faults.

"Further, it is empty in that it transcends the categories of above, below, the cardinal and intermediate directions, intervals, and time. It is empty in that it is all-pervasive and all-encompassing. There is outer emptiness in that all outer appearances cannot be established as bearing substantial characteristics or as being truly existent. There is inner emptiness in that your own inner mind transcends having any ground or root. There is the great uniform pervasiveness of nonexclusive emptiness in that between the outer and inner, there is no dualistic differentiation of the apprehended and the apprehender. This is emptiness as a door of liberation.

"The ground dharmakāya, the sugatagarbha, is free of signs that can be expressed in words, it transcends metaphorical approximations, and it is devoid of anything that could be actually demonstrated. This is the absence of signs as a door of liberation. [334]

"Regarding ultimate reality, the sugatagarbha, or 'the sugatas of the three times,' the notion that this is a result of merely practicing physical and verbal virtues, and that it entails going to some other realm and being liberated there, is to think that the panoramic sweep of all-pervasive space is an object or agent of coming and going. This is an extremely confused and muddled notion!

"What is the path? It is holding to your own place within yourself. What is realization? It is truly knowing your own essential nature and mode of existence. What is liberation? It is simply your own awakening to your own essential nature. It is utterly deluded to grasp at anything else as the state or location of liberation and to strive for that. Ultimately, since there is not even a goal to aspire for, this is the absence of aspiration as a door of liberation.

"O my child, Faculty of Pristine Awareness, you will not be liberated merely by my talking and your hearing like this. Investigate and analyze the nature of that which has already been explained. Let experience arise from the depths, stabilize your continuum of conscious awareness, and then teach fortunate people who are suitable vessels. By transferring my Enlightened View Lineage to individuals who practice single-pointedly, there is no doubt that they will soon achieve liberation." [335]

Saying this, he disappeared.

Teachings of Mañjuśrī, the Lion of Speech

On another occasion when I encountered Mañjuśrī, the Lion of Speech, in a meditative experience of clear light, I asked him, "O Teacher, protector of the world, although I have correctly ascertained how all appearances of the physical world and its sentient inhabitants are nothing other than my own appearances, please reveal to me whether or not the distinct names and pure realms of all the buddhas are established as autonomously existent objects."

The teacher replied, "O great being, listen! The qualities of precious spontaneous actualization constitute the inner glow of the ground dharmakāya, the sugatagarbha. With this as the basis, the displays of the buddhafields and the male and female deities, together with their palaces, are naturally perfect in the ground itself—and this perfection is wisdom. Presenting them as existing in other realms is skillful means. The perfection of their sublime qualities in the ground itself is ultimate, while explanations of their existing in other physical worlds with their sentient inhabitants are relative. Moreover, the spontaneous actualization of the ground itself as displays of the kāyas and facets of primordial consciousness is the definitive meaning. All explanations of the buddhafields and the names of male and female deities and so on [336] as entities with real characteristics existing in other realms constitute provisional meanings.

"The following are presentations of the ultimate as relative, in accordance with the ways of saṃsāra. Here is how all the jinas are subsumed within the five kāyas: The great ultimate reality of the uncontrived, naturally present existence of all phenomena included in the world of appearances of saṃsāra and nirvāṇa as the ground absolute space, the great emptiness, is called *dharma.* Due to the unimaginable range of dispositions and specific faculties, there is an unimaginable range of entrances to the path, experiences, and goals to be achieved. Their natural presence is called *kāya.*

"The natural perfection of the displays of the spontaneously actualized kāyas and facets of primordial consciousness as enjoyments is called *saṃbhogakāya.* The displays of emanations that are none other than the ground, without any mental activity of thinking to send forth emanations, are teacher nirmāṇakāyas, created nirmāṇakāyas, living-being nirmāṇakāyas, and material nirmāṇakāyas. The consciousness that grasps at the self is like a container of water, and the sublime qualities of the absolute space of the sugatagarbha are like the planets and stars in the sky. When these occur simultaneously, emanations as dependently related events appear to be of four kinds. In reality, the physical world and its sentient inhabitants are none other than displays of the three kāyas.

"The aspect of the essential nature [of the sugatagarbha] as emptiness is called *dharmakāya,* the aspect of its nature as spontaneous actualization is called *saṃbhogakāya,* [337] and the aspect of its distinct appearances is called *nirmāṇakāya.* Moreover, the ground itself is the essential nature of all of saṃsāra and nirvāṇa, and in this essential nature everything is of one taste, so it is called *svabhāva*; and because all sublime qualities and facets of primordial consciousness are assembled in an aggregate, as it were, it is called *kāya.*

"Since [the ground of being] is unchanging throughout the three times and does not transform into any other essential nature, it is called *immutable.* Since it cannot be injured by anything else, it is called invulnerable. Since it cannot be destroyed by itself or anything else, it is indestructible. Since it is the universal basis of saṃsāra and nirvāṇa, it is real. Since it cannot be contaminated by good or bad qualities, it is incorruptible. Since it is devoid of movement, it is stable. Since it can penetrate even the subtlest cognitive obscurations, it is unobstructable. Since it cannot be overcome by any object or condition, it is invincible.

"Thus, the nature of existence of the ultimate, indestructible *vajra* is imbued with four pledges: It is impossible for sentient beings to realize it, apart from those beings who possess the necessary karma and good fortune. Once it has been realized and put into practice, it is impossible for you not to acquire indwelling confidence in it. When confidence is acquired, it is impossible for you not to be liberated. As for the extent of your liberation, it is impossible for you not to become enlightened.

"The natural presence of these five kāyas in the ground itself is ultimate, while explanations of them as being distinct [338] constitute the relative path of skillful means.

"In accordance with beings' obsessions with families, here is the basis for speaking of the families of deities: Since the ground of being is such that the defilements of habitual propensities are cleansed in absolute space, it is said to be *cleansed*. Since the facets of primordial consciousness and sublime qualities are naturally fulfilled, it is said to be *fulfilled*. Since it is imbued with the seven vajra qualities, it is called the *vajra family*. Since it is the origin of all kāyas and facets of primordial consciousness, it is called the *jewel family*. Since it is not sullied by faults or defilements, it is called the *lotus family*. Since it thoroughly accomplishes enlightened activities, it is called the *karma family*. The term *family* refers to the respective associations embraced by each one.

"The following are teachings on the five buddhafields, presented in accordance with people's obsessions with land: Ghanavyūha [Compact Display] is so called because of the spontaneously actualized, compact density of sublime qualities in the absolute space of the ground. Abhirati [Higher Joy] is so called because it is imbued with great joy that is not created by any object, condition, or agent. Śrīmat [Endowed with Glory] is so called because it is imbued with a glorious bounty of facets of primordial consciousness and sublime qualities. Sukhāvatī [Land of Bliss] is so called because it is imbued with the taintless primordial consciousness of bliss and emptiness. Karmaprasiddhi [Perfection of Excellent Deeds] is so called because it brings to perfection all actions of purification and liberation.

"The term *field* refers to absolute space, and the term *realm* indicates that it is none other than that absolute space. [339]

"Since the sublime qualities of the ground cannot be measured, it is called *immeasurable*, and since it fills all of saṃsāra and nirvāṇa, it is called a *palace*.

"When the natural glow of the omnipresent absolute space of the ground is made manifest by all-pervasive great wisdom, all the facets of primordial consciousness and sublime qualities of the domain of the ground sugatagarbha are illuminated. Because [the ground] is imbued with the seven indestructible vajra qualities and is free of wavering and movement throughout the three times, it is an immutable vajra. Because it is the source of all the dharmas of the path and fruition, and because it is imbued with a bounty of sublime qualities, it is called a source of jewels. The illumination of the ground is limitless, so it is boundless illumination. Since all authentic aims naturally emerge within it, it is said to accomplish aims.

"Since all phenomena of saṃsāra and nirvāṇa appear in the manner of coming and going in the true vajra, the space of emptiness, this is called Vajraḍākinī. The self-emergent aspect of all the facets of primordial consciousness and sublime qualities, which are like a treasury of jewels, is

Ratnaḍākinī. The aspect of freedom from all attachments is Padmaḍākinī. The self-emergence of actions of the spontaneously actualized kāyas and facets of primordial consciousness—not performed with deeds or accomplished with effort—is Karmaḍākinī. Since the afflictive and cognitive obscurations are cleansed in the absolute space of phenomena, [340] and the facets of primordial consciousness and sublime qualities are naturally brought to fulfillment, it is called Buddha; and since all phenomena of saṃsāra and nirvāṇa appear in the aspects of coming and going in the expanse of the space of great emptiness, it is called ḍākinī.

"Thus, the manifestation of the ground dharmakāya, the sugatagarbha, the great reality that totally pervades saṃsāra and nirvāṇa, is the ground pristine awareness, which is the great freedom from extremes; and all ultimate sādhanas are synthesized as follows:

"Self-mastery—through your conviction that the ground pristine awareness is the synthesis of all the [Three] Jewels—is the ultimate, unsurpassed, real taking of refuge in the nature of existence.

"Throughout the course of beginningless lifetimes, you have grasped at true existence and have fixated on objects, causing you to become very small minded. Now, having come to a decisive understanding of saṃsāra and nirvāṇa as continuous displays of the one pristine awareness, the scope of your mind is expanded. This is the most sublime of all methods for generating bodhicitta.

"The dualistic mind that grasps at the apprehender and the apprehended is the great demon of conditioned existence that causes you to wander among the three realms of saṃsāra. With discerning wisdom, expel this into emptiness devoid of objects.

"The experience of the wisdom that realizes identitylessness is the wheel of protection of bodhicitta, which cannot be vanquished or destroyed.

"The descent of the great blessing of primordial consciousness, pristine awareness, into the darkness of ignorance [341] constitutes the actual descent of blessings.

"With the realization of how appearances arise as ornaments of pristine awareness, the arrays of naturally occurring sensory experiences become offerings.

"The transformation of the substrate into the dharmakāya is the enlightenment of the primordial ground of being. The actualization of the wisdom that knows the nature of existence [of that ground] just as it is, along with the all-knowing and all-illuminating wisdom that perceives the full range [of phenomena], is the synthesis of the mysteries of all the jinas and jinaputras.

"The assembly of haughty guardians of the teachings represents the path of skillful means for your initial realization; the array of bodhisattvas represents the path of skillful means for the mastery of the eighth bodhisattva ground and higher; and the array of buddhas and buddhafields represents the path of skillful means for manifest buddhahood.

"Explanations of the ignorance of the substrate as Maheśvara and of all the configurations of thoughts that arise from it as the eight classes of guardians of the teachings, dharmapālas, gods, and demons are expressions of skillful means.

"The appearances of creative expressions of great primordial consciousness emerging of themselves from the manifestation of the dharmakāya, the primordial ground of being, are classified and presented as paths of skillful means, and the manifestation of ultimate buddhahood is the sādhana. All sādhanas and maṇḍalas are synthesized and perfected in this. [342]

"The invitation consists of manifesting the essential nature by transforming all phenomena of the three realms of saṃsāra into displays of the one great ultimate reality.

"Holding your own ground within yourself, without movement or change within the three times, is the request to remain.

"When you encounter your own face as the dharmakāya—the primordial ground of being, the sovereign view—your experience of great wonder is the homage of encountering the view.

"The display of phenomena as ultimate reality is the great offering.

"The wonder and confidence upon truly perceiving the mode of existence of the Great Perfection of saṃsāra and nirvāṇa is the actual praise.

"The individual, distinct appearances of various phenomena are arrays of the enlightened body. Their spontaneous perfection and actualization is the display of the enlightened speech. Primordially pure absolute space, free of the extremes of conceptual elaboration, is the display of the enlightened mind.

"The qualities of realizing how the displays of the kāyas and facets of primordial consciousness are spontaneously actualized, without being sought after, include mastery over the four kinds of enlightened activity; and these are characteristics of the pristine awareness of the Great Perfection.

"Know that the four empowerments are likewise simultaneously perfected in the enlightened body, speech, mind, qualities, and activities within yourself.

"Thus, truly knowing and realizing the nature of perfection is certainly the Great Perfection. As a result of failing to know this, [343] you have wandered in saṃsāra in the past. Although perfection is primordial, it has been obscured by ignorance. This is like water that is naturally liquid freezing into a solid, and like having no relief from poverty due to failing to recognize gold and jewels.

"Ultimately, the facets of primordial consciousness and sublime qualities of the ground sugatagarbha are perfected as creative displays of this ground. Explanations of them as individual supporting maṇḍalas and supported deities are presented as skillful means to guide disciples who grasp at things as permanent in ultimate, effortless absolute space, and they depend on relative paths entailing effort. Therefore, using the three essential points of luminosity, purity, and emptiness, those disciples are led to the fruition of supreme absolute space."

With these words, he disappeared.

Teachings of the Lake-Born Vajra of Orgyen

On yet another occasion, I met the glorious Lake-Born Vajra and asked him, "O Omnipresent Lord and Primordial Protector, why are there teachings on the generation and accomplishment of buddhafields, celestial palaces, and deities?"

He replied, "These worlds that extend throughout space are the outer rūdra of the reified view of the self. The remedy for it is the purification of buddhafields created from emanated light. Inwardly, grasping at your dwelling place, possessions, and body [344] is the inner rūdra of the reified view of the self. The remedy for it is meditation on celestial palaces and deities. At all times and in all circumstances, the cohesive, uninterrupted latent consciousness of that which appears as a self called 'I' is the secret rūdra of the reified view of the self. This is the common thread running through all appearances and mindsets of saṃsāra. The remedy for it is firmly holding to divine pride.

"If they do not know these vital points, some people disregard the visualizations of the stage of generation and the maintenance of divine pride and apply themselves to verbal recitations alone. Some people practice while reifying the deities and buddhafields. But since it is impossible to achieve enlightenment in those ways, recognize these vital points."

With these words, he disappeared.

Teachings of Ekajaṭī

On yet another occasion, when I had a vision of the Lady of Absolute Space, Ekajaṭī, I asked, "O sole grandmother of saṃsāra and nirvāṇa, what is the name of this yāna that is displayed in the secret space of the Lady of Absolute Space, the great emptiness of saṃsāra and nirvāṇa?"

She replied, "O mother's little boy, I have fully granted you the Enlightened View Lineage of the Buddhas, which is like providing you with a body. I have reared you, as though suckling you with mother's milk, with the Symbolic Lineage [of the Vidyādharas]. I have fostered your wisdom by providing you with the heartfelt advice of the Aural Lineage [of Ordinary Individuals]. [345] Revealing this to all those fortunate disciples who are connected to it by way of their karma and prayers is meaningful.

"My name is given to the king of all yānas. All sounds express my name. The essential secret—this perfected display as the unsurpassed space of the mother ḍākinī—has numerous synonyms, but I say they are included in seven names.

"Since this Dharma involves two great kinds of secrecy, it is called *secret*. Since it protects you from the dangers of concepts of the self and engaging with its characteristics, it is called *mantra*. It is called the ultimate, indestructible *vajra*. Since the sublime qualities of all paths are distilled in it, it is called *yāna*.

"Since it is present as the ultimate mode of being of all phenomena, it is called *reality*. Since it is the foremost of all that is to be realized, it is called *ultimate*. Since it is purified of all faults and stains, it is called *pure*. Since it fully embraces all kāyas, facets of primordial consciousness, and sublime qualities of the path and fruition, it is called *full*. Since it is the basis for the emergence of everything appearing as various displays of purity and equality, and since it is present as the sole life force of the three vajras, it is called *citta*, or heart—that is, mind.

"It is the *perfection* of saṃsāra and nirvāṇa. Since it synthesizes and unifies all the yānas, it is the universal basis of all yānas and is therefore called *great*. [346]

"Since it transcends all the edges and corners of concepts, it is called *bindu*. Since saṃsāra and nirvāṇa are of one taste in bodhicitta, it is called *sole*.

"Since the nature of pristine awareness, the sugatagarbha, is lucid, luminous, and free of contamination, it is called *clear light*. Since it is imbued with the seven indestructible vajra qualities, it is called *vajra*. Since it abides as the distilled essence of all phenomena of saṃsāra and nirvāṇa, it is called *essence*.

"Since all phenomena of *saṃsāra and nirvāṇa* are fully *embraced* and *consummated* in the nature of the sugatagarbha, it is called the *consummation of saṃsāra and nirvāṇa*.

"Since it is free of birth, death, aging, and degeneration, it is called *youthful*. Since it does not breach the periphery of spontaneous actualization, it is called *vase*. Since it is like an accumulation and compilation of all facets of primordial consciousness and sublime qualities, it is called *kāya*."

With these words, she disappeared.

With that general explanation having been presented, I shall give a more specific account of the manner in which all sublime qualities of the paths of the nine stages of yānas are perfected.

Śrāvakas are so called because they see that everything that appears as a self, which is the basis of grasping at "I" and "self," is devoid of inherent nature. Pratyekabuddhas are so called because they realize all outer and inner things solely as dependently related illusory appearances. Bodhisattvas are so called because for them, the power of realizing emptiness arises in the nature of compassion, effortlessly subsuming all aspects of skillful means and wisdom. [347]

The sublime qualities of these three yānas that lead you away from the origins of suffering are perfect, such that the higher approaches subsume the lower ones.

In kriyā tantra, you please the deity by means of austerities and ritual purifications. In upāya tantra, you achieve siddhis by oral recitations and samādhi. In yoga tantra, there is the yoga of śamatha and vipaśyanā in which you witness the blessings of absolute space, devoid of characteristics, within the great maṇḍala of the vajra, absolute space.

All the sublime qualities and functions of these three yānas that evoke pristine awareness by means of austerities are perfect and complete within the single, coemergent absolute space of your own inexpressible mind, the essence of siddhis.

All the qualities of the father tantra, mahāyoga, are pure from the very beginning in the supreme dharmakāya, ultimate reality endowed with seven attributes, or the indivisibility of the two higher levels of truth.

In orally transmitted anuyoga, the son of the union of primordial being and the maṇḍala of spontaneously actualized primordial consciousness is great bliss, in which appearing phenomena are perfected in great purity and equality in the maṇḍala of bodhicitta.

The nature of existence of the Great Perfection is clear light, in which the precious, spontaneously actualized appearances of the ground of being [348] and phenomena naturally arise without bias or partiality in the one absolute space, which has no periphery or center. All such appearances, undifferentiated like gold and its glow, are simultaneously subsumed in the dharmakāya—unchanging pristine awareness, the great freedom from extremes—and the absolute space of the ground of being, the sugatagarbha. These individual accounts are presented simply for the sake of leading disciples stage by stage.

Teachings of Śrī Siṃha

On another occasion when I encountered the king of vidyādharas, Śrī Siṃha, I asked, "O Teacher, please show me the path of the Great Perfection."

He replied, "The Great Perfection is the great, universal basis of saṃsāra and nirvāṇa, the great absolute space in which saṃsāra, nirvāṇa, and the path are perfect and complete. Knowing its mode of being is the view. Gaining mastery over this great, original, primordial ground, you awaken and expand within yourself, which is meditation that is devoid of a referent. This is like a drop of water merging with the ocean, becoming the ocean without modifying it. It is like the space inside a vase merging with the space outside it, such that it expands infinitely into space without modifying it.

"Although there is no outer or inner with respect to the ground of being and the mind, self-grasping superimposes boundaries between outer and inner. [349] Just as water in its naturally fluid state freezes solid due to currents of cold wind, likewise the naturally fluid ground of being is thoroughly established as saṃsāra by cords of self-grasping.

"Recognizing how that is so, relinquish good, bad, and neutral bodily activities, and remain like a corpse in a charnel ground, doing nothing. Likewise, relinquish the three kinds of verbal activity and remain like a mute; and also relinquish the three kinds of mental activity and rest without modification, like the autumn sky free of the three contaminating conditions. This is called *meditative equipoise*. It is also called *transcendence of the intellect*, for by relinquishing the nine kinds of activity, activities are released without doing anything, and nothing is modified by the intellect. In the context of this vital point, you will acquire great confidence within yourself.

"Moreover, at all times while moving about, sitting, shifting positions, and engaging in oral recitations and mental activities, without losing the perspective of the view, regard appearing phenomena as being like illusions. Without losing the confidence of meditation, be consciously aware of the nature of phenomena. Without allowing your conduct to become careless, properly devote yourself to the four kinds of activity. This is the natural liberation of meditation that transcends the intellect. [350]

"As for the vital point of conduct, do not go astray in your conduct due to your view, thinking that 'Everything is emptiness, so however I behave, I will not be contaminated by faults.' Avoid nonvirtues of the body, speech, and mind as if they were poison. Serene, subdued, and conscientious, behave as if you were entering the presence of a supreme judge.

"On the other hand, if you fixate on other virtues of the body, speech, and mind as if they were of the utmost importance, this will overwhelm the authentic view and meditation. If you spend your whole life merely accumulating merit within saṃsāra, it will be as if you were bound with chains of gold. Without overemphasizing proper conduct at the expense of the view, be like an unconquerable snow lion standing proudly in the snow.

"Furthermore, if you follow after those who say that you must cultivate compassion in some other way, even though you have realized the view of emptiness, this will be like someone who has water but seeks moisture elsewhere, like someone who has fire but seeks warmth elsewhere, or like someone who has wind but says coolness must come from somewhere else.

"The decisive ascertainment of saṃsāra and nirvāṇa as great emptiness is the unsurpassed bodhicitta—the compassion of viewing saṃsāra and nirvāṇa as displays of purity and equality. [351]

"Even though you have correctly identified and recognized the vital points and nature of the view and meditation, if you decide that this alone is sufficient and then fixate on mundane activities, it will result in wasting your life in various activities of attachment and aversion. By so doing, all your view and meditation will be overwhelmed by delusive activities of saṃsāra.

"Appearances of meditative experiences occur when your mind and consciousness shift in unprecedented ways. Pleasurable, soothing experiences of bliss propel you to rebirth as a god of the desire realm. Vivid experiences of luminosity propel you to rebirth as a god of the form realm. A nonconceptual sense of vacuity, in which awareness is withdrawn in an unconscious, blank, unmindful state like deep sleep, propels you to rebirth in the four dimensions of the formless realm. Lacking any knowledge of the view of emptiness, you may determine that the mind is empty merely in the sense that it is not established as something substantial. Resting the mind single-pointedly in this state of vacuity is a view that propels you to the peak of mundane existence and to rebirth as a god who lacks discernment.

"Moreover, outer upheavals include various apparitions appearing to your senses, such as visions of gods and demons arising as bad omens. Inner upheavals include the occurrence of various illnesses and pains in the body. Secret upheavals include random mood swings. If you are aware of the deceptive flaws of all of these and come to a decisive understanding of them, [352] they will vanish of their own accord. If you cling to their true existence and obsessively fixate on hopes and fears, they can become life threatening, resulting in psychotic episodes, fits, seizures, and so on. Succumbing to fixating on them as divine and demonic appearances causes meditative adepts to degenerate into being merely ordinary."

With these words, he disappeared.

Teachings of Zurchung Sherap Drakpa

On yet another occasion, when I encountered Zurchung Sherap Drakpa in the Blazing Volcano Charnel Ground in the self-appearing, actual Akaniṣṭha, I asked, "O guru, please grant me practical instructions that are your heart essence expressed with few words but comprehensive meaning."

He replied, "O you who have assembled accumulations, prayers, and karmic momentum for incalculable eons, listen! If you wish to ascend to the state of omniscient buddhahood, please your guru, with constant admiration and reverence, in all your activities. Continuously cultivate affection and pure perception regarding your friends. With heartfelt compassion for sentient beings, strive for liberation and the state of omniscience. Constantly bearing in mind the impermanence of all composite phenomena, [353] abandon mundane activities and dwell in a state of inactivity. This is the unsurpassed quintessence of all Dharmas.

"Three vital points are offering service to the sublime guru by not squandering his practical instructions; honoring your samayas without hypocrisy, as the life-principle stone of the gods and guardians; and devoting your whole life to the Dharma, so that you know there is nothing left unfinished at the time of death.

"Guarding your samayas and vows as if they were your own life force is the vital point to prevent contemplatives from degenerating into ordinary people. Cultivating contentment with regard to sensory pleasures is how to not get caught up in negative objects. Recognizing that saṃsāra has no essence is how to cut through the fixations of attachment and aversion. Recognizing that mundane activities are never finished and accomplished, that they are like lines of smoke from an incense clock, is the pith instruction for bringing activities to a close.

"First you gain knowledge in reliance upon training. Then you gain experience in your own mindstream and realization by means of investigation and analysis. But liberation is not achieved merely by such knowledge and realization, just as hunger is not satisfied if you have food but don't eat it. Just as darkness does not appear once dawn has broken, when you have given up the nine kinds of activity, [354] you acquire stability within yourself due to the power of meditation. When there is no fragmentation of the panoramic sweep of pristine awareness, indwelling confidence is acquired within your own pristine awareness.

"Still, that by itself will not bring you to enlightenment. When phenomenal appearances have been extinguished into ultimate reality, there is an infinite expansion into the great, all-encompassing sphere of the absolute space of phenomena, devoid of even a trace of the appearances and mindsets of saṃsāra. You have then reached the state of liberation.

"Within this experience, even the subtlest of cognitive obscurations have been utterly cleared away, and mastery is gained over great primordial consciousness that knows reality as it is and perceives the full range of phenomena. So you achieve buddhahood in the dharmakāya, which is like space, and the three kāyas arise as displays of uniform pervasiveness.

"Son of the family, the defining characteristic of the mind is ignorance of the ground of being, with concepts subject to origination and cessation emerging as its creative displays. The defining characteristic of pristine awareness is the realization of the ground of being, with a great, atemporal state of relaxation as its creative display. The ground pristine awareness is knowing the mode of existence of the ground of being. The path pristine awareness is lucid, clear consciousness, free of contamination, by which you experience ultimate reality. All-pervasive pristine awareness, in which these two aspects are simultaneously conjoined, is the Great Perfection.

"The term *mentation* refers to the consciousness that experiences all appearances that emerge as apparitions of thoughts. The term *mental consciousness* refers to the unimpeded avenue for the six objects that emerge as appearances. [355] The *ground wisdom* correctly knows the nature of saṃsāra and nirvāṇa to be great emptiness. The *path wisdom* is the identification of unadulterated, open, unimpeded consciousness. The simultaneous conjunction of these two is called *pervasive wisdom.*

"The unimpeded avenue for appearing objects that emerge as sensory appearances is called *conditioned consciousness.* Thoughts that reify these appearances as things are called *karmic energies.* With the conjunction of these subtle and coarse aspects of mental consciousness, saṃsāra is thoroughly established. The *primordial consciousness that knows reality as it is* correctly knows the nature of ultimate reality, the sugatagarbha. When the mode of existence of suchness, ultimate reality, is actualized, unimpeded, all-knowing, all-cognizing awareness is the *primordial consciousness that perceives the full range of phenomena.* The uniform pervasiveness [of these two] is called the *originally pure primordial consciousness of equality.*

"An ethically neutral state results from the influence of ignorance of the ground of being. Various karmic energies move within the space of the substrate, like various dreams appearing during sleep, and this is the basis and root of the whole of saṃsāra. Within the wide-open clarity of ultimate reality, free of the extremes of conceptual elaboration—the great purity and equality of saṃsāra and nirvāṇa—[356] all appearing phenomena are the spacious dharmakāya, Samantabhadra.

"Son of the family, all reflections of the moon and other things in water are displays of the water and are none other than water. All unmoving and moving things in the physical world and its sentient inhabitants are displays of space and are none other than space. All of saṃsāra and nirvāṇa consists of displays of the one ultimate reality and is none other than ultimate reality.

"Thus, when the great depth and luminosity of the ground dharmakāya is actualized, its essential nature is the dharmakāya, the purity and equality of saṃsāra and nirvāṇa; its manifest nature is the saṃbhogakāya, replete with the facets of primordial consciousness and sublime qualities; and the nirmāṇakāya is self-illuminating compassion, free of obscuring veils. Its displays are called *ultimate*.

"Ignorance of the essential nature of the originally pure ground of being is the substrate. Appearances arise from its radiance and displays of mental factors arise as its creative expressions, and they are called *relative*.

"Having recognized in this way the nature of all displays, encompassments, and uniform pervasiveness, you simply rest in ultimate reality and come to certainty in the natural abiding of great, intellect-transcending, spacious, vacuous, ineffable ultimate reality. Until great, omniscient primordial consciousness is attained, practice with intense, unflagging enthusiasm. Adhere to this supreme vital point!" [357]

With these words, he expanded into the absolute space of ultimate reality.

This text was written in response to heartfelt requests by Pema Lungtok Gyatso and Khyenrap Gyatso, two tulkus who have been connected to me over many lifetimes by their karma and prayers. I, Traktung Düdjom Dorjé Trolö Tsal, codified this from the treasury of the vast expanse of apparitional displays. The ḍākinīs prophesied that sixty-eight sublime individuals would serve as custodians of this Dharma. By the command of the great Orgyen, this was the first occasion on which auspicious circumstances came about [for these teachings to be written down]. My own sublime son, the outstanding scholar Sönam Tenzin (Dodrup Rinpoché), carefully edited the manuscript.

The Fine Path to Liberation

An Explanation of the Stages of the Preliminary Practices for Manuals Such as "Buddhahood Without Meditation"

by
Sera Khandro

[2] FIRST, REGARDING the explanation of the stages to be discussed, the compassionate *jinas*, who are expert in skillful means, have taught an inconceivable number of Dharmas, entrances to the path, and resultant accomplishments in accordance with the temperaments, capacities, and inclinations of disciples. However many teachings they have given, if you synthesize their meaning, they consist of two [*yānas*]: the causal, [Sūtrayāna] with characteristics, and the resultant, secret mantra, Vajrayāna. If you classify them internally, in the causal yāna there are the Śrāvakayāna, the Pratyekabuddhayāna, and the Bodhisattvayāna. In the resultant yāna [3] there are three classes of outer tantras: *kriyā tantra*, *upa tantra*, and *yoga tantra*. The three classes of inner tantras are the father tantras of the [stage of] generation known as *mahāyoga*, the mother tantras of the transmission of *anuyoga*, and the nondual tantras of the Great Perfection known as *atiyoga*. As a tantra states:

> In the past, between the causal and resultant [yānas], among the causal [yānas] there are three [divisions], and among the resultant [yānas] there are two. In the second,[14] there are six categories in accordance with the level of one's faculties.

As for the topic to be discussed here, among the canonical and treasure teachings, this is exceptional due to four qualities: its short lineage, its unerring practical instructions, its great blessings, and its revelation of the descent of the lineage. [4] The meaning of the vast and profound revealed treasures of the Great Perfection, atiyoga, is impeccable, and it includes the three divisions of the mind, expanse, and pith instructions. This is a commentary on the principal, very secret, unsurpassed teaching from a direct vision of Samantabhadra called *Buddhahood Without Meditation*, and it begins with the way to listen to the Dharma, followed by the actual explanation of the meaning of that treatise.[15]

14. This refers to the resultant vehicle, with its three inner tantras and three outer tantras.

15. This second section refers to the commentary to *Buddhahood Without Meditation* called *Garland for the Delight of the Fortunate*, which immediately follows this short, preliminary text on the way to listen to the Dharma.

I. The Way to Listen to the Dharma

First, regarding the way to listen to the Dharma, there are (A) the general explanation and (B) the specific explanation.

A. The General Explanation

It is extremely important that you expel the miserable attitude of thinking only about yourself, by considering that "Among all sentient beings dwelling since beginningless time in *saṃsāra*, there is not even one who has not been my father or mother. So in order for them to be freed from the miserable ocean of saṃsāra and to achieve the truly perfected state of buddhahood, I shall authentically practice the profound, sublime Dharma." In this way, bring forth the indefatigable Mahāyāna motivation of *bodhicitta* to achieve the well-being of others. As Maitreyanātha declared:

> The generation of bodhicitta aspires to
> truly perfected buddhahood for the sake of others. [5]

Especially concerning the practice of the profound path of the secret mantra, Vajrayāna, the goal aspired for and the resolution of bodhicitta are crucial. As the *Lamp for the Three Methods* states:

> Because of its lack of confusion regarding even a single point,
> its many methods, which are not difficult,
> and its mastery by those with sharp faculties,
> the Mantrayāna is exceptional.

This secret mantra, Vajrayāna, has many methods that can be practiced without needing to undergo great hardships. The root of its many profound methods for actualizing the fruition [of enlightenment] depends on the transformation of your aspirations. As it is written:

> The contributing condition for all Dharmas
> dwells on the summit of your aspirations.

You must listen to the sublime Dharma with a pure body, speech, and mind—not grasping at the ordinary, autonomous existence of the teaching, the teacher, and so on—but rather imagining them to be imbued with five perfections: The perfect place is the pristine buddhafield of the absolute space of phenomena, Akaniṣṭha. The perfect teacher is the primordial lord, the *dharmakāya*, Samantabhadra. The perfect retinue is [6] the Enlightened View Lineage of the Buddhas and the Symbolic Lineage of the Vidyādharas, visualized as male and female bodhisattvas, gods, and goddesses. The perfect Dharma is the Mahāyāna Dharma of the unsurpassed fruition—the Great Perfection. The perfect time is imagined as the fourth time—one of perfect symmetry, an eternal, continuous cycle, free of movement and change. By such means your body, speech, and mind must be purified, enabling blessings to flow into your mindstream.

On all occasions—whether you are teaching or listening to the Dharma or practicing meditation—you must carefully examine your own mindstream and listen in a way that is free of the following three faults: Like an upside-down container, however the words of Dharma are expressed, you do not hear them or retain the slightest bit of their meaning. Like a leaky container, even though you hear the mere sounds of the Dharma, your conceptual mind is unstable regarding their meaning from start to finish. Like a toxic container, even though you retain the words of the Dharma, they do not act as remedies for your mental afflictions, because your mindstream is not sustained by the pure spirit of emergence and bodhicitta. These faults must be avoided, as is said in the sūtras: "O monks, listen well and attentively and bear in mind what you hear, and I shall teach you." By listening well to the Dharma, [7] the fault of a toxic container is dispelled. By listening attentively, the fault of an upside-down container is dispelled. And by bearing the teachings in mind, the fault of a leaky container is remedied.

When you listen to the Dharma, you should avoid everything that is incompatible with the Dharma, such as the egoistic pride of thinking you are highly knowledgeable, lack of faith in your Dharma friends and the guru, lack of interest in the Dharma, and allowing your eyes and other senses to be distracted elsewhere. Instead, when you listen to the Dharma, you should take delight in receiving the sublime Dharma, and with firm reverence and faith purify the faults of the six contaminants[16] and focus solely on the welfare of sentient beings, as is written in the *Condensed Perfection of Wisdom Sūtra*:

> By abiding in delight, reverence, and supreme faith,
> obscurations and mental afflictions are dispelled and defilements
> are left behind.
> By applying yourself to the welfare of sentient beings, heroic
> wisdom is perfected.
> O valiant disciples, follow such conduct.

16. The six contaminants are (1) pride, (2) lack of faith, (3) lack of dedication to practice, (4) distraction, (5) dullness, and (6) depression.

Here is how to practice the six perfections: Setting out the Dharma seat and offerings is generosity. Listening to the Dharma while restraining your body, speech, and mind is ethical discipline. Enduring harm by others at that time is patience. Requesting the guru to teach the Dharma is enthusiasm. [8] Listening without distraction to the meaning of the Dharma is meditation. Inquiring by means of investigation and analysis into the points of uncertainty is wisdom. These are the six aspects of a listener. The *Tantra of Manifest Realization* states:

> Beautifully offering flowers, a seat, and so forth;
> restraining your conduct in the room;
> refraining from harming all living creatures;
> offering prayers of supplication to the guru;
> retaining the guru's teachings without distraction; and
> making critical inquiries in order to dispel your uncertainties:
> these are the six aspects of the lamp.

Accordingly, listening to the Dharma while properly bringing to mind everything regarding your motivation and conduct is very important, so this is a sublimely important point.

B. The Specific Explanation

Regarding the specific explanation, there are five topics: (1) the cultivation of admiration and reverence for the guru, (2) the cultivation of love and affection for your *vajra* siblings and friends, (3) the cultivation of compassion for sentient beings, (4) the cultivation of the spirit of emergence regarding saṃsāra, and (5) meditation on the impermanence of composite phenomena.

1. The Cultivation of Admiration and Reverence for the Guru

In general there are said to be six kinds of teachers from whom you receive teachings,[17] but the one who grants empowerments, explains the tantras, and provides pith instructions is the root guru who is imbued with the three kindnesses. Nowhere in the sūtras or tantras are there accounts of anyone achieving enlightenment without devotion to a guru. It is empirically evident that all the *siddhas* of the past without exception [9] developed the sublime qualities of the grounds and paths and achieved *siddhis* by first devoting

17. The six kinds of teachers are (1) teachers who grant samayas and vows, (2) teachers who grant oral transmissions, (3) teachers who explain the tantras, (4) teachers who provide pith instructions, (5) teachers who bestow empowerments, and (6) teachers who perform work.

themselves to their gurus who were physically present and those who were not. Therefore, even though the guru is truly a buddha, free of all faults and replete with all sublime qualities, the mindstreams of ordinary individuals like us are easily swayed by the influences of our social environments, historical eras, friends, and so on. For this reason, it is important that you first thoroughly examine the guru, both closely and from a distance. Then, eliminate the faults of your own speculations and negative attitudes and devote yourself to the guru. Finally, offer your services by pleasing the guru in three ways,[18] and without letting your *samayas* deteriorate or be broken, emulate the thoughts and behavior of your guru, as if you were shaping yourself in his mold. Because of the degenerate nature of the current era, it is difficult to find a guru who has all the attributes described in the collections of tantras. Nevertheless, the guru to whom you devote yourself must have all these positive qualities:

- Purity of the three kinds of vows
- Great erudition
- Compassion for sentient beings
- Knowledge of the collections of the three outer divisions of the teachings and of the meaning of the inner secret mantra, Vajrayāna Dharma
- For the guru's own sake, the actualization of realization and the perfect achievement of positive qualities and the abandonment of negative ones
- For the sake of others, [10] the ability to provide training in the sublime Dharma by way of body, speech, and mind in inconceivable ways, in accordance with the temperaments and capabilities of individual students
- The ability to assemble fortunate students by the four means of gathering others.[19]

It is important to devote yourself to such a spiritual mentor, and specifically to a guru who reveals the profound points of pith instructions in the secret mantra, Vajrayāna. Due to the unbroken lineage of ripening empowerments

18. The three ways to please the guru are by means of (1) offering material goods, (2) offering service, and (3) devoting yourself to practice.

19. The four means of gathering others are (1) pleasing others by giving them material things or whatever they need, (2) teaching the Dharma to lead others to liberation, (3) helping others in their Dharma practice by giving them encouragement, and (4) showing others a good example by always practicing what you teach.

and liberating teachings, his mindstream is ripened and liberated. The guru's [conduct] does not conflict with the root of commitments taken at the time of an empowerment, namely the samayas and vows of enlightened body, speech, and mind, and so on. He has few mental afflictions and obsessive thoughts, his mindstream is calm and subdued, and he has internalized the meaning of all the tantras and the pith instructions pertaining to the ground, path, and fruition. Having seen the signs of the stages of generation and completion, he has correctly actualized the nature of existence. Having renounced [the concerns of] this life, he constantly dwells in solitary retreat. Imbued with great altruism, he brings living beings onto the path of Dharma by every suitable means. By practicing in accordance with such a guru's instructions, you receive swift blessings of the lineage, and excellent qualities manifest.

A guru who has all these sublime qualities is the regent of all buddhas of the past, [11] the source of all buddhas of the future, and an emanation of all buddhas of the present. His body is the Saṅgha, his speech is the sublime Dharma, and his mind is the Buddha. His enlightened body is the guru, his enlightened speech is the personal deity, and his enlightened mind is the ḍākinī. His enlightened body is the nirmāṇakāya, his enlightened speech is the saṃbhogakāya, and his enlightened mind is the dharmakāya. The synthesized essential nature of the objects of refuge is the compassionate root guru. Regarding him as an actual buddha, reverently offer prostrations with your body, reverently offer prayers of supplication with your speech, and with your mind reverently visualize the guru in the center of your crown, your throat, and your heart. While merging your mind and so on with that of the guru, by unpretentiously pleasing him in the three ways with your body, speech, and mind, it is of vital importance that you maintain continuous faith, pure perception, admiration, and reverence. Even if you know the three collections of teachings as if by heart, if you lack admiration and reverence for your guru, there will not be even the slightest benefit for your mindstream. As it is written:

> The guru is the Buddha, the guru is the Dharma,
> and the guru is also the Saṅgha.
> The master of everything is the guru.
> The guru is the glorious Vajradhara.

Drikung Kyobpa Rinpoché [1143–1217] declared:

> If the sun of admiration and reverence does not rise
> on the snow mountain of the four *kāyas* of the guru,

> the stream of blessings will not flow. [12]
> So earnestly devote your mind to admiration and reverence for
> him.

Accordingly, if you single-pointedly pray to the guru, without a vacillating mind or uncertainty, his realizations will be transferred to you, and you will achieve all the supreme and common siddhis.

2. The Cultivation of Love and Affection for Your Vajra Siblings and Friends

The guru, your spiritual mentor, and your vajra siblings and friends are like guides on the path to the land of omniscience and liberation, so you should devote yourself to them with love and affection. Although there are four internal divisions of vajra siblings,[20] here the coupling of siblings and friends is like that of twins—so on all occasions and in all ways restrain your conduct by way of body, speech, and mind with affection and loving-kindness, without any duplicity regarding the samayas. Viewing everything they say as credible, as if they were your gurus, cultivate pure perception with the admiration and reverence of seeing their conduct as symbolic of the Dharma, whatever they do. You should never be separated from them, as if they were your own heart, and you should hold them dear with love and affection. The *Awesome Lightning of Primordial Consciousness* states:

> With affection for your vajra siblings,
> for all your siblings, for those with whom you are and are not
> close, and
> for those who have entered the authentic path, [13]
> always avoid even the mere thought of contempt.
> Bring forth the power of love and affection,
> and look after each other as you would your own eyes.

Until you actualize liberation and the omniscient state of perfect buddhahood, you must accompany your vajra siblings and friends. So it is important

20. The four internal divisions of vajra siblings are (1) *general* brothers and sisters, who are all the sentient beings possessing buddha nature, (2) *distant* brothers and sisters, who are all the practitioners belonging to the retinue of the Buddha, (3) *close* brothers and sisters, who are Vajrayāna practitioners, and (4) *inseparable* brothers and sisters, who belong to the retinue of the same guru. Those who receive empowerment together from the same maṇḍala are like siblings with the same father.

that you love them and do not let your samayas degenerate. If they degenerate, you and everyone else will wander about in miserable states of existence, so you must properly guard your samayas and ardently love your vajra siblings.

3. The Cultivation of Compassion for Sentient Beings

Among all sentient beings throughout space, there is not one who has not been your father or mother, but under the influence of the delusive appearances of their own karma, those sentient beings, who have been your parents, experience only suffering, without even the briefest occasion of happiness. Resolve that "In order to purify and cleanse the appearances of their karma, habitual propensities, and suffering, and to achieve the precious state of authentic, omniscient buddhahood, I shall generate bodhicitta to achieve perfect enlightenment and shall dredge the depths of the ocean of the three realms of saṃsāra." [14] With this heartfelt motivation, you should cast off the attitude of self-centeredness and cultivate compassion for the sake of sentient beings, like Prince Courage.[21] The *dohā*s of the glorious Saraha state:

> One whose view of emptiness is devoid of compassion
> does not reach the supreme path.
> Even if you cultivate compassion alone,
> you will remain here in saṃsāra, but where is liberation?
> One who has both
> does not remain either in mundane existence or in *nirvāṇa*.

Accordingly, loving-kindness, compassion, and bodhicitta are indispensable for Dharma practitioners. At all times, whatever path you follow, they are like your pillar of life, so you should practice them correctly.

4. The Cultivation of the Spirit of Emergence Regarding Saṃsāra

Wherever we are born in saṃsāra, whether in its heights, its depths, or in between, it never transcends the nature of suffering—an ever-shifting display of misery and a delusive cycle of pain, nothing more. Therefore, by reflecting on the ways in which the activities of saṃsāra are devoid of essence, resolve

21. Tib. *snying stobs can*. This is a reference to Prince Great Courage (*rgyal bu snying stobs chen po*), one of three sons of the king at Namo Buddha in Nepal, the other two being Great God (*lha chen po*) and Great Mighty One (*mthu thob chen po*). When Prince Great Courage saw a tigress in the forest that was dying of starvation, he offered his body to her so that she could save her starving cubs. The prince was a previous incarnation of Buddha Śākyamuni when he was a bodhisattva.

that "I shall renounce all activities of this life, such as subduing my enemies and protecting my friends, and devote myself solely to practicing the sublime Dharma." With this firm intention, [15] you should go by yourself to an unpopulated, solitary place and let your practice pervade your whole life. Otherwise, if you have attachment to those who are close to you and aversion to those who are distant, while craving and clinging to such things as food, clothing, and enjoyments as if this were a city of *gandharva*s, your practice will act as a cause for higher and lower rebirths, with no occasion for happiness, and you must experience only misery. The great Orgyen declared:

> Here in saṃsāra there is never
> as much happiness as would fit on the tip of a needle.
> Even slight happiness is the suffering of change.

Accordingly, it is very important that you come to a complete and decisive certainty that the activities of saṃsāra have no essence, and then strive solely for the essence—the sublime Dharma.

5. Meditation on the Impermanence of Composite Phenomena

All outer appearances of the firm and solid physical world, the numerous inner sentient beings who move about and inhabit the physical world, and all the beautiful intervening appearances of the five sensory fields are finally impermanent and subject to destruction. Apart from that, however composite phenomena may appear, they are not self-sustaining, like clouds in the sky, and all activities are like last night's dream or like rainbows in the sky, [16] never remaining. So continually meditate on death and impermanence, and with the thought that "death is coming," until you cast off that sense of dread, without laziness or procrastination, you must bring your life and spiritual practice to culmination. The noble Mokchokpa commented:

> The experiences of those in whom [the awareness of]
> death has not arisen are like autumnal mist.
> The nobility of those in whom [the awareness of]
> death has not arisen is like that of a king's consort.
> The courage of those in whom [the awareness of]
> death has not arisen is like ice in the summertime.

Accordingly, impermanence is a motivating force for Dharma, so you should by all means bring forth this certainty in your mindstream at all times and on all occasions. Leave your homeland behind, adopt another region, disregard hardships, let your body and life force be an object [of abuse], live happily in a cave as your home, let wild animals be your companions, entrust your heart to the guru and the Dharma, and bring your life and spiritual practice to culmination. This is the most cherished, sublime point.

Whatever kind of practice you adopt, with meditative objects belonging to the stages of generation and completion, the above five topics are indispensable. They are the most important things to practice, like a heart treasure for all Dharma practitioners, [17] so each of you should definitely take them to heart. This concludes the explanation of the stages to be discussed. This is just a synopsis of auxiliary elements of the Dharma from the root text, adapted by Dewé Dorjé as requisites for practice.[22]

May there be virtue!
Sarva maṅgalam!

22. Tib. *bde ba'i rdo rje*. This is Sera Khandro's personal name.

Garland for the Delight of the Fortunate

A Supremely Clear Elucidation of Words and Their Meaning:
An Explication of the Oral Transmission of the Glorious Guru,
as Notes on the Nature of Reality, the Great Perfection,
"Buddhahood Without Meditation"

by
Sera Khandro

Homage [20]

Homage to self-emergent pristine awareness, indivisible from the three kāyas,
inconceivably emanated as apparitional displays for guiding others, out of compassion,
to the spontaneously actualized kāyas, facets of primordial consciousness, and the perfection of sublime qualities,
in the space of the lucid expanse of the absolute space of phenomena, free of extremes.
With faith I bow a hundred times to the three ultimate refuges:
the Buddha, whose expansive, sublime qualities of freedom and realization awaken us from the sleep of ignorance,
the Dharma of scripture and realization that pacifies mental afflictions,
and the *ārya* Saṅgha, imbued with knowledge and freedom.
Protect us, Second Buddha Padmakara [Padmasambhava],
Orgyen, the self-emergent nirmāṇakāya, transcending causes and conditions,
in the center of a lotus on an island,
who emanates clouds of *vīra*s and ḍākinīs of the three places.[23] [21]
Homage to Düdjom Dorjé, Protector of the Wheel,[24]
the extraordinary chariot of the essence of the supreme yāna, and
to Samantabhadra, manifesting as a spiritual mentor
in order to guide disciples.
Immersed in the expanse of realization of the ocean of profound meanings,
fathoming countless definitive Dharmas,
you[25] are the true Vajradhara, who knows reality as it is

23. In this context, the "three places" refers to the three kāyas of the Buddhas: dharmakāya, saṃbhogakāya, and nirmāṇakāya.

24. The epithet "Protector of the Wheel" refers to the presence of the Buddha being continuous like the movement of a revolving wheel.

25. The author Sera Khandro here refers to her lama and consort, Drimé Özer.

and perceives the full range of phenomena.
To train disciples, the actual Vajradhara displays the realm of the Secret Mantra[yāna]
in the lucid absolute space of the wheel of Dharma.
Having cleansed the snowy peak of the supreme yāna, [22]
you have caused the rain of Dharma teachings of the three classes and nine expanses to fall.
Homage to the assemblies of vīras and ḍākinīs, those lords of Dharma,
who terrify the hosts of creatures who disparage [the Dharma].
For the sake of myself and others, I shall lucidly present
the vital essence of the view of all the jinas of the three times,
the Great Perfection of pith instructions on the pinnacle of the nine yānas,
this oral transmission of the guru, the lord of treasure revealers,
without contaminating the higher or lower teachings with my own fabrications.
May the lords of Dharma, the vīras and ḍākinīs,
the guardians of the teachings, and the lords of treasures grant their permission.

In this commentary to *Buddhahood Without Meditation*, teachings on the nature of the Great Perfection, [23] there are (I) the explanation of the auxiliary elements of the text and (II) the actual explanation of the meaning of the text. As for the first, the explanation of the auxiliary elements of the text has already been presented.[26]

II. The Actual Explanation of the Meaning of the Text

In this section there are three parts: (A) the virtuous introduction, (B) the virtuous meaning of the text, and (C) the virtuous conclusion.

A. The Virtuous Introduction

In this section there are three parts: (1) the meaning of the title, (2) the homage, and (3) the explanation of the introduction. [24]

26. Although Sera Khandro's preceding commentary, the *Fine Path to Liberation*, is presented as a separate text with its own title, its outline is continuous with the one in this commentary; hence we begin here with the heading "II. The Actual Explanation of the Meaning of the Text."

1. The Meaning of the Title

"Buddhahood Without Meditation: Advice for Revealing Your Own Face as the Nature of Reality, the Great Perfection," Is Presented Here.

The nature of the earth [element] is emptiness, and emptiness appears as the earth [element]. This likewise applies to the [elements of] water, fire, air, and so on. The nature of the outer appearances of the physical world is emptiness, and emptiness appears as the physical world. The nature of the inner, animate sentient beings who inhabit the physical world is emptiness, and emptiness appears as the sentient inhabitants. The nature of the five sensory objects is emptiness, and emptiness appears as the five sensory objects. Therefore, since the nature of all phenomena is emptiness, this is **the nature of reality.**

The ground is perfection because it perfects the phenomena of saṃsāra, including the aggregates, elements, and sense bases. The path is perfection because it perfects the various yānas, including the inconceivable entrances to the path and resultant attainments. The fruition is perfection because it is primordially present as the great nature of the twenty-five resultant dharmas of the kāyas, the facets of primordial consciousness, and so forth. In short, this is **perfection**, for it perfects the nine stages of the yānas, together with their results.

It is **great** because it synthesizes all the yānas, unifies their meaning, and summarizes their essence. [25]

This is **advice for revealing your own face**, for this is a profound method, or path, for revealing the pristine awareness that is present in the ground dharmakāya as your own unmanifested face of Samantabhadra.

This is **without meditation**, for pristine awareness identifies itself within itself as the nature of existence of suchness, it is decisively determined, the ground is sustained by itself, indwelling confidence and liberation flow forth directly from it, and you are manifestly united with your true nature without even the slightest bit of meditation on anything else.

This is **buddhahood**, for it arouses you from a state of ignorance like that of deep sleep and fulfills all the facets of primordial consciousness and sublime qualities.

This **is presented here**, indicating that this extraordinary advice is present here.

The purpose [of the title] is so that people of superior faculties can fathom the synthesized meaning of the text from start to finish; people of middling faculties can know where this belongs in terms of the Hīnayāna and Mahāyāna, like the appellations of soldiers training for war and archers training in archery; and even people of inferior faculties can easily find their way to this volume, like putting a name on a medicine jar. The *Laṅkāvatāra Sūtra* states:

> If names are not designated,[27] [26]
> everyone becomes confused;
> so the Protector, using skillful means,
> applies names to phenomena.

2. The Homage

> **With unshakable faith I pay homage to the Omnipresent Lord and Primordial Protector, the display of the supreme cities of apparitions of primordial consciousness.**

The dharmakāya, the *sugatagarbha*, pervades all beings, from the dharmakāya, Samantabhadra, down to the mindstream of a leech. Just as a sesame seed is saturated with oil, it is **Omnipresent**. If you wonder who this Omnipresent Lord is, he is the dharmakāya, Samantabhadra, so he is the **Lord**. He does not emerge due to fresh causes and new conditions but is rather self-emergent from time immemorial, so he is **Primordial**. He is a **Protector** because he is the protector and defender of both mundane existence and nirvāṇa. He [manifests as] **apparitions of primordial consciousness**, because he emanates as the five kāyas and the five buddha families from the causal five facets of primordial consciousness. The buddhafield of the buddha family emanates from the causal primordial consciousness of the absolute space of phenomena. This likewise applies to the [buddhafields of the] vajra, jewel, lotus, and karma families arising from mirror-like primordial consciousness, the primordial consciousness of equality, discerning primordial consciousness, the primordial consciousness of accomplishment, and so on. All these apparitional manifestations are displays in the expanse of ultimate reality of the mind of the dharmakāya, Samantabhadra, so they are a **display**. [27]

As for the term *city*, taking the analogy of human cities in this world, such as Beijing in China and such regions as Kapilavastu and Varanasi in India, a city is so called because it is a gathering place for eighteen types of craftsmen and for a continuous stream of merchants and travelers coming and going.

27. Emending *ming du gdags par mdzad na* ("are designated") to *ming du gdags par ma mdzad na* ("are not designated").

Likewise, with regard to the pure cities of deities, which are as inconceivably numerous as the grains of sand in the Ganges River, in the central region is the buddhafield of the buddha family. To the east is the buddhafield of the vajra family, to the south the buddhafield of the jewel family, to the west the buddhafield of the lotus family, and to the north the buddhafield of the karma family. All of these are foremost and unique among all cities, so they are **the supreme cities.**

Even *devas* and māras cannot separate the sugatagarbha from the mindstreams of individuals who have faith and reverence for it, so it is **unshakable.** Among the three kinds of faith—admiring faith, protective faith, and irreversible faith—this is faith that combines all three. [28] Or it is called irreversible faith regarding your acquired belief that, as a result of identifying and acquiring indwelling confidence in pristine awareness, the dharmakāya, the sugatagarbha, you will not return to saṃsāra.

Homage is offered with this **faith,** and in this regard there are the foremost homage of encountering the view, the middling homage of familiarization with meditation, and the inferior homage imbued with the three recognitions.[28] The foremost homage of encountering the view entails simultaneous wonderment, belief, and comprehension regarding your own view. What is this? Wonderment is at the immutable, nonconceptual primordial consciousness of the absolute space of the essential nature of reality; belief is in the synthesis and perfection of all the noncomposite, spontaneously actualized qualities of the kāyas, facets of primordial consciousness, the path, and its fruition in the maṇḍala of pristine awareness, bodhicitta; and due to your confidence in the revelation of the absolute space of the equality of the three kāyas, there is comprehension regarding the lack of even the slightest interest in seeking results elsewhere. In short, **I pay homage** with words of reverence for the displays of the purity and equality of saṃsāra and nirvāṇa.

3. The Explanation of the Introduction

In the explanation of the introduction, there are four parts: (a) individuals who lack the proclivity for the path, (b) individuals who [29] do not seek the path, (c) individuals who seek the path but do not find it, and (d) individuals who have a dispensation for the path.

28. The three recognitions can be interpreted in various ways, such as recognizing all forms as the nirmāṇakāya, all sounds as the saṃbhogakāya, and all thoughts as the dharmakāya.

a. Individuals Who Lack the Proclivity for the Path

> **Nowadays, when the five kinds of degeneration are on the rise, due to the uncouth nature of sentient beings and their powerful, negative karma, every one of them clings to this life—which is no more than an episode in a dream—makes long-term plans for living indefinitely, and shows no concern for meaningful pursuits pertaining to future lifetimes. Therefore, those who strive for the states of liberation and omniscience appear no more often than stars in the daytime.**

The five kinds of degeneration are said to be the worsening of mental afflictions, views, era, lifespan, and sentient beings. In the past eon of completeness,[29] mental afflictions were weak and the five poisons were dormant. However, in this current era people behave with coarse mental afflictions and the five poisons are turbulent, so this is the degeneration of mental afflictions. In the past eon of goodness,[30] everyone without exception had authentic views that avoided the extremes of eternalism and nihilism. However, nowadays people either fall to the extreme of eternalism or to the extreme of nihilism, and no one avoids both those extremes, so this is the degeneration of views. In the past eon of goodness, there weren't even words for turmoil, disease, war, famine, and so on. However, the current era is one in which turmoil, disease, war, famine, and so on are on the rise, so this is the degeneration of the era. [30] In the past eon of goodness, everyone was able to live for countless years or for eighty thousand years. However, in this current era, people are worn out by the age of twenty and are approaching death by thirty, so this is the degeneration of lifespan. In the past eon of goodness, when sentient beings saw one another they would look at each other with smiling eyes, greet each other with friendly words, and look after each other with altruism. Nowadays when sentient beings see each other they all consider each other to be enemies, taunt each other with harsh words, and prepare to beat and kill each other, so this is the degeneration of sentient beings.

During this era when the five kinds of degeneration are on the rise, due to the great magnitude of sentient beings' barbarism and negative karma, everyone clings to and is attached to this human life—which is no more than an episode in a dream—makes long-term plans for living indefinitely, subdues their enemies, protects their friends, erects buildings, plows fields

29. This was the first eon, in which humans were able to keep the four root precepts in completeness.

30. This is the eon in which one thousand buddhas appear.

and farms, and increases their wealth in order to add to their possessions and enjoyments. In the meantime, no one shows any concern for meaningful pursuits pertaining to future lifetimes. For these reasons, [31] it is said that people striving for the states of liberation and omniscience are seen more rarely than stars in the daytime. These are individuals who lack the proclivity for the path.

b. Individuals Who Do Not Seek the Path

> **Although some people bear death in mind and enthusiastically practice Dharma, they let their lives pass while engaging in mere verbal and physical spiritual practices and striving for higher rebirths as gods and humans.**

Even if people bear death in mind and enthusiastically practice Dharma, by spending their lives engaging merely in spiritual practices of physical prostrations and circumambulations, verbal recitations of liturgies, and the mental cultivation of good attitudes, they are striving for nothing more than higher rebirths as gods and humans, without any of them striving for the omniscient state of buddhahood. These are individuals who do not seek the path.

c. Individuals Who Seek the Path but Do Not Find It

> **Some, while lacking even the faintest understanding of the view of emptiness, ascertain their own minds as empty, merely identify the nature of discursive thoughts or inactive consciousness, and then passively remain in that state. As a result, they are simply propelled into rebirths as gods in the desire and form realms, without coming even a hair's breadth closer to the path to omniscience.**

Some, while lacking even the faintest understanding of the view of emptiness, when apprehending the external physical world, its sentient inhabitants, and their own internal bodies as ethically neutral, ascertain just their own minds as empty. Then they either take thoughts as the path or else are introduced by some foolish teacher merely to the nature of inactive consciousness and then rest in that state, while remaining totally passive with regard to the nine kinds of activity of the body, speech, and mind.[31] [32] When they abide doing

31. Tib. *bya ba dgu sprugs.* The nine kinds of activity include the body's (1) outer activities, such as walking, sitting, and moving about, (2) inner activities of prostrations and

nothing, the experience of bliss propels them to the desire realm, the experience of luminosity propels them to the form realm, or the experience of nonconceptuality propels them to the formless realm. When this occurs, if they take it to be the pinnacle of meditation and have confidence in that, the result is that they are merely propelled into rebirths as gods of the desire and form realms, without coming even a hair's breadth closer to the path to omniscience. These are individuals who seek the path but do not find it.

d. Individuals Who Have a Dispensation for the Path

> **Therefore, if there are a few individuals who have accrued vast accumulations [of merit and knowledge] over the course of countless eons, conjoined them with fine prayers, and established a karmic connection with the ultimate Dharma, I have bestowed this as their inheritance. Those who have no karmic connection with me and who lack the particular fortune of mastering the Dharma of the Great Perfection will engage in either projection or denial regarding this teaching and will thereby banish their own minds into the wilderness. You people who are not like that and whose fortune is equal to my own, attend to this advice—and by investigation, analysis, and familiarization, recognize saṃsāra and nirvāṇa as great emptiness, and realize its nature.**

For that reason, as the sustenance and inheritance for those few individuals who have accrued vast accumulations [of merit and knowledge] over the course of countless eons, conjoined them with fine prayers, and established a karmic connection with the ultimate Dharma, I, Kunzang Düdjom Dorjé, have revealed this. Those who have no karmic connection with me and who lack the karma and fortune to master the Dharma of the Great Perfection may project faults where there are no faults in this teaching and may deny good qualities that do exist. Such people banish their own minds into the wilderness, far from this clear-light Dharma of the Great Perfection. [33] You people who are not like that and whose fortune is equal to my own, by first

circumambulations, and (3) secret activities of ritual dancing, performing mudrās, and so on; the speech's (4) outer activities, such as all kinds of delusional chatter, (5) inner activities, such as reciting liturgies, and (6) secret activities, such as counting propitiatory mantras of your personal deity; and the mind's (7) outer activities, such as thoughts aroused by the five poisons and the three poisons, (8) inner activities of mind training and cultivating positive thoughts, and (9) the secret activity of dwelling in mundane states of dhyāna. See GD 297.

attending to this advice, then investigating and analyzing it, and finally familiarizing yourself with it, recognize the nature of the one great emptiness of all the phenomena of saṃsāra and nirvāṇa, and recognize them as displays of the one great emptiness and as the sphere of the one great emptiness. Realize its nature! So it is said. This concludes the virtuous introduction.

B. The Meaning of the Text

> **Among the three categories—the category of the mind, the category of the expanse, and the category of pith instructions—of [the teachings on] the nature of reality, the Great Perfection, this is called the category of secret pith instructions. In this regard there are three sections: view, meditation, and conduct. First, the view is determined and authentically realized by way of four themes: nonexistence, oneness, uniform pervasiveness, and spontaneous actualization. This is a sublime, essential point.**

There are three categories of the mind, expanse, and pith instructions in this Dharma of the nature of reality, the Great Perfection. Among them, first, this is the view of the category of the mind: the thorough investigation of the mind, the examination of which is primary among the body, speech, and mind, and the examination of the mind's origin, location, destination, form, shape, color, and so on. This is followed by the actualization of the clear light, in which luminosity and cognizance are undifferentiated. Finally, the unification of appearances and mindsets is asserted to be the culmination of the view.

Second, this is the view [34] of the category of the expanse: after indivisibly unifying and then meditating on external absolute space and internal pristine awareness, the unification of the absolute space of phenomena and pristine awareness is asserted to be the culmination of the view. Since these two involve seeking the view on the basis of meditation, their pace is a bit slow.

Third, among the outer cycle, the inner cycle, the secret cycle, and the very secret, unsurpassed cycle within the category of pith instructions, this is called the category of very secret, unsurpassed pith instructions. With regard to the correct practice of these instructions, there are four sections: (1) determining the ground by way of the view, (2) how to practice by cultivating the path, (3) teachings on the conduct that is the support of those two, and (4) the way in which the fruition is actualized.

1. Determining the Ground by Way of the View

The view is presented in the manner of the landing of a great *garuḍa.* As an analogy, when the king of garuḍas seeks food on the ground, he soars up into the sky and carefully examines whether or not the food is guarded and protected and so on, and when he determines that it is not, without any vacillation or uncertainty he eats the food. Likewise, because meditation is sought on the basis of the view, [35] all phenomena included in the world of appearances of saṃsāra and nirvāṇa are determined in terms of (a) nonexistence, (b) oneness, (c) uniform pervasiveness, and (d) spontaneous actualization. The true realization of the absolute space of equality of the three kāyas is the sublime, most essential point.

Teachings of Avalokiteśvara

a. Determining the Manner of Nonexistence

i. Determining the Apprehending Subject, Your Personal Identity, as Identityless

> **First, to determine the manner of nonexistence, there are the determination of personal identity and the determination of phenomenal identity. First, as for so-called personal identity, the mere appearance of the existence of a self during waking experience, dreaming experience, the intermediate period, and future lifetimes is called *personal identity*. As soon as this appearance occurs, there is a latent consciousness that takes it to be "I," and this is called *subsequent consciousness* or *discursive thinking*. This consciousness clarifies [the appearance of the self] and then stabilizes and fortifies it.**

HERE IS THE etymology of the term *person*: a person is one whose mindstream is *filled* with the two obscurations and their habitual propensities, and who is *contaminated* due to acting as a basis for the contaminated, closely held aggregates.[32] As for the term *self*, this latent consciousness of the mere appearance of the existence of a self where none exists in waking experience, dreaming experience, the intermediate period, and future lifetimes is called *personal identity*. As soon as this occurs, a latent consciousness grasps that which is not an "I" as being an "I" and that which is not a self as being a self. This subsequent consciousness and discursive thinking clarify, stabilize, and fortify [the appearance of the self], [36] and this is called *grasping at the apprehending subject, personal identity*.

This consciousness that grasps at the "I" is called the *causal ignorance of yourself alone*. From it emerges the ignorant consciousness that reifies the

32. This etymologizes "person" (Tib. *gang zag*): filled (*gang*), contaminated (*zag*).

distinction between objects and subjects, and this is called *connate ignorance*. From it emerges the individual naming of all phenomena appearing in the external physical world and its internal sentient inhabitants. Grasping at the referents [of these names] as distinct and the fortification of them as separate things is called *speculative ignorance*. Due to the functioning of these three kinds of ignorance, the three realms appear as saṃsāra, and there is delusion and bondage. The cause of this is the demon of grasping at the "I" and the self. The supreme paṇḍita and siddha Karma Lingpa wrote:

> The demon of grasping at the "I" and self
> is the great demon of the three realms of saṃsāra.

Accordingly, it is imperative to cut the taproot of grasping at the "I" and the self.

Investigating the source from which the so-called "I" first arises leads to the conclusion that no such source exists.

If you wonder whether the so-called "I" descends from the sky above, consider: If this space were the "I," then the "I" would emerge from the "I." Dust particles emerge from the earth, water drops from water, sparks from fire, and cool breezes from air. Likewise, if this space were the "I," [37] then the "I" would emerge from the "I." But the "I" does not emerge from space that is not the "I"; dust particles do not emerge from something that is not earth; water drops do not emerge from something that is not water; sparks do not emerge from something that is not fire; and cool breezes do not emerge from something that is not air. Likewise, the "I" does not emerge from space that is not the "I."

Further, if you wonder whether the "I" emerges from the elements of earth, water, fire, or air, consider: If the elements of earth, water, fire, or air were the "I," the "I" would emerge from the "I" just as dust particles emerge from earth, water drops from water, sparks from fire, and cool breezes from air. If the elements of earth, water, fire, and air were the "I," then the "I" would emerge from the "I." But the "I" does not emerge from the elements of earth, water, fire, and air that are not the "I," just as particles of dust do not emerge from that which is not earth, water drops do not emerge from that which is not water, sparks do not emerge from that which is not fire, and cool breezes do not emerge from that which is not air. Accordingly, the "I" does not emerge from the elements of earth, water, fire, and air that are not the "I." Likewise, the "I" does not emerge from the domain of the five outer elements.

If you wonder whether the "I" emerges from something substantial, consider: It is impossible for something insubstantial to emerge from something that is substantial. If the "I" emerges as something substantial, then the form, shape, color, and so on of the "I" [38] should be directly visible to the eyes and really graspable by the hands. But this is not the case.

If you wonder whether you emerge from within your own body, examine and investigate from the tips of the hair on your head down to the tips of your toes, and you will absolutely find no objective "I" that emerges from these places. Therefore, it inevitably turns out that the so-called "I" has no initial source.

This is how to investigate whether or not the so-called "I" has a location and is an agent bearing real characteristics that can be individually identified in the interim period [between its origin and cessation].

The head is called the *head*; it is not the "I." Likewise, the scalp is called *skin*; it is not the "I." The bones are called *bones*; they are not the "I." Likewise, the eyes are *eyes* and not the "I." The ears are *ears* and not the "I." The nose is the *nose* and not the "I." The tongue is the *tongue* and not the "I." The teeth are *teeth* and not the "I." The brain, too, is not the "I." Moreover, regarding the flesh, blood, lymph, channels, and tendons, each has its own name and is not the "I." This is revealing.

Moreover, the arms are *arms* and not the "I." The shoulders are likewise not the "I," nor are the upper arms, the forearms, or the fingers. The spine is the *spine* and not the "I." The ribs are not the "I," nor are the chest, lungs, heart, diaphragm, liver, or spleen. The intestines and kidneys are not the "I," nor are urine or feces. Furthermore, the word "I" is not attributed to the legs. The thighs are called *thighs* and not "I," and the hips are similarly not the "I," nor are the calves, the soles of the feet, or the toes.

In short, the outer skin is not called "I"; the intervening flesh and fat are called *flesh* and *fat*, not "I"; the inner bones are called *bones* and not "I"; and the innermost marrow is called *marrow* and not "I." Consciousness, too, is so called and is not named "I." Therefore, emptiness as the nonexistence of a

location and agent during the interim [between the origination and cessation of the self] is certain.

If you think there certainly must be some place where [the "I"] is located during the interim period [between its origination and cessation], consider: The "I" is not located in the domain of the five elements. If it were located there, when the elements are destroyed or damaged, you should experience pain within, but that doesn't happen. If you investigate your own body inwardly, the head is called *head*, not "I." Likewise, the scalp is called *scalp*; it is not called "I." Bones are called *bones*; they are not called "I." Similarly, the eyes are called *eyes*, not "I." The ears are called *ears*, not "I." The nose is called *nose*, not "I." The tongue is called *tongue*, not "I." Likewise regarding the teeth, brain, flesh, blood, [39] lymph, channels, and tendons, they are all called by their own names and are not called "I." Similarly, the arms are called *arms*, not "I." Regarding the shoulders, upper arms, forearms, and fingers, each is called by its own name and is not called "I." Likewise, the spine is called *spine* and not "I," and the same goes for the ribs, chest, lungs, heart, diaphragm, liver, spleen, intestines, kidney, urine, feces, legs, thighs, hips, calves, soles of the feet, and toes. The outer skin [40] is called *skin*, the intervening flesh and fat are called *flesh* and *fat*, the inner bones are called *bones*, and the innermost marrow is called *marrow* and not "I." Moreover, consciousness is called *consciousness* and not "I." Therefore, emptiness as the nonexistence of a location and agent during the interim period [between the origination and cessation of the self] is certain.

Finally, you should likewise come to a decisive understanding that this transcends all destinations and the agents who go to them. The apparent existence of something that in fact does not exist is like a hallucination. Uttering the names [of such things] is like talking about the horns of a hare.

Finally, if you think there must certainly be a destination to which one goes, consider: When the "I" has no origin or location, it certainly has no final destination. However, if it did, would the "I" that appears during the waking state and the "I" that appears while dreaming be one or two? If they were one and the same, the swelling on "my" body from being hit with sticks and stones and the wounds inflicted by weapons in a dream last night should be present on my body today during waking experience. But they are not. If you think they are different, consider: In one year there are 360 days and 360 nights,[33] making 720 daily cycles, so there should also be 720 bodies. When they turn into corpses, the four primary directions of east, south, west, and north, as well as the eight intermediate directions, should all be filled with corpses. [41] But they are not. If they were living until they deceased, [all the directions] should be filled with great legions of "me." If this were the case, they should be visible to the eyes, really graspable with the hands, and evident to the senses. But they are not.

Therefore, if you wonder whether the "I" becomes utterly nonexistent, consider: A nonexistent "I" would have no way of going to a realm of nonexistence. If it were existent, the "I" would have to be established as truly existent, but since it has already been determined that it is not to be found, it will still not be found. So this finally transcends all destinations and the agents who go to them.

For these reasons, the appearance of the "I" as existing even though it does not exist is [like] the appearance of strands of hair in the sky due to a disease of the eyes, and all references to the name ["I"] are like talking about the horns of a hare or sky lotuses. They do not bear even the slightest trace of true existence. As the *All-Creating Sovereign Tantra* states:

> The root of saṃsāra is "I" and "mine."
> If this nonexistent and delusive root is cut,
> the self-emergent, all-creating sovereign dissolves into yourself.

This concludes [42] the discussion of determining the apprehending subject, personal identity, as identityless.

ii. Determining the Apprehended Objects, Phenomenal Identity, as Identityless

> **Second, to determine the identitylessness of phenomena, there are (A') searching for the bases of designation of names, (B') dissolving grasping at the permanence of things, (C') counteracting the flaws of benefit and harm, and (D') collapsing the false cave of hope and fear.**

In the discussion of determining the apprehended object, phenomenal identity, as identityless, there are four parts:

33. There are 360 days in the year according to traditional Indian and Tibetan calendars.

A' Searching for the Bases of Designation of Names

> **First, if you seek out the referents of all names, you will see that they do not exist and are nothing more than imputations upon the merely natural displays of thoughts; for it is impossible for any phenomenon to be established as self-sustaining upon its own basis of designation. For instance, upon what is the so-called head designated and why? Is it so designated because it is the first part of the fetus to develop, or because it is round, or because it appears above? In fact, the head does not arise as the first part of the fetus; everything that is round is not called a *head*; and if you examine *above* and *below*, you will find that they do not exist in space. Likewise, hair is not the *head*. Skin is only skin and is not called a *head*. Bones are called *bones* and not a *head*. The brain is not the *head*, nor are the eyes, ears, nose, or tongue.**
>
> **If you think that none of these individually is the *head*, but their collective assembly is called a *head*, consider: If you severed a creature's head, pulverized it into its constituent molecules and atoms, and showed this to anyone in the world, no one would call it a *head*. Even if you reconstituted these molecules and atoms with water, it would not be called a *head*. Therefore, know how the so-called head is nothing more than a verbal expression, with no objective basis for this utterance.**

All names are designated, even though they do not exist. Know that grasping at them as existent, while being ignorant of the fact that they do not exist, is speculative ignorance. For instance, on what is the so-called head designated and why? If you think it is so designated because it is the first part of the fetus to develop, note that in fact the head does not arise as the first part of the fetus, which gradually develops from the *cakra* of emanation at the navel. So that is not a justification for calling it a *head*. If you think it is called a *head* because it is round, note that all things that are round, such as peas and pills, are not named a *head*. If you think that something is called a *head* because it appears above, note that if you impute *above* and *below* on space, you will see that space has no above or below.

If you think that the appearance of an indigo color is above, note that most tantras state that the lapis lazuli light from the southern face of Mount Meru is the indigo color that strikes the ocean and appears as the color of the intervening space. In some tantras it is said that this space [43] is the indigo color of depth.

To draw a parallel, the color of a small body of water appears to be pale, and when this water is poured into a container, it is of a pale color. A bit deeper body of water appears to be indigo, but when this is poured into a container it is pale in color, not blue. If you look at a very deep body of water, it looks dark blue in color, but when that water is poured into a container, once again it is pale, not dark blue. Likewise, it is said that this space appears to be indigo due to its great depth.

In that case, you may wonder whether the references to *above* and so forth are lies. Among the perfect buddhas' Dharma teachings, some are intended for specific periods, occasions, people, and so forth, so they are not categorically the same. In most treatises it is said that if you kill your parents, it is a deed of immediate retribution, but as it states in the *Letter of Consolation for King Ajātaśatru* [558–491 BCE]:

> One's father and mother (craving and grasping) are to be killed.
> The king (the substrate consciousness) overcomes the two
> kinds of hygiene (wrong view regarding your impermanent
> aggregates and grasping at the superiority of your own ethics
> and view). [44]
> If one conquers a region together with its inhabitants (the mind
> and mental factors),
> that person will become pure.

There is no reason why the categories of *above* and *below* must be absolute.[34] So if you think there is something established as self-sustaining in the basis of designation of the head, consider: Hair is called *hair*, not the *head*; the tips of hair are called *tips of hair*; the midsections of hair are called *midsections of hair*; and the roots of hair are called *roots of hair*. The scalp is called the *scalp*, not the *head*; the skull is called the *skull*, not the *head*; and the brain is called the *brain*, not the *head*. Likewise, the eyes are called *eyes*; the ears are called *ears*; the nose is called *nose*; and the tongue is called *tongue*, and not the *head*.

If you think that none of these individually is the *head* but that their collection is called *head*, consider: If you severed a creature's head, ground it into particles, pulverized them into molecules and those into atoms, and then showed them to the people of this southern kingdom of Jambudvīpa, they

34. The point here is that the terms "above" and "below" are not lies, nor are they absolute; rather, they are provisional and relative in the sense that they are subject to interpretation, circumstance, and setting.

would call them *particles* and not a *head*. Even if you formed them into a lump with water, it would be called a *lump*, not a *head*.

Furthermore, are the head that appears in the waking state and the head that appears in a dream one or two? If they are one, [45] the swelling that resulted from your head being beaten with rocks and sticks last night in a dream and the wounds inflicted on it by a weapon should be present on your head during the waking state. But they are not. On the other hand, if you think they are different, consider: In one year there are 360 days and 360 nights, so there are 720 days and nights, implying that you should have 720 heads. If so, they should either be stacked upon each other like palm fronds, or else they should be layered from inside to outside like the layers of bark of a box-tree. If this is the case, then you should be able to directly see them with your eyes, really hold them in your hands, and experience them through your senses. But it is not so.

Therefore, the *head* is nothing more than a verbal expression, while the basis of that verbalization has no objective existence. It is necessary to correctly recognize exactly how this is so.

> **Likewise, regarding the *eyes*—that name is not attributed to all pairs of spheres. The sclera is not an *eye,* nor are tears, veins, or blood. An *eye* is none of these individually, nor is it the assembly of their particles, or the lump of them reconstituted with water. That which sees forms is consciousness, not the eyeballs, which is evidenced by the fact that visual perception takes place in dreams and in the intermediate period.**

Likewise, if you think there is something self-sustaining in the basis of designation of the *eyes*, consider: Regarding the *eyes*, any pair of spheres is not called *eyes*. The sclera is called *sclera*, but it is not an *eye*; [46] tears are called *tears*, but they are not an *eye*; the veins in the eye are called *veins in the eye*, but they are not an *eye*; blood is called *blood*, but it is not an *eye*. Each of these is called by its own name, and it is not an *eye*.

If you think that each of these individually is not designated as an *eye*, but that their assembly is called an *eye*, consider: If you took the eye of a creature, ground it into particles, pulverized them into molecules and those into atoms, and then showed them to the people of this southern kingdom of Jambudvīpa, they would call them *particles* and not an *eye*. Even if you formed them into a lump with water, that would be called a *lump*, not an *eye*.

If you think something is called an *eye* because it sees forms, consider: If you took the eyes of many dead creatures and stuck them into the eye sockets of someone who was blind, that person should be able to see, but it is not so.

Furthermore, are the eyes in a dream and the eyes during the waking state the same or different? If they are the same, and if last night you dreamed that you became blind, then you should have been blind when you awoke this morning, but it is not so. If you were blind during the waking state today, [47] even though you saw various forms during your dreams last night, during the waking state today your eyes don't see even a single form.

Alternatively, if you think they are different, consider: In one year there are 360 days and 360 nights, so there are 720 days and nights, implying that you should have 720 pairs of eyes. If so, from time immemorial until the present, your eyes should either be stacked upon each other like palm fronds, or else they should be layered from inside to outside like the layers of bark of a box-tree. If this is the case, then you should be able to directly see them with your eyes, really hold them in your hands, and experience them through your senses. But it is not so.

If you think that if you were to become blind, you would never see anything again, consider: If you think that it was your eyes that first saw forms, then you would think that forms would not be seen once you became blind; and in the end, it seems that no forms would be seen. However, if you close your eyes today during the waking state [48] and fall asleep, there is something that sees various forms in your dreams—even though your eyes during the waking state today don't see even a single form. Likewise, during the intermediate period and thereafter, you will have died, leaving your present body behind as a corpse. Nevertheless, there is something that sees during the intermediate period and thereafter. Apart from the primordially present consciousness of your own mind simply seeing its own forms, this eyeball has never seen even a single form. For this reason the Bhagavān[35] declared, "Visual consciousness is limitless."

> **Likewise, regarding the *ears*—neither the auditory canals nor the skin are the ears, and the flesh, channels, ligaments, blood, and lymph all have their own names, so they are not the *ears*. The powder that would result from reducing them to tiny particles is not the *ears*, nor is the lump that would be formed by reconstituting them with water. If you think that the name *ear* is attributed to that which hears sounds, check out what hears sounds in a dream, the waking state, and the intermediate**

35. In this instance, "Bhagavān" refers to Gautama Buddha.

period. It is only the primordially present consciousness of your mind and not the ears.

Likewise, if you think there is something self-sustaining in the basis of designation of the *ears*, consider: Regarding the *ears*, the auditory canals are called *auditory canals*, so they are not the *ears*. The skin is called *skin*, so it is not the *ears*. The flesh is called *flesh*, so it is not the *ears*. The channels and ligaments are called *channels* and *ligaments*, so they are not the *ears*. The blood is called *blood*, so it is not the *ears*. The lymph is called *lymph*, so it is not the *ears*. They are all called by their own names, so they are not called *ears*.

If you think that none of these individually is designated as an *ear*, [49] but their combined assembly is called an *ear*, consider: If you severed a creature's ear, ground it into particles, pulverized them into molecules and those into atoms, and then showed them to the people of this southern kingdom of Jambudvīpa, they would call them *particles* and not an *ear*. Even if you formed them into a lump with water, it would be called a *lump*, not an *ear*.

If you think that something is called an *ear* because it hears sounds, consider: If you took the ears of many dead creatures and stuck them into the ear sockets of someone who was deaf, that person should be able to hear, but it is not so.

Furthermore, are the ears in a dream and the ears during the waking state the same or different? If they are the same, and if last night you dreamed that you became deaf, then you should have been deaf when you awoke this morning, but it is not so. If you were deaf during the waking state today, even though you heard various sounds during your dreams last night, during the waking state today your ears don't hear even a single sound.

Alternatively, if you think they are different, consider: In one year there are 360 days and 360 nights, [50] so there are 720 days and nights, implying that you should have 720 pairs of ears. If so, from time immemorial until the present, your ears should either be stacked upon each other like palm fronds, or else they should be layered from inside to outside like the layers of bark of a box-tree. If this is the case, then you should be able to directly see them with your eyes, really hold them in your hands, and experience them through your senses. But it is not so.

If you think that if you were to become deaf, you would never hear anything again, consider: If you think that it was your ears that first heard sounds, then you would think that sounds would not be heard once you became deaf; and in the end, it seems that no sounds would be heard. However, if you close your eyes today during the waking state and fall asleep, there is something that hears various sounds in your dreams, even though your ears during the waking state today don't hear even a single sound. Likewise, during the intermediate period and thereafter, you will have died, leaving your present body behind as a corpse. Nevertheless, there is something that hears during the intermediate period and thereafter. This is nothing other than the primordially present consciousness of your own mind simply hearing its own sounds. [51] For this reason the Bhagavān declared, "Auditory consciousness is limitless."

> **Likewise, regarding the *nose*—the nostrils, skin, cartilage, flesh, channels, and ligaments all have their own names, so they are not called a *nose*. Moreover, that which smells odors is consciousness itself, so you should investigate what smells odors in a dream and in the intermediate period.**

Likewise, if you think there is something self-sustaining in the basis of designation of the *nose*, consider: Regarding the *nose*, the nostrils are called *nostrils*, so they are not a *nose*. Skin is called *skin*, so it is not a *nose*. Cartilage is called *cartilage*, so it is not a *nose*. Flesh is called *flesh*, so it is not a *nose*. Channels and ligaments are called *channels* and *ligaments*, so they are not a *nose*. They are all called by their own names, so they are not called a *nose*.

If you think that none of these individually is designated as a *nose*, but their combined assembly is called a *nose*, consider: If you severed a creature's nose, ground it into particles, pulverized them into molecules and those into atoms, and then showed them to the people of this southern kingdom of Jambudvīpa, they would call them *particles* and not a *nose*. Even if you formed them into a lump with water, it would be called a *lump*, not a *nose*.

If you think that something is called a *nose* because it smells odors, consider: If you took the noses of many dead creatures and stuck them into the facial cavity of someone whose nose had been severed, that person should be able to smell, but it is not so. [52]

Furthermore, are the nose in a dream and the nose during the waking state the same or different? If they are the same, and if last night you dreamed that your nose was cut off, then your nose should be cut off during the waking state today, but it is not so. If your nose was cut off during the waking state today, even though you smelled various odors during your dreams last night, during the daytime today your nose doesn't smell even a single odor.

Alternatively, if you think they are different, consider: In one year there are 360 days and 360 nights, so there are 720 days and nights, implying that you should have 720 noses. If so, from time immemorial until the present, your noses should either be stacked upon each other like palm fronds, or else they should be layered from inside to outside like the layers of bark of a box-tree. If this is the case, then you should be able to directly see them with your eyes, really hold them in your hands, and experience them through your senses. But it is not so.

If you think that if your nose were cut off, you would never smell any odors again, consider: [53] If you think that it was your nose that first smelled odors, then you would think that odors would not be smelled once your nose was cut off; and in the end, it seems that no odors would be smelled. However, if you close your eyes today during the waking state and fall asleep, there is something that smells various odors in your dreams, even though your nose during the waking state today doesn't smell even a single odor. Likewise, during the intermediate period and thereafter, you will have died, leaving your present body behind as a corpse. Nevertheless, there is something that smells odors during the intermediate period and thereafter. This is nothing other than the primordially present consciousness of your own mind simply smelling its own odors. For this reason the Bhagavān declared, "Olfactory consciousness is limitless."

> **Likewise, regarding the *tongue*—its flesh, skin, blood, veins, and nerves all have their own names, so they are not called a *tongue*. If they were pulverized into a powder, this would not be called a *tongue*, and if it were reconstituted into a lump, it would still not be called a *tongue*. This applies to all the following instances as well.**

Likewise, if you think there is something self-sustaining in the basis of designation of the *tongue*, consider: Regarding the *tongue*, the flesh is called *flesh*, so it is not a *tongue*. Skin is called *skin*, so it is not a *tongue*. Blood is called *blood*, so it is not a *tongue*. Veins and nerves are called *veins* and *nerves*, so they are not a *tongue*. They are all called by their own names, so they are not called *tongue*.

If you think that none of these individually is designated as a *tongue*, [54] but their combined assembly is called a *tongue*, consider: If you severed a creature's tongue, ground it into particles, pulverized them into molecules and those into atoms, and then showed them to the people of this southern kingdom of Jambudvīpa, they would call them *particles* and not a *tongue*. Even if you formed them into a lump with water, it would be called a *lump*, not a *tongue*.

If you think that something is called a *tongue* because it experiences tastes, consider: If you took the tongues of many dead creatures and stuck them into the oral cavity of someone whose tongue had been cut out, that person should be able to experience tastes, but it is not so.

Furthermore, are the tongue in a dream and the tongue during the waking state the same or different? If they are the same, and if last night you dreamed that your tongue was cut out, then your tongue should be cut out during the waking state today, but it is not so. If your tongue was cut out during the waking state today, even though you experienced various tastes during your dreams last night, during the waking state today your tongue doesn't experience even a single taste.

Alternatively, if you think they are different, consider: In one year there are 360 days and 360 nights, so there are 720 days and nights, [55] implying that you should have 720 tongues. If so, from time immemorial until the present, your tongues should either be stacked upon each other like palm fronds, or else they should be layered from inside to outside like the layers of bark of a box-tree. If this is the case, then you should be able to directly see them with your eyes, really hold them in your hands, and experience them through your senses. But it is not so.

If you think that if your tongue were cut out, you would never experience any tastes again, consider: If you think that it was your tongue that first experienced tastes, then you would think that tastes would not be experienced once your tongue was cut out; and in the end, it seems that no tastes would be experienced. However, if you close your eyes today during the waking state and fall asleep, there is something that experiences various tastes in your dreams, even though your tongue during the waking state today doesn't experience even a single taste. Likewise, during the intermediate period and thereafter, you will have died, leaving your present body behind as a corpse. Nevertheless, there is something that experiences tastes during the intermediate period and thereafter. This is nothing other than the primordially present consciousness of your own mind simply experiencing its own tastes. For this reason the Bhagavān declared, [56] "Gustatory consciousness is limitless."

> **Likewise, regarding the *arms*—the shoulders are not the *arms*, nor are the upper arms, forearms, fingers, knuckles, flesh, skin, bones, or marrow. Likewise, regarding the *shoulders*—the skin is not the *shoulders*, nor are flesh, bones, their assembled particles, or the lump reconstituted with water. The basis of designation of the name *shoulder* is empty in that it has no objective existence. Likewise, by investigating the upper arms and forearms, it becomes apparent that each component has its own name, with flesh being called *flesh*, bones called *bones*, skin**

called *skin*, and marrow called *marrow*. Not even an atom can be established as their basis of designation.

Likewise, if you think there is something self-sustaining in the basis of designation of the *arms*, consider: Regarding the *arm*, the shoulder is called *shoulder*, so it is not an *arm*. The upper arm is called *upper arm*, so it is not an *arm*. The lower arm is called *lower arm*, so it is not an *arm*. The fingers and knuckles are called *fingers* and *knuckles*, so they are not an *arm*. Flesh is called *flesh*, so it is not an *arm*. Skin is called *skin*, so it is not an *arm*. Bones are called *bones*, so they are not an *arm*. Marrow is called *marrow*, so it is not an *arm*. If you think that none of these individually is designated as an *arm*, but their combined assembly is called an *arm*, consider: If you severed a creature's arm, ground it into particles, pulverized them into molecules and those into atoms, and then showed them to the people of this southern kingdom of Jambudvīpa, they would call them *particles* and not an *arm*. Even if you formed them into a lump with water, it would be called a *lump*, not an *arm*.

Therefore, is something called an *arm* because it performs tasks? If you think that if this arm didn't exist, there would be nothing that performs tasks and actions, [57] consider: Are the arm in a dream last night and the arm during the waking state today the same or different? If they are the same, and if last night you dreamed that you had a crippled arm, then your arm should be crippled during the waking state today, but it is not so. If your arm was crippled during the waking state today, even though you plowed a field, built a house, and performed various tasks during your dreams last night, during the waking state today your arm doesn't perform even a single task.

Alternatively, if you think they are different, consider: In one year there are 360 days and 360 nights, so there are 720 days and nights, implying that you should have 720 pairs of arms. If so, from time immemorial until the present, your arms should either be stacked upon each other like palm fronds, or else they should be layered from inside to outside like the layers of bark of a box-tree. If this is the case, then you should be able to directly see them with your eyes, really hold them in your hands, [58] and experience them through your senses. But it is not so.

If you think that if your arm were crippled, you would never perform any tasks again, consider: If you think that it was your arm that first performed tasks, then you would think that tasks and activities would not be performed once your arm was crippled; and in the end, it seems that no tasks or activities would be performed. However, if you close your eyes today during the waking state and fall asleep, there is something that performs tasks and activities in your dreams, even though your arm during the waking state today doesn't perform even a single task. Likewise, during the intermediate period and thereafter, you will have died, leaving your present body behind as a corpse. Nevertheless, there is something that performs tasks during the intermediate period and thereafter. This is nothing other than the primordially present consciousness of your own mind simply performing its own tasks. Therefore, the basis of designation of the name *arm* is empty in that it has no objective existence.

Likewise, if you think there is something self-sustaining in the basis of designation of the *shoulders*, consider: Regarding the *shoulder*, the skin is called *skin*, so it is not called a *shoulder*. The flesh is called *flesh*, so it is not called a *shoulder*. The bones are called *bones*, so they are not called a *shoulder*. [59] If you think that none of these individually is designated as a *shoulder*, but their combined assembly is called a *shoulder*, consider: If you took a creature's shoulder, ground it into particles, pulverized them into molecules and those into atoms, and then showed them to the people of this southern kingdom of Jambudvīpa, they would call them *particles* and not a *shoulder*. Even if you formed them into a lump with water, it would be called a *lump*, not a *shoulder*. Therefore, the basis of designation of the name *shoulder* is empty in that it has no objective existence.

Likewise, if you think there is something self-sustaining in the basis of designation of the *upper arm*, consider: Regarding the *upper arm*, flesh is called *flesh*, so it is not called an *upper arm*. Bones are called *bones*, so they are not called an *upper arm*. Skin is called *skin*, so it is not called an *upper arm*. Marrow is called *marrow*, so it is not called an *upper arm*. They all have their own names, so they are not called an *upper arm*. If you think that none of these individually is designated as an *upper arm*, but their combined assembly is called an *upper arm*, consider: If you took a creature's upper arm, ground it into particles, pulverized them into molecules and those into atoms, and then showed them to the people of this southern kingdom of Jambudvīpa, [60] they would call them *particles* and not an *upper arm*. Even if you formed them into a lump with water, it would be called a *lump*, not an *upper arm*. Therefore, the basis of designation of the name *upper arm* is empty in that it has no objective existence.

Likewise, if you think there is something self-sustaining in the basis of designation of the *forearm*, consider: Regarding the *forearm*, flesh is called *flesh*, so it is not called a *forearm*. Skin is called *skin*, so it is not called a *forearm*. Bones are called *bones*, so they are not called a *forearm*. Marrow is called *marrow*, so it is not called a *forearm*. They all have their own names, so they are not called a *forearm*. If you think that none of these individually is designated as a *forearm*, but their combined assembly is called a *forearm*, consider: If you cut off a creature's forearm, ground it into particles, pulverized them into molecules and those into atoms, and then showed them to the people of this southern kingdom of Jambudvīpa, they would call them *particles* and not a *forearm*. Even if you formed them into a lump with water, it would be called a *lump*, not a *forearm*. Therefore, the basis of designation of the name *forearm* is empty in that it has no objective existence, for there has never been even an atom that is established as its truly existent basis of designation.

> **By investigating the bases of designation of the *body* and the *aggregates*, it becomes apparent that the *body* does not refer to the spine or ribs, or to the chest, flesh, skin, or bones. The heart, lungs, liver, diaphragm, spleen, kidneys, and intestines are all called by their own names, so the bases of designation of the *body* and *aggregates* are empty in that they have no objective existence: they are emptiness.** [61]

Likewise, if you think there is something self-sustaining in the bases of designation of the *body* and the *aggregates*, consider: The spine is called the *spine* and not the *body* or *aggregates*. The ribs are called the *ribs* and not the *body* or *aggregates*. The chest is called the *chest* and not the *body* or *aggregates*. Flesh is called *flesh* and not the *body* or *aggregates*. Skin is called *skin*, and not the *body* or *aggregates*. Bones are called *bones* and not the *body* or *aggregates*. Likewise, the heart is called the *heart* and not the *body* or *aggregates*. The lungs are called *lungs* and not the *body* or *aggregates*. The liver is called the *liver* and not the *body* or *aggregates*. The diaphragm is called the *diaphragm* and not the *body* or *aggregates*. The spleen is called the *spleen* and not the *body* or *aggregates*. The kidneys are called *kidneys* and not the *body* or *aggregates*. The intestines are called *intestines* and not the *body* or *aggregates*. They are all called by their own names, so they are not called *body* or *aggregates*.

If you think that none of these individually is designated as the *body* or *aggregates*, but these names are attributed to their combined assembly, consider: [62] If you took a creature's corpse, it would be called a *corpse* and not a *body* or *aggregates*. If you ground it into particles, pulverized them into molecules and those into atoms, and then showed them to the people of this southern kingdom of Jambudvīpa, they would call them *particles* and not a *body* or *aggregates*. Even if you formed them into a lump with water, it would be called a *lump*, not a *body* or *aggregates*. Therefore, the bases of designation of the names *body* and *aggregates* are empty in that they have no objective existence.

> **Likewise, by investigating the *legs*, it becomes apparent that the hips are not the *legs*, nor are the thighs, calves, or ankles. Similarly, the name *hips* does not refer to flesh, skin, bones, channels, or ligaments. Regarding the *thighs* as well, this name does not refer to any of the skin, flesh, bones, channels, or ligaments. This goes for the *calves*, too. These names would not be applied if they were pulverized into powder, nor would they refer to the lump formed from that powder mixed with water.**

Likewise, if you think there is something self-sustaining in the bases of designation of the *legs*, consider: The hips are called *hips* and not *legs*. The thighs are called *thighs*, the calves are called *calves*, and the ankles, *ankles*. Their outer skin, underlying flesh, internal bones, and core marrow are called by their respective names and not *legs*. If you think that none of these individually is designated as the *legs*, but this name is attributed to their combined assembly, consider: If you severed a creature's legs, ground them into particles, pulverized them into molecules and those into atoms, and then showed them to the people of this southern kingdom of Jambudvīpa, they would call them *particles* [63] and not *legs*. Even if you formed them into a lump with water, it would be called a *lump*, not *legs*.

If you think that it is the legs that walk and stand, so that if there were no legs, there would be nothing to walk or stand, consider: Are the legs in a dream last night and the legs during the waking state today the same or different? If they are the same, and if last night you dreamed that you had crippled legs, then your legs should be crippled during the waking state today, but it is not so. If you had crippled legs during the waking state today, even though you walked from one place to another, stood upright, danced, and so on during your dreams last night, during the waking state today your legs wouldn't walk or stand even once.

Alternatively, if you think they are different, consider: In one year there are 360 days and 360 nights, so there are 720 days and nights, implying that you should have 720 pairs of legs. If so, from time immemorial until the present, your legs should either be stacked upon each other like palm fronds, [64] or else they should be layered from inside to outside like the layers of bark of a box-tree. If that is the case, then you should be able to directly see them with your eyes, really hold them in your hands, and experience them through your senses. But it is not so.

Therefore, if you think that if your legs became crippled you would never again walk or stand, consider: If you think that it was your legs that first walked and stood upright, then you would think you couldn't walk once your legs were crippled; and in the end, it seems that you would never walk again. However, if you close your eyes today during the waking state and fall asleep, there is something that walks and stands upright in your dreams, even though your legs during the waking state today don't walk or stand even once. Likewise, during the intermediate period and thereafter, you will have died, leaving your present body behind as a corpse. Nevertheless, there is something that walks and stands during the intermediate period and thereafter. This is nothing other than the primordially present consciousness of your own mind simply dancing in its own expanse. Therefore, the basis of designation of the name *legs* is empty in that it has no objective existence.

Likewise, if you think there is something self-sustaining in the bases of designation of the *hips*, consider: [65] Flesh is called *flesh* and not *hips*. Skin is called *skin* and not *hips*. Bones are called *bones* and not *hips*. Channels and ligaments are called *channels* and *ligaments* and not *hips*. They are all called by their own names and not *hips*.

If you think that none of these individually is designated as the *hips*, but this name is attributed to their combined assembly, consider: If you severed a creature's hips, ground them into particles, pulverized them into molecules and those into atoms, and then showed them to the people of this southern kingdom of Jambudvīpa, they would call them *particles* and not *hips*. Even if you formed them into a lump with water, it would be called a *lump*, not *hips*. Therefore, the basis of designation of the name *hips* is empty in that it has no objective existence.

Likewise, if you think there is something self-sustaining in the basis of designation of the *thigh*, consider: The outer skin is called *skin* so it is not called a *thigh*. The underlying flesh is called *flesh*, so it is not called a *thigh*. The internal bones are called *bones*, so they are not called a *thigh*. The channels and ligaments are called *channels* and *ligaments*, so they are not called a *thigh*. The core marrow is called *marrow*, so it is not called a *thigh*. If you think that none of these individually is designated as a *thigh*, [66] but this name is attributed to their combined assembly, consider: If you severed a creature's thigh, ground it into particles, pulverized them into molecules and those into atoms, and then showed them to the people of this southern kingdom of Jambudvīpa, they would call them *particles* and not a *thigh*. Even if you formed them into a lump with water, it would be called a *lump*, not a *thigh*. Therefore, the basis of designation of the name *thigh* is empty in that it has no objective existence.

Likewise, if you think there is something self-sustaining in the basis of designation of the *calf*, consider: The outer skin is called *skin*, so it is not called a *calf*. The underlying flesh is called *flesh*, so it is not called a *calf*. The internal bones are called *bones*, so they are not called a *calf*. The channels and ligaments are called *channels* and *ligaments*, so they are not called a *calf*. The core marrow is called *marrow*, so it is not called a *calf*. If you think that none of these individually is designated as a *calf*, but this name is attributed to their combined assembly, consider: If you severed a creature's calf, ground it into particles, pulverized them into molecules and those into atoms, and then showed them to the people of this southern kingdom of Jambudvīpa, they would call them *particles* and not a *calf*. Even if you formed them into a lump with water, it would be called a *lump*, [67] not a *calf*. Therefore, the basis of designation of the name *calf* is empty in that it has no objective existence.

> **If you seek the basis of designation of a *mountain* externally, it becomes apparent that earth is not a *mountain*, nor are shrubs, trees, stones, boulders, or water.**

Likewise, to take an example from the external universe such as a *mountain*, if you think there is something self-sustaining in the basis of designation of a *mountain*, consider: Earth is called *earth*, so it is not called a *mountain*. Similarly, shrubs are called *shrubs*, so they are not called a *mountain*. Trees are called *trees*, so they are not called a *mountain*. Stones are called *stones*, so they are not called a *mountain*. Boulders are called *boulders*, so they are not called a *mountain*. Trees are called *trees*, so they are not called a *mountain*. Water is called *water*, so it is not called a *mountain*. Moisture is called *moisture*, so it is not called a *mountain*.

If you think that none of these individually is designated as a *mountain*, but this name is attributed to their combined assembly, consider: If you removed one chunk and then showed it to the people of this southern kingdom of Jambudvīpa, they would call it a *chunk of earth* or a *chunk of stone*, and not a *mountain*. If you ground it into particles, pulverized them into molecules and those into atoms, and then showed them to the people of this southern kingdom of Jambudvīpa, they would call them *particles* and not a *mountain*. Even if you formed them into a lump with water, it would be called a *lump*, not a *mountain*. Therefore, the basis of designation of the name *mountain* is empty in that it has no objective existence. [68]

> **If you seek the basis of designation of a *building*, it becomes apparent that neither mortar, nor stones, nor lumber is a *building*. Moreover, just as walls are called *walls* and not a *building*, likewise there is nothing in the exterior or interior that is established as a *building*.**

Likewise, if you think there is something self-sustaining in the basis of designation of a *building*, consider: Clay is called *clay*, so it is not called a *building*. Stones are called *stones*, so they are not called a *building*. The walls are called *walls* and pillars are called *pillars*, so they are not called a *building*. The lower floors are called *lower floors*, so they are not called a *building*. The beams are called *beams*, so they are not called a *building*. Similarly, the exterior is called the *exterior*, so it is not called a *building*. The interior is called the *interior*, so it is not called a *building*.

If you think that none of these individually is designated as a *building*, but this name is attributed to their combined assembly, consider: If you removed one chunk and then showed it to the people of this southern kingdom of Jambudvīpa, they would call it a *chunk of clay* or a *chunk of stone* and not a *building*. If you ground it into particles, pulverized them into molecules and those into atoms, and then showed them to the people of this southern kingdom of Jambudvīpa, they would call them *particles* and not a *building*. Even if you formed them into a lump with water, it would be called a *lump*, not a *building*. Therefore, the basis of designation of the name *building* is empty in that it has no objective existence.

> **Although you may seek the bases of designation of a *human being*, a *horse*, a *dog*, and so on, it becomes apparent that their eyes, ears, noses, tongues, flesh, blood, bones, marrow, channels, and ligaments, together with their consciousnesses, all have their own names, so the bases of designation of a *human being*, a *horse*, and a *dog* have no objective existence. These [names] are indicative of everything else.**

Likewise, if you think there is something self-sustaining in the bases of designation of a *human being*, a *horse*, and a *dog*, consider: [69] Eyes are called *eyes*, so they are not called a *human being*, a *horse*, or a *dog*. Ears are called *ears*, so they are not called a *human being*, a *horse*, or a *dog*. A nose is called a *nose*, a tongue is called a *tongue*, and the outer skin is called *skin*. The underlying flesh is called *flesh*, the blood is called *blood*, the inner bones are called *bones*, and the core marrow is called *marrow*. Channels are called *channels*, ligaments are called *ligaments*, and together with consciousnesses, each has its own name, so they are not called a *human being*, a *horse*, or a *dog*. Therefore, the bases of designation of the names *human being*, *horse*, and *dog* are empty in that they have no objective existence; and it is said that these [names] are indicative of everything else.

Furthermore, among material objects, the name *drum* is not attributed to the wood, leather, exterior, or interior. Moreover, the term *knife* is not attributed to the metal, blade, back of the blade, tip, or haft. None of these is established as the object designated *knife*. Names and their referents change. For example, when a knife is formed into an awl, its name changes, and when this is made into a needle, all its previous names disappear.

For instance, with material things, to take a *drum* as an example, its wood is called *wood*, so it is not called a *drum*. Its leather is called *leather*, its exterior is called its *exterior*, and its interior is called its *interior*, so they are not called a *drum*. Therefore, the basis of designation of a *drum* is empty in that it has no objective existence.

Likewise, regarding a *knife*, its metal is called *metal*, so it is not called a *knife*. Its blade is called a *blade*, the back of the blade is called the *back of the blade*, its tip is called a *tip*, and its haft is called a *haft*. [70] Therefore, the basis of designation of a *knife* is empty in that it has no objective existence.

Names change. For example, if you make an awl out of a knife, it is called an *awl*, so it is not called a *knife*. When a needle is made from an awl, it is called a *needle*, not an *awl*. Likewise, all its earlier names disappear. If one reed is hollow inside, you should know that all are hollow. Therefore, know how everything in reality is merely mentally designated, so not even a fraction of an atom is established as truly existent.

In dependence upon the teachings I have received during a dream from my guru, the supreme ārya, the Great Compassionate One (Avalokiteśvara), I have thoroughly realized both the so-called "personal identity" [as identityless] and this search for the bases of designation of names.

Teachings of the Lake-Born Vajra of Orgyen

THEN THIS IS how the displays of dependently related events arise as appearances from emptiness:

> **On one occasion when I encountered the illusory body of the primordial consciousness of the Lake-Born Vajra of Orgyen, he granted me these instructions on perceiving appearances as illusory: "In order to be introduced to the dependent origination of the confluence of causes and conditions, consider this: Lucid, luminous absolute space, as the ground, having the potential to manifest any kind of appearance, serves as the cause; and consciousness that grasps at the 'I' serves as the contributing condition. In dependence upon the confluence of these two, all appearances manifest like illusions. Thus, absolute space, as the ground, the mind that arises from its creative power, and all the outer and inner phenomena that are appearances of this mind are called *dependently related events*, for they are interrelated as a sequence of events, like the sun and its rays.**
>
> **"This is like the appearance of an illusion that arises in dependence upon the interaction of transparent, clear space, the primary cause, with the magical substances, mantras, and mind that views the object, the contributing conditions."**

The instructions on perceiving appearances as illusory that were granted when [Düdjom Lingpa] encountered the illusory body of the primordial consciousness of the Lake-Born Vajra of Orgyen are an introduction to the dependent origination of the confluence of causes and conditions. In this regard, the great Orgyen [Padmasambhava] declared:

> Live like an illusion, a mirage, a dream, a reflection,
> a city of gandharvas, and an echo; [71]

know that the phenomena of saṃsāra and nirvāṇa
are like the ten analogies of illusion of known objects, including
the moon in water, a bubble, a hallucination, and an
emanation.[36]

Here is an introduction to dependent origination in terms of the ten analogies of illusion: As for the cause, lucid, luminous absolute space, as the ground, having the potential to manifest any kind of appearance, serves as the cause. As for the condition, the consciousness that grasps at the "I," together with incidental thoughts, serves as the contributing condition. When these two—the cause and the contributing condition—are brought together, various dependently related events emerge as appearances in the ocean of the realm of phenomena, even though they don't exist. On what do they depend? On the ground. To what are they related? To the nondual union of the ground and the various appearances of the ocean of the realm of phenomena. What events emerge? Various appearances of the ocean of the realm of phenomena, even though they don't exist.

As for an analogy, they are like illusions. Take the example of an illusionist who goes to a frightening region with deep ravines, thorny trees, gravel, towering peaks, and deep valleys, where a great crowd of spectators has assembled. Casting his magical substances and mantras into the sky, he imagines that in the center of a great plain that would take a horseman eighteen days to ride around is a four-sided, nine-storied castle [72] with four entrances and a tenth floor consisting of a treasury above the ninth floor. Surrounding it is a metallic mountain composed of various precious substances, and inside it are eighteen great craftsmen. The entire landscape is covered with white, red, yellow, green, and blue flowers; it is filled with lovely, beautiful birds and attractive forest creatures; and there is a continuous stream of an inconceivable number of Chinese, Tibetan, and Mongolian people, horses, elephants, and so forth, coming and going. By imagining all this, images like these visually appear to the spectators over yonder. These images are dependently related events, emerging from the confluence of causes and conditions. As for the causes, the lucid, clear sky, which has the potential to manifest any kind of appearance, and the eyes of the spectators, which have the ability to manifest any kind of visual form, serve as the causes. As for the contributing conditions, the magical substances, the mantras, and the imagination of the

36. Padmasambhava, *Natural Liberation: Padmasambhava's Teachings on the Six Bardos*, commentary by Gyatrul Rinpoche, trans. B. Alan Wallace (Boston: Wisdom Publications, 1998), 55.

illusionist serve as the contributing conditions. When these two are brought together, the dependently related events of the illusory appearances emerge, even though they don't exist.

On what basis do they depend? On the sky. To what are they related? To the nondual union of the sky and the illusory appearances. What events emerge? The illusory appearances, even though they don't exist. [73]

> **"In this way, all appearing phenomena manifest due to the power of grasping at the 'I,' even though they don't exist. This is like the appearance of a mirage due to the confluence of a lucid clear sky, warmth, and moisture."**

The vast environment of the outer physical world, the multitude of inner sentient inhabitants, and all the beautiful intervening objective appearances of the five senses are like a mirage in that they manifest due to the power of the consciousness that grasps at the "I," even though they don't exist. A mirage, too, is a dependently related event emerging from the confluence of causes and conditions. Regarding its cause, the lucid, clear sky, having the potential to manifest any kind of appearance, serves as the cause. Regarding its contributing conditions, the coexistence of warmth and moisture on the ground serve as its contributing conditions. When these two are conjoined, the appearances of a mirage emerge, even though they don't exist. On what do they depend? On the sky. To what are they related? To the nondual union of the sky and the appearances of the mirage. What events emerge? The appearances of the mirage, even though they don't exist.[37]

> **"All waking appearances, dream appearances, and appearances during the intermediate period and thereafter appear, even though they don't exist, and confusion arises due to reifying them. As an analogy, during a dream, instead of thinking, 'This is a dream' and recognizing it as delusive, you apprehend it as an enduring, objective world and fixate on it."**

During a dream, regarding the vast environment of the outer physical world, the many inner sentient inhabitants, [74] and all the beautiful intervening

37. In this commentary Sera Khandro adds this note: "According to the root text, the next line should read, 'All waking appearances, dream appearances . . .' Perhaps a word was omitted or there may be an error, so this should be checked." Translator: It appears that this error has been corrected in the current edition of the root text.

objective appearances of the five senses, instead of thinking that "this is a dream; I exist in some other world," you reify it. Likewise, regarding your constructed house, plowed fields, and all your accumulated wealth and enjoyments, you think these have all existed since the times of your fine ancestors. Moreover, just as you think of your enemies and friends and the owners of this place and that place, getting bound up in reifying and fixating on objects in a dream, so do you become confused by reifying and fixating on all the appearances of the waking state, dreams, the intermediate period, and thereafter, which are like the appearances of a dream, and which don't actually exist. Such confusion is like the analogy of a dream.

These are dependently related events emerging from the confluence of causes and conditions. Regarding the cause, the lucid, luminous space of awareness as the ground, having the potential to manifest any kind of appearance, serves as the cause. Regarding the contributing conditions, the consciousness and experiences of a person who is asleep serve as the contributing conditions. When those two are conjoined, the dependently related appearances of a dream emerge, even though they don't exist. On what do they depend? On the ground [the space of awareness]. To what are they related? To the nondual union of the ground and the appearances of the dream. What events arise? The appearances of the dream, even though they don't exist. [75]

> **"The appearances of various phenomena as something 'other' due to the dominant condition of inwardly grasping at the 'I' are like the appearances of reflections arising from the interaction of your face and a mirror."**

While the "I" does not exist, there is grasping at the "I," and while the self does not exist, due to the contributing condition of demarcating the self that is apprehended as a self, the physical world, its sentient inhabitants, and appearances seem to be "other." This is like the analogy of a reflection. Such appearances are dependently related events emerging from the confluence of causes and conditions. Regarding the cause, a lucid, clear mirror, having the potential to manifest all kinds of appearances, serves as the cause. Regarding the contributing condition, the presentation of a person's face and form over yonder serves as the contributing condition. When these two are conjoined, the dependently related appearances of a reflection emerge, even though they don't exist. On what do they depend? On the mirror. To what are they related? To the nondual union of the mirror and the appearances of the reflection. What events arise? The appearances of the reflection, even though they don't exist.

> **"Due to being completely ensnared by the reification of the self, the worlds of the six cities appear to arise one after another. These are like the appearances of a city of gandharvas manifesting in an area such as a plain at sunset, which occur as visions grasped by the mind."**

While the "I" does not exist, there is grasping at the "I," and while the self does not exist, due to being completely ensnared by the reification of grasping at the self, the worlds of the six realms appear to arise one after another. Due to the arousal of the mental affliction of hatred in this life, negative, nonvirtuous karmas are accumulated one after another. [76] From the time you are afflicted by a mortal disease until the time your breath ceases, craving and clinging catalyze the negative, nonvirtuous karmas accumulated due to the arousal of the mental affliction of hatred. Just as a fire flares up when it is strengthened by being blown on, hatred causes the appearances of hell to flare up, even though they don't exist. Such appearances are dependently related events emerging from the confluence of causes and conditions. As for the cause, the lucid, luminous space of awareness as the ground, having the potential to manifest any kind of appearance, serves as the cause. As for the condition, the catalytic effect of craving and clinging when you are about to die serves as the contributing condition. When these two—the cause and the conditions—are brought together, the dependently related appearances of hell emerge, even though they don't exist. On what do they depend? On the ground. To what are they related? To the nondual union of the ground and the appearances of hell. What events arise? The appearances of hell, even though they don't exist.

Due to the arousal of the mental affliction of attachment in this life, negative, nonvirtuous karmas are accumulated one after another. From the time you are afflicted by a mortal disease until the time your breath ceases, craving and clinging catalyze the negative, nonvirtuous karmas accumulated due to the arousal of the mental affliction of attachment. Just as a fire flares up when it is strengthened by being blown on, [77] attachment causes the appearances of the *preta* realm to flare up, even though they don't exist. Such appearances are dependently related events emerging from the confluence of causes and conditions. As for the cause, the lucid, luminous space of awareness as the ground, having the potential to manifest any kind of appearance, serves as the cause. As for the condition, the catalytic effect of craving and clinging when you are about to die serves as the contributing condition. When these two—the cause and the conditions—are brought together, the dependently related appearances of the preta realm emerge, even though they don't exist.

On what do they depend? On the ground. To what are they related? To the nondual union of the ground and the appearances of the preta realm. What events arise? The appearances of the preta realm, even though they don't exist.

Due to the arousal of the mental affliction of delusion in this life, negative, nonvirtuous karmas are accumulated one after another. From the time you are afflicted by a mortal disease until the time your breath ceases, craving and clinging catalyze the negative, nonvirtuous karmas accumulated due to the arousal of the mental affliction of delusion. Just as a fire flares up when it is strengthened by being blown on, delusion causes the appearances of the animal realm to flare up, even though they don't exist. Such appearances are dependently related events emerging from the confluence of causes and conditions. [78] As for the cause, the lucid, luminous space of awareness as the ground, having the potential to manifest any kind of appearance, serves as the cause. As for the condition, the catalytic effect of craving and clinging when you are about to die serves as the contributing condition. When these two—the cause and the conditions—are brought together, the dependently related appearances of the animal realm emerge, even though they don't exist. On what do they depend? On the ground. To what are they related? To the nondual union of the ground and the appearances of the animal realm. What events arise? The appearances of the animal realm, even though they don't exist.

Due to the arousal of the mental afflictions of the five poisons in this life, defiled, complex virtues of the ten kinds are enacted. From the time you are afflicted by a mortal disease until the time your breath ceases, craving and clinging catalyze the defiled ten virtues[38] or the five poisons. Just as a fire flares up when it is strengthened by being blown on, appearances of the human realm flare up, even though they don't exist. Such appearances are dependently related events emerging from the confluence of causes and conditions. As for the cause, the lucid, luminous space of awareness as the ground, having the potential to manifest any kind of appearance, serves as the cause. As for the condition, the catalytic effect of craving and clinging when you are about to die serves as the contributing condition. When these two—the cause and the conditions—are brought together, the dependently related appearances of the human realm emerge, even though they don't exist. On what do they depend? On the ground. To what are they related? To the nondual union of the ground and the appearances of the human realm.

38. Such virtues are called "defiled" (Tib. *zag bcas*) because they are contaminated by self-grasping.

[79] What events arise? The appearances of the human realm, even though they don't exist.

Due to the arousal of the mental affliction of envy in this life, negative, nonvirtuous karmas are accumulated one after another. From the time you are afflicted by a mortal disease until the time your breath ceases, craving and clinging catalyze the sinful, nonvirtuous karmas accumulated due to the arousal of the mental affliction of envy. Just as a fire flares up when it is strengthened by being blown on, envy causes the appearances of the *asura* realm to flare up, even though they don't exist. Such appearances are dependently related events emerging from the confluence of causes and conditions. As for the cause, the lucid, luminous space of awareness as the ground, having the potential to manifest any kind of appearance, serves as the cause. As for the condition, the catalytic effect of craving and clinging when you are about to die serves as the contributing condition. When these two—the cause and the conditions—are brought together, the dependently related appearances of the asura realm emerge, even though they don't exist. On what do they depend? On the ground. To what are they related? To the nondual union of the ground and the appearances of the asura realm. What events arise? The appearances of the asura realm, even though they don't exist.

Due to the arousal of the mental affliction of pride in this life, combined with mental grasping at *dhyāna*, [80] from the time you are afflicted by a mortal disease until the time your breath ceases, craving and clinging catalyze any of the great, middling, or lesser dhyānas and the negative, nonvirtuous karma accumulated from the arousal of the mental affliction of pride. Just as a fire flares up when it is strengthened by being blown on, the appearances of the deva realm flare up, even though they don't exist. Such appearances are dependently related events emerging from the confluence of causes and conditions. As for the cause, the lucid, luminous space of awareness as the ground, having the potential to manifest any kind of appearance, serves as the cause. As for the condition, the catalytic effect of craving and clinging when you are about to die serves as the contributing condition. When these two—the cause and the conditions—are brought together, the dependently related appearances of the deva realm emerge, even though they don't exist. On what do they depend? On the ground. To what are they related? To the nondual union of the ground and the appearances of the deva realm. What events arise? The appearances of the deva realm, even though they don't exist.

This is like the analogy of a city of gandharvas. Such appearances are dependently related events emerging from the confluence of causes and conditions. Regarding the cause, the lucid, clear sky, having the potential to manifest any kind of appearance, and the visions of someone with a water constitution who has cultivated the dhyānas serve as the cause. Regarding the contributing condition, a plain at sunset and [81] the edge of a moist bowl serve as the contributing conditions. When these two are conjoined, the dependently related appearances of a city of gandharvas emerge, even though they don't exist. On what do they depend? On the sky. To what are they related? To the nondual union of the sky and the appearances of a city of gandharvas. What events arise? The appearances of a city of gandharvas, even though they don't exist.

> **"While the appearances to the physical senses have never been established as real, your own diverse experiences of seeing, hearing, experiencing, and feeling appear as something 'other,' like echoes."**

Regarding the appearances to the physical senses, all the appearances of forms as visual objects, sounds as auditory objects, odors as olfactory objects, tastes as gustatory objects, and sensations as tactile objects have never been established as real. All the forms seen with the eyes, sounds heard with the ears, odors smelled with the nose, tastes experienced with the tongue, and tactile sensations felt with the body are like the analogy of an echo. The sound of an echo is a dependently related event emerging from the confluence of causes and conditions. Regarding the cause, a high rock wall with a smooth surface and the ears of someone nearby serve as the cause. Regarding the contributing condition, shouting serves as the contributing condition. When these two are conjoined, the dependently related appearance of an echo emerges, even though it doesn't exist. On what does it depend? On the rock wall. To what is it related? To the nondual union of the rock wall and the appearances of echoes. [82] What event arises? The sound of an echo, even though it doesn't exist. In the absence of a self, there is grasping at a self over here, and in the absence of an "other," there is the appearance of the "other" over there. That's all.

> **"All appearances are not other than the ground, and they are of one taste with the ground itself, just as all the planets and stars reflected in the ocean are not other than the ocean and are of one taste with the water itself."**

Whatever appearances arise, be they ever so vast and numerous, all are not other than the ground and are of one taste with the ultimate reality of that ground. This is like the analogy of the planets and stars reflected in the ocean.

However vast and numerous the appearances of the planets and stars in the ocean may be, they are not other than the ocean, and they are of one taste with the water itself. Such appearances are dependently related events emerging from the confluence of causes and conditions. Regarding the cause, the lucid, clear ocean, having the potential to manifest any kind of appearance, serves as the cause. Regarding the contributing condition, the conjunction of the sky, planets, and stars serves as the contributing condition. When these two are conjoined, the dependently related reflections of the planets and stars emerge, even though they don't exist. On what do they depend? On the ocean. To what are they related? To the nondual union of the ocean and the appearances of the planets and stars. What events arise? The reflections of the planets and stars, even though they don't exist.

> **"Due to grasping at the 'I,' 'self' and 'other' appear as if truly existent in the panoramic sweep of the expansive, all-pervasive absolute space of the ground. These appearances are like bubbles emerging from water."** [83]

In the great, uniform pervasiveness of the nonobjective, panoramic sweep of the all-pervasive absolute space of the ground—the groundless, rootless manifestation of the great, omnipresent nature of saṃsāra and nirvāṇa—under the influence of grasping at the "I," something is established as being "over here" in relation to something "over there," and something is established as being "over there" in relation to something being "over here." This results in the appearances of "self" and "other" as truly existent, which are like water bubbles. As for the analogy, when bubbles emerge from water, even though they do not exist as anything other than the water itself, the water and bubbles appear to be separate. Such appearances are dependently related events emerging from the confluence of causes and conditions. Regarding the cause, the lucid, clear ocean, having the potential to manifest any kind of appearance, serves as the cause. Regarding the contributing condition, a disturbance caused by natural waves or by something else serves as the contributing condition. When these two are conjoined, the dependently related appearances of water bubbles emerge, even though they don't exist. On what do they depend? On the ocean. To what are they related? To the nondual union of the ocean and the appearances of water bubbles. What events arise? The appearances of water bubbles, even though they don't exist.

As another analogy, when a rainbow appears, even though it is not other than the vast expanse of empty sky, the rainbow and the sky appear separately, even though the rainbow does not exist apart from the sky. [84] Such appearances are dependently related events emerging from the confluence of causes and conditions. Regarding the cause, the lucid, clear sky, having the potential to manifest any kind of appearance, serves as the cause. Regarding the contributing conditions, the confluence of the appearance of the sun, darkening clouds, and the moisture of rain serve as the contributing conditions. When these two are conjoined, the dependently related appearance of a rainbow emerges, even though it doesn't exist. On what does it depend? On the sky. To what is it related? To the nondual union of the sky and the appearances of a rainbow. What event arises? The appearance of a rainbow, even though it doesn't exist.

> **"The lucid luminosity of the empty absolute space of the ground is crystallized into self-appearances to mental consciousness. Due to this becoming reinforced, various delusive appearances manifest, which are like hallucinations caused by pressure on the nerves of the eyes or by disturbances in the channels due to the vital energies."**

In the lucidity and luminosity of the empty absolute space of the ground, appearances of the self where there is no self are crystallized by mental consciousness. Due to this becoming reinforced, various delusive appearances manifest, which are like the appearances of hallucinations. Such appearances are dependently related events emerging from the confluence of causes and conditions. Regarding the cause, the lucid, clear eyes, having the potential to manifest any kind of appearance, serve as the cause. Regarding the contributing conditions, pressure on the nerves of the eyes by pressing them with a finger or a disturbance in the channels caused by vital energies serve as the contributing conditions. When these two are conjoined, the dependently related appearances of hallucinations emerge, even though they don't exist. On what do they depend? On the eyes. [85] To what are they related? To the nondual union of the eyes and the appearance of hallucinations. What events arise? The appearances of hallucinations, even though they don't exist.

> **"Although various appearances from the ground manifest to a consciousness that grasps at the 'I,' they do not waver from or occur outside of that ground. As an analogy, when someone who has mastered the samādhi of emanation and transformation settles in meditative equipoise in such samādhi, various emanations appear, even though they have no ground or root and do not exist as real objects."**

Although all the various appearances from the ground appear as emanations of the absolute space of the sugatagarbha to the consciousness that grasps at the "I," which is like a water vessel, they do not waver from the ground, and these appearances in the ground do not emerge as truly existent. They are like emanations. Consider the analogy of someone who has mastered the *samādhi* of emanation and transformation and settles in the meditative equipoise of such samādhi with the thought "May emanations emerge!" Even though others have no intention of seeing various emanations, when that person settles in the meditative equipoise of such samādhi, various emanations appear, although they have no ground or root and do not exist as real objects.

Such appearances are dependently related events emerging from the confluence of causes and conditions. Regarding the cause, lucid, clear space, having the potential to manifest any kind of appearance, and the person who is capable of emanation and transformation, serve as the causes. [86] Regarding the contributing conditions, other people's eyes and the samādhi of emanation and transformation serve as the contributing conditions. When these two are conjoined, the dependently related appearances of emanations emerge, even though they don't exist. On what do they depend? On the sky. To what are they related? To the nondual union of the sky and the appearances of emanations. What events arise? The appearances of emanations, even though they don't exist.

Therefore, in accordance with this presentation of ten analogies of illusion, all phenomena are nothing but dependently related events emerging from the confluence of causes and conditions, with no true existence. Not even a single atom exists. As the Lord of Sages [Buddha Śākyamuni] declared:

> There are no phenomena
> other than dependently related events,
> so there are no phenomena
> other than emptiness.

From the ultimate reality of pristine awareness:

> **"O my incredible child, gradually meditate in this way, and you will become an illusory yogin by realizing the illusory nature of appearances."**
>
> **So saying, he disappeared.**

Teachings of Vidyādhara Düdul Dorjé

B′ Dissolving Grasping at the Permanence of Things

On one occasion Vidyādhara Düdul Dorjé spoke these words to me:

The vajra is the eternal vajra;
for its meaning, look to space itself!

Elaborating on this point, he said, "Behold! This empty space is the ground of the appearances of all physical worlds and their sentient inhabitants. To provide analogies, the ground of the appearances of reflections is a mirror, for reflections are not established as anything other than the mirror. The ground of the appearances of images of the moon in water is water, for these images are not established as anything other than the water. The ground of the appearances of rainbows is space, for rainbows are not established as anything other than space.

"This space cannot be injured, so it is invulnerable. Space cannot be conquered or destroyed, so it is indestructible. Space abides as the ground of the appearances of the phenomenal world, so it is real. Space cannot be affected by good or bad qualities, so it is incorruptible. Space is unmoving and unfluctuating, so it is stable. Space can penetrate even the minutest particles, so it is unobstructable. Space cannot be harmed by anything whatsoever, so it is completely invincible."

When Vidyādhara Düdul Dorjé [1615–72][39] directly appeared in a vision, he said:

39. Düdjom Lingpa's previous incarnation Vidyādhara Düdul Dorjé was a treasure revealer and an incarnation of Drokpen Khyeuchung Lotsawa, one of the twenty-five principal disciples of Padmasambhava.

The vajra is the eternal vajra;
for its meaning, look to space itself! [87]

This mind vajra, pristine awareness, never changes within the three times of past, present, and future, so it is said to be the *eternal vajra.* Its meaning is space, inconceivable absolute space itself. In this regard there are three aspects: external space, internal space, and secret, inconceivable space. As for external space, all phenomena included in the vast outer physical worlds; the multitudes of inner, animate sentient inhabitants; the well-displayed intervening appearances of the five senses; your own body, aggregates, elements, and sense bases; and all the appearances and mindsets of ordinary sentient beings are external space. Once this has been determined by way of the authentic teachings of the jinas, the authentic pith instructions of the sublime guru, and your own authentic pristine awareness, the true realization of the manner in which they do not exist and are not established as real is internal space. The realization of the indivisibility of external space and internal space—in which luminosity and emptiness are indivisible as the one taste of your own pristine awareness, the great dharmakāya—is the secret, inconceivable space.

The elaboration on this point [88] begins with the exclamation "Behold!" This empty space is the ground of the appearances of all physical worlds and their sentient inhabitants. To provide analogies, the ground of the appearances of all reflections is a mirror, all reflections are displays of a mirror, and all reflections are not established as anything other than a mirror. The ground of the appearances of all images of the moon in water is water, all images of the moon in water are displays of water, and all images of the moon in water are not established as anything other than water. The ground of the appearances of all rainbows is the sky, all images of rainbows are displays of the sky, and all rainbows are not established as anything other than the sky.

The ground of appearances of all physical worlds and their sentient inhabitants is space, all physical worlds and their sentient inhabitants are displays of space, and all physical worlds and their sentient inhabitants are not established as anything other than space. This space is imbued with the seven vajra qualities. Even if this space were struck by many hundreds of thousands of kinds of weapons of devas and māras, it would be uninjured, so it is invulnerable. This space does not change by itself, nor can it be destroyed by anything else, so it is [89] indestructible. Although this space abides as the ground of appearances of all of saṃsāra and nirvāṇa, it is changeless in its own nature, so it is real. This space is not adulterated by the faults of bad sentient beings, by the virtues of the excellent buddhas, or by lovely or ugly colors, so it is incorruptible. This space is unfluctuating, for it is not moved by time or place, so it is stable. This space can penetrate even the minutest particles, whereby everything is penetrated as a display of space, so it is unobstructable. This space cannot be harmed by anything else, so it is invincible to everything. In these ways it is imbued with the seven vajra qualities.

> **"Since all other substances can be injured by weapons, they are vulnerable. Since they can be conquered and destroyed by circumstances, they are destructible. Since they can change into one thing or many, they are unreal. Since they can be affected by other things, they are corruptible. Since they move and fluctuate, with no enduring stillness, they are unstable. They can be obstructed by certain things, and since they can be nullified by other influences, they are vincible. Such things, having the characteristic of not being established as truly existent, are empty.**
>
> **"Moreover, by pulverizing coarse materials, they are reduced to particles. Decomposing these particles by a factor of seven results in molecules. The empty, partless atoms that result from decomposing these molecules by a factor of seven are characterized by not being established as real.**
>
> **"If you think they existed at first but were then reduced to nothing due to being acted upon, take heed of the appearances of dreams, which are not established as real from the very moment they manifest, regardless of whether or not they have been acted upon, either by observation or by physical contact."**

Three kinds of vajras are relative truths: The wheel of Brahmā made from the bones of the Brahman Zhothung, the bow and arrow of Rāhula, the vajra of Indra, and the trident of Īśvara are said to bear the seven vajra qualities. However, when the bones of the deceased Brahman Zhothung were taken from a cavern in Mount Meru, melted, and made into the forms of hand implements such as a wheel, [90] they didn't have even one vajra characteristic, let alone seven. To the north of the region Nyenchen Tanglha there is a so-called vajra diamond, but when that object was first broken, it was spherical; when it was broken a second time, it became rectangular; when it was broken a third time, it became crescent-shaped; and when it was broken a fourth time, it became triangular. From that time onward it was said that it couldn't be destroyed by anything, but when the one object turned into many, it didn't have even one vajra characteristic, let alone seven. In China's Beijing there is a so-called iron vajra diamond. However, even though it is said that nothing can melt it except fire, since it can be melted by fire, it doesn't have even one vajra characteristic, let alone seven.

Likewise for all other substances, when they are struck by weapons, they are injured, so they lack the quality of invulnerability and are instead vulnerable. They can be conquered and destroyed by other influences, so they lack the quality of indestructibility and are instead destructible. A single substance can become two or more, so it lacks the quality of reality and is instead unreal. Substances can be stained by the impurities of white, [91] yellow, red, multiple colors, gray, and so forth, so they lack the quality of incorruptibility and are instead corruptible. They shift and fluctuate as they move from one time and place to another with no enduring stillness, so they lack the quality of stability and are instead unstable. All material things can be obstructed by something, so they lack the quality of unobstructability and are instead obstructable. They can be nullified by other influences, so they lack the quality of invincibility and are instead vincible.

Thus, all appearing phenomena have the qualities of being nonexistent and not established as real, from the time that they first manifest. From the very moment they appear, they are empty, with no basis or root. Something coarse such as a stone can be ground into powder that can be pulverized into particles; these can be reduced to molecules, which can be reduced by a factor of seven to atoms, which can be reduced by a factor of seven to partless particles; and these partless particles, consisting of nothing, with an empty nature and the characteristic of not being established as real, are empty, with no basis or root, from the very moment they appear.

If you think those coarse things existed at first but were then reduced to nothing due to being acted upon by someone's hand, [92] note that while dreaming, something coarse such as a stone can be ground into powder that can be pulverized into particles; these can be reduced by a factor of seven to molecules, which can be reduced by a factor of seven to partless particles; and these partless particles, consisting of nothing, are in the dream reduced to emptiness. However, during the waking state today, that appearance is first not seen, then not touched, and finally not acted upon by the mouth and hands to pulverize it into particles, reduce them by a factor of seven to molecules, reduce those by a factor of seven to partless particles, or reduce those partless particles, consisting of nothing, to emptiness. This is revealing. The vajra has thus been determined by way of its seven qualities.

Now, to determine the nature of consciousness by way of its emergence and cessation:

"Observe how appearances emerge and cease due merely to opening and closing your eyes or lowering and raising your feet. If you think it is not that the previous appearances cease and vanish as the subsequent ones emerge, but rather that the earlier ones go elsewhere, with all the former and later appearances being truly existent, look at the appearances of a dream. In particular, it is impossible for some substantial nature to exist except as something designated as a relative [truth] upon the interrelations of causes and effects. So consider this issue well.

"Well then, these accounts of space having the seven vajra qualities are presented using metaphors to show how space is devoid of movement and change due to its insubstantiality. They demonstrate how ultimate reality is present as the essential nature, which is inexpressible by speech or thought and is devoid of change. It is worthwhile to apply these accounts to explanations of the distinctions between substantiality and insubstantiality and between reality and unreality. So when the moon is symbolically pointed out with a finger, you should look at the moon and not be satisfied with looking merely at the tip of the finger. If you do not decisively recognize appearances as empty by repeatedly familiarizing yourself with these points, you will not come the slightest bit closer to the path of omniscience."

When you open and close your eyes and lower and raise your feet, appearances manifest even though they do not exist. Their nature is that as they manifest, so do they cease, and as they cease, so do they emerge. Thus, if you think it is not that the previous appearances cease and vanish as the subsequent ones emerge, but rather that the earlier ones go elsewhere, and the soil, stones, mountains, boulders, fruit trees, and forest along the way all truly exist as they did before, just as they appeared, and that the arising and ceasing outer and inner appearances of your home truly exist [93] as they did before, consider: When you were traveling from your home region to another region in a dream last night, just as the soil, stones, mountains, boulders, fruit trees, and forest along your route appeared on your way there, so did you dream that on your return trip they truly existed, just as they appeared to truly exist on your outbound journey; and you dreamt that all the materials and utilities on the outside and inside of your home were truly existent, corresponding to the earlier arising and passing of their appearances outside and inside. However, during the waking state today, not even one of those previous appearances is established as real. This is revealing.

For example, imagine that someone's shoe was carried away by a stream, and the next year that person and a companion came to that place on the shore of the stream and the person who lost his shoe commented, "This was where my shoe was carried away by the stream." His companion would be correct in replying, "It wasn't carried away by this stream." Why? When its owner returned here from someplace else, the water that carried off his shoe was already gone. Likewise, for bodhisattvas who have achieved bodhisattva grounds, during the time it takes to slowly lift dice into the air and bring them down,[40] they know the creation and destruction of a great eon. Likewise, yogins must all understand how to create and destroy a great eon [94] within a single day. As Ācārya Āryadeva wrote:

> It is impossible for those of little wisdom
> even to be skeptical about this Dharma;
> if they are even skeptical about it,
> this will shred mundane existence.

The duration of a finger snap is a moment, one sixtieth of a moment is an instant, one fortieth of an instant is a flash, and in just a flash an eon is created and destroyed. Likewise, once you have repeatedly familiarized yourself with this, if you do not gain a decisive understanding that all the phenomena included in the appearing worlds of saṃsāra and nirvāṇa are shifting displays of one great emptiness within the circumference of one great emptiness, you have not come the slightest bit closer to the path of omniscience.

> **"My child, endowed with the pinnacle of conscious awareness, carefully attend to this point, and by realizing all appearances as space itself, become a yogin of the uniform pervasiveness of space!"**
>
> **With these words, he disappeared.**

40. Emending *dar gyi cho lung* ("silken sleeve snap") to *dal gyis cho lo* ("slowly lift dice into the air and bring them down").

Teachings of Longchenpa, Drimé Özer: An Introduction in the Form of a Question-and-Answer Session for the Sake of Developing Certainty

By gaining a strong conviction about the above points, I understood all appearances to be empty from their own side. Nevertheless, regarding the outer appearances of the physical world, its inner, animate sentient inhabitants, and all the intervening appearances of the five kinds of sensory objects, I still thought they would be left behind when I departed for other realms, and that all sentient beings existed with their own individual mindstreams. During that period my guru, Drimé Özer, appeared to me in a dream and gave me the following introduction in the form of a question-and-answer session.

He said, "O son of the family, the outer appearances of the physical world, its inner, animate sentient inhabitants, and the intervening appearances of the five kinds of sensory objects are like illusory apparitions that dissolve into the space of awareness. Accordingly, once they have disappeared into the vacuous space of the substrate, eventually, due to the projections resulting from the movements of karmic energies, there is an appearance of your own body, giving rise to a physical world, its sentient inhabitants, and all sensory appearances. As fixation arises toward them, delusion sets in. Finally, this appearing world once again disappears into the vacuous space of the substrate, like a rainbow dissolving into the sky. Then waking appearances emerge like before."

THUS, [95] by gaining a strong conviction about the above points, I knew that all appearances are empty from their own side. Nevertheless, regarding the outer appearances of the physical world, its inner, animate sentient inhabitants, and all the intervening appearances of the five kinds of sensory objects, I still thought they would be left behind as I went from one realm to another among the six realms of animate beings and so on, and that each sentient being existed with an individual mindstream. During that period, when my guru, Drimé Özer [Longchenpa], appeared to me in a pure dream, there occurred the following question-and-answer session. This was an introduction to determining the nature of dream images and the appearances of birth and death and of going and coming, such that they are not established as real objects from the very moment they first arise.

O son of the family, the outer appearances of the vast physical world, its numerous inner, animate sentient inhabitants, and the fine display of the intervening appearances of the five kinds of sensory objects all appear as if they were truly existent. As an analogy, just as illusory apparitions dissolve into the space of awareness, when you fall asleep and dream, [all appearances] disappear into the vacuous space of the substrate. This is called the *actual substrate* and [96] the *substrate of descent*. It is an embryonic, semiconscious, muddled state of unconsciousness in which the creative expressions of the radiance [of primordial consciousness] are impeded. There are five states of mindlessness: the states of deep sleep, of fainting, of death, and of sexual union of a male and female, as well as the state aroused by meditative experience. They are also called the *substrate of descent*. As Vidyādhara Jikmé Lingpa [1729–98] says:

> From the domain of the substrate, the projections of the movements of karmic energies and
> habitual propensities shroud the womb of the ultimate reality of the mind.

From the realm of the substrate, the arousal of ever-so-subtle grasping is the grasping of karmic energies. Due to this, in the realm of the substrate, the luminosity that emerges like the first light of dawn is the substrate consciousness. From it arises a tenacious consciousness that grasps at an "I" where none exists, and this is prior afflictive mentation. From it, due to the mere appearance of your own body, all the coarse phenomena that appear as the physical world and its sentient inhabitants manifest, even though they do not exist. This includes subtle, veiled afflictive mentation, from which [97] indiscernible concepts of the six kinds [of consciousness] emerge as lucid, clear mentation. This is mentation. From it emerge appearances of form, sound, smell, taste, and tactile sensations; and the presentations of these potentials are the five kinds of sensory consciousness, which are objects. The actual emergences of the appearances of form, sound, smell, taste, and tactile sensations are that which is apprehended, while the mind that closely holds these appearances is the mind that apprehends the occurrences of subtle thoughts. The whole of saṃsāra emerges from the fortification of grasping at the duality of the apprehender and the apprehended.

Thus, the domain for the emergence of dream appearances is the substrate consciousness. From it arises the consciousness that grasps at the "I," which enters into the basis of the subtle consciousness of the five senses, giving rise to dream appearances. The grasping at the "I" enters into the basis of the five coarse senses, giving rise to waking appearances. From the consciousness of the mere appearance of your body—in the absence of a self—emerge all physical worlds, sentient inhabitants, and sensory objects of the world of dream appearances. Delusion occurs due to grasping at this as truly existent and fixating on it; and then the phenomenal world of the dream, with all its physical worlds and their sentient inhabitants, dissolves into the vacuous space of the substrate, like a rainbow dissolving into the sky. Then, due to the apparitions of the movements of karmic energies [98] from the domain of the substrate, waking appearances emerge like before.

> **I responded, "I think this body of mine is not a mere appearance but definitely arose from the causes and conditions of a father and mother."**
>
> **He replied, "If you think your body arose from a father and mother like that, tell me: What are the beginnings and ends of your fathers and mothers, and what are their origins, locations, and destinations?"**
>
> **I answered, "I believe they exist, but I can't remember them. I think it's impossible for there to be a body without parents."**
>
> **He countered, "Check to see who are the parents of a body in a dream, the intermediate period, a hell realm, and so on."**
>
> **Consequently, I gained a decisive understanding that this body is not established as anything other than a mere appearance.**

When I told him that I thought the body is not a mere appearance, but rather that it is created from the causal influence of a father, the contributing condition of a mother, and the tangible connection of these two—my material body being ascertained to arise as something truly existent—the guru replied, "If you think this body of yours arose in that way from the cause and condition of your father and mother, tell me: From the beginningless past until now, what are the beginnings and ends and the origins, locations, and destinations of fathers? And what are the beginnings and ends and the origins, locations, and destinations of mothers?"

I answered, "I believe they exist, but I can't remember them. However, I think it's impossible for there to be a body without parents."

He countered, "In that case, even though you don't remember the beginnings and ends of your fathers and mothers from the beginningless past until now, check out the beginnings and ends and the origins, locations, and destinations of the fathers and mothers of bodies in a dream. Likewise, examine the beginnings and ends and the origins, locations, and destinations of the fathers and mothers of bodies in the intermediate period. And look for the beginnings and ends and the origins, locations, and destinations of the fathers and mothers of bodies in the resuscitating hell, in which bodies perish and are resuscitated many tens of thousands of times." [99] Consequently, I decisively recognized that this body is a mere appearance and is not established as truly existent.

> **I commented, "O guru, I think that when my body is in bed covered with bedclothes and dream appearances arise, my body and the human environment remain unchanged."**
>
> **The guru replied, "Examine the dream appearances of the vast outer physical world, its numerous inner sentient inhabitants, and the well-displayed intervening appearances of the five senses to see whether they are located in the head, the limbs, or the upper or lower parts of your body."**
>
> **Consequently, I became certain that such was not the case.**

"O guru, I think that when my body is in bed covered with bedclothes and I am sleeping, my human environment, including my house, remains without changing, but all the physical worlds and their sentient inhabitants that are dream appearances arise from some other realm."

The guru replied, "Examine all the vast outer physical worlds, including great mountains, houses, and landscapes; and their numerous inner sentient inhabitants, from the smallest creatures up to human beings; and the well-displayed intervening appearances of the five senses—forms appearing as visual objects, sounds as auditory objects, odors as olfactory objects, tastes as gustatory objects, and sensations as tactile objects—that occur when you are dreaming to see whether they emerge as objects located in your head, limbs, or the exterior, interior, upper, or lower parts of your body today."

If you believe they are located inside your head, your head is filled with your brain and so on, so there is no way the vast landscapes that appear in a dream could fit inside your head. Likewise, your limbs [100] are filled with their own flesh, blood, bones, marrow, and so forth, so these vast landscapes couldn't fit in them either. If you think they are located in your upper body, it is filled with lungs, the liver, and so on, so the vast landscapes that appear in a dream couldn't fit in there either. If you think they are located in your lower body, it is filled with intestines and so on, so the vast landscapes that appear in a dream couldn't fit in there either.

Consequently, I became certain that such was not the case.

> **Nevertheless, I persisted, "Guru, perhaps dream appearances arise when consciousness goes elsewhere. Then, when it reenters the body, waking appearances arise."**
>
> **The guru replied, "Well, if that were so, this body would be like a hotel, in which case, identify and report to me what is the door to this hotel, as it were, by which consciousness comes and goes. In addition, you must identify where the mind is located. If the mind is located in the upper part of the body, why is pain experienced when the lower part is pricked with a thorn? Likewise, if it resides in the lower part, there would be no reason for pain to be experienced in the upper part. It doesn't make sense for it to fluctuate in size, such that a tiny consciousness enters the body through an orifice, increases in size until it pervades the body, and then shrinks again as it departs through that orifice. If that were so, once awareness is separated from the material body, why wouldn't consciousness reenter the corpse after death?**
>
> **"Where do dream appearances go? Do they go above, below, or in one of the cardinal or intermediate directions? Do you believe they are the same as the waking appearances of the physical world and its sentient inhabitants or different? If you believe they are the same, does sleep define their boundaries or not? If it does, then they are not waking appearances; and if it doesn't, they are not dream appearances. On the other hand, it is invalid to believe that these appearances exist, while imagining that they are above or below, outside or inside."**

I persisted, "Guru, perhaps dream appearances arise when consciousness goes elsewhere, and then when it reenters the body, waking appearances arise."

The guru replied, "Well, if that were so, since this body would be like a hotel, there must be something like a door to this hotel by which consciousness comes and goes. So you should identify that hotel door and show it to me!"

I replied, "I think it must exist, but I don't remember where."

He countered, "For example, you may pass in and out of a hotel door on one occasion, [101] but from then on you would recognize this door due to your previous experience. If every year you passed in and out daily, 720 times, even if you didn't identify it on one occasion, you must identify it on another! If you still don't identify it, this should show you that the door does not exist by its own inherent nature."

In addition, you must identify where your mind is located. If it is located in the upper part of the body, why are suffering and pain experienced when the lower part is pricked with a thorn? If it resides in the lower part, why would pain be experienced in the lower part if the upper part were pricked with a thorn? It doesn't make sense for consciousness to fluctuate in size, such that a tiny consciousness like a mustard seed leaves through an orifice at the beginning of a dream, increases in size and fills the body when it returns to the body, and then diminishes in size so that it can leave again through that little portal. But if we assume you are right, then when you die, upon the separation of your material body and awareness, you might think it's not the time for you to die because you are still young. So why wouldn't your consciousness reenter your corpse if it could? [102]

As for the place to which a dream appearance goes, is it above or below this world of the waking state? Where is it among the four cardinal or eight intermediate directions? Are the physical world and its sentient inhabitants that arise in the waking state and those that arise at night while dreaming the same or different? If you believe they are the same, does sleep define their boundaries or not? If it does, then they are not the same as waking appearances; and if it doesn't, then they are not different. On the other hand, if waking appearances today and dream appearances last night are different, there is no way that one could be above or beneath the other or outside or inside the other, or that those two could not be ascertained in the same region!

> **I replied, "Guru, then how is this to be decided? Where should I stand? Sublime guru, please show me."**
>
> **The guru replied, "Throughout beginningless lifetimes you have never been born; there have been only appearances of birth. You have never died; there have been only appearances of a change of place, like dream appearances and waking appearances. Regarding the eyes, ears, nose, tongue, and body,**

> **all things that are seen as forms, heard as sounds, smelled as odors, experienced as tastes, and felt as tactile sensations are simply your own appearances arising to yourself, without their ever existing, even in the slightest way, as something else.**
>
> **"If you think that things exist autonomously as something else since you can directly see them with your eyes, really hold them in your hands, and experience them through your senses, consider: All the forms, sounds, odors, tastes, and tactile sensations in a dream appear at the time to be truly existent. But from the next day onward, they have no objective existence. This should tell you something."**

I replied, "Guru, then how is this to be decided? Where should I stand? Supreme guru, please show me."

The guru replied, "Throughout beginningless lifetimes you have never been born; there has been nothing more than the appearance of birth. You have never died; there has been only the appearance of death." For example, once you make the transition from a dream, waking appearances merely emerge; and once you make the transition from waking appearances, dream appearances merely emerge. [103] Apart from that, birth and death do not exist from their own side.

Regarding the myriad forms that appear as visual objects, sounds that appear as auditory objects, odors that appear as olfactory objects, tastes that appear as gustatory objects, sensations that appear as tactile objects, and various phenomena that appear as mental objects, all are nonexistent. Nevertheless, they are seen, heard, smelled, tasted, and felt simply as your own appearances arising to yourself, without their ever truly existing, even in the slightest way, as something else.

You may think things autonomously exist as something else since you can directly see them with your eyes, really hold them in your hands, and experience them through your senses. If an attractive form is seen, it is recognized as attractive. If an unattractive form is seen, it is recognized as unattractive. If a neutral form is seen, it is recognized as neutral. The same holds true for attractive, unattractive, and neutral sounds, smells, tastes, and tactile sensations. If you think that that which is directly seen with your eyes, [104] really held in your hands, and experienced through your physical senses exists, consider: Last night when you were dreaming, with these eyes you may have seen beautiful forms, such as the bodies of gods, humans, and *sugatas*, as well as unattractive forms that were disagreeable; but with these eyes during the waking state today, not one of them is seen. Likewise, with these ears pleasant sounds are heard, such as those of a lute and a flute, as well as unpleasant sounds, such as the irritating noises of a donkey and a dog; but with these ears during the waking state today, not one of them is experienced. With this nose fine fragrances are smelled, such as those of musk, camphor, and saffron, as well as foul odors, such as those of rotting corpses of horses and dogs; but with this nose during the waking state today, not one of them is smelled. With this tongue sweet tastes are experienced, such as those of molasses, sugar, and honey, as well as unpleasant tastes, such as bitter and sour; but with this tongue during the waking state today, not one of them is tasted. With this body soft sensations are experienced, such as those of fine silk clothing and fleece, as well as unpleasant, harsh sensations; [105] but with this body during the waking state today, not one of them is experienced. It is said that from the very moment they arise, such appearances do not truly exist, so this shows that dream and waking appearances are alike.

> **"Throughout your beginningless succession of lifetimes, you have never moved from one place to another, and you have never lived anywhere else. This condition is equivalent to appearances in a dream. If you think there is a difference in the reality or unreality of dream appearances and waking appearances, observe for yourself: From the time you were born until now, are all the dream and waking appearances of working, farming, striving, saving, and planning the same or not? If you carefully examine them without regard for their duration and quantity, you will definitely recognize that they are alike.**
>
> **"Moreover, if dream appearances were unreal and waking appearances were real, this would mean that dream appearances are delusive and waking appearances are not delusive. In that case, you would have to believe that you are a sentient being while dreaming and a buddha during the waking state! If both are delusive appearances, it is pointless to distinguish one as being real and the other as unreal, for something is called a delusive appearance if it appears and is apprehended as something it is not.**
>
> **"Until now you have eaten enough food to fill Mount Meru and drunk an ocean of liquid, but still you are not full. You have worn a galaxy of clothing, but still you are not warm. Know that this indicates that these are mere appearances and are not established as real."**

Throughout your beginningless lifetimes in saṃsāra, you have never moved from one place to another, and you have never lived anywhere else. This is suggested by appearances in a dream. If you think dream appearances and waking appearances are unlike each other in terms of how real or unreal they are, consider: That which you dream tonight will not be dreamed tomorrow. If you think the appearances that are present in the waking state today are also present tomorrow, consider: Going back to the time since you were ten years old, what friends did you accompany, what conversations did you have, what food did you eat, and where are the food and other things you accumulated? Going back to the time since you were ten years old, in your dreams what friends did you accompany, what conversations did you have, what food did you eat, and where are the food and other things you accumulated on those occasions? If they exist, you should be able to directly see them with your eyes, really hold them in your hands, and experience them through your senses, but it is not so. [106] They have all been forgotten, and objects that are remembered are alike in terms of how real or unreal they are. Dream appearances emerge upon the substrate consciousness, and waking appearances emerge upon the mentation of the substrate. So due to the difference of one looking outward and the other looking inward, one is apprehended more firmly than the other.

Even if you examine them in terms of their durations, there are thirty *ghaṭikās*[41] during the day and thirty during the night, so there are sixty ghaṭikās during a full day and night, and the durations of daytime and nighttime appearances are the same. Even if you examine them in terms of their quantities, in one year there are 360 appearances of the day, 360 appearances of the night, and 720 appearances of the day and night, so they are the same in quantity. Investigate this carefully and you will come to certainty!

Although you have eaten enough food to fill Mount Meru and drunk an ocean of liquid, you still don't seem to be full. Although you have worn a galaxy[42] of clothing, you still don't seem to be warm. The appearances of this life alone indicate that none of them are established as truly existent.

41. One *ghaṭikā* equals twenty-four minutes.

42. The Tibetan here reads *lho sprin*, or "southern cloud," in contrast to the root text, which reads *stong gsum*, an abbreviation of *stong gsum gyi 'jig rten*. I have emended the commentary in accordance with the root text. The Tibetan term *stong gsum gyi 'jig rten*, literally "three-thousandfold world," means one thousand to the third power, or one billion worlds; each has a Mount Meru and four continents. There are said to be a countless number of these throughout the vastness of space.

> **"It is a great mistake not to recognize that what appears as your body is empty and to cling to it as real. This is a consuming demon, since the efforts you make for the sake of your body eat away at the fruit of omniscience. It is a murderous executioner, since it links one cycle of existence to the next, displaying the appearances of birth and death. It cuts your life force, since, for the sake of your body, you seek happiness from clothing and so on, and you are imprisoned by clinging to attachments and aversions that perpetuate hopes and fears; thus, your lifeline to liberation is cut. And it asphyxiates you, for it robs you of the breath of eternal bliss. Therefore, all those who cling to the objective appearances of the six kinds of consciousness are like deer that mistake a mirage for water and run to it. There is not even an iota of an essence that is established as real."**

If you single-pointedly practice the sublime Dharma in this life, you may realize the fruition of omniscience [107] in one lifetime; but without applying yourself to the Dharma, for the sake of this appearance of a body—although the body doesn't exist—if you exert yourself in acquiring food for your mouth, clothes for your back, and so on, you are like a consuming demon that eats away at the fruit of omniscience.

There is no way to avoid death at the end of a rebirth, so you also become a murderous executioner who continuously displays the appearances of birth and death. If, however, you achieve the omniscient state of enlightenment while merely satisfying your hunger and thirst and protecting your extremities with clothing, you may achieve the life force of liberation in this lifetime. But without doing so, if you grasp at the mere appearance of a body as a real body and apply yourself solely to concerns of this life—such as acquiring fine, warm, and soft clothing and excellent, delicious food for the sake of your body, devoting yourself only to pleasure, hoping for the good and fearing the bad, with hostility toward your enemies and attachment to your relatives, subduing your enemies and caring for your family—you become a murderer who cuts your lifeline to liberation. [108]

If you meditate on the meaning of the clear-light Great Perfection in this life, you may achieve the eternally blissful fruition of omniscience in one lifetime and with one body. But if you do not do so, this asphyxiates you, for it robs you of the breath of omniscience.

If you enter the gateway of the secret mantra, Vajrayāna, in this life, and properly keep your samayas without letting them degenerate, you have the ability to achieve the state of Vajradhara in this lifetime and with this body.

However, if you do not properly keep them, but rather pass the time solely in the nonvirtuous activities of subduing your enemies and protecting your relatives of this life, your samayas will degenerate, so you will be a demon who causes the breakage of samayas.

Therefore, those who cling to the objective appearances of the six kinds of consciousness are like deer that mistake a mirage for water and run to it. There is not even an iota of an essence that is established as real, so realize the empty nature of all objective appearances. From the moment they arise, all appearing phenomena cannot be established as having an inherent nature, for they are like rainbows or flashes of lightning in the sky.

> **"Even though you know appearances to be empty in this way, they might remain as before, as if they were truly existent, without turning into nothing. So if you wonder why it is necessary to know this, consider: If you do not know that the essential nature of the object of meditation is emptiness, all your meditations will certainly turn out to be ethically neutral.**
>
> **"Furthermore, you may wonder why the mere realization of emptiness should reveal the nature of nonexistence, given that mere understanding and mere realization resulting from all other visualizations and meditations are not liberating. Moreover, if everything is primordially empty, you may think that it makes no difference whether or not you know everything to be empty. If so, consider this: Know that saṃsāra and nirvāṇa and liberation and delusion come about due to the differences between awareness and unawareness and between knowing and not knowing. Realize that awareness is essential."**

If you think that even if you know that appearances are empty, that which is empty does not become nothing, consider: This is not so, for the essential nature of meditation is emptiness, so [109] if you do not truly know the nature of existence and mode of being of everything, you will be misled by reifying external appearances and by grasping at your own body with attachment. Then, even if you penetratingly meditate on the mere luminosity of the mind, since you do not accurately perceive emptiness, all your meditations will certainly turn out to be ethically neutral. Therefore, true knowledge and awareness of the view of the ground emptiness are vitally important, so you must know and realize that the nature of all phenomena is emptiness.

Again, you may retort, "If what you say is true, by merely visualizing a deity, one's body will become a deity; by merely reciting mantras, one's spoken words will ripen as empty mantras; and by merely cultivating samādhi, one may be able to realize the mind as clear light. But since the mere understanding and realization of these facts is not liberating, the mere realization of emptiness doesn't annihilate all phenomena, and that would not constitute a reason for such realization being necessary." Moreover, it is possible that some people think that if [everything] has always been empty, [everything] beneath, upon, and above the earth would be empty, so it would be the same whether or not one knows everything to be empty. [110] Therefore, you must recognize the nature of all phenomena to be emptiness, for saṃsāra and nirvāṇa and liberation and delusion come about due to the differences between awareness and unawareness and between knowing and not knowing. Thus it is said that knowledge and awareness are of the utmost importance.

> **"Some people may think that if you can't understand this on your own, then hearing teachings and contemplating them will be of no use. But since beginningless time you have failed to realize this on your own and have wandered in saṃsāra. Know that through studying and training you will realize emptiness, thereby gaining the view that accords with all the tantras, oral transmissions, and pith instructions.**
>
> **"Furthermore, whether you realize emptiness after undergoing great hardships in studying, training, and so on, or you realize emptiness without experiencing the slightest difficulty, there is no difference in the quality of your realization. For example, whether you discover gold after undergoing great hardships or you find it under your bed without the slightest difficulty, there is no difference in the quality of the gold."**

Some people may think that if you don't know this on your own, then understanding that results from studying and training will be of no use. But since beginningless time until now you have failed to realize the view on your own, and under the influence of ignorance you have wandered in saṃsāra. On your own, you still won't realize emptiness. Therefore, know that through studying and training—by way of the authentic teachings of the jinas, the authentic pith instructions of the guru, and your own authentic pristine awareness—you must realize emptiness and the view that accords with all the tantras, oral transmissions, and pith instructions.

From the side of emptiness, there is not even a hair's breadth of difference in realizing it after studying, training, and undergoing great hardships as opposed to realizing emptiness without experiencing even the slightest difficulty. [111] For example, whether you discover gold after undergoing great hardships or find it under your bed without the slightest difficulty, there is no difference in the quality of the gold. And there is no difference in the nature of the blessings received by meeting the Lord of Lhasa[43] whether someone undergoes great hardships [to meet him] or someone from Lhasa meets him without any difficulty at all.

> **"The consciousness that analytically ascertains all appearances as emptiness is called *discerning wisdom*. The continuum of subsequent consciousness that definitely ascertains saṃsāra and nirvāṇa as great emptiness is called the *wisdom that realizes identitylessness*. Once these two types of wisdom have been generated in your mindstream, there is first realization, then experience, and finally acquiring indwelling confidence. This is a crucial point.**
>
> **"Moreover, if you say that it is incorrect to assert that the body and so forth are not established except as mere appearances, because if the body of someone who has realized them as empty is touched by fire or water or struck by an arrow, a spear, or a club, then pain arises, consider: Until you reach absolute space, in which phenomena are extinguished in ultimate reality, dualistic appearances do not subside; and until they vanish, appearances of benefit and harm will uninterruptedly arise. But in reality, even the fires of hell do not burn."**
>
> **With these words, he disappeared.**

The consciousness that analytically ascertains all the phenomena included in the world of appearances of saṃsāra and nirvāṇa as being of the nature of great emptiness is called *discerning wisdom*. Once saṃsāra and nirvāṇa have been definitely ascertained as great emptiness, the continuum of subsequent consciousness is called the *wisdom that realizes identitylessness*. Therefore, first there is recognition and realization, then there is experience and familiarization, and finally there is the acquisition of indwelling confidence.[44] This is said to be of the utmost importance.

43. The Lord of Lhasa is the famous statue of the Buddha that resides in the central temple in Lhasa.

44. This varies from the sequence presented in other teachings of Düdjom Lingpa, where one acquires first understanding, then experience, then realization, and finally indwelling confidence.

If someone with mere understanding and realization says, "If you have realization of emptiness and I poke you with fire, you appear to burn; if you are doused with water, you appear to chill; [112] and if you are struck by an arrow, a spear, a club, and so on, you appear to be injured and hurt," consider: Until all appearances of phenomena are extinguished in the absolute space of ultimate reality, dualistic appearances of grasping at "self" and "other" do not subside. Until they vanish, if you are touched with fire, there is the appearance of burning; if you are doused with water, there is the appearance of chilling; if you are struck by an arrow, a spear, a club, and so on, there are the appearances of being injured and hurt. Thus, an uninterrupted stream of appearances of benefit and harm arises. But in reality, the self exists in such a way that even the fires of hell do not burn, the cold of the cold hells does not freeze, and being pierced by the arrows, spears, and clubs of the asuras does not cause death. This shows that all these appearances are mere appearances and are not truly existent.

With these words, he disappeared.

Teachings of Saraha

C′ Counteracting the Faults of Benefit and Harm

> **On another occasion when I had a vision of Mahāsiddha Saraha, I asked the great lord of siddhas, "By what means are obscurations purified? How are deities to be realized? By what means can one be freed of demons and obstructive beings? Please explain!"**
>
> **He replied, "O great being, you must counteract the faults of benefit and harm. As for so-called obscurations, ignorance of the essential nature of the ground as emptiness is called an *obscuration* and *ignorance*, and the entrenchment of such ignorance is called a *habitual propensity*. These cannot be purified by ordinary efforts, such as striving at physical and verbal spiritual practices. Rather, obscurations are naturally purified as a result of ascertaining ultimate reality by means of discerning wisdom."**

On another occasion when I had a vision of Mahāsiddha Saraha, I asked the great lord of siddhas, "By what means are obscurations purified? How are deities to be realized? By what means can one be freed of demons and obstructive beings? Please explain!"

"O great being," he replied, "you must counteract the faults of benefit and harm. [113] As for so-called obscurations, ignorance of the essential nature of the ground emptiness is called an *obscuration* and *ignorance*; and the entrenchments of such ignorance and all the actions committed under its influence are fortified in the domain of the substrate and are called *habitual propensities*." These cannot be purified by strenuously applying yourself merely to spiritual practices such as performing prostrations or circumambulations with the body, chanting recitations with the speech, or cultivating good thoughts with the mind. For example, this would be like sweeping the dust on the ground because you wish to dispel the clouds in the sky. If you wish to purify the obscurations and habitual propensities of ignorance, when all the phenomena included in the world of appearances of saṃsāra and nirvāṇa are ascertained with discerning wisdom as the ground of great ultimate reality, then the obscurations and habitual propensities of ignorance will naturally be purified. Therefore, you must determine the nature of the beneficial virtues of the body and speech and the harmful vices of the body, speech, and mind.

> **"Where are all beneficial virtues of the body and speech located? Where is the storehouse in which they are accumulated? By investigating and analyzing the origin from which they arise, their location, and the destination to which they go, if you find that none of them have any objective existence, then what do they benefit? By investigating what it could mean to benefit the empty ultimate nature of mind—in terms of its exterior, interior, middle, top, or bottom—you will become certain that such benefit has no objective existence. Then you will see that there is nothing more than an accumulation of merit within saṃsāra."**

First, to determine the nature of beneficial virtues of body, speech, and mind, all spiritual practices of physical prostrations and circumambulations, verbal recitations, [114] and mental good thoughts should be piled up like a heap of grain, and they should be accumulated in some place like a king's storehouse. If they are, you should be able to directly see them with your eyes, really hold them in your hands, and experience them through your senses, but it is not so. If there is an initial origin from which the beneficial virtues of the body, speech, and mind arise, then if they arise from the domain of the five external elements, do they arise from the earth element, the water element, the fire element, or the air element? If they do, you should be able to directly see this with your eyes, really hold it in your hands, and experience it through your senses, but it is not so.

Do the beneficial virtues of the body, speech, and mind arise from something substantial or something insubstantial? If they arise from something substantial, you should be able to directly see their source with your eyes, really hold it in your hands, and directly experience it through your senses, but it is not so. If they arise from something insubstantial, there should exist some physical virtues of the body, speech, and mind that arise from something insubstantial. If this were so, then you should be able to directly see with your eyes, really hold in your hands, and directly experience through your senses the form, shape, color, and so on of these virtues of the body, speech, and mind, but this is not the case. [115]

If there is some intervening location where these beneficial virtues of the body, speech, and mind exist, once you have examined the body from the tips of the hair on your head down to the tips of your toenails, you should be able to say, "This is the spot!" If such a place exists, you should be able to directly see it with your eyes, really hold it in your hands, and experience it through your senses, but it is not so.

If there is some destination where the beneficial virtues of the body, speech, and mind finally go, it must be somewhere in one of the four cardinal directions of the east, south, west, and north, in one of the intermediate directions, or above, below, or in between. If such a place exists, you should be able to directly see it with your eyes, really hold it in your hands, and experience it through your senses, but it is not so.

Therefore, once you have determined this in terms of their origin, location, and destination, if you think that even though they don't exist, virtues bring benefit, consider: From which side is the empty ultimate nature of mind benefited—its exterior, interior, middle, top, or bottom? You should be able to directly see this cleansing with your eyes, really hold it in your hands, and directly experience it through your senses, but it is not so.

Therefore, apart from the mere imputation by your own mind, when you become certain that virtue does not truly exist from its own side and has no objective existence, you will see that it is nothing more than a merely temporary accumulation of merit within saṃsāra.

> **"Likewise, in what cardinal or intermediate direction are the heaps of accumulated vices located? Where is their storehouse? Investigate how they harm the exterior, interior, middle, top, or bottom of the empty mind. Now if you carefully examine the streams of consciousness of people who have constantly applied themselves to physical and verbal virtues and those of others who have devoted their whole lives to perpetrating evil, you will find that there is not one iota of difference between them in terms of the perpetuation of all their attachment and hostility, hope and fear. If they are liberated, they are freed due to their streams of consciousness being freed; and if they are deluded, they are bewildered due to their streams of consciousness being bewildered. There is not even the slightest difference in terms of their streams of consciousness wandering in saṃsāra without being liberated. Therefore, virtue and vice are**

> **different merely insofar as they generate temporary happiness and suffering, but other than this, they do nothing more than perpetuate saṃsāra."**

Likewise, the heap of accumulated vices that harm the body, speech, and mind [116] should be piled up like a mound of grain, and they should be accumulated in some place like a king's storehouse. If they are, you should be able to directly see this with your eyes, really hold it in your hands, and experience it through your senses, but it is not so. Determine the nature of their origin, location, and destination like before. If you think that that which inflicts harm is vice, consider: If it harms the exterior, interior, middle, top, or bottom of the ultimate nature of the empty mind, you should be able to see that which harms and fouls the mind, really hold it in your hands, and experience it through your senses, but it is not so. Therefore, apart from the mere imputation by your own mind, vice does not have even an iota of true existence from its own side.

Now if you carefully examine the stream of consciousness of one person who has devoted his whole life to physical, verbal, and mental virtues and that of someone else who has devoted his whole life to practicing physical, verbal, and mental vices, you will find that there is not one iota of difference between them in terms of the perpetuation of all their attachment to relatives and hostility toward their enemies and hope for the good and fear of the bad. In that case, if they are liberated, they are freed due to their streams of consciousness being freed; and if they are deluded, they are bewildered due to their streams of consciousness being bewildered, and they wander in saṃsāra. There is no difference in terms of their streams of consciousness, and they do not transcend saṃsāra. If there is no difference apart from merely temporary happiness and [117] temporary suffering, they do nothing more than perpetuate saṃsāra.

> **"If you do not determine the nature of virtue in this way, you will confuse the virtue of accumulating temporary merit with the path to liberation, so you will not achieve the fruition of omniscience. If you fail to determine the nature of vice, you will not know that ignorance of your own essential nature is an obscuration and the basis of delusion, so you will not recognize the cause of delusion. Consequently, you will have no alternative but to remain endlessly deluded in saṃsāra. So recognize the crucial importance of determining this."**

If you think that even if you don't determine the nature of virtue, there is no one who performs virtue, and even if you don't determine the nature of vice, everyone will equally engage in vice, and that therefore, there is no need to determine the nature of virtue and vice, consider: Their nature is not to be determined so that you won't perform virtue and you will commit negative deeds. Rather, if their nature is not determined in this way, you will confuse the virtue of accumulating temporary merit within saṃsāra with the path to liberation, so you will not achieve the fruition of omniscience. If you fail to determine the nature of vice, you will not know that ignorance of your own essential nature is an obscuration and the basis of delusion, so you will have no alternative but to remain endlessly deluded in saṃsāra. Therefore, determining the nature of virtue and vice is of the utmost importance.

Thus, if you think that regardless of whatever virtue or vice you commit, no consequences will arise, you are wrong. Since the virtuous thought that "this is virtue" is a trace of the ground sugatagarbha, whatever virtues you perform by way of your body, speech, and mind [118] enable you merely to achieve the favorable states of existence of gods and humans. But you will be bound by the limitation that they will not bring you the slightest bit closer to the path of omniscience. Moreover, whatever nonvirtuous karma you accumulate by way of a basis, intention, enactment, and culmination, this will consequently cast you into the three miserable states of existence, depending on the relative strengths of the motivations of any of the three poisons, which complete the enactment of the vice. However, since neither of these two transcends saṃsāra, they are nothing more than mere accumulations of merit within saṃsāra.

With an aspiration focused on the hereafter, you may enter solitary retreat; but when meditating on emptiness, you may become dissatisfied due to not gaining any desired experiences and hence exert yourself toward some other defiled virtues that seem to be very profound. Then, when seeing the excellent qualities of meditating on emptiness, you may meditate and so forth on the meaning of emptiness. However, like the aphorism "you can't sew with a two-pointed needle, and you can't accomplish your aim with a two-pointed mind," you become bound by the limitation of not being able to acquire indwelling confidence in the meaning of ultimate reality. For this reason, you must determine the nature of both virtue and vice. Apart from this, due to engaging in the ordinary activities of the three mental afflictions of attachment, hostility, and delusion, [119] you will achieve nothing more than various defiled virtues.

On the other hand, no virtue can compare to the meaning of ultimate reality. When you meditate on the meaning of this, you are free of activity by way of mentally fabricated, conceptual, virtuous, or nonvirtuous deeds; and there is not the slightest distinction between good and bad in terms of their obscuring your essential nature. As the great, omniscient Longchenpa stated:

> The sun of ultimate, self-emergent pristine awareness
> is obscured by the clouds of positive virtues and negative vices.
> With the flash of lightning of striving to embrace and reject [virtue and vice],
> the rain of delusive appearances of joy and sorrow falls,
> nurturing the harvest of the seeds of saṃsāra as the six realms of existence.
> Alas, pity every single pathetic sentient being!
> With regard to the essence of the ultimate, definitive meaning,
> just as it is the same whether you are bound by cords of gold or rope,
> it is the same whether you are bound by virtuous or nonvirtuous thoughts.
> When there are no clouds, white or black,
> the sun of ultimate reality shines in the sky of the absolute space of phenomena.[45]

> **"By investigating the initial origin, interim location, and final destination of so-called benevolent and protective gods, you will see that they have no objective existence. In which of the objects of form, sound, smell, taste, and tactile sensations appearing as sensory objects is their existence established? If you think they exist in the domain of one of the elements of the physical world and its sentient inhabitants, investigate within molecules and atoms, examine the individual names and constitutions of the elements, and see how these gods could be of benefit."**

To determine the nature of benevolent gods, by investigating their initial origin, their interim location, and their final destination, [120] you will see that they have no objective existence. If something called a *god* appears to your

45. Longchen Rabjam, *The Precious Treasury of the Way of Abiding* (*Gnas lugs mdzod*), trans. Richard Barron (Junction City, CA: Padma Publishing, 1998), 21.

senses, there should be something you could call the god's form, sound, smell, taste, or touch, but there is nothing that can be established as truly existent.

If you think gods arose from the elements of the physical world and its sentient inhabitants, to take the element of earth as an example: Even if earth is reduced to particles, particles to molecules, and molecules to atoms, they are still called *earth*, and there is no way that something called a *god* could emerge from them. Likewise, each of the elements is called by its own name, not by the name *god*. If you think a god is something separate, consider: If a god is something insubstantial, there is no way it could benefit you as a substantial being. If a god is something substantial, there is no way you could be unaware of it when it looks after and befriends you. If you are aware of it at that time, you should be able to directly see the god's form, shape, and color with your eyes, you should be able to really hold it in your hands, and it should be evident to your senses. But it is not so.

If you think a local god is a powerful, ferocious *dharmapāla* who lives on a certain mountain and is benevolent, how is he of benefit? If that mountain is a god, when he provides protection, that mountain should come and protect you. If he doesn't, [121] there is no way he can be of benefit. If he dwells inside the mountain, he must have some way out. If he doesn't, he must come out by digging through the earth. If he exists beneath the mountain, then you should certainly witness him when you dig down to look for him, but it isn't so.

If you think that ever since the times of your ancient ancestors, if offerings are made, incense is burned, and prayer flags are strung, the god looks after and befriends you, but if offerings aren't made, disease and calamities ensue, consider: There is no way a nonphysical god could help anything that is physical. If the god is something physical, when burnt offerings are made of fragrant trees, silk brocade, and so forth, there should be someone who partakes of them. But there isn't. The smoke of the incense disappears into the sky, the burnt offering substances turn into ash, and the remains are carried away by the wind. Apart from that, there is no one who takes off with them. Likewise, regarding the stringing of so-called prayer flags in multicolored silk cloth, with each passing phase of the year they decompose due to moisture, tear away and are consumed by rain, and then disappear; but it's obvious that nothing called a *god* actually partakes of them.

On the other hand, if you think that when you went to a terrifying rock on a clay mountain somewhere, because [122] you mined into the earth and removed boulders there was an incredible hailstorm, with thunderbolts, thunder, and lightning flashes, and you barely escaped being killed, consider: For example, imagine that when you were dreaming last night, you went to a mountain with a snow-clad summit, grass covering its sides, forests blanketing its base, and a powerful and terrifying local god as its inhabitant. There you shouted into a forbidden valley, hacked with an axe in a forbidden forest, cut the grass with a sickle in a forbidden meadow, gouged into the earth with a hoe in a forbidden ground, and scooped up water with a bucket from a forbidden stream. As a result, a stream of fog like the tail of a yak emerged from the grassy mountainside and drifted up into the sky, immediately producing incredible thunderbolts, thunder, and lightning flashes. Although these appearances were unbearable, during the daytime today you don't see even a single hailstone.

In the same way, benevolent gods are nothing more than your own subjective appearances, but they actually have no basis or root, and they have never had even an iota of true existence. If you therefore conclude that there is nothing to actualize that is called a *deity*, you are wrong. From the creative power of your own realization, you actualize something as existent that didn't exist before. You possess the cause of actualizing a deity from the absolute space of nonexistence such that it [123] directly appears to your senses, so you establish its existence. Not knowing that you possess this, you apprehend and actualize an autonomous god as something over there. For example, there is not even the slightest difference between blowing into a yak's horn and shouting into an empty valley. Therefore, it is said that whatever deity you actualize, if you actualize it with your own unimpeded consciousness, it is established solely by means of your own mind's concepts.

> **"By investigating malevolent demons in the same way, you will see that they have no objective existence either. All joys and sorrows are dreamlike mental appearances, so no benefit or harm by gods or demons occurs from their bases of designation. If you think demons inflict harm, consider: Since they lie outside the domains of form, sound, smell, taste, and tactile sensations, that which is called a *demon* is nothing more than a mere name. By investigating how it can inflict harm, you will see it as not anything existent—nothing other than nonobjective and empty.**
>
> **"Out of delusion, people view the upper and lower portions of the body as good and bad respectively. Since the upper body appears to be clean, they regard it as if it were a god, and since the lower body appears unclean, they regard it as if it were a demon. This results in a continuous stream of hope and fear, and due to the tight bondage of self-grasping, a continuous stream of joyful and miserable experiences arises. All these consist of**

nothing more than experiential appearances of saṃsāra, without even an iota of true existence as anything else. This is simply illustrated with the metaphor of a dream."

Likewise, by investigating the initial origin, the interim location, and the final destination of so-called demons, you will see that they have no objective existence. If something called a *demon* appears as a sensory object, there should be something you could call the demon's form, sound, smell, taste, and tactile sensations; but none of these is established as truly existent.

If you think demons arise from the elements of the physical world and its sentient inhabitants, consider: Take the element of earth as an example—if earth is reduced to particles, particles to molecules, and molecules to atoms, they are still called *earth*, and there is no way that something called a *demon* emerges from them. Likewise, each of the elements is called by its own name, [124] not by the name *demon*.

If you think a demon inhabits someone, and if you investigate and examine that person from the tips of the hair on his head down to the tips of his toenails, you will not find its dwelling place anywhere. If you think consciousness is a demon, there is no way one person could have two streams of consciousness. If you think the basis of your disease is a demon, consider: Did that demon hold the disease in its hand and then insert it into your belly? On the other hand, if it strikes you with something like an arrow or a spear, of course you may retaliate, but there is nothing to retaliate against.

If in a dream last night you dreamt of an old man wearing a golden crown and thought he was a king, all the old men wearing golden crowns today during the daytime should also be kings, but it isn't so. If you dreamt of an old woman and thought she was a demoness, then all the old women during the daytime today should be demonesses as well, but it isn't so. If you dreamt of a poorly clothed child and thought he was a *serak*,[46] all the children during the daytime today would have to be seraks as well, but they aren't.

Therefore, if you think every single disease is due to demons, when you eat meat, the hand you use to cut it with a knife must be a demon, too. Likewise, if you overeat, [125] this must be a demon. If you stay out in the sun, at first it seems pleasant, but if the heat becomes unbearable after a while, this must be a demon, too—but it isn't. Likewise, all joys and sorrows are dreamlike mental experiences. So no benefit or harm is established as existing from the bases of designation of gods or demons, and thus they are seen as nothing more than nonobjective and empty.

Likewise, out of delusion, people view the upper and lower portions of

46. Tib. *bse rag*. A type of preta that consumes the vital essence of food and wealth.

the body as good and bad respectively. They think of hats as clean and store them in the upper part of the house, while regarding shoes as foul and storing them down below. They regard the upper part of a house as good, as if it were a god, and the lower part as bad, as if it were a demon. To take another matter as an example, if a dark-complexioned person comes, the family may say, "He is ugly. Don't let him stay upstairs. Either send him away or let him stay downstairs."[47]

Regarding the divine aspect of the upper part of a house, even if you look in every nook and cranny, you don't find the god's hideout. And regarding the demonic aspect of the lower part of a house, you don't discover where the demon lurks. Therefore, even though so-called gods and demons have never been established as real, that which doesn't exist appears to exist and [126] is nothing more than your own delusive perception. Not even a particle is truly existent. Therefore, there arises a continuous flow of hope for the good, while holding it to be divine, and fear of the bad, while holding it to be demonic. Furthermore, due to the tight bonds of your own self-grasping, a continuous stream of pleasant and unpleasant experiences arises, and all of them are simply of the nature of saṃsāra, without their having even an iota of existence as anything else. Therefore, this is simply illustrated by a dream.

> **"The essential point of all this is knowing the way things exist, which dispels obstacles to meditation. After this has cleared away all obstacles of lack of conviction and distrust toward meditation, you will acquire indwelling confidence and be filled with conviction and freedom from doubt regarding the meaning of ultimate reality. Freed of the obscuration of ignorance, this will provide you with mastery over the great, continuous displays of pristine awareness.**
>
> **"This is also the root of the profound practices of pacification and the severance of māras. Do not seek any divinity other than your own pristine awareness. You will come to the decisive recognition that there are no demons other than discursive thoughts. And this recognition is indispensable for all sādhanas and rituals for dispelling obstacles. If you have such knowledge, you are certainly a great, illusory yogin who realizes all phenomena as being like illusions.**
>
> **"O little one whose pristine awareness transcends the mind,**

47. This refers to the Tibetan aesthetic preference for a pale complexion and prejudice against those with a darker complexion.

teach this to your disciples and they may all become Mahāyāna yogins of this great mystery."

Saying this, he vanished from sight.

Knowledge of the essential meaning of this point and the nature of being dispels obstacles to all kinds of meditation. Whatever obstacles you need to dispel, this eliminates the obstacles of disbelief and distrust toward meditation. Thus you will practice meditation with conviction and freedom from doubt regarding the meaning of ultimate reality, and by doing so you will acquire indwelling confidence. Due to acquiring confidence, you will be freed from the obscuration of ignorance, acquire the confidence of mastery over the great, continuous displays of pristine awareness, and achieve liberation.

Therefore, this is the root of the profound practices of pacification and the severance of māras.[48] If you ascertain that there are no autonomous deities other than your own pristine awareness, and no autonomous demons other than discursive thoughts, [127] you will exile the four māras[49] into absolute space. Furthermore, this is indispensable in rituals for dispelling obstacles. If you realize all phenomena as mere illusions, by means of the liberation and guidance of this illusion-like knowledge, you will become an illusory yogin who can liberate and guide all illusion-like beings from miserable states of existence. Like the aphorism "on the basis of human existence, your accumulations [of merit and knowledge] are perfected," you will greatly fulfill your own and others' aspirations.

Otherwise, while under the influence of ordinary mental afflictions, by merely stabbing an effigy out of anger and craving, not only will you fail to subdue demonic spirits, this will result in rebirth in a miserable realm [even though] the basis of a negative deed is not completed with the triad of the intention, enactment, and culmination. So he said.

He called out, "O little one whose pristine awareness transcends the mind, teach this to your disciples and they may all become Mahāyāna yogins of this great mystery." Then he disappeared.

48. Padampa Sangyé introduced into Tibet a system of Dharma called *pacification* (Tib. *zhi byed*), the actual meditation practice of which is *severance of māras* (*bdud gcod*). Severance meditation involves imaginatively offering up your entire being as a means to realizing the empty nature of all phenomena, severing all clinging to the appearances of the three realms, and realizing that all gods and demons are none other than your own appearances.

49. The four māras are those of mental afflictions, of the aggregates, of the Lord of Death, and of the sons of the gods (symbolizing laziness and attachment to sense pleasures).

Teachings of Vajrapāṇi

D' Collapsing the False Cave of Hope and Fear

On one occasion when I encountered the glorious Vajrapāṇi in a pure vision of clear light, I asked him, "O Jina, great Vajradhara, is so-called buddhahood something I awaken to within myself, or do I need to go elsewhere to become enlightened?"

He replied, "Behold! Fortunate son of the family, if you think that so-called buddhas are people who live in a vast realm, noble individuals of fine and flawless countenance, peaceful and cooling, clear and free of blemishes, handsome and attractive, consider: Who are their parents? If they were born from mothers, they would fall to the extreme of birth. If they dwell somewhere, they would fall to the extreme of having a permanent location. If they were to cease to exist, they would fall to the nihilistic extreme of disappearing. In short, nothing that has a self-sustaining, truly existent nature of arising, ceasing, and remaining has a mode of existence free of the two extremes. These appearances that seem to arise and cease are nothing more than imputations.

"Moreover, if you reify that which is authentically enlightened, you will bind yourself. If there is a real difference between the ultimate natures of saṃsāra and nirvāṇa, then references to the equal mode of existence of mundane existence and the peace [of nirvāṇa] are nothing more than empty words. Many people, clinging to nirvāṇa as substantially existent, fall into the trap of hope and fear. There are many accounts of the enjoyments in the pure realms, but if you think of their vast qualities and reify them, that still constitutes grasping at the identities of phenomena. However you name them, in reality, viewing the tathāgatas as being eternal and truly existent is nothing more than viewing them as identities of persons."

On another occasion when I directly encountered the kāya of pristine awareness, [128] the glorious Vajrapāṇi, in the nature of a pure vision of clear light, I asked him, "O Jina, great Vajradhara, is so-called buddhahood something I awaken to within my own ground as Samantabhadra, or do I need to travel from one place to another to become enlightened? Which of these two alternatives is true?"

He replied, "Behold! Fortunate son of the family, if you think that so-called buddhas are people who live in a vast realm, noble kings of fine and flawless countenance, who are peaceful in that they calm discursive thoughts, cooling in that they are free of the burning heat of mental afflictions, clear and free of blemishes, and handsome and attractive, consider: Who are the parents of these buddhas? If they were born from fathers and mothers, they would fall to the extreme of birth. If you think they dwell somewhere, they would fall to the extreme of eternalism. If they were to be eternally terminated, they would fall to the extreme of nihilism."

Thus, due to being bound and limited by the three faults of birth, cessation, and abiding, they would definitely have to be sentient beings.

Likewise, if vast, physical worlds and multitudes of sentient inhabitants were instances of *pure realms*, [129] these realms would be objects of grasping at the identities of phenomena, and the bodies of these corporeal buddhas would be identities of persons. If they did not transcend the two types of grasping at the identities [of persons and of phenomena], they would be reduced to the status of sentient beings.

> **"If you think a buddha has eyes, he would also have visual consciousness. As soon as visual consciousness is established, the emergence of visual appearances is inevitable. They are known as the objects apprehended by the eyes. Once such objects are established, subtle conceptual states of mind that closely hold to forms inevitably arise. These are the mental states of visual apprehension. The dualistic conceptualization of the apprehender and the apprehended is called *mind*, and anyone who has a mind is known as a *sentient being*.**
>
> **"Likewise, if you think a buddha has ears, he must have auditory consciousness as well as sounds. If you think he has a nose, he must have olfactory consciousness as well as smells. If you think he has a tongue, he must have gustatory consciousness as well as tastes. If you think he has a body, he must have tactile consciousness as well as tactile sensations. And all these would be their apprehended objects. The assemblies of concepts**

closely holding these objects are the mental states that apprehend them. As before, whoever has a mind is called a *sentient being*."

If you think that such a substantially existent buddha has eyes, he must also have visual consciousness. If the eyes [visual faculties], together with visual consciousness, are established, the emergence of visual appearances is inevitable. As soon as visual appearances emerge, they are objects apprehended by the eyes. Once such objects are established, subtle conceptual states of mind that closely hold to forms inevitably arise. These are the mental states of visual apprehension. Whoever has a mind is known as a *sentient being*.

If you think that such a substantially existent buddha has ears, he must also have auditory consciousness. If the ears, together with auditory consciousness, are established, [130] the emergence of auditory appearances is inevitable. As soon as auditory appearances emerge, they are objects apprehended by the ears. Once such objects are established, subtle conceptual states of mind that closely hold to sounds inevitably arise. These are the mental states of auditory apprehension. Whoever has a mind is known as a *sentient being*.

If you think that such a substantially existent buddha has a nose, he must also have olfactory consciousness. If the nose, together with olfactory consciousness, is established, the emergence of olfactory appearances is inevitable. As soon as olfactory appearances emerge, they are objects apprehended by the nose. Once such objects are established, subtle conceptual states of mind that closely hold to smells inevitably arise. These are the mental states of olfactory apprehension. Whoever has a mind is known as a *sentient being*.

If you think that such a substantially existent buddha has a tongue, he must also have gustatory consciousness. If the tongue, together with gustatory consciousness, is established, the emergence of gustatory appearances is inevitable. As soon as gustatory appearances emerge, they are objects apprehended by the tongue. Once such objects are established, subtle conceptual states of mind that closely hold to tastes inevitably arise. [131] These are the mental states of gustatory apprehension. Whoever has a mind is known as a *sentient being*.

If you think that such a substantially existent buddha has a body, he must also have tactile consciousness. If the body, together with tactile consciousness, is established, the emergence of tactile appearances is inevitable. As soon as tactile appearances emerge, they are objects apprehended by the body. Once such objects are established, subtle conceptual states of mind that closely hold to tactile sensations inevitably arise. These are the mental states of tactile apprehension. Whoever has a mind is known as a *sentient being*.

> **"Regarding so-called buddhas, if it were possible for there to be buddhas who did not transcend dualistic grasping, their qualities could also be transferred to sentient beings, just like the qualities of one human being can be transferred to another. If you think buddhas teach Dharma to others, then the teachers would appear as selves, the Dharma would appear as the teaching, and those who are taught would appear as sentient beings; and if buddhas were apprehended as such, they would not have even a sesame seed's worth of qualities superior to those of sentient beings. So they would all be sentient beings.**
>
> **"If you think a buddha has a pleasant environment, a beautiful form, fine companions, great enjoyments and pleasures, and no anger or attachment, and that these are the exceptional qualities of a buddha, then a buddha would be no better than a god of the form realm. So such a buddha would not be anything more than a sentient being either."**

Therefore, buddhas must be of such a nature that they transcend dualistic grasping. Otherwise, if it were possible for buddhas to exist autonomously, their qualities could be transferred to sentient beings, like those of one human being can be transferred to another. There is no way that the qualities of a buddha can be transferred to the mindstream of a sentient being.

If you think that buddhas are so called because they are teachers of Dharma to others, then the teachers would appear as selves, the Dharma would appear as the teaching, and those who are taught would appear as sentient beings. [132] If buddhas were apprehended as such, they would not have even a sesame seed's worth of qualities superior to those of sentient beings. So all buddhas would be sentient beings.

If you think a buddha has a pleasant environment, a beautiful form, fine companions, great enjoyments and pleasures, and no anger or attachment, and that these are the exceptional qualities of a buddha, then a buddha would be no better than a god of the form realm. So such a buddha would not be anything more than a sentient being either.

> **"In terms of the definitive meaning, your own ground, Samantabhadra, is called the *sugatas of the three times*. Ultimately, a buddha has never come into the world or taught Dharma.**

> **Many of the tantras, oral transmissions, and pith instructions clearly explain how the self-appearing teacher manifests to disciples themselves. Observe and realize this point."**

Therefore, that which is called *buddha*—your own ground, Samantabhadra—has never been deluded in the past, it does not dwell in delusion in the present, and it will never be deluded in the future. The sugatas of the three times are called *buddhas*. An autonomously existent buddha has never come to the world from some other realm, nor has he taught Dharma. This is stated in many tantras, oral transmissions, and pith instructions. As it is stated in the *Diamond-Cutter Sūtra* (*Vajracchedikā Sūtra*):

> Those people who see me as form
> or know me as sound
> have entered a false path;
> those people do not see me. [133]

The self-appearing teacher manifests to disciples themselves, so observe and realize how an autonomously existent buddha does not exist anywhere else.

To determine the nature of saṃsāra—

> **"Furthermore, it is incorrect to think that there are other kinds of realms of saṃsāra that are established as existent, and that many sentient beings migrate from one of those places to another and successively experience joys and sorrows. If the appearance of your previous body being discarded were true, whence would you obtain your body in the intermediate period? If sentient beings these days can die merely from wounds, from burns on their arms and legs, or from cold wind on a single winter's day, then when a body is formed that experiences the heat and cold of hell realms, why doesn't it die even though it has been boiled and burned for a long time?**
>
> **"Likewise, if death can occur nowadays due to starvation for only a few months or even days, why don't sentient beings in the preta realms perish due to being starved for eons?**
>
> **"Therefore, all sentient beings in the six states of existence, as well as those in the intermediate period, manifest merely like appearances in a dream; but apart from that, they are empty and are not established as real. They are deluded due to**

> **obsessively grasping at the true existence of things that have no objective existence."**

Saṃsāra is like a jar with a trapped bee that flies sometimes to the top, sometimes to the bottom, and sometimes to the midsection, but never escapes the jar. Likewise, these three realms do not transcend saṃsāra. You are utterly mistaken if you think that they are established as the environments and sentient beings of the six states of existence in the three realms, that many beings migrate to those places, and that while roving from one to another they definitely experience joys and sorrows.

If your previous body were discarded, whence would you obtain a body in the intermediate period? If your body in the intermediate period were discarded, whence would you obtain a body that experiences the heat and cold of the hell realms? For instance, when you are born in the resuscitating hell, the entire ground is molten metal, [134] all the mountains are surrounded by molten metal, and all activities resound with the noise of the messengers of the Lord of Death killing and maiming. Many hell beings are gathered there, and when they see each other—like seeing a crippled enemy—they maim and kill one another. Then, as soon as a voice from the sky declares, "Be resuscitated!" they are restored. If such is the case, what were the causes and conditions from which they arose? Apart from their mere appearances, they do not truly exist. This is as Jinaputra Śāntideva wrote:

> Who created the floor of heated iron?
> Whence arose those billowing flames?
> The Sage declared that all of this has arisen from the evil mind.[50]

If you still maintain that the hell realms, suffering, and so forth are autonomously existent, consider that once a body is formed that experiences the heat and cold of hell, it doesn't die as a result of being boiled, burned, and maimed. Yet if the mere wounds and burns on the feet and arms of the sentient beings nowadays exist from their own side as causes of death, why doesn't death result from being boiled, burned, and maimed in hell for eons?

Likewise, if death is [135] caused by a cold wind on a single winter's day, why don't beings die after they have been born in a cold hell and have suffered from cold for eons? If beings nowadays can die from starvation after

50. Śāntideva, *A Guide to the Bodhisattva Way of Life*, trans. Vesna A. Wallace and B. Alan Wallace (Ithaca, NY: Snow Lion Publications, 1997), 48.

just a few months or weeks, why don't pretas die if they suffer from hunger and thirst for eons? It follows that these two are incompatible.

Therefore, all sentient beings in the six states of existence, as well as those in the intermediate period, arise like appearances in last night's dream. From the very moment they appear, they are nonexistent and are not established as real. Just by the fact of their appearing, they are empty and bear no objective existence. Beings are deluded due to obsessively grasping at their true existence.

> **"If you determine the nature of delusive appearances in that way and realize them as not truly existent, as empty, and as having no objective existence, you have dredged saṃsāra from its depths. If you decisively understand that buddhas do not exist apart from your own ground and you acquire confidence within yourself, you will actually attain what is called the *natural liberation of a multitude of buddhas*."**

Thus, all delusive appearances and deluded grasping are not truly existent and are of the nature of the one great emptiness. They are of one taste in the nature of the one great emptiness, and they are the great uniform pervasiveness of nonobjectivity. If you determine this by realizing it, you will dredge saṃsāra from its depths. Why? Because all the appearances in the three realms of saṃsāra are none other than the deluded thoughts of a single sentient being. [136] For example, although birth, movement, and appearances in a dream seem to be different, as soon as the person wakes from sleep, they all fundamentally vanish. Likewise, when a single sentient being becomes a buddha, one would have to assert that all sentient beings become buddhas.

In this regard, there are the general assertion of the philosophical schools and the manner of realization of yogins. According to the former, one must assert that even if the private appearances to an individual cease for that person's mind, the delusive mode of appearances in general is not destroyed. But this is taught merely as a provisional meaning in order to avoid the false conclusion that there would subsequently be no point in working for the sake of sentient beings. According to the latter, all appearances of the phenomena of saṃsāra and nirvāṇa are none other than the eight gateways of spontaneous actualization.[51] When you become a buddha, the eight gateways dissolve

51. The eight gateways of spontaneous actualization (Tib. *lhun grub sgo brgyad*) are (1) the gateway of compassion, (2) the gateway of light, (3) the gateway of the kāyas, (4) the gateway of the facets of primordial consciousness, (5) the gateway of nonduality, (6) the

into their own inner luminosity, and you abide as the youthful vase kāya. At that time, outward appearances are not established as being different, just as dreams implode by waking from sleep.

If you think that yogins assert this from their own side, but different modes of appearances exist in the mindstreams of others, then the mode of existence of equality—in which all of saṃsāra and nirvāṇa is realized as being none other than your own appearances—would be false, [137] for there would be the duality of purity and impurity. Therefore, from the perspective of the essential nature, ultimate reality, you must know that there is no one who is not a buddha, for everything is the self-appearance of pristine awareness. From the perspective of relative truth, however things are regarded, there is no inconsistency in their being simply dependently related events.

In point of fact, if you wish to realize the equality of saṃsāra and nirvāṇa, do not think that so-called buddhas exist in some other realm. The essential nature of your own ground—nonconceptual primordial consciousness—has never been deluded in the past, it does not dwell in delusion in the present, and it will never be deluded in the future. Due to the manifestation of your own ground, Samantabhadra, you will decisively know that no autonomous buddhas exist anywhere else. Once pristine awareness has acquired its own confidence, by itself, in itself, a multitude of buddhas naturally achieve their own self-liberation.

> **"O Lord of Space, Omnipresent Vajra, determine that all the phenomena of saṃsāra and nirvāṇa are nonexistent and empty, and realize their nature of nonexistence."**
>
> **Saying this, he disappeared.**

---

gateway of liberation from extremes, (7) the gateway of the impurity of saṃsāra, and (8) the gateway of the purity of primordial consciousness.

Teachings of Dorjé Drolö

b. The One Nature of All Phenomena as the Ground, Absolute Space [138]

After considering it for a long time, a decisive understanding of nonexistence arose, so that I knew that all the appearances of the physical world and its sentient inhabitants are empty from their own side. Nevertheless, many kinds of emptiness seemed to be ethically neutral. At that point I had a vision of the supreme Dorjé Drolö chanting the melody of *Hūṃ*, which reveals saṃsāra and nirvāṇa as displays of emptiness.

On that occasion I asked, "O great and supreme special deity, although I understand saṃsāra and nirvāṇa to be empty, this emptiness seems to be without benefit or harm. Why is that?"

He replied, "O my child, Lord of Space, reduce all of saṃsāra and nirvāṇa to emptiness; reduce emptiness to the essential nature of reality; reduce this essential nature to the ground of being; reduce saṃsāra and nirvāṇa to displays of this ground; and reduce the entirety of saṃsāra and nirvāṇa to this very ground.

"The reflections of the planets and stars in the ocean are none other than the ocean. The physical world and its sentient inhabitants are none other than space. Saṃsāra and nirvāṇa are none other than displays of ultimate reality. This unifying principle and ultimate reality are all-pervasive and all-encompassing. Understand these metaphors and what they exemplify. Thus you will become a yogin who embraces saṃsāra and nirvāṇa."

So saying, he disappeared.

AFTER CONSIDERING the meaning of emptiness for a long time, there arose merely a certainty that all things were nonexistent and unestablished. Although I knew that all appearances of the outer physical world and its inner sentient inhabitants are empty from their own side, the many kinds of emptiness seemed to be ethically neutral. At that point I had a vision of the special deity, the supremely great Dorjé Drolö, as he was chanting the melody of *Hūṃ*, by which one realizes saṃsāra and nirvāṇa as displays of emptiness.

I asked, "O great and supreme special deity, I have determined the nature of all of saṃsāra and nirvāṇa, and though I merely know their mode of existence as emptiness, I have not acquired the confidence of ascertaining saṃsāra and nirvāṇa as displays of one emptiness. So emptiness seems to be without benefit or harm. To what is this attributed?"

He replied, "O great being, Lord of Space, reduce all of saṃsāra and nirvāṇa to emptiness."

The nature of earth (water, fire, and air) is emptiness; and the nature of emptiness appears as earth (water, fire, and air). The nature of form (sound, smell, taste, and tactile sensations) is [139] emptiness; and the nature of emptiness appears as form (sound, smell, taste, and tactile sensations). The nature of all phenomena included in the world of appearances of saṃsāra and nirvāṇa is emptiness; and the nature of emptiness appears as all phenomena included in the world of appearances of saṃsāra and nirvāṇa.

Reduce emptiness to the essential nature of reality. The essential nature of earth (water, fire, and air) is emptiness; and the essential nature of emptiness appears as earth (water, fire, and air). The essential nature of form (sound, smell, taste, and tactile sensations) is emptiness; and the essential nature of emptiness appears as form (sound, smell, taste, and tactile sensations). The essential nature of all phenomena included in the world of appearances of saṃsāra and nirvāṇa is emptiness; and the essential nature of emptiness appears as all phenomena included in the world of appearances of saṃsāra and nirvāṇa.

Reduce this essential nature to the ground of being. The ground of appearances of earth (water, fire, and air) is emptiness; and emptiness, as the ground of appearances, manifests as earth (water, fire, and air). The ground of appearances of form (sound, smell, taste, and tactile sensations) is emptiness; and emptiness, as the ground of appearances, manifests as form (sound, smell, taste, and tactile sensations). [140] The ground of appearances of all phenomena included in the world of appearances of saṃsāra and nirvāṇa is emptiness; and emptiness, as the ground of appearances, manifests as all phenomena included in the world of appearances of saṃsāra and nirvāṇa.

Reduce saṃsāra and nirvāṇa to displays of the ground of being. As a metaphor, however vast and numerous are the appearances of planets and stars in the ocean, they are not other than the ocean, and they are displays of the ocean. However vast and numerous are all the phenomena included in the world of appearances of saṃsāra and nirvāṇa, they are none other than the ultimate reality of the ground of being. They are displays of the ultimate reality of the ground of being, so they are displays.

Reduce the entirety of saṃsāra and nirvāṇa to this very ground. As a metaphor, all the appearances of the planets, stars, and reflections in the ocean must be reduced to water itself, and they are not other than water. The entirety of all the planets, stars, and reflections must be reduced to water itself. Likewise, however vast and numerous are the appearances of the physical world and its sentient inhabitants throughout the extent of space, they must be reduced to space. They are not other than space, and however vast and numerous are the appearances of the physical world and its sentient inhabitants, [141] the entirety of them must be reduced to space itself.

Likewise, you must reduce all phenomena included in the world of appearances of saṃsāra and nirvāṇa to ultimate reality, the ground of being. They are not other than ultimate reality, the ground of being. The entirety of all phenomena included in the world of appearances of saṃsāra and nirvāṇa must be reduced to this very ground.

In summary, all phenomena included in the world of appearances of saṃsāra and nirvāṇa are displays of ultimate reality, and this is the unifying principle, all-pervasive and all-encompassing. Correctly understand these metaphors and what they exemplify, and by so doing you will become a yogin who embraces saṃsāra and nirvāṇa.

So saying, he disappeared.

Teachings of Vajradhara

The Distinction Between Liberation and Delusion

Seven years later, when the dharmakāya teacher Vajradhara appeared to me in a pure dream, I asked him, "O Teacher, Bhagavān, how is one freed on the path of liberation and omniscience, and how is one deluded on the impure path of saṃsāra? May the Teacher explain!"

He replied, "O great being, listen! The distinction between the emergence of buddhas and sentient beings is the difference between knowledge and ignorance. The fundamental primordial protector, Samantabhadra, is of the nature of the four kāyas and five facets of primordial consciousness. His empty essential nature is the dharmakāya, his luminous nature is the saṃbhogakāya, his self-liberating compassion is the nirmāṇakāya, and his pervasive and encompassing nature throughout all of saṃsāra and nirvāṇa is the svabhāvikakāya.

"The *primordial consciousness of absolute space* is so called because it accommodates all phenomena; *mirror-like primordial consciousness* is so called because it is lucid, luminous, and free of contamination; the *primordial consciousness of equality* is so called because saṃsāra and nirvāṇa are displays of purity and equality; *discerning primordial consciousness* is so called because of the unimpeded nature of the primordial consciousness that knows and perceives; and the *primordial consciousness of accomplishment* is so called because it accomplishes its tasks by way of purification and liberation."

THEN, SEVEN YEARS LATER, when the dharmakāya teacher Vajradhara appeared to me in a pure dream, I asked him, "O Teacher, Bhagavān, how is one freed on the path of liberation and omniscience, and how is one deluded on the impure path of saṃsāra? [142] May the Teacher explain!"

He replied, "O great being, listen! Buddhas have gained mastery over the ground, while sentient beings are deluded due to the power of ignorance. The difference in their manifestations stems from knowledge and ignorance."

How so? Buddhas correctly perceive and know the nature of existence of the ground sugatagarbha and manifest as buddhas. Sentient beings manifest as sentient beings due to not knowing and not realizing this.

The reality is that the primordial ground, the original protector, Samantabhadra, is of the nature of the four kāyas and the five facets of primordial consciousness. In this regard there are (i) the manner in which the ground pristine awareness is perfected as the four kāyas and five facets of primordial consciousness, and (ii) the manner in which the path pristine awareness manifests as the four kāyas and five facets of primordial consciousness.

i. The Manner in Which the Ground Pristine Awareness Is Perfected as the Four Kāyas and Five Facets of Primordial Consciousness

The empty essential nature [of the ground of being], the aspect that is free of all the extremes of conceptual elaboration, is the dharmakāya; its luminous nature, the aspect of its unimpeded inner glow, is the saṃbhogakāya; its appearances of creative displays of compassion, the aspect that is liberated right where it is, is the nirmāṇakāya; and the ground of the indivisibility of those three kāyas, [143] the aspect that pervades and encompasses all of saṃsāra and nirvāṇa, is the *svabhāvikakāya*. These are the four kāyas.

Emptiness, as the aspect that provides the possibility for all phenomena, is the primordial consciousness of the absolute space of phenomena. Emptiness, as the mirror-like aspect that is lucid and luminous—and is not a mere emptiness of materiality, but rather one that is lucid, luminous, and free of contamination—is mirror-like primordial consciousness. In the absolute space of the ultimate nature of the ground, the aspect of all phenomena included in saṃsāra and nirvāṇa as displays that are equally nonexistent and equally pure is the primordial consciousness of equality. The primordial consciousness that knows reality as it is has mastery over the ground and knows the mode of existence of the ground. The primordial consciousness that perceives the full range of phenomena has mastery over the path and knows the mode of existence of the path. The aspect of mastery over saṃsāra, nirvāṇa, and the path due to the unimpeded primordial consciousness that knows reality as it is and perceives the full range of phenomena is discerning primordial consciousness. The aspect of the primordially pure essential nature of ultimate reality, the purity of the adventitious stains of relative truth, and the natural liberation of thoughts entailing dualistic appearances of the apprehender and the apprehended right where they are is the primordial consciousness of accomplishment. These are established as self-emergent in the nature of the five facets of primordial consciousness.

ii. The Manner in Which the Path Pristine Awareness Manifests as the Four Kāyas and Five Facets of Primordial Consciousness [144]

> **"The path pristine awareness that liberates you as a self-emergent buddha manifests in the nature of the four kāyas and five facets of primordial consciousness. The display of the essential nature of pristine awareness—all-pervasive, extending to the limits of space, without objective existence, a great uniform pervasiveness with no ground or root—is free of conceptual elaboration, and is therefore the dharmakāya. Regarding its nature as self-illuminating, it is the saṃbhogakāya; regarding its unimpeded luminosity of primordial consciousness, it is the nirmāṇakāya; and regarding its being the common ground of saṃsāra and nirvāṇa, it is the svabhāvikakāya.**
>
> **"Having determined the nature of the ground, the realization of the one taste of saṃsāra and nirvāṇa in the absolute space of ultimate reality is the primordial consciousness of the absolute space of phenomena. Without reducing emptiness to a mere immateriality, lucidity and luminosity free of contamination, like a stainless mirror in which anything can appear, is mirror-like primordial consciousness. The awareness of the equal purity of saṃsāra and nirvāṇa in great emptiness is the primordial consciousness of equality. The unimpeded luminosity of primordial consciousness that discerns the displays of pristine awareness is discerning primordial consciousness. By gaining mastery over pristine awareness, activities of purification and liberation are naturally accomplished, so this is the primordial consciousness of accomplishment."**

Regarding the path pristine awareness that liberates you as a self-emergent buddha manifesting in the nature of the four kāyas and five facets of primordial consciousness, the display of the essential nature of pristine awareness—all-pervasive, extending to the limits of space, without objective existence, a great uniform pervasiveness with no ground or root, the great nature that totally pervades saṃsāra and nirvāṇa—is the dharmakāya, free of conceptual elaboration. Its nature as self-illumination is the saṃbhogakāya; the unimpeded consciousness of its own essential nature, the unimpeded luminosity of primordial consciousness, and the unimpeded understanding of itself constitute the nirmāṇakāya; and the indivisible ground of the three kāyas as the common ground of saṃsāra and nirvāṇa is the svabhāvikakāya. These are the four kāyas.

When the nature of the ground is first determined by way of the view, the authentic realization of the one taste of saṃsāra and nirvāṇa in the absolute space of ultimate reality is the primordial consciousness of the absolute space of phenomena.

Without reducing emptiness to a mere immateriality, lucidity and luminosity free of contamination, like a stainless mirror in which anything can appear, is mirror-like primordial consciousness. Authentic knowledge of the equal purity of saṃsāra and nirvāṇa in great emptiness [145] is the primordial consciousness of equality. The unimpeded luminosity of primordial consciousness that discerns the displays of pristine awareness is discerning primordial consciousness. When mastery is gained over pristine awareness, you see the primordially pure essential nature and the pristine purity of the manifest nature; all thoughts of dualistic appearances are purified in primordially free, unconditioned absolute space; and activities imbued with the two purities[52] are accomplished by themselves. This is the primordial consciousness of accomplishment.

Implicitly, the four kinds of enlightened activity are also spontaneously actualized. When you directly perceive primordial consciousness, pristine awareness, the 84,000 mental afflictions and all the illnesses, demons, interferences, and obstacles created by them are pacified, so this is pacifying enlightened activity. All the excellent qualities of scriptural knowledge and realization expand, so this is enriching enlightened activity. Power is gained over the entire appearing world of saṃsāra and nirvāṇa in the expanse of the ultimate nature of pristine awareness, so this is powerful enlightened activity. All thoughts of dualistic appearances of the apprehender and the apprehended and all the enemies, demons, and assemblies of obstructive beings created by them are banished into the absolute space of the ultimate nature of pristine awareness, so this is wrathful enlightened activity. This is spontaneous actualization of the four kinds of activity. [146]

"Without knowing this mode of being, many people take as their path a passive state of consciousness that does not distinguish between the mind and pristine awareness. They grasp

52. The two purities are the purities of freedom from afflictive obscurations and of freedom from cognitive obscurations.

at outer appearances as ethically neutral entities bearing their own intrinsic characteristics. Inwardly, they are tightly bound by the chains of reifying their own bodies as ethically neutral and permanent. In between these two [the outer and inner], as it were, they gain stability in a mere unimpeded, luminous, and cognizant state of consciousness. However, while it is possible that this may constitute a virtue that propels them to the two higher realms of existence, they will not achieve the states of liberation and enlightenment. So this is a flawed approach.

"Authentically knowing how all the phenomena included in saṃsāra and nirvāṇa are of one taste in the nature of suchness, ultimate reality, is the *wisdom that knows reality as it is*. Even while dwelling in the essential nature of pristine awareness, the self-emergence of unimpeded consciousness that is all-knowing and all-cognizing is the *wisdom that perceives the full range of phenomena*. Although such wisdom is unimpeded, it does not merge with objects, like a drop of mercury [does not merge with soil] when it falls on the ground.

"The mind views saṃsāra and nirvāṇa as autonomous, reifies appearances, and is unaware of the nature of existence of the ground. From this mind emerge thoughts that arise and pass, merging with their objects, like drops of water falling on dry ground."

It is necessary to correctly know this mode of being and to distinguish between the mind and pristine awareness. Due to their ignorance of this mode of being, there are many who take a merely passive state of consciousness to be the path; they reduce outer appearances to the status of ethically neutral entities and grasp at them as real things bearing their own intrinsic characteristics. Inwardly, they reduce their own bodies to the status of an ethically neutral entity and become tightly bound by the chains of reifying their own bodies as something permanent. In between the outer and inner, they regard as the most sublime meditation a state of unimpeded, luminous, and cognizant consciousness. There are many who practice in this way, but the results are indeterminate, just as when water drips into a hole in the ice, or it freezes due to a cold wind, or it melts when exposed to warmth. Even if they achieve stability in such practice—constituting a kind of virtue that propels them to the two higher realms of existence, the form and formless realms—they will not achieve the states of liberation and enlightenment. They will remain in bondage due to the flaw of not realizing emptiness and the view.

Authentically knowing how all phenomena included within saṃsāra and nirvāṇa are of one taste in the nature of suchness, ultimate reality, and that they are equally nonexistent and equally pure [147] is the *wisdom that knows reality as it is*. Even while dwelling in the essential nature of pristine awareness, without slipping into an uncomprehending state of bewilderment, the state of being untainted by objects, without grasping at objects, without cutting off objects, and without falling under the influence of objects, is the *wisdom that perceives the full range of phenomena*. This is self-emergent primordial consciousness, pristine awareness, which is unimpeded, all-knowing, and all-cognizing. Emerging from itself, it does not merge with objects, just as a drop of mercury [does not merge with soil] when it falls on the ground.

The mind views saṃsāra and nirvāṇa as autonomous and truly existent, it reifies appearances, and it is unaware of the ground of being. From this mind emerge thoughts that arise and pass, merging with their objects, being defiled by objects, grasping at objects, cutting off objects, and falling under the influence of objects, like drops of water falling on dry ground.

The original, universal ground is like space, its essential nature is empty, its manifest nature is luminous, and its compassion has the potential to manifest in all manner of ways. From the aspect of the manifest nature of this ground emanate appearances of five spontaneously actualized lights generated by a lattice of vital energies bearing five colors of light rays. The essential nature serves as their basis of manifestation, and when they arise outwardly as luminosity, a subtle, dualistic, faint consciousness emerges from the aspect of compassion, [148] and it is able to discern objects. This is also called *unripened awareness*. If it is identified, buddhahood is achieved; and if it is not, you are propelled down into the three realms of saṃsāra.

In the first instant of consciousness, Samantabhadra arises as pristine awareness; in the second instant, the five lights are known to be self-appearing; and in the third instant, they dissolve into the ground of being, and you manifestly achieve the state of Samantabhadra, buddhahood, which is the ultimate fulfillment of your own and others' needs.

This state is endowed with the six qualities of the youthful vase kāya, those six qualities being (1) superior to the ground, (2) appearing as your own essential nature, (3) discerning, (4) liberated in activity, (5) not emerging from anything else, and (6) dwelling in your own ground.

First, this is greater than the substrate, for it arises as a spontaneously actualized wheel of five lights and is therefore superior to the ground. Second, the five lights appear as the essential nature of pristine awareness itself, so it appears as your own essential nature. Third, the five lights are recognized as your own appearances, and since you distinguish between delusion and liberation, it is discerning. Fourth, confidence is acquired in the midst of activity, resulting in buddhahood, so there is liberation in activity. Fifth, since all facets of primordial consciousness and sublime qualities, including twenty-five resultant qualities, are perfected within you, this state does not emerge from anything else. [149] Sixth, instead of the ground merely appearing as something ethically neutral, in reality the buddha dwelling within you becomes manifest, so this is dwelling in your own ground. These are the six qualities.

As for the manner in which the six qualities of Samantabhadra are achieved, they do not arise from the mind, for without needing to reject the mind and all the adventitious thoughts that emerge from it—as they are not present in the ground—you achieve buddhahood within yourself. They do not arise from scriptures, for without having any other guru who reveals pith instructions, pristine awareness as self-emergent primordial consciousness emerges as your guidance. They do not arise from causes, for without Samantabhadra performing even an iota of defiled virtue, you are liberated by the qualities of fruition being perfected within yourself. They are self-appearing, for the spontaneously actualized wheel of five lights appears as the essential nature of pristine awareness itself. They are self-arising, for pristine awareness arises of itself in the form of the five lights. They are self-liberated, for pristine awareness perceives its own essential nature for itself, and it is naturally liberated within itself. These are the six qualities of the youthful vase kāya. Once these six qualities of Samantabhadra are achieved, mastery is gained over the ground, and you manifestly act as a buddha of the pure ground of being. [150]

Here is how you become deluded on the path of impure saṃsāra:

> **"As a result of ignorance obscuring your own face of buddhahood of the pure ground, which has mastery over the ground of being, all the kāyas and facets of primordial consciousness of the natural inner glow of the ground subside into that inner glow. The outer radiance is projected externally, with the aspects of the five lights manifesting as displays of the five elements.**
>
> **"Here is how this occurs: Due to the primordial consciousness of the absolute space of phenomena being obscured by ignorance, its outer radiance appears as indigo light. This is called the *inner element*, *great element*, and *quintessence of space*. Due to reifying and clinging to this light, it appears as**

space, and this is called the appearance of the *outer element*, *derivative element*, and *residue*.

"Due to mirror-like primordial consciousness being obscured by ignorance, its inner glow subsides, resulting in its outer radiance appearing as white-colored light. This is the quintessence of water, its great element, and its inner element. Due to reifying and clinging to this light, it appears as water, and this is its residue, derivative element, and outer element.

"Due to the primordial consciousness of equality being obscured by ignorance, its inner glow subsides, resulting in its outer radiance appearing as yellow-colored light. This is the quintessence of earth, its inner element, and its major element. Due to reifying and clinging to this light, it appears as earth, and this is its residue, derivative element, and outer element.

"Due to discerning primordial consciousness being obscured by ignorance, its inner glow subsides, resulting in its outer radiance appearing as red-colored light. This is the quintessence of fire, its inner element, and its major element. Due to reifying and clinging to this light, it appears as fire, and this is its residue, derivative element, and outer element.

"Due to the primordial consciousness of accomplishment being obscured by ignorance, its inner glow subsides, resulting in its outer radiance appearing as green-colored light. This is the quintessence of air, its inner element, and its major element. Due to reifying and clinging to this light, it appears as air, and this is called its residue, derivative element, and outer element.

"Due to the condition of these lights and radiances remaining within, the various colors and appearances of the five elements manifest uninterruptedly."

When wisdom rides the vital energy arising as the life force (with the merging of vital energy and the primordial consciousness of compassion), like a horseman on his mount, and the five lights arise as outer luminosity, this very consciousness is obscured by ignorance, and that is the causal ignorance of yourself alone. Connate ignorance is due to the lack of recognition of the five lights as your own appearances, and speculative ignorance differentiates subject and object. These three kinds of ignorance constitute the causal conditions.

To distinguish among the four kinds of contributing conditions: The arising of the ground of being itself as the five lights is the causal condition. The aspect of discerning wisdom is the dominant condition. The differentiation of subject and object is the objective condition. The simultaneous manifestation of these three as the sudden emergence of the appearances of saṃsāra is the immediate condition. These are the four contributing conditions. There is also a custom of presenting the previously mentioned three kinds of ignorance as causes and the immediate condition as a contributing condition, making for three causes and four conditions. The omniscient Jikmé Lingpa writes:

> The ground itself abiding as if it were a house is the causal condition.
> The arising of discernment in that regard is the dominant condition.
> The subsequent distinction of subject and object is the objective condition.
> The simultaneous presence of these three is the immediate condition. [151]

Without recognizing the five lights as your own appearances, your own face of buddhahood of the pure ground is obscured by ignorance. Consequently, all the kāyas and facets of primordial consciousness of the natural inner glow of the ground subside into that inner glow. Here is how the outer glow is projected externally, emerging as the five lights: When the primordial consciousness of the absolute space of phenomena is obscured by ignorance, all the displays of the kāyas and facets of primordial consciousness of the inner glow (appearances of the nature of the five lights) subside into the inner glow (which is the inner luminosity of the kāyas and facets of primordial consciousness). Its outer glow arises externally, manifesting in the aspect of indigo light. This is the inner element, the great element, and the quintessence of the element of space. When reifying and clinging to it arise with the thought that "this light is indigo," it is the element of space, and this is its outer element, derivative element, and residual element.

When mirror-like primordial consciousness is obscured by ignorance, all the displays of the kāyas and facets of primordial consciousness of the inner glow subside into the inner glow. Its outer glow arises externally, manifesting in the aspect of white light. This is the quintessence of the element of water, [152] the great element, and the inner element. When reifying and clinging to this light arise with the thought that "this light is white," it is the element of water and its residual element, minor element, outer element, and derivative element.

When the primordial consciousness of equality is obscured by ignorance, all the displays of the kāyas and facets of primordial consciousness of the inner glow subside into the inner glow. Its outer glow arises externally, manifesting in the aspect of yellow light. This is the quintessence of the element of earth, its inner element, and its great element. When reifying and clinging to this light arise with the thought that "this light is yellow," it is the element of earth and its residual element, minor element, outer element, and derivative element.

When discerning primordial consciousness is obscured by ignorance, all the displays of the kāyas and facets of primordial consciousness of the inner glow subside into the inner glow. Its outer glow arises externally, manifesting in the aspect of red light. This is the quintessence of the element of fire, its inner element, and its great element. [153] When the bondage of reifying and clinging to this light arise with the thought that "this light is red," it is the element of fire and its residual element, minor element, outer element, and derivative element.

When the primordial consciousness of accomplishment is obscured by ignorance, all the displays of the kāyas and facets of primordial consciousness of the inner glow subside into the inner glow. Its outer glow arises externally, manifesting in the aspect of green light. This is the quintessence of the element of air, its inner element, and its great element. When this light is named and reified with the thought that "this light is green," it is the element of air and its residual element, minor element, outer element, and derivative element.

The natural glow subsides into the inner glow, and the outer glow manifests externally, much like the fading light rays of the setting sun in the external world. Thus, this is the meaning of these glows of light appearing externally and continuously as various colors and as the five elements, due to their inner presence.

> **"The creative power of these five bases of delusion manifests in the following ways. Due to the obscuration of the ground by ignorance, the actual substrate, which is space-like and immaterial, devoid of thoughts and appearances, is like deep sleep and fainting. Immersion in this state is of the essential nature of delusion, a vast field of ignorance.**
>
> **"The arousal of the karmic energies of an eon from that state is the essential nature of envy. Due to its activity, luminosity emerges from emptiness, and this is the substrate consciousness, which is present in the essential nature of hatred.**

The ego-grasping that arises from it with respect to the mere appearance of the self is afflictive mentation, which is present in the essential nature of pride. Mentation arises from this, and it establishes the potential for appearances to emerge from immaterial emptiness, thus bringing forth luminosity; and this is present in the essential nature of attachment. These constitute the five essential natures arising as outer creative expressions of the inner glow.

"The essential nature of the five poisons is like fire, from which afflictive thought formations emerge like sparks."

With the solidification of the five external elements serving as the cause, here is how the creative power of the five bases of delusion manifests: [154] This is the foundation of all of saṃsāra and nirvāṇa, all suffering, all habitual propensities, and all kinds of karma. Due to the obscuration of the ground by ignorance, the actual substrate, which is space-like and immaterial, devoid of thoughts and appearances, in which all lustrous expressions cease, is like deep sleep and fainting. This is called the *substrate*. Immersion in this state is of the essential nature of delusion, a vast field of ignorance. The essential nature of the substrate is ignorance, and its creative power emerges as delusion. What does it obscure? It obscures the kāya of Vairocana. Where is this obscured? It is obscured in the aggregate of form.

The arousal of the karmic energies of an eon from that state is the essential nature of envy. Its essential nature is ignorance, and its creative power emerges as envy. What does it obscure? It obscures the kāya of Amoghasiddhi. Where is this obscured? It is obscured in the aggregate of compositional factors.

Due to the activity of those karmic energies, luminosity emerges from emptiness in the domain of the substrate, and this is the *substrate consciousness*, which is present in the essential nature of the mental affliction of hatred. Its essential nature is ignorance, [155] and its creative power emerges as hatred. What does it obscure? It obscures the kāya of Vajrasattva.[53] Where is this obscured? It is obscured in the aggregate of consciousness.

Ego-grasping that arises from [the substrate consciousness] with respect to the mere appearance of the self is *afflictive mentation*, which is present in the essential nature of the mental affliction of pride. Its essential nature is ignorance, and its creative power emerges as pride. What does it obscure? It obscures the kāya of Ratnasaṃbhava. Where is this obscured? It is obscured in the aggregate of feeling.

53. In other contexts hatred is said to obscure the kāya of Akṣobhya.

Mentation arises from [afflictive mentation], and it establishes the potential for appearances to emerge in that immaterial emptiness, thus bringing forth luminosity. This is called *mentation*, and it is present in the essential nature of the mental affliction of attachment. Its essential nature is ignorance, and its creative power emerges as attachment. What does it obscure? It obscures the kāya of Amitābha. Where is this obscured? It is obscured in the aggregate of recognition.

In these ways, even when the elements of the five lights and the five derivative elements manifest as the five aggregates, skillful means and wisdom are nondual. How is this? The five lights are the female consorts, and the five elements are the male consorts; the five elements are the female consorts,[54] and the five aggregates are the male consorts; emptiness is the female consort, and appearances are the male consort. Thus, skillful means and wisdom are united. [156] Karma Lingpa writes:

> The absolute space of gods and goddesses of the pristine appearing worlds is spontaneously perfected deities and consorts as the elements and derivative elements (the five lights emerge from the natural glow of the five facets of primordial consciousness, and with the infiltration of grasping, the five elements and so forth emerge).

A tantra states, "Nondual skillful means and wisdom fill the expanse." Accordingly, although primordial purity is present in the nature of deities, under the influence of conceptualization, it appears as the elements and aggregates. All these five bases of delusion manifest from the inner glow as the creative power of the five essential natures. This may be likened to sparks of afflictive thoughts emerging from the fiery essential nature of the five poisons, which manifest as their creative power.

> **"In this way, objects unimpededly emerge as appearances in the uniformly pervasive emptiness and luminosity of the substrate and mentation. Consequently, due to the simultaneous confluence of the movements of karmic energies as the contributing conditions and the potential of the ground for manifesting appearances as the primary cause, the appearances of**

54. In other contexts it is said that the five great elements are the male consorts, and the five derivative elements are the female consorts.

various forms emerge in dependence upon the ground and without relation to anything other than the ground.

"Whatever objects emerge as appearances of form are called by mere convention *visual consciousness*. Therefore, appearing objects, which may be likened to the ocean, are called *objects*, and the appearances of forms, which may be likened to [reflections of] planets and stars, are said to be *that which is apprehended*.

"Consequently, a subtle, apprehending mental consciousness attributes names to these forms, invests them with meaning, and reifies them. Thoughts arise that cling to forms as pleasant, unpleasant, and neutral, and they are called the *mind of visual apprehension*.

"Likewise, the unimpeded objects that emerge as sounds are called *objects*, the appearances that emerge as sounds are said to be *that which is apprehended*, and the mental consciousness that adheres to them is called the *apprehending mind*. As described above, these are dependently related events arising from the assembly of causes and conditions.

"Likewise, the appearances that emerge as smells are merely conventionally named *olfactory consciousness*, the appearances that emerge as tastes are merely named *gustatory consciousness*, and the appearances that emerge as tactile sensations are merely named *tactile consciousness*. But they do not actually appear to those various orifices, which is made clear by the appearances in dreams and the intermediate period."

In this way, the six kinds of objects unimpededly emerge as appearances of forms, sounds, smells, tastes, and tactile sensations in the uniformly pervasive emptiness and luminosity of the substrate and mentation, and this is called *mentation*. Then, due to the simultaneous confluence of the movements of karmic energies as the contributing conditions and the potential of the ground for manifesting appearances as the primary cause, the appearances of various forms emerge in dependence upon the ground and without relation to anything other than the ground. [157]

Whatever objects emerge as appearances of form are called by mere convention *visual consciousness*, and they are no more than that. As an analogy, appearing objects, which may be likened to the ocean, are called *objects*, and the appearances of forms, which may be likened to reflections of planets and stars, are said to be *that which is apprehended*.

The apprehender imputes names upon each of these forms, apprehends each of their referents, and observes each entity, leading to the arousal of thoughts that cling to them as pleasant, unpleasant, and neutral. This is a subtle mental consciousness called the *mind of visual apprehension*.

Likewise, the objects that emerge unimpededly as sounds in the lucid, clear space of mentation are called *objects*. The appearances that emerge as sounds due to the activation of karmic energies are said to be *that which is apprehended*. The mental consciousness that names each of these sounds, apprehends each of their referents, observes each entity, and then clings to them as pleasant, unpleasant, and neutral is called the *mind of auditory apprehension*. This occurs, as described above, as a dependently related event arising from the assembly of causes and conditions. The causal space of the lucid, luminous ground, which has the potential for manifesting appearances, serves as the primary cause. The creative powers of the movements of karmic energies serve as the contributing conditions. [158] When those two—the primary cause and the contributing conditions—are simultaneously assembled, the dependently related events of the appearances of sounds emerge, even though they do not exist. On what do they depend? On the ground of being. To what are they related? To the nondual union of the ground of being and the appearances of sounds. What events arise? The appearances of sounds, even though they don't exist.

Likewise, the objects that emerge unimpededly as smells in the lucid, clear space of mentation, free of contamination, are called *objects*. The appearances that emerge as smells due to the activation of karmic energies are said to be *that which is apprehended*. The mental consciousness that names each of these smells, apprehends each of their referents, observes each entity, and then clings to them as pleasant, unpleasant, and neutral is called the *mind of olfactory apprehension*. This occurs, as described above, as a dependently related event arising from the assembly of causes and conditions. The causal space of the lucid, luminous ground, which has the potential for manifesting appearances, serves as the primary cause. The creative powers of the movements of karmic energies serve as the contributing conditions. When these two—the primary cause and the contributing conditions—are simultaneously assembled, the dependently related events of the appearances of smells emerge, even though they do not exist. On what do they depend? On the ground of being. To what are they related? To the nondual union of the ground of being and the appearances of smells. What events arise? The appearances of smells, even though they don't exist. [159]

Likewise, the objects that emerge unimpededly as tastes in the lucid, clear space of cognition, free of contamination, are called *objects*. The appearances that emerge as tastes due to the activation of karmic energies are said to be *that which is apprehended*. The mental consciousness that names each of these tastes, apprehends each of their referents, observes each entity, and then clings to them as pleasant, unpleasant, and neutral is called the *mind of gustatory apprehension*. This occurs, as described above, as a dependently related event arising from the assembly of causes and conditions. The causal space of the lucid, luminous ground, which has the potential for manifesting appearances, serves as the primary cause. The creative powers of the movements of karmic energies serve as the contributing conditions. When these two—the primary cause and the contributing conditions—are simultaneously assembled, the dependently related events of the appearances of tastes emerge, even though they do not exist. On what do they depend? On the ground of being. To what are they related? To the nondual union of the ground of being and the appearances of tastes. What events arise? The appearances of tastes, even though they don't exist.

Likewise, the objects that emerge unimpededly as tactile sensations in the lucid, clear space of mentation, free of contamination, are called *objects*. The appearances that emerge as tactile sensations due to the activation of karmic energies are said to be *that which is apprehended*. The mental consciousness that names each of these tactile sensations, apprehends each of their referents, observes each entity, and then clings to them as pleasant, unpleasant, and neutral is called the *mind of tactile apprehension*. This occurs, as described above, as a dependently related event arising from the assembly of causes and conditions. The causal space of the lucid, luminous ground, which has the potential for manifesting appearances, serves as the primary cause. [160] The creative powers of the movements of karmic energies serve as the contributing conditions. When those two—the primary cause and the contributing conditions—are simultaneously assembled, the dependently related events of the appearances of tactile sensations emerge, even though they do not exist. On what do they depend? On the ground of being. To what are they related? To the nondual union of the ground of being and the appearances of tactile sensations. What events arise? The appearances of tactile sensations, even though they don't exist.

In short, you must understand that with the meeting of consciousness and its object, the five types of sensory consciousness act as the primary cause. You must understand that for all of them, the pervasive emptiness and luminosity of the ground and mentation serves as the primary cause, the creative powers of the movements of karmic energies serve as the contributing conditions, and due to the assembly of these two—the primary cause and contributing conditions—the appearances of forms, sounds, smells, tastes, and tactile sensations are merely dependently related events. If you think that apart from this there are appearances to the various sense apertures, you must become clear by examining how various appearances manifest in dreams and in the intermediate period, even without the presence of a coarse body.

Even though there are different types of appearances due to the influence of the body, with regard to the five sensory modes of consciousness there are no differences in terms of good or bad in their apprehension of objects. For example, a single body of liquid variously appears to a god as ambrosia, to an animal as something to drink or as a place to live, to a preta as pus and blood, and to a hell being as burning embers or boiling liquid. In reality, the appearances arising by way of just one body of liquid [161] are merely dependently related events.

Thus, delusion arises due to the reification of outer, inner, and secret apprehended objects and apprehending subjects. Concepts of forms belonging to the outer physical world and its sentient inhabitants are apprehended objects, while mental consciousness that clings to them as good, bad, and neutral constitutes the apprehending mind. These are the outer apprehended objects and apprehending mind. It is as if the five senses meet with their objects, and the generic ideas [of these forms] arise to mentation. For example, when there is a meeting of consciousness and an object while thinking "conch," this constitutes the inner apprehended object and the apprehending mind. When there is a subliminal appearance of the self and a subtle appearance—even in the absence of any coarse appearance of form manifesting as the physical world and its sentient inhabitants to an earlier afflictive mentation—this is an apprehended object, and the subtle concept of grasping at "mine" is an apprehending mind. These constitute the secret apprehended object and apprehending mind. The inner and outer apprehended object and apprehending mind emerge from the root of the secret apprehended object and apprehending mind. In reality, apart from the reification of the secret apprehended object and apprehending mind, there are no distinctions among the three apprehended objects and apprehending minds.

> **"Some people take appearances to be the mind, and they may think that all outer appearances are discursive thoughts and really their own minds, but it is not so. This is demonstrated by the fact that appearances change from the very moment they arise, with former moments sequentially passing away and giving rise to later ones, while the mind does not take on the nature of any of these moments, which would render it nonexistent. Thus, as appearances to the eight types of consciousness sequentially emerge in their natural order, saṃsāra fully manifests. As they reabsorb back into the substrate consciousness, they subside into the peak of mundane existence."**

There are also people who assert that appearances are the mind, and according to their tradition, [162] all appearances directly reveal themselves as discursive thoughts and their own minds, but appearances and the mind are not the same. This is demonstrated by the fact that from the very moment that appearances arise, they change. If appearances and the mind were the same, when the mind thought about India, then appearances should also depart for India; and when the mind thought about China, appearances should also go to China. When the mind ceases, appearances would also have to cease and vanish, but it is not so. If you think they are different, that is not the case either. When the mind is absent, appearances do not arise, because the mind that experiences them is absent.

How, then, do they appear? As explained above, they are simply dependently related events arising from the assembly of causes and conditions. As an analogy, the ocean does not consist of [reflections of] planets and stars, and no [reflections of] planets and stars [in the ocean] are established apart from the ocean. While the appearances of the moon and other reflections are not really in the water, it is certain that they appear as dependently related events arising from the confluence of causes and conditions. The above point should be understood by way of these analogies and their referents.

Thus, due to appearances to the eight types of consciousness sequentially emerging in their natural order, saṃsāra fully manifests. Then, due to their reabsorption, they subside into the peak of mundane existence. How does this happen? In terms of relative truth, when this eon first arose, in a dimension without any basis, [163] energies congealed as a dark mountain in the form of a crossed vajra. Upon it formed a serene, clear, pure ocean, and upon this formed the powerful golden ground. It is said that a crescent-shaped fire maṇḍala emerged in the nature of [the ocean and ground], and from the confluence of moisture and warmth, sentient beings gradually came to inhabit the formless, form, and desire realms.

Ultimately, however, that is not the case. Emptiness with no basis is the immaterial substrate. Energies manifesting as a dark mountain in the form of a crossed vajra are the karmic energies of grasping. The so-called serene, clear, pure ocean is the substrate consciousness. The so-called powerful golden ground is afflictive mentation, and the so-called crescent-shaped fire maṇḍala that manifests as the nature of [the ocean and ground] is mental consciousness. The so-called confluence of moisture and warmth is the simultaneous confluence of the lucid, luminous space of the ground of being and mental consciousness. The so-called gradual formation of the formless, form, and desire realms is the establishment of the substrate as the formless realm, [the substrate] consciousness as the form realm, and mentation and the five senses as the desire realm. Moreover, that which appears as the body is the desire realm, that which distinctively appears as speech is the form realm, [164] and nonapparent mentation is the formless realm. These are explained as the three realms.

Then, the relative assertions that the world is eventually destroyed seven times by fire, one time by water, and one time by wind actually refer to the following: the destructions by fire refer to the six types of consciousness dissolving into mental consciousness; the destruction by water refers to the dissolution of the configurations of mental consciousness into the substrate consciousness; and the destruction by wind refers to the dissolution of the substrate consciousness into the karmic energies, resulting in the grasping of the karmic energies subsiding into space. Finally, the assertion that [everything dissolves] into baseless emptiness refers to swooning into the space of the great vacuity of the substrate.[55] So you should understand in this way how during a single day and night yogins experience the whole fourfold cycle of the formation, presence, destruction, and emptiness of an eon.

> **"In this way the whole world of appearances of saṃsāra and nirvāṇa is none other than the ground of being, and it is of one taste in that very ground. As an analogy, you must understand that even though various reflections of the planets and stars appear in the ocean, in reality they are of one taste in the water. The revelation of all phenomena to be your own appearances is the essential teaching of Vajradhara."**
>
> **Saying this, he disappeared from view.**

In this way the liberating and delusive appearances of the worlds of saṃsāra and nirvāṇa manifest like illusions, yet they are all of the same taste in the ground of being and are none other than the essential nature of the space of that ground. So they are reduced to oneness.

As an analogy, even though various appearances of reflections of the planets, stars, and so forth appear in the lucidity and clarity of the ocean, in reality they are of one taste in the water. Understand this analogy and that to which it is analogous. [165] Thus, all appearing phenomena are your own appearances that simply arise to yourself, without even the minutest particle existing objectively from its own side. The decisive understanding of this point is the essential teaching of Vajradhara.

Saying this, he disappeared from view.

55. This refers to those occasions when one loses consciousness of appearances, which dissolve into the substrate.

Teachings of Hūṃchenkāra

c. The Instructions on Not Allowing the Uniform Pervasiveness of Equality to Be Defiled by the Faults of Conceptual Elaboration

On yet another occasion when I met the great vidyādhara Hūṃchenkāra, I asked him, "What is this array of appearances like?"

He replied, "O great being, the five kinds of sensory consciousness are like space, in which anything may emerge. Discursive thoughts are like substances and mantras used by an illusionist, such that illusion-like arrays of appearances arise due to their simultaneous conjunction. Consciousness that closely attends to them is like a spectator.

"Thus, all substances that are offered and donated are like illusory substances. The approach of the illusion-like yoga is to dissolve them into emptiness with purifying mantras, and then use enriching mantras to immeasurably increase the appearances of these offerings to the six senses of the objects of worship, so that they are well pleased. Further, by means of the illusion-like yoga, you generate appearances like a city of gandharvas to emanation-like sentient beings; and by transforming these dream-like appearances, you liberate and guide them and so forth, and by so doing you gain mastery over the great yoga of illusion.

"No matter how many planets and stars are reflected in a lake, the reflections are encompassed within the water itself. No matter how many physical worlds and their sentient inhabitants there are, they are encompassed within a single space. And no matter how vast and numerous are the appearances of saṃsāra and nirvāṇa, they are encompassed within the single ultimate nature of mind. Observe how this is so!"

On yet another occasion when I met the great vidyādhara Hūṃchen-kāra, I asked him, "What is this array of appearances like?" He replied, "O great being, the five kinds of sensory consciousness are like space, in which anything may emerge. Discursive thoughts are like substances and mantras used by an illusionist."

Due to the simultaneous conjunction of the five kinds of sensory consciousness and discursive thoughts, all the arrays of appearances of the outer physical world, its inner, animate sentient inhabitants, and the five types of sensory stimuli are like the apparitions of an illusionist. The mental consciousness that closely identifies with them is like a spectator. You must correctly understand their nature. [166]

A yogin who realizes this uses purifying mantras to dissolve all offerings and gifts, which are like illusory substances, into emptiness. He then uses enriching mantras to immeasurably increase their appearances to the six senses of the beings to whom he makes offerings and gifts, and imagines that they are well pleased by these offerings. This is the sublime avenue of illusion-like yoga for implicitly perfecting the two accumulations [of merit and of knowledge] on the path of yoga. As it is said:

> As a samaya for the Ratna family,
> one constantly makes gifts of four kinds.[56]

Once you have taken the samayas of the preliminary phase of an empowerment, it is important that you apply yourself to them constantly.

Therefore, in the manner of a smoke offering, as if you were an illusionist, first clearly visualize yourself in the form of any personal deity. With a purifying mantra, purify in emptiness the smoke offerings together with a ritual stove, as if they were the substances and mantras of an illusionist. With an enriching mantra, imagine the ground, intervening space, and sky filled with every single object of form, sound, smell, taste, and tactile sensation, transforming them all into space treasuries, as if they were apparitions. Imagine the revered Three Jewels, who are like spectators, as guests filling the sky like shining constellations of stars; [167] noble protector guests filling the intervening space like billowing clouds; and guests who deliver karmic retribution to obstructive beings, slightly elevated above the ground and filling the sky like dust particles. On the ground, imagine the six types of beings, who are guests worthy of compassion, gathered like an assembly of gods and men.

Then, emanate and present the smoke offerings in the forms of all kinds

56. The four kinds of gifts are those of material goods, Dharma, fearlessness, and loving-kindness.

of enjoyments to the six senses of these guests, imagining the guests to be like water vessels. Imagine that these enjoyments arise to their six faculties like planets and stars until they fade into space, and that their nature is inexhaustible. Imagine that all the guests are delighted and thoroughly pleased, and that your habitual propensities are purified, that dullness is dispelled, that you obey all commands, and that you have favorable friends and circumstances. Finally, as if the illusionist's apparitions are dissolving into space, you as the one who makes the offerings, the offering substances, and the guests to whom offerings are made all disappear, and you conclude with prayers of dedication.

In the morning, water offerings are to be made as follows: Once again visualize yourself, as if you were an illusionist, in the form of your personal deity, either as Śākyamuni [168] or the Great Compassionate One (Avalokiteśvara), white in color, complete with all the correct hand implements and ornaments. Likewise, with a purifying mantra, purify in emptiness the water and its containers, and from emptiness visualize a vast, jeweled container arising from the syllable *Traṃ*, in which that substance is generated. Above it visualize a white *Oṃ*, red *Āḥ*, and blue *Hūṃ*, one stacked upon another. Increase them with an enriching mantra, and then simultaneously imagine a rain of white *Oṃ*s, red *Āḥ*s, and blue *Hūṃ*s descending, and visualize from the palms of yourself as your personal deity a stream of ambrosia flowing out and dissolving into the seed syllables inside the container. As a consequence of this, visualize the ambrosia of the taintless primordial consciousness of bliss and emptiness, white and red with a tint of blue, as all kinds of offering substances of form, sound, smell, taste, and tactile sensation arising as objects to the six senses. As you offer them to the revered Three Jewels, the noble protectors, malevolent beings who are karmic creditors, and the six kinds of sentient beings deserving of compassion, imagine that they partake of these equally distributed offerings with their tongues in the forms of vajras and hollow rays of light, and that they achieve a state free of strife and conflict, filled with joy and delight. Visualize the remaining offerings as flames presented to the mouth of the king of pretas, and by dedicating the merits, [169] imagine that the beings to whom you have made these offerings are all satisfied, that all their delusive appearances and habitual propensities cease, and that they achieve enlightenment. At the conclusion, dissolve everything into space and offer prayers of dedication.

At night, burnt offerings are to be made as follows: Visualize yourself as your personal deity in the illusory rainbow body form of Ārya Avalokiteśvara, white in color and bearing the ornaments of a saṃbhogakāya. Purify in emptiness the burnt offerings and ritual stove in front of you. From emptiness, emanate from the syllable *Raṃ* a vast stove, inside of which the burnt offerings appear as an inexhaustible space treasury of forms, sounds, smells, tastes, and tactile sensations in the space of the six senses of all the kinds of guests. Invite the four classes of guests, who are like spectators effortlessly receiving whatever kinds of enjoyments they desire, and imagine that the two higher types of guests[57] experience the supreme satisfaction of the taste of bliss and emptiness and achieve the supreme and common siddhis. Imagine that the two lower types of guests achieve liberation. At the conclusion, seal the offering by imagining that the three aspects[58] disappear, and then dedicate the merit.

At dusk, the offering of your body is to be made as follows: This offering of your body is the foremost of all gifts. In the past, the king known by the name Great Courage gave his body to a tigress, [170] the king known as Power of Love sacrificed his body to the five *yakṣa*[59] brothers, Princess Mandhebhadra gave her body to a tigress, and Drimé Kunden gave away his son and wife. Those were all blessed deeds of bodhisattvas, and such actual conduct is rare. Machik Lapdrön writes in this regard:

> If gifts of horses and cattle merit one hundred,
> gifts of your children and wife merit a thousand,
> and the gift of your body merits a hundred thousand.

In this world, this body is cherished above all things; so if it is given away, due to that accumulation of merit with this as an object, the accumulation of knowledge without an object is perfected. Therefore, first of all visualize this big, plump, sleek, glistening body as being as vast as a galaxy. In its center, visualize the central channel like an erect pillar in an empty building, with its upper end at the crown of your head like an opening at the top of a cave, and its lower end beneath your navel like a blocked bamboo joint. [Inside this channel] imbued with four qualities,[60] at the level of your heart imagine the essential nature of your energy-mind and consciousness as a white *bindu*, like the egg of a *masar*[61] bird, [171] luminous, shining, sleek, twirling, and about to shoot upward like a meteor.

57. The revered Three Jewels and the noble protectors.

58. The one who makes the offering, the offering itself, and those to whom the offerings are made.

59. Tib. *gnod sbyin*. A type of nonhuman being belonging to the class of devas or demons.

60. The four qualities are straight, subtle, lucid, and opulent.

61. Tib. *bya ma sar.*

Then, as you utter *Phaṭ* the first time it merges with space; the second time it emerges from space; and the third time you instantly transform into Black Machik Tröma, your body indigo in color, with one head and two hands. Your right hand brandishes a curved flaying knife in the sky, symbolizing your mastery of appearances, and your left hand holds at your heart a blood-filled skull cup, symbolizing your enjoyment of the three realms as blood. Your right leg is bent, with your heel pointing to your *bhaga*, and your left leg is extended, trampling a corpse upon a lotus and sun disk. Your mouth is open, with your tongue coiled and your sharp, white fangs bared. Vajra fire blazes from your facial hair and eyebrows, your three eyes move fiercely, and you scowl like a tidal wave. In the midst of your orange hair, at the apex of conditioned existence, there is the black head of a pig whose squeal rouses all sentient beings from the slumber of delusion.

A three-pointed *khaṭvāṅga*, of the nature of your consort, Heruka, rests on your left shoulder, and you bear the eight garments of a charnel ground and are adorned with the six types of bone ornaments. Imagine yourself as an illusory kāya [172] of the primordial consciousness of appearances and emptiness, in the midst of a blazing fire of primordial consciousness. Simply brandishing a curved flaying knife in your right hand, you flay the skin off a corpse lying on the ground and spread it over the whole earth. Upon it is a threefold hearth of dry, moist, and old self-appearing skulls, symbolizing the three kāyas, as large as Mount Meru. The aggregate of form is cast from above into the hearth of skulls, where it disintegrates into many pieces. Beneath the hearth of skulls, the air element emerges from the syllable *Yaṃ* and the fire element arises from the syllable *Raṃ*, causing the air element to move. With the blazing of the fire, the skulls heat up, melting and boiling their contents, such that the bubbles spill over and fall on the skin-covered ground. The whole earth and intervening space are filled with a mountain of flesh to feed upon, an ocean of blood to drink, a river bank of bones to chew, a soup of grease and fat, and bones and marrow to suck.

Having expanded these inexhaustible ornamental wheels of sensual pleasures into a space treasury, a rain of white *Oṃ*s, red *Āḥ*s, and blue *Hūṃ*s blessed by the body, speech, and mind of all the *tathāgata*s falls from space, dissolving into the ambrosia, which takes on a sheen of white and red with a tint of blue. Just by experiencing the rain touching your mouth, [173] you are liberated in the blessing of this great ambrosia of primordial consciousness. From the vapor of the bubbles are emanated incredible arrays of outer, inner, and secret offerings. Imagine that with the first utterance of *Phaṭ* the sounding of thighbone trumpets catches the attention of the guests, with the second they set out from their abodes, and with the third they all converge.

In the sky are the revered guests of the Three Jewels—the Buddha, Dharma, and Saṅgha—the gurus, personal deities, and ḍākinīs, the dharmakāya, saṃbhogakāya, and nirmāṇakāya, and all the sublime gurus endowed with the three lineages,[62] clustered together like a shimmering constellation. In the intervening space are the noble protector guests, including the eight devas, eight *nāga*s, eight planets, nine terrifying ones,[63] ten guardians of the directions, twenty-eight constellations, four classes of great kings, and so on, gathered like billowing clouds. Elevated slightly above the ground are the guests who deliver karmic retribution to malevolent beings; they include assemblies of *pārthivas*[64] who are male spirits, demonesses who are female spirits, assemblies of nāgas, *grahas*,[65] and *kṣamāpatis*,[66] the eighteen *phungsi driwo* demons,[67] fifteen childish great demons,[68] the mother *hāriṇī*[69] and her five hundred sons, nine demons of attachment to mundane existence,[70] ten temple demons,[71] minor demons of sudden winds,[72] [174] and so on, all gathered in the sky like a host of dust particles.

On the ground are the six kinds of sentient beings deserving of compassion, including hell beings, pretas, animals, asuras, humans, gods, and so on, appearing like an assembly of gods and men.

From your heart [as the goddess] are emanated countless activity ḍākinīs, who make offerings by scooping with jeweled ladles with their right hands and pouring into skull cups in their left hands. The revered guests, the Three Jewels, partake of the vital essence of the ambrosia through their tongues,

62. The three lineages are the Enlightened View Lineage of the Buddhas, the Symbolic Lineage of the Vidyādharas, and the Aural Lineage of Ordinary Individuals.

63. Tib. *'jigs byed dgu*; Skt. *navabhairava*.

64. Tib. *rgyal po*. Demonic beings who emerge from the aggregates of grasping at the "I" and consist of the conceptual mental factors that reify appearances. Such a being is created by conceptually focusing on it, and it arises as an apparition of hatred.

65. Tib. *gdon*. Malevolent demonic beings who torment one in lifetime after lifetime.

66. Tib. *sa bdag*. Earth spirits whose actual nature is that of delusion produced by the causes and conditions of ignorance.

67. Tib. *phung sri gri bo*.

68. Tib. *byis pa'i gdon chen*.

69. Tib. *'phrog ma*. Malevolent demonic beings who steal one's collections of merit and knowledge.

70. Tib. *srid pa'i chags pa'i 'dre*.

71. Tib. *gtsug lag khang gi gdon*.

72. Tib. *glo bur lhags pa'i 'dre phran*.

which take on forms of tubular gems, vajras, lotuses, and rays of light, and their minds are satisfied by the taste of bliss and emptiness. Imagine that your two accumulations [of merit and knowledge] are perfected, that the two types of [afflictive and cognitive] obscurations are purified, and that you achieve the supreme and common siddhis.

Imagine that the noble protector guests enjoy the vital essence of the ambrosia by way of their tongues in the form of hollow swords and that they are satisfied by the taste of bliss and emptiness. Imagine that this atones for your transgressions, that you realize limitless, bountiful enlightened activities, and that your outer, inner, and secret obstacles are dispelled.

By equally dedicating the flesh and blood, white and sweet substances,[73] and ambrosia to the guests who deliver karmic retribution to malevolent beings, imagine that they achieve freedom from strife and conflict; their debts of karmic retribution and killing are paid; [175] all harmful behaviors of viciousness, hostility, and disturbance are pacified; and precious bodhicitta arises in their mindstreams. Imagine that their negative karma, the causes and conditions for delusion, and their habitual propensities are exhausted, and that they achieve enlightenment.

For the six types of guests who are deserving of compassion, imagine that the offerings transform into Dharma and medicine to dispel their individual kinds of suffering, into streams of water to purify their negative karma, and into whatever kinds of sensual enjoyments they desire. By dedicating offerings to them in this way, imagine that they are contented and satisfied, and that the six kinds of beings are freed from their individual kinds of suffering. All their vices, obscurations, and habitual propensities are purified, and they experience visions of enlightened teachers and their retinues in the pure realms of the five buddha families, including Abhirati and so on, so that they dredge the depths of saṃsāra.

Then, gathering all the scattered remains inside the skull cups, bless them in the ambrosia of primordial consciousness, and give them to the remaining humble guests who are feeble, sluggish, crippled, deaf, blind, or mute. When you do so, they are satisfied with enjoyments in accordance with their individual desires, and they are each freed of their sufferings. The humble ones become endowed with the power of nobility; those who are weak, with the power of abundant self-mastery; [176] the sluggish, with swift, wrathful power; the crippled, with miraculous legs; the blind, with eyes of primordial consciousness; the deaf, with all-hearing auditory faculties; and the mute, with eloquent tongues. Imagine that they are utterly delighted and smiling,

73. The three white substances are milk, curd, and butter, and the three sweet substances are honey, sugar, and molasses.

and that the supreme, taintless primordial consciousness of bliss and emptiness arises in all their mindstreams.

In addition, imagine guests who did not have time to come—yakṣas who dwell on the seashore at the foot of Mount Meru, those who dwell on the second terrace of Mount Meru, those who dwell on its summit, old female pretas, and female *terma* protectors. Imagine guests who did not heed the invitation to attend—male māras holding skulls, female māras who send illnesses, big-bellied grahas, grahas with boils, and so on—all these beings experiencing only the miseries of their own karmic appearances. Imagine sending forth ambrosia to their abodes, such that they are all contented and satisfied, all the fears of their delusive appearances and miseries vanish into space as if they were awakened from sleep, and they achieve enlightenment.

At the end, you as the dedicator, the four kinds of guests as the objects of dedication, and all the dedicated substances, together with the illusion-like apparitional appearances, merge into the space of the nirmāṇakāya with the first recitation of *Phaṭ*. [177] With the second recitation you merge into the space of the saṃbhogakāya, and with the third recitation you merge into the space of the dharmakāya. Then rest for a little while in meditative equipoise in the bare nature of objectless uniform pervasiveness.

Then, like a bubble emerging from water, imagine all gods and demons of the world of appearances in front of you, as you instantaneously visualize yourself in the form of the Great Compassionate One. Imagine teaching them the Dharma, and due to white rays of light emanating from your body, all the male beings achieve the state of Avalokiteśvara and all the female beings achieve the state of the venerable Tārā. Their hands are all pressed together in *mudrās* and their legs are moving about. Imagine that they depart for Sukhāvatī with a whooshing sound, like a flock of vultures lofting into the sky. Place your awareness in a state devoid of an object and dedicate the virtue to perfect enlightenment.

When you make supplications and offerings to the guardians of the teachings without mental emanations like illusory apparitions, the gods are not pleased, so they provide no benefit, only harm. First visualize yourself as any of the personal deities, and from your heart, imagine black light thoroughly pervading the world, completely assembling all injurious beings, enemies, and malevolent beings, who merge indivisibly with the *torma*[74] offering. [178] By gathering them together, imagine that the enemies and malevolent beings

74. Tib. *gtor ma*; Skt. *bali*. A ritual offering in which the nutritive essence of the universe is synthesized and that acts as a source of all desirable things.

of the ten fields[75] are completely assembled, so that none are left elsewhere. Finally, imagine creative expressions of primordial consciousness from space descending as a rain of various weapons, creating a mountain of flesh and an ocean of blood as vast as space that liberates them from their infractions.

Then, with a purifying mantra, purify all the contaminations of the offering substances in emptiness. From the nature of emptiness a syllable *Aḥ* emerges from your heart, giving rise to a vast skull cup, white on the outside, red on the inside, and as enormous as a galaxy. Inside it, from gathering together the quintessence and vital essence of the five elements and the torma substances, there emerges a mountain of flesh, an ocean of blood, river banks of bones, mountains of the three white substances and three sweet substances, an ocean of milk and yogurt, various kinds of fruits, various sorts of offering substances and ritual instruments, various kinds of forest creatures, domestic animals, water-dwelling birds and predators, powerful armor, sharp weapons, and various beautiful silken garments, soft to the touch.

In addition, imagine an inconceivable, inexhaustible array of offerings, including ritual offerings, sensory enjoyments, medicine, tormas, blood, and the seven royal possessions,[76] [179] all having a nature such that they satisfy the desires of each of the beings to whom they are offered. Bless them with the six mantras and six mudrās. Imagine the bountiful array of offerings in front of you as a natural display of primordial consciousness, and in the midst of fire, rainbow light, and clouds of smoke, visualize the male lineage of the protectors of the teachings, the female lineage of goddesses, and the eight classes of *mattas*,[77] each with his or her own bodily color, hand implements, and clothing, as described in the classic treatises. Imagine them mounted upon swift steeds, wearing mighty armor, brandishing sharp weapons, and imbued with wrathful and wondrous splendor. In the meantime, from the domains of the five elements invite countless protectors of the teachings bearing similar forms, and repeatedly visualize them merging with

75. According to the tantras, enemies of the Dharma who are to be vanquished must have ten qualities, namely, that they: (1) destroy the Dharma, (2) disparage the Three Jewels, (3) rob the Saṅgha of its possessions, (4) revile the Mahāyāna, (5) harm the body of the guru, (6) denigrate their vajra siblings and others, (7) obstruct others' Dharma practice, (8) are utterly devoid of love and compassion, (9) break their vows and samayas, and (10) hold false views regarding the laws of karma.

76. The seven royal possessions are the (1) precious wheel, (2) precious jewel, (3) precious queen, (4) precious minister, (5) precious elephant, (6) precious steed, and (7) precious general.

77. Tib. *dregs brgyad*. Spirits belonging to an eightfold class of haughty gods and demons.

the deities you have generated. Do not interrupt this with human words, do not let your bodily warmth dissipate from your meditation cushion, and without forgetfulness, distinctly call out their names.

If you actualize them, they will be established as existent from the space of nonexistence. As an analogy, they will be directly established as if you had constructed a building by compounding earth, stone, and wood. Even those mattas who present themselves as autonomously existent do not exist as something else, for all the appearances of the creative power of pristine awareness [180] are merely designated as protectors of the teachings of the Secret Mantrayāna by the skillful means and compassion of the jinas; they have no other existence apart from those designations.

As a result of making supplications and offerings to them, while recognizing them as being like conjury and illusory apparitions, imagine that they partake of the offerings by taking in the vital essence of the tormas through hollow tubes of light from the weapons of their tongues. With their minds satisfied by the taste of bliss and emptiness, imagine that they blaze with magnificent power and that they limitlessly realize the four kinds of enlightened activity of practicing yogins.

Moreover, when making offerings of grain and so forth, imagine immeasurable clouds of offerings being emanated from your heart as your personal deity, and offer them to the dharmapālas, who are pleased by this. At the end, you enjoin them to perform any tasks that you desire, and without their departing or assembling, imagine that all detrimental obstacles to reaching the grounds and paths on the way to enlightenment are dispelled and that they assist you in increasing all favorable circumstances. They then remain in your life-principle stone[78] and in the space of your life-force cakra.

When you actualize the dharmapālas, you must visualize them as being permanent, firm, and enduring. When you finally die, if you think of yourself as disintegrating into space, as if you were an illusory apparition, [181] there is no need to visualize them dissolving or ask them to leave.

Such is the unsurpassable yogic experience of realizing saṃsāra and nirvāṇa as illusory. You yogins who realize all phenomena as being like illusions, shift the appearances of sentient beings to self-appearances that are not other than yourselves.

Then, skillfully take care of all the karmic deeds that sentient beings have experienced and will experience and that have been accumulated since beginningless time, as follows: (1) Imagine ferocious, pernicious beings as if they

78. Tib. *bla rdo*. A stone symbolizing your life principle that may be used as a ritual talisman.

were appearances of a city of gandharvas, and engage in the wrathful enlightened activity of annihilating those beings. (2) To mercifully and compassionately care for those who are filled with passionate desires, visualize pacifying enlightened activity. (3) Transforming many eons into a single instant, imagine annihilating pernicious beings with the thought of drawing in their life forces, purifying their vices, and sending them to a pure land. (4) Take care of those with passionate desires by bringing them to a higher state: like waking them from a dream, you are able to forcefully unite them with the realm of original purity in which delusion is impossible. Thus, the ability to master the great, illusory yoga arises from the essential point of realizing all phenomena as illusions. [182]

(1) First, as for the activity of liberating ferocious, pernicious beings through destruction, the triad of the fortress of the view, the highway of meditation, and the life force of visualization is very important. Regarding the fortress of the view, the knowledge that saṃsāra and nirvāṇa are not other than your own appearances is the fortress of the view. The highway of meditation is not mistaking pristine awareness for the mind by never being separated from the samādhi of your personal deity. The life force of visualization requires the vitality transmission[79] and the purification transmission.[80]

In this regard there are three visualizations: In the upper portion of your body, instantly visualized in the form of your personal deity, imagine the gurus of the lineage of teachings; in the middle area at the hips, visualize the assemblies of personal deities; and in the lower portion of your body, imagine all the ḍākinīs and dharmapālas, like planets and stars brilliantly reflected in the ocean. After transforming the nature of all the sentient beings who inhabit the world into that of your personal deity, the visualization of them engaging in the activity of killing and liberating enemies and malevolent beings is the vital point of their not turning back against you.

The Supreme Son Kīla is the Youthful Vajra, with his upper body visualized as a wrathful king having three faces and six arms. His lower body is visualized as a three-sided *kīla*[81] made of meteorite metal, as if it were created in a blacksmith's charcoal hearth, and as a mass of snakes vomited from the mouth of a sea monster. On the upper globe above the handle of the kīla, visualize the palace of the five peaceful buddhas; [183] on the bulbous handle

79. Tib. *tshe lung*. The purpose of this is to draw in the vitality of the subject.

80. Tib. *khrus lung*. The purpose of this is to purify the subject.

81. Tib. *phur ba*. A three-edged ritual dagger that may be used as an object of devotions such as prostrations, offerings, and circumambulations.

of the kīla, visualize the palace of the nine blood-drinking deities; and on the lower globe of the kīla, visualize the palace of the glorious kīla protectors. Imagine rays of light being emitted from the three syllables at his three places, drawing in all the empowerments, blessings, and siddhis of the jinas and dissolving them into the kīla, such that simply due to the mightiness of their bodies, the sounding of their voices, and the movements of their minds the kīla receives the empowerment to simultaneously liberate the three realms. This is the vital point of unconquerableness.

For the direct visualization of enemies and malevolent beings as your meditative objects, imagine a dark blue syllable *Eḥ* being emitted from your heart as your personal deity, from which emerges the kāya of the five poisons as a black slaughterhouse of Karma Yama. Its interior is cloaked in the darkness of delusion, an ocean of the blood of attachment boils beneath it, its center is wracked by the dark wind of envy, its corners crumble with landslides from the cliffs of pride, and its exterior blazes with the flames of hatred. Its three corners symbolize the spontaneous actualization of the three kāyas, and its three levels symbolize the release of the three poisons into space. It is unassailable by the forces of māras and *yamas*. [184] On the exterior fortifications are sharp, pointed spears aligned in a row. Inside it, rays of light emanate from the syllables *Nṛiḥ* to the enemies and *Triḥ* to the malevolent beings, instantly drawing in and dissolving the life principle, vitality, and life force of enemies and malevolent beings throughout all the realms of galaxies. As a result of this transformation, the enemies and malevolent beings weep with their mouths, show distress with their eyes as if someone had died, and wring their hands in misery. With their feet and hands bound by chains, they involuntarily lose their white and red bodhicitta; and as if they had been cast naked into a barren wasteland, they have no protector or refuge. Imagine these pathetic, breathless beings trembling and shaking with fear. Moreover, wherever the nature of the life principle, vitality, and life force of enemies descends in these external worlds, imagine that there is nothing that can prevent the death of the enemies. This is the sublime, vital point of them [the enemies] not spreading elsewhere.

Among the three restorations, the first is the restoration of yourself. Imagine immeasurable syllables of *Hūṃ* being emanated from your heart as your personal deity, completely filling all dimensions of saṃsāra and nirvāṇa. Like salt dissolving into water, visualize all the buddhas, buddhafields, and physical worlds with their sentient inhabitants of the three realms dissolving into the *Hūṃs*. [185] Imagine them all being drawn inward and dissolving into yourself, resulting in your transforming into the universal splendor of all of saṃsāra and nirvāṇa.

As for the restoration of the kīla, directly visualize the Supreme Son Kīla, the Youthful Vajra. Sparks from the kīla are emitted like sparks from a fire, completely filling all the worlds of appearances of saṃsāra and nirvāṇa. As before, imagine all the phenomena included in both saṃsāra and nirvāṇa merging into the kīla, like salt dissolving into water. Imagine all the power, might, and strength of all of saṃsāra and nirvāṇa being drawn in and perfected.

As for the restoration of enemies and obstructive beings, directly visualize enemies and obstructive beings as an effigy from which black light is emitted, retracting and dissolving into the effigy the life principle, vitality, and life force, as well as the merit and enjoyments, of all enemies, obstructive beings, and malevolent beings, like drops of water that completely disperse into a pool of water. Thus, all malevolent beings are retracted and perfected.

To use the messengers to make a summons, imagine yourself as the deity, emanating from your heart countless messengers holding hooks, nooses, iron chains, and bells, together with a black karmic energy that terminates the eon. They carry away the life principle, vitality, and life force of all enemies and obstructive beings from the sky and dissolve them into the effigy, [186] like a kite carried by the wind, like a hurricane driving mist from the sky, and like deer driven away by hunting dogs.

During the intervals between each of the seven times you make the summons, you must repeatedly take hold of the life principles of the enemies. Their consciousnesses are to be summoned. The life principle circles consciousness like a watchdog circles its master, so they must be crazed by summoning, binding, and restraining, and they must be bound with the deity, mantras, and samādhi. It is the life principle that must be extinguished. The cord that connects the body and mind is said to be the noble gods of the ancestors. It is the life force that must be cut. From time to time, by merely brandishing a kīla as if you were churning yogurt, you stir up the aggregates, elements, and sense bases of the enemies and obstructive beings. Like butter emerging from milk, imagine the essential nature of their life principles turning into white *Nṛiḥ* syllables, which are drawn up from the aperture in the kīla, as if you were sucking up drops of water. Imagine them repeatedly dissolving into the spaces between the sun and moon on your seat as your personal deity.

After the repeated appearances of indications of summoning in that way, when signs appear of [the enemies'] life principles, the activity of binding them is as follows: From your heart, imagine before you blue and red light in the form of cords being emitted, completely ensnaring and firmly binding the life principles, vitalities, and life forces, as well as the bodies, speech, and minds of the enemies, such that [187] all their abilities and powers to move and fly away are restrained and suppressed, like stones cast to the ground.

Regarding the isolation of the *daemon*[82] [from one's enemy], some say that this isolation should be done just at the time of liberating activity, but not before then. Prior to that, repeatedly bind the life principle, and afterward perform the isolation. If the isolation is done prematurely, the life force will be powerful, and there is the danger that it will be lost together with the daemon. As for the actual isolation, instantaneously perform the isolation and liberation at the mouth of an incarceration box[83] by imagining two *piśācīs*,[84] one with an owl's head and one with a raven's head, each having a woman's body covered with feathers, and emanating a foul odor that causes one's enemies and malevolent gods to become crazed and to faint. The two roaring like lions, fighting, and beating their wings at the mouth of the incarceration box cause all the daemons who protect enemies and malevolent beings to faint and fall into insanity. Enemies and malevolent beings are cast away and flee, following which innumerable replicas of the two piśācīs are emanated, scratching them with their talons, pummeling them with their wings, and chopping them up and devouring them with their beaks. Finally, imagine that they are banished into the darkness inside a mountain on the far side of the ocean, so dazed that they can never return. [188] While reciting and chanting expelling mantras, burn incense and fan it with a feather.

Regarding causing insanity in enemies and malevolent beings, imagine drawing together the karmic energies of all sentient beings of the three realms, and visualize these energies in the form of a black wind that penetrates the tips of the ring fingers of enemies and malevolent beings and enters their life-force channels. Due to the movement of these energies, imagine that the enemies and malevolent beings are utterly crazed as you recite *Jva la pa ya* and so on.

Then, the vitality transmission, the purification transmission, the abode transmission,[85] and so on, are as follows: Visualize the Supreme Son Kīla like

82. Tib. *lhan cig skyes pa'i lha.* A god that accompanies an individual from birth, serving as that person's protector, similar to the concept of daemon in classic Greek mythology.

83. Tib. *'brub khung.* A triangular ritual container, often made of metal, black on the outside and red on the inside, and sometimes marked with skulls. It is visualized in various ways: as the absolute space of ultimate reality, as the miserable states of existence, as the womb of the consort, or as a prison.

84. Tib. *phra men.* One of eight flesh-eating protector deities with a bird's head and a woman's body or with a carnivorous animal's head and a man's body.

85. Tib. *gnas lung.* The purpose of this is to send the subject to a pure land.

before, merely pointing to the bodies of enemies and malevolent beings. By stirring up their aggregates, elements, and sense bases, like milk emerging from stirred yogurt, the essential nature of the life principles of the enemies transforms into shimmering white *Nṛiḥ* syllables; these are completely drawn into the tip of the kīla, like drops of water being gulped down. Dissolving into the kīla, like yogurt filling a pouch, imagine that the kīla is filled with fire, which satisfies the kīla with their life principles. Again, by stirring up their aggregates, elements, and sense bases, the essential nature of their vitality and merit transforms into shimmering green *Nṛiḥ* syllables, which are completely drawn into the tip of the kīla. Imagine that all their contaminants and faults are purified from within, and then they emerge from the upper tip of the kīla and [189] dissolve into yourself, greatly increasing your own vitality and merit. This increases the lifespan of the yogin.

Again, the visualization of white rays of light being emitted from the tip of the kīla and completely purifying all the vices, obscurations, karma, and mental afflictions in the mindstreams of enemies and malevolent beings is the purification transmission.

Then, when the hearts of the enemies and malevolent beings are struck with the kīla, their consciousnesses turn into white bindus marked with the syllable *Aḥ*. They are drawn up inside the kīla as if being sucked through a straw, and all their afflictive and cognitive obscurations are completely purified, like impurities removed from a white crystal. With the utterance of *Phaṭ*, imagine that from the lower bulb [of the kīla] their consciousnesses are transferred to nirmāṇakāyas, from the handle their consciousnesses are transferred to saṃbhogakāyas, and from the upper bulb their consciousnesses are transferred to the dharmakāya. Then, like shooting stars, they dissolve into the heart of the principal deity visualized in front of you. Imagine that they achieve enlightenment in the expansive awareness of the four kāyas and five facets of primordial consciousness, thereby satisfying the enemies by way of the abode [transmission].

Finally, imagine various weapons that are emanations of the enlightened activities of all the jinas raining down on their form aggregates, [190] and liberating their three poisons into the expanse of the three kāyas, their five poisons into the expanse of the five facets of primordial consciousness, and their 84,000 mental afflictions into the expanse of the 84,000 collections of Dharma. This is the visualization of liberating activity.

As for pounding them in a mortar, imagine all the aggregates, elements, and sense bases of the enemies and malevolent beings being drawn into the mortar of the secret space of the wrathful goddess Black Röljé. With the supreme method of [her consort] Blazing Pulverizer, they are pounded with his flaming pestle, such that they are ground down to tiny particles and dust. Recite the *Ta thā ya* mantra three times, visualizing that they are being beaten with the vital points of samādhi and that their flesh and blood turns into the essential nature of the ambrosia of primordial consciousness with the form of a mountain of flesh and an ocean of blood. Imagine that the first portion is offered to the assemblies of personal deities, satisfying their minds with the taste of bliss and emptiness and perfecting their two accumulations [of merit and knowledge]. The remaining mountain of flesh and ocean of blood is served in an open pit[86] and evenly distributed into the mouths of the guardians of the teachings and dharmapālas. It passes through their throats, providing unimpeded, great enjoyment, and into their bellies, [symbolizing] great, all-encompassing ultimate reality. By offering every bit of the remains, imagine that they are extremely pleased, thereby satisfying the guardians with flesh and blood. These constitute the four satisfactions.

If the vital points of the view and meditation are met, it is said [191] that a Mantrayāna practitioner may achieve buddhahood upon the triangular incarceration box.[87] If these points are absent, it will be no more beneficial than child's play, so it is important that you sustain these vital points.

(2) Second, here are the stages of purifying with great compassion the abode of your followers who have attachment.[88] There is no difference between guiding beings from their abode following death and liberating and guiding them, except merely in terms of the peacefulness or wrathfulness of the methods.

First, in front of yourself visualized in the form of your personal deity, imagine a dome of light of the five facets of primordial consciousness, with no doors or cracks and with no exit apart from an opening at its top. In its center, generate a white syllable *Nṛiḥ*, from which rays of light are emitted, causing the consciousnesses of the deceased person, all beings of the three realms with the four kinds of birth, the six classes of beings, and those in the intermediate period to dissolve into the *Nṛiḥ*. Imagine that they transform into pleasing, youthful forms, like when they were alive, wearing celestial garments of five-colored silk, complete with all their elements and sense bases, kneeling down with palms pressed together, holding eight-petaled lotuses as

86. Tib. *hom khung*. A triangular pit in which offerings are made.

87. Tib. *e khang khar*. A triangular box, symbolizing the space maṇḍala, in which one's enemies are placed and then struck with a kīla.

88. This refers to the pacifying enlightened activity of purifying their abode of saṃsāra and leading them to a pure land.

an offering. You should imagine them to be dwelling peacefully with faith and reverence.

It is said that a consciousness after death, with no physical basis, [192] goes wherever it intends, so the generation and dissolution of your samādhi is very important. Therefore, from your heart as your personal deity, hook-shaped rays of light are emitted, drawing in the targeted consciousnesses wherever they exist in the three realms and the three worlds, like fish drawn in with a hook. Imagine them repeatedly dissolving into the nametag.[89] Then emanate and offer all kinds of enjoyments, including forms, sounds, smells, tastes, and tactile sensations, to the six senses of malevolent spirits and malevolent beings who hinder and obstruct the liberation and omniscience of the deceased. This purifies their karmic debts from past actions, clears away their killing debts, and settles their [other] debts. Having thoroughly satisfied them, imagine that they return to their own abodes without creating any hindrances or obstacles.

If they don't go and are about to inflict harm, imagine that from the pores of your body visualized as your personal deity, and from your abode, throngs of ferocious beings, foul odors, bursts of flames, weapons, and so forth are emanated, expelling all malevolent beings to the far side of the great ocean. Drawing them back in, imagine them filling a five- or six-layered wheel of protection, which cannot be penetrated [193] or destroyed by anything, and which can never be seen by enemies and malevolent beings. Then teach Dharma to the deceased and imagine that their obscurations of the three poisons are purified by being cleansed with vase water of the nature of the three kāyas. By cleansing them with the ambrosia of primordial consciousness having the nature of the five kāyas, the five facets of primordial consciousness, and the six perfections, their afflictive and cognitive obscurations are completely purified. Then imagine that they are thoroughly purified, like wiping away the dust on a white crystal and washing away its contaminants with water.

Then, regarding guiding beings from their abode, the accumulation of negative karma by way of hatred, avarice, delusion, envy, pride, and attachment necessarily leads to experiences of the suffering of hell beings, pretas, animals, asuras, gods, and so forth. Imagine that many eons of such miseries are simultaneously transformed in an instant, manifesting appearances of hell beings, pretas, animals, asuras, gods, and humans. Then emanate a space treasury of clouds of offerings to the six great sages, including the sage

89. Tib. *ming byang*. A paper depicting an image and name of a person, into which that person's consciousness is invoked.

of hell, such that the accumulations [of merit and knowledge] are perfected and obscurations are purified. Imagine that you act as a master who provides protection from the sufferings of heat and cold of hell beings, the hunger and thirst of pretas, the stupidity and dullness of animals, [194] the conflicts of asuras, the death, transmigration, and descent of gods, and the birth, aging, sickness, and death of humans. Then you are entrusted as their guide.

As for settling karmic debts, the deceased, over the course of beginningless lifetimes, has accumulated karma of the mental afflictions of hatred, avarice, delusion, envy, pride, attachment, and so forth. At this time, imagine that with the ripening of actions such as killing, stealing, and dominating, wish-fulfilling tormas are dedicated to the male and female beings to whom the deceased is indebted, so that they are all satisfied and contented, karmic debts are settled, killing debts are cleared away, and [other] debts are repaid. Then imagine that they are enlightened.

(3) As for the purification transmission, purification occurs with the stream of blessings of the mirror-like primordial consciousness of all the assemblies of deities of the vajra family, including Bhagavān Vajrasattva; the discerning primordial consciousness of all the assemblies of deities of the lotus family, including Bhagavān Amitābha; the primordial consciousness of the absolute space of phenomena of all the assemblies of deities of the buddha family, including Bhagavān Vairocana; the primordial consciousness of accomplishment of all the assemblies of deities of the karma family, including Bhagavān Amoghasiddhi; [195] the primordial consciousness of equality of all the assemblies of deities of the jewel family, including Bhagavān Ratnasaṃbhava; and the great, self-emergent primordial consciousness of the mind of the buddhas, including Śākyamuni. Imagine that all the causal seeds and habitual propensities aroused by hatred, avarice, delusion, envy, pride, and attachment are thereby completely purified, like wiping the dust from a crystal or washing the rust from a mirror with water.

Regarding the vitality transmission, from your heart as your personal deity, rays of light are emitted like the conflagration at the end of the eon. The causal seeds and habitual propensities [of the deceased] for being reborn as a hell being, a preta, an animal, an asura, a god, a human, and so forth are visualized as follows: On the soles of the [deceased's] feet is the black seed syllable *Duḥ* of hell beings, at the genital region is the dark red seed syllable *Preḥ* of pretas, at the navel is the grey seed syllable *Triḥ* of animals, at the throat is the pale green seed syllable *Suḥ*[90] of asuras, at the crown is the white seed syllable *Aḥ* of devas, and at the heart is the dark green seed syllable *Nṛiḥ*

90. Emending *Sumḥ* to *Suḥ*.

of humans. Like fine hairs burnt in a flame, imagine that they are instantly incinerated. In that very moment, imagine that the deceased falls unconscious, as if he were deep asleep. [196]

When the deceased regains consciousness, his appearances shift, and he becomes seated on an eight-petaled lotus on an empowerment platform at the eastern gate of the maṇḍala. He then gradually offers homage at each gate in stages, starting from the eastern gate, and makes supplications to the gatekeepers. When he meets the deities of the maṇḍala, a red syllable *Raṃ*, together with the warmth of blessings, is emitted from your heart as his personal deity, striking the disciple [the deceased], and immediately consuming masses of the habitual propensities of his fully ripening karma.

His consciousness then takes on the form of a white syllable *Aḥ*, which is drawn into the mouth of the principal deity visualized in front of him, as if it were a drop of water being sucked in. Imagine that the syllable passes through the deity's body and emerges from the left side of the consort's ribs and transforms into the body of his personal deity, and in that form the disciple retakes his place on the empowerment platform at the eastern gate like before. Then the disciple is again visualized as the deity, and from absolute space, primordial consciousness beings descend and merge into the disciple. Then gradually bestow upon the disciple the common empowerments of pristine awareness; the empowerments of the enlightened body, speech, and mind; and the four empowerments and their related rituals. At this time, imagine that from your heart and the heart of the deity in front, two deities are emanated and dissolve into the disciple, so that he fully receives the four empowerments.[91]

Then, to provide satisfaction by means of the sensual pleasures of food and drink, [197] purify the offered substances so that they disappear into emptiness. From emptiness emerges the syllable *Oṃ*, from which appears a vast, jeweled container. Inside it, the three seed syllables [*Oṃ*, *Aḥ*, *Hūṃ*] dissolve into light and emanate an ornamental wheel of inexhaustible sensual pleasures of all kinds, offered as objects to the six senses.

As for the offerings—the aggregates, elements, and sense bases of the deceased are presented as offerings to the bhagavāns, the sugatas of the five families of jinas, thereby completing [the deceased's] collections [of merit and knowledge] and purifying his obscurations. Imagine that he attains enlightenment with his five aggregates of the nature of the five families of sugatas,

91. The four empowerments are (1) the vase, or water, empowerment, (2) the secret, or crown, empowerment, (3) the wisdom–primordial-consciousness, or vajra, empowerment, and (4) the word, or bell, empowerment. See glossary; GD 255–57, 271; VE 248–49.

his five elements of the nature of the five consorts, including Ākāśadhātvīśvarī (the consort of Vairocana), and his five mental afflictions of the nature of the five facets of primordial consciousness. As for dedicating the butter lamps, by dedicating the butter lamps as being of the nature of the five facets of primordial consciousness, imagine that all the bewilderment of ignorance on the part of the deceased is cleared away, and that the illumination of the five facets of primordial consciousness expands to perfection.

(4) Then, to elevate [the deceased] to a higher abode, visualize him as the deity like before, and in the center of his body, imagine the central channel imbued with four qualities. Upon the junction of the central channel at the heart, the essential nature of the vital energy, mind, and consciousness transforms into a white bindu marked with the syllable *Aḥ*. With the first recitation of *Phaṭ*, [198] imagine that appearances of a buddhafield manifest; with the second recitation they are recognized; and with the third recitation the [deceased] acquires firm confidence and perfect power.

Then imagine that all the contaminants of afflictive and cognitive obscurations converge in that same nametag, which is incinerated by fire that burns the three poisons into the three kāyas, fire that burns the five poisons into the five facets of primordial consciousness, and fire that burns the 84,000 mental afflictions into the 84,000 collections of Dharma. Visualize that the remains of [the deceased's rebirths in] saṃsāra merge into absolute space.

By means of such illusion-like yoga, the practices of liberating and guiding, which are like illusory displays, are taught for the sake of realizing the illusion-like nature of all phenomena. The appearance of that which doesn't exist as being existent is like getting angry at your own shadow. By intensely clinging to objects, various phenomena appear in the ocean of the domain of mental phenomena, and you become deluded. For example, however many distinct planets and stars appear in a body of water, in reality they are all displayed by that one body of water. Likewise, observe how all the appearances of saṃsāra and nirvāṇa are embraced by the one ultimate nature of mind.

Regarding actual uniform pervasiveness, there are the uniform pervasiveness of the ground, the uniform pervasiveness of the path, and the uniform pervasiveness of the fruition. First, the ground is imbued with the ultimate nature of mind, the sugatagarbha. Before sentient beings were deluded, it was never contaminated by habitual propensities of faults and stains, [199] so this is the uniform pervasiveness of the ground. Second, even when sentient beings are deluded, they simply fail to see the characteristics of the ground due to the influence of delusion. The ground, which is naturally pure, abides in the nature of the kāyas and great primordial consciousness. This is the uniform pervasiveness of the path. Third, even when you finally achieve buddhahood, the nature of the ground, which has never been contaminated by habitual propensities of faults and stains, becomes manifest; it is not augmented by any new virtues whatsoever. This is like the essential nature of the sun not being affected for better or worse before being obscured by clouds, while it is obscured, or after the clouds have cleared away. Maitreyanātha declared:

> Its nature is immutable,
> the same afterward as it was before.

And the *Ornament of Clear Realization* (*Abhisamayālaṃkāra*) states:

> With no difference before and after,
> suchness is pure.

"The ultimate nature of mind, which is called the *sugatagarbha*, is a uniform pervasiveness uncontaminated by faults. For example, even if it were possible for space to be filled with buddhas, there is uniform pervasiveness in that there is no object that could be benefited by their primordial consciousness and sublime qualities. And even if there were autonomous sentient beings throughout the whole of space, there is uniform pervasiveness in that there is no object that can be harmed by them.

"The ground dharmakāya, the sugatagarbha, has no place, object, or agent of origination, so it is free of the extreme of origination. Since it transcends any time of cessation and any agent that ceases to exist, it is free of the extreme of cessation. Since it is invisible even to the eyes of the jinas due to not falling to the extreme of real existence, it is free of the extreme of permanence. Since it is the universal basis of saṃsāra and nirvāṇa, without being totally nonexistent, it is free of the extreme of nihilism. Because it is beyond all locations, objects, and agents of going, it is free of the extreme of going. Since no location, object, or agent of coming is established as real, it is free of the extreme of coming.

"In the expanse of the ground sugatagarbha, all phenomena of saṃsāra and nirvāṇa appear distinctly and individually; like [reflections of] planets and stars in the ocean, they are free of the extreme of unity. However the modes of saṃsāra and nirvāṇa arise, they are of one taste in the ground sugatagarbha; just as the planets and stars reflected in the ocean are not other

> **than the ocean, this is free of the extreme of diversity. Since it does not fall to any of the eight extremes of conceptual elaboration, its uniform pervasiveness is unsullied by faults."**

Accordingly, the ultimate nature of mind, which is called the *sugatagarbha*, is empty, uncontaminated by faults, [200] and is the uniform pervasiveness of the nature of suchness, which is unstained by faults. Apart from your own awareness, there are no autonomous buddhas whatsoever. Assuming that such buddhas did exist and, for example, it were possible for space to be filled with buddhas, you might think that their primordial consciousness and sublime qualities must improve the ground sugatagarbha. But since there is no object to be benefited, all-pervasive emptiness is unstained by faults.

Apart from your own appearances, there are no autonomous sentient beings whatsoever. Assuming that such sentient beings did exist and it were possible for such autonomous beings to exist throughout space, you might think that their karma, mental afflictions, vices, and obscurations, together with their habitual propensities, would impair the ground sugatagarbha. But since there is no object to be harmed, all-pervasive emptiness is unsullied by faults.

This ground dharmakāya, imbued with the sugatagarbha, is free of the eight extremes of conceptual elaboration and is imbued with the three doors of liberation.

First, this is how it is free of the eight extremes of conceptual elaboration. The glorious protector Ārya Nāgārjuna declared:

> That which dependently arises [201]
> is unceasing and unborn,
> neither annihilated nor permanent,
> free of coming and going,
> neither diverse nor a unity;
> with its teaching on complete freedom from conceptual
> elaboration,
> homage to the sublime medicine
> of the perfectly awakened Buddha!

The ground sugatagarbha is free of all places, objects, and agents of origination.

Does the ground sugatagarbha arise from earth (water, fire, or air)? No. Earth (water, fire, and air) appear as such from the sugatagarbha. Earth (water, fire, and air) are displays of the sugatagarbha. The elements appear as such from the sugatagarbha, and they are its displays, so the sugatagarbha does not arise from the domain of the five outer elements.

If you investigate and analyze any appearing phenomenon, you find that its origination does not exist in the present. To take a flower as an example, it is a mistake to think that its full origination [202] takes place in the present. For those things that have already arisen, their origination is in the past, and for those things that might arise from now on, their origination is in the future. During the interim, origination is not something that occurs in the present. Réchungpa states:

> Past thoughts have ceased and are gone,
> future thoughts have not arisen,
> and the present cannot be ascertained.

Accordingly, the sugatagarbha is a uniform pervasiveness, uncontaminated by faults, that does not fall to the extreme of origination.

The ultimate nature of mind, the sugatagarbha, is beyond the past and beyond agency. Whatever appearing phenomenon you investigate and analyze, you find that its cessation does not take place in the present. To take a flower as an example, it is a mistake to think that the cessation of the flower that has already initially arisen takes place in the present. For those things that have finished arising, their cessation is in the past,[92] and for those things that are still arising, their cessation is in the future. During the interim, their cessation is not something that occurs in the present. Therefore, the sugatagarbha is a uniform pervasiveness, uncontaminated by faults, that is free of cessation.

It is a mistake to think that the ultimate nature of mind, the sugatagarbha, is included among real, existent things. Not falling to the extreme of real existence, [203] it has never been seen, is not seen, and will never be seen with the eyes of the jinas, the perfectly enlightened buddhas, the bhagavāns; so it is a uniform pervasiveness, uncontaminated by faults, that is free of the extreme of permanence.

It is a mistake to think that the ground sugatagarbha is utterly nonexistent. Not being utterly nonexistent, it is the sublime, universal basis of all phenomena included in the world of appearances of saṃsāra and nirvāṇa. So it is a uniform pervasiveness, uncontaminated by faults, that does not fall to the extreme of annihilation. As Vidyādhara Jikmé Lingpa declared:

92. The implication here is that by the time one becomes aware of something that has already arisen, its cessation has already occurred, and for those things that have not yet arisen, their cessation lies in the future.

It is not existent, for it is not seen by the jinas.
It is not nonexistent, for it is the basis of all of saṃsāra and nirvāṇa.

The sugatagarbha is of a nature that transcends all locations, objects, and agents of going. It is a mistake to think that the dharmakāya sugatagarbha goes to the east, south, west, or north. The east, south, west, and north appear as such from the sugatagarbha, and the east, south, west, and north are its displays. As an analogy, even regarding mundane phenomena, going is not something that exists in the present. If you think that when you lift your foot in taking a step, [204] that going occurs in the present, consider that once your foot has pressed on the ground, the going has passed, and the need to go now is a future going. During the interim, going is not something that occurs in the present, so the sugatagarbha is a uniform pervasiveness, uncontaminated by faults, that does not fall to the extreme of going.

The ground sugatagarbha is something that is not established as real in terms of a location, object, or agent of coming. It is a mistake to think that the sugatagarbha comes from the east, south, west, or north, for the east, south, west, and north appear as such from the sugatagarbha, and they are displays of the sugatagarbha. Even with respect to mundane phenomena, if they are investigated and analyzed it is found that coming does not occur in the present. If you think that when you lift your foot in taking a step, that coming occurs in the present, consider that once your foot has pressed on the ground, the coming has passed, and the need to come now is a future coming. During the interim, coming is not something that occurs in the present, so the ground sugatagarbha is a uniform pervasiveness, uncontaminated by faults and free of the extreme of coming.

It is a mistake to think that the dharmakāya, the sugatagarbha, is of the nature of a single entity. In the expanse of the ground sugatagarbha, all the phenomena of the world of appearances [205] of saṃsāra and nirvāṇa arise and are illuminated individually, without being blended together, like the reflections of planets and stars arising in the ocean. So it is a uniform pervasiveness, uncontaminated by faults and free of the extreme of unity.

However vast and numerous the aspects of saṃsāra and nirvāṇa that may arise, they are of one taste in the ground sugatagarbha, just as the reflections of planets and stars in the ocean are not other than the ocean. So the sugatagarbha is a uniform pervasiveness, uncontaminated by faults and free of the extreme of diversity. Therefore, this ultimate nature of mind, the sugatagarbha, is a uniform pervasiveness uncontaminated by faults, which does not fall to any of the eight extremes of conceptual elaboration.

Second, it is endowed with the three doors of liberation:

> **"Further, it is empty in that it transcends the categories of above, below, the cardinal and intermediate directions, intervals, and time. It is empty in that it is all-pervasive and all-encompassing. There is outer emptiness in that all outer appearances cannot be established as bearing substantial characteristics or as being truly existent. There is inner emptiness in that your own inner mind transcends having any ground or root. There is the great uniform pervasiveness of nonexclusive emptiness in that between the outer and inner, there is no dualistic differentiation of the apprehended and the apprehender. This is emptiness as a door of liberation.**
>
> **"The ground dharmakāya, the sugatagarbha, is free of signs that can be expressed in words, it transcends metaphorical approximations, and it is devoid of anything that could be actually demonstrated. This is the absence of signs as a door of liberation.**
>
> **"Regarding ultimate reality, the sugatagarbha, or 'the sugatas of the three times,' the notion that this is a result of merely practicing physical and verbal virtues, and that it entails going to some other realm and being liberated there, is to think that the panoramic sweep of all-pervasive space is an object or agent of coming and going. This is an extremely confused and muddled notion!**
>
> **"What is the path? It is holding your own ground within yourself. What is realization? It is truly knowing your own essential nature and mode of existence. What is liberation? It is simply your own awakening to your own essential nature. It is utterly deluded to grasp at anything else as the state or location of liberation and to strive for that. Ultimately, since there is not even a goal to aspire for, this is the absence of aspiration as a door of liberation."**

Further, [ultimate reality] is something that is empty in that it transcends the categories of above, below, the cardinal and intermediate directions, intervals, and time. Although people grasp at such categories as above, below, and the cardinal and intermediate directions, in reality such categories do not exist. For example, when you ascend to the peak of a mountain to the east, which is named *east*, that eastern mountain is located next to a central mountain. From that point onward, there are eastern mountains. This center that was identified is located next to a western mountain. [206] This likewise applies to all the cardinal and intermediate directions and to above and below. Therefore, all the categories of above, below, and the cardinal and intermediate directions cannot be apprehended [by themselves]. Grasping at that which cannot be apprehended as something that can be apprehended is a case of lying to yourself. The great Orgyen declared:

> Those who grasp at directions where none exist
> ensnare and delude themselves—how sad!

Since emptiness pervades and totally encompasses all of saṃsāra and nirvāṇa, it is empty. All outer appearances are called existent even though they do not exist. In reality, since they cannot be established as bearing substantial characteristics or as being truly existent, there is outer emptiness. Moreover, if your own inner mind is investigated, it is found to be devoid of origination, cessation, and abiding, and it transcends all grounds and roots. So there is inner emptiness. Outer appearances and the inner apprehending mind are merely designated as being different, but the apprehended and the apprehender are not differentiated or established as being dual, so there is a great uniform pervasiveness. Thus, nonexclusive emptiness[93] is emptiness as a door of liberation.

The ground dharmakāya, the sugatagarbha, is not established as bearing the signs of form, shape, or color. [207] It is devoid of articulable signs and is inexpressible by speech or thought. It cannot be illustrated by way of metaphors, and it transcends analogies. It is empty of the substantial reality of any object that can be demonstrated, so this is the absence of signs as a door of liberation.

Ultimate reality, the sugatagarbha, is a sugata of the three times, for it has never been deluded in the past, it does not dwell in delusion in the present, and it will never be deluded in the future. If you think that as a result of merely engaging in physical prostrations and circumambulations, verbal recitations, and the mental cultivation of good thoughts, mind training, mundane dhyānas, and the virtues of samādhi, you will go to some other realm and be liberated there, this notion that the panoramic sweep of all-pervasive space is an object or agent of coming and going is extremely confused and muddled!

93. Tib. *dor ba med pa'i stong pa*; Skt. *anakāraśūnyatā*. Nonexclusive emptiness is one of twenty kinds of emptiness.

Therefore, what is the path? It is holding your own ground within yourself. What is realization? It is first determining with discerning wisdom the nature of all phenomena within the world of appearances of saṃsāra and nirvāṇa, then experiencing the wisdom of realizing identitylessness, and thus knowing ultimate reality [208] as your own essential nature and mode of existence.

What is liberation? It is definitely awakening to your own essential nature, without being transferred to some other realm or hoping for some other place in which to be liberated. It is utterly deluded to grasp at anything else as the state or location of liberation and to strive for that. For these reasons, apart from making a commitment within yourself, the absence of even the aspiration for some other result is the absence of aspiration as a door of liberation.

> **"O my child, Faculty of Pristine Awareness, you will not be liberated merely by my talking and your hearing like this. Investigate and analyze the nature of that which has already been explained. Let experience arise from the depths, stabilize your continuum of conscious awareness, and then teach fortunate people who are suitable vessels. By transferring my Enlightened View Lineage to individuals who practice single-pointedly, there is no doubt that they will soon achieve liberation."**
>
> **Saying this, he disappeared.**

O my child, Faculty of Pristine Awareness, you will not be liberated simply by hearing these explanations of realizing all phenomena within the world of appearances of saṃsāra and nirvāṇa as an equality embraced by a single ultimate nature of mind. By investigating, analyzing, and familiarizing yourself with the mode of existence and nature of being of that which has been explained, experience will arise from the depths of your being. By so doing, experience the four kinds of unshakable confidence[94] regarding the ultimate nature of mind, and correctly reveal this meaning to your fortunate disciples of the family who have a combination of earlier prayers and karmic momentum and who are suitable vessels for gaining mastery of the Dharma of the Great Perfection. [209] If they single-pointedly put this into practice, all the

94. Tib. *gdeng bzhi, gding bzhi.* These four confidences are (1) the confidence that even if one were to have visions of three thousand buddhas, one would not feel the slightest faith in them; (2) the confidence that even if one were surrounded by a hundred thousand māras and murderers, one wouldn't feel even a trace of fear; (3) the confidence of having no hope in the maturation of cause and effect; and (4) the confidence of fearlessness regarding saṃsāra and the miserable states of existence. *See* GD 298.

blessings of the Enlightened View Lineage of Vidyādhara Hūṃchenkāra will be transferred to them, like a *tsatsa*[95] being replicated. Before long, in one lifetime and with one body, they will reach the state of Jina Vajradhara, and they will certainly achieve liberation!

Saying this, he disappeared.

95. Tib. *tsha tsha.* A small, sculptural image of an enlightened being, formed by pressing clay or other substances into a mold.

Teachings of Mañjuśrī, the Lion of Speech

d. Explaining How All Virtues without Exception Are Thoroughly Established as Being of the Nature of Precious, Spontaneously Actualized Displays of the Inner Glow

> **On another occasion when I encountered Mañjuśrī, the Lion of Speech, in a meditative experience of clear light, I asked him, "O Teacher, protector of the world, although I have correctly ascertained how all appearances of the physical world and its sentient inhabitants are nothing other than my own appearances, please reveal to me whether or not the distinct names and pure realms of all the buddhas are established as autonomously existent objects."**
>
> **The teacher replied, "O great being, listen! The qualities of precious spontaneous actualization constitute the inner glow of the ground dharmakāya, the sugatagarbha. With this as the basis, the displays of the buddhafields and the male and female deities, together with their palaces, are naturally perfect in the ground itself—and this perfection is wisdom. Presenting them as existing in other realms is skillful means. The perfection of their sublime qualities in the ground itself is ultimate, while explanations of their existing in other physical worlds with their sentient inhabitants are relative. Moreover, the spontaneous actualization of the ground itself as displays of the kāyas and facets of primordial consciousness is the definitive meaning. All explanations of the buddhafields and the names of male and female deities and so on as entities with real characteristics existing in other realms constitute provisional meanings."**

On another occasion when I encountered Mañjuśrī, the Lion of Speech, in a meditative experience of clear light, I asked him, "O Teacher, protector of the world, although I have truly fathomed how all appearances of the physical world and its sentient inhabitants are nothing other than my own appearances, please reveal to me whether or not the distinct names and pure realms of all the buddhas are established as autonomously existent objects."

The teacher replied, "O great being, listen! [210] The sublime qualities of precious, spontaneous actualization constitute the inner glow of the ground dharmakāya, the sugatagarbha. With this as the basis, the displays of the buddhafields and the male and female deities, together with their palaces, are naturally perfect in the ground itself—and this perfection is wisdom. Presenting them as existing in other realms is skillful means.

"The perfection of all the kāyas and sublime qualities in the ground itself is ultimate, while explanations of their existing in other physical worlds with their sentient inhabitants are relative. Moreover, the spontaneous actualization of the ground sugatagarbha as displays of the kāyas and facets of primordial consciousness is the definitive meaning. All explanations of the buddhafields and the names of male and female deities and so on as entities with real characteristics existing in other realms constitute provisional meanings."

> **"The following are presentations of the ultimate as relative, in accordance with the ways of saṃsāra. Here is how all the jinas are subsumed within the five kāyas: The great ultimate reality of the uncontrived, naturally present existence of all phenomena included in the world of appearances of saṃsāra and nirvāṇa as the ground absolute space, the great emptiness, is called *dharma*. Due to the unimaginable range of dispositions and specific faculties, there is an unimaginable range of entrances to the path, experiences, and goals to be achieved. Their natural presence is called *kāya*.**
>
> **"The natural perfection of the displays of the spontaneously actualized kāyas and facets of primordial consciousness as enjoyments is called *saṃbhogakāya*. The displays of emanations that are none other than the ground, without any mental activity of thinking to send forth emanations, are teacher nirmāṇakāyas, created nirmāṇakāyas, living-being nirmāṇakāyas, and material nirmāṇakāyas. The consciousness that grasps at the self is like a container of water, and the sublime qualities of the absolute space of the sugatagarbha are like the planets and stars in the sky. When these occur simultaneously, emanations as dependently**

related events appear to be of four kinds. In reality, the physical world and its sentient inhabitants are none other than displays of the three kāyas."

The following are presentations of the ultimate as relative, in accordance with the ways of saṃsāra. Generally, both saṃsāra and nirvāṇa arise from the creative power of precious spontaneous actualization, and this is none other than the creative power of the sugatagarbha itself; all of saṃsāra and nirvāṇa consists of nothing other than your own apparitions. Therefore, all teachings that are presented in accordance with the ways of saṃsāra are relative. [211] They are skillful means for leading disciples who grasp at the permanence of the absolute space of ultimate reality—which is free of conceptual elaboration—and who are dependent upon a relative, effortful path. Thus, in terms of the delusive appearances of sentient beings, many avenues arise for accumulating merit. To take prostrations as an example, merely rising up and bending to the ground does not accumulate merit. Rather, positive thoughts of faith, reverence, and admiration involved in the intention to prostrate actually generate a heap of merit, for they are facets of the ground sugatagarbha.

Likewise, regarding circumambulations, virtue is not accumulated by merely lifting and placing your feet in the act of walking; or regarding offering water, by the mere act of filling bowls; or regarding verbal recitations, by the mere act of uttering words. The heartfelt, positive thoughts in all of these are facets of the ground sugatagarbha, so they are the actual virtue.

Similarly, for the accumulation of nonvirtuous karma, for example, (1) the basis, namely the recognition of someone as a sentient being, (2) the intention, namely the arousal of the violent intention to kill, (3) the enactment, [212] namely the performance of the deed with respect to a sentient being, and (4) the culmination, namely the termination of that being's life or taking satisfaction in such a deed, constitute nonvirtue. Likewise, if you dream of accumulating merit, say, in a temple in a dream, and the next day you take satisfaction in thinking you have done so, that is virtue; and the same is true for nonvirtue.

Whatever good and bad thoughts arise, they are all facets of the sugatagarbha, so this is the meaning of virtue and vice and of the variety of appearances of joys and sorrows. Moreover, non-Buddhists also hope for the results of their own practices, and by applying themselves to their own paths, they achieve their respective results. Thus, their own paths are facets of truth and of the sugatagarbha, so it is said that you must not disparage non-Buddhists.

Likewise, Bönpos have adopted teachings similar to Buddhism, and they call them the "great elements."[96] It is said that if you are very diligent, like Bolek Tokden,[97] you achieve the rainbow body by way of twenty-one bindus led by the syllable *A*. Thus it is said that you must not disparage Bönpos either. [213] Similarly, all Buddhist yānas, from the Śrāvakayāna on up, also take the sugatagarbha as their path. Thus, according to people's specific temperaments, capacities, and motivations, they all achieve their own results, so their paths are all true. However, even though they all derive their own paths from the sugatagarbha, none of them see the actual path itself. As an analogy, even though an unimaginable array of beings with various capacities of mouths and stomachs may all drink their own portions of the ocean, never do they gulp down the whole ocean.

The generation of bodhicitta is an inconceivable method of expanding the mind for beginners, so the generation of bodhicitta is very important for them. Even a hundred, a thousand, ten thousand, or a hundred thousand physical and verbal virtues cannot match it. Nevertheless, if emptiness is realized, there is no need to cultivate compassion by some other means. However, most people nowadays say that even if emptiness is realized, compassion must be cultivated by other means. This is like having fire, but saying that you must search for heat elsewhere. For a yogin who has realized emptiness, there is no distinction between the object of compassion [214] and the agent of compassion, for such a person has ascended to the great openness that is devoid of an object. Therefore, such a yogin experiences ultimate bodhicitta. Patching the ground of being with other thoughts is tantamount to the buddhas placing their hopes in sentient beings, so this is a very poor method.

Regarding the teachings of the Buddha, none are the final word. There is an unimaginable array of provisional meanings, definitive meanings, indirect meanings, non-implied meanings, and so on. Although many scholars may write commentaries to a mere four lines of the Buddha's teachings, it is difficult for any of them to realize their actual meaning, just as many sentient beings may drink from the ocean, but none can drink it all down in one gulp. Everything consists of none other than your own appearances and the apparitions of the sugatagarbha.

Mañjuśrī declared:

> Earth is discerned as the life force,
> and water is discerned as the life force.

96. Tib. *khams chen*.

97. Tib. *bo leg rtogs ldan*. A Bönpo master.

Accordingly, some sentient beings regard the earth as the life force, some regard water as the life force, some regard air as the life force, others regard space as the life force, and so on. Now I, as a yogin who has accomplished the practice of taking the vital essence,[98] sustain myself, as it were, by meditating on air, space, and so on as food. [215]

Therefore, with the intention to lead disciples who lack good fortune and who grasp at permanence on the relative, effortful path—using skillful means to guide them to the effortless absolute space of ultimate reality—all the kāyas and facets of primordial consciousness of the ground sugatagarbha are fabricated as having real characteristics. The deities, celestial palaces, and so on to be actualized are fabricated in accordance with the ways of saṃsāra, and all teachings about a pure realm far away called Vaiśālī constitute paths of skillful means.

In this regard, in order to guide people who cling to bloodlines, who are deluded with respect to the lineages of the five great bloodlines of Mutsaga, Achakdru, Apodong, Sekhyungdra, and the two Pa-ngas, who are counted as one, all the jinas are subsumed within and are displayed as the five kāyas. Thus, all phenomena included in the world of appearances of saṃsāra and nirvāṇa consist of all phenomena in the physical world and its sentient inhabitants, in the great expanse of the ground, absolute space, emptiness, free of conceptual elaboration. As an analogy, just as the nature of all the reflections of planets and stars in the ocean is water, and the nature of all physical worlds and their sentient inhabitants is space, all appearances of entities are none other than the nature of the ground. [216] Great ultimate reality, uncontrived and naturally present, is called *dharma*. The natural presence of an unimaginable range of dispositions and specific faculties, entrances to the path, experiences, and goals to be achieved, which are gathered and heaped up, as it were, is called *kāya*.[99]

In the absolute space of the ground sugatagarbha, all the displays of the spontaneous actualization of the kāyas, facets of primordial consciousness, and sublime qualities are naturally perfect as primordial enjoyments in the great ultimate reality of the ground, and they are called *saṃbhoga* [complete enjoyment]. Regarding sentient beings who are obscured by ignorance, karma, and mental afflictions, from the moment that the consciousness that grasps at the self arises, all appearances in the dream state, in the waking state, and in the hereafter, along with all sense qualities of the physical world and

98. Tib. *bcud len grub pa*.

99. This etymologizes "dharmakāya" (Tib. *chos kyi sku*): dharma (*chos*) kāya (*sku*).

its sentient inhabitants, are naturally perfected as enjoyments, without doing anything or effortfully accomplishing anything. Moreover, once enlightenment is achieved, all displays of purity, liberation, spontaneous actualization, kāyas, and facets of primordial consciousness are naturally perfected as enjoyments, without doing anything or effortfully accomplishing anything, so they are called *saṃbhoga*. All qualities of wisdom and primordial consciousness are spontaneously actualized as an aggregate, as it were, so this is called *kāya*.[100] [217]

Emanations from the ground sugatagarbha do not emerge with the mental activity of thinking them forth. Regarding the teacher nirmāṇakāyas, created nirmāṇakāyas, living-being nirmāṇakāyas, and material nirmāṇakāyas, the consciousness that grasps at the self is like a container of water, and the qualities of the absolute space of the sugatagarbha are like the planets and stars in the sky. When they come together, the four kinds of dependently related emanations appear. *Teacher nirmāṇakāyas* are displays of the absolute space of the sugatagarbha, arising like the planets and stars in the sky reflected in the lucid water vessel of your own self-grasping. Now, such nirmāṇakāyas include the guru, or spiritual mentor, who reveals the meaning of the primordial consciousness that is present in your own being. Likewise, this is also the case for realizations arising in dependence upon the written word. The methods and so on for realizing your own nature in dependence upon daytime appearances, nighttime appearances, meditative experiences, and so forth are the self-appearing teachers who appear to you.

Living-being nirmāṇakāyas arise from your own self-grasping thoughts as objective companions, similar in form to yourself as a biped, or like other creatures with many legs or no legs, or as creatures with wings, claws, [218] hooves, horns on their mouths, horns on their heads, and so on. All such continuous appearances as the forms of various creatures that are born, die, go, and come are called *living-being nirmāṇakāyas*.

Created nirmāṇakāyas include paintings and statues as representations of the bodies of enlightened beings, texts as representations of the speech of enlightened beings, and stūpas and so on as representations of the minds of enlightened beings. These are emanations of your own sugatagarbha arising to yourself, and they are called *created nirmāṇakāyas*.

Material nirmāṇakāyas include requisites such as clothing, ornaments, and household goods, as well as an unimaginable array of luxuries that are

100. This etymologizes "saṃbhogakāya" (Tib. *longs spyod rdzogs pa'i sku*): saṃbhoga (*longs spyod rdzogs*) kāya (*sku*).

objects for your use and that arise simply from your own appearances. Such appearing phenomena are called *material nirmāṇakāyas*.

These four kinds of nirmāṇakāyas are self-appearing emanations of the sugatagarbha in the objective expanse of consciousness that grasps at the self. They appear like reflections of planets and stars in water, arising as dependently related events due to the simultaneous confluence of the causes and conditions of a vessel of water and the planets and stars in the sky. Therefore, as long as the space of self-grasping by disciples remains, they arise continuously, [219] just as reflections unpredictably and continuously appear in a lucid, clear pool of water until it dries up. In reality, the physical world and its sentient inhabitants are none other than displays of the three kāyas.

> **"The aspect of its essential nature as emptiness is called *dharmakāya*, the aspect of its nature as spontaneous actualization is called *saṃbhogakāya*, and the aspect of its distinct appearances is called *nirmāṇakāya*. Moreover, the ground itself is the essential nature of all of saṃsāra and nirvāṇa, and in this essential nature everything is of one taste, so it is called *svabhāva*; and because all sublime qualities and facets of primordial consciousness are assembled in an aggregate, as it were, it is called *kāya*.**
>
> **"Since [the ground of being] is unchanging throughout the three times and does not transform into any other essential nature, it is called *immutable*. Since it cannot be injured by anything else, it is called invulnerable. Since it cannot be destroyed by itself or anything else, it is indestructible. Since it is the universal basis of saṃsāra and nirvāṇa, it is real. Since it cannot be contaminated by good or bad qualities, it is incorruptible. Since it is devoid of movement, it is stable. Since it can penetrate even the subtlest cognitive obscurations, it is unobstructable. Since it cannot be overcome by any object or condition, it is invincible.**
>
> **"Thus, the nature of existence of the ultimate, indestructible *vajra* is imbued with four pledges: It is impossible for sentient beings to realize it, apart from those beings who possess the necessary karma and good fortune. Once it has been realized and put into practice, it is impossible for you not to acquire indwelling confidence in it. When confidence is acquired, it is impossible for you not to be liberated. As for the extent of your liberation, it is impossible for you not to become enlightened.**

"The natural presence of these five kāyas in the ground itself is ultimate, while explanations of them as being distinct constitute the relative path of skillful means."

The aspect of its essential nature as emptiness is called *dharmakāya*, the aspect of its nature as spontaneous actualization is called *saṃbhogakāya*, and the aspect of the distinct appearances of all phenomena is called *nirmāṇakāya*. Thus, from this present moment of impure appearances of saṃsāra onward, there are no phenomena that are not included among the body, speech, and mind of all the jinas; and in the infinite expanse of purity, they are primordially awakened.

How is this so? All appearances are perfect in the absolute space of the [jinas'] bodies, their spontaneous actualization is perfect in the absolute space of their speech, and their essential nature is perfect in the absolute space of their minds. Similarly, the desire realm is already primordially pure in the absolute space of the nirmāṇakāya, the form realm is already primordially pure in the absolute space of the saṃbhogakāya, and the formless realm is already primordially pure in the absolute space of the dharmakāya. Likewise, the ground itself is the essential nature of all of saṃsāra and nirvāṇa, and in this essential nature everything is of one taste, so it is called *svabhāva*. Moreover, this great self[101] that embodies the essence of the nonconceptual primordial consciousness of ultimate reality and all the sugatas [220] is the essential nature of the absolute space of the one taste as the essential nature of all of saṃsāra and nirvāṇa. In the absolute space of that essential nature, all facets of primordial consciousness and sublime qualities are assembled as an aggregate, as it were, so it is called *kāya*.[102]

Likewise, since [the ground of being] is unchanging throughout the three times and does not transform into any other essential nature, it is called the *immutable* vajra. Since the ground sugatagarbha is unmoving and unchanging throughout the three times and does not turn into anything good or bad, it is immutable. Since it is indestructible and is imbued with the seven vajra qualities, it is called *vajra*. Moreover, it is invulnerable to all mental afflictions, karma, and habitual propensities of mental afflictions. It can never be destroyed by objects or conditions. Since it is the great, primordial ground of all of saṃsāra and nirvāṇa, with its essential nature being eternally pure, it is real. Since it cannot be contaminated by any good or bad qualities, it is

101. Tib. *bdag nyid chen po*; Skt. *mahātmā*.

102. This etymologizes "svabhāvikakāya" (Tib. *ngo bo nyid kyi sku*): svabhāva (*ngo bo nyid*) kāya (*sku*).

incorruptible. Since it is devoid of movement in space and change in time, it is stable. Since it is ultimate reality that can penetrate the absolute space that transcends the causal influences of even the subtlest cognitive obscurations, it is totally unobstructable. Since it cannot be changed by anything in saṃsāra or nirvāṇa, [221] it is invincible to everything. So it is imbued with these seven vajra qualities.

For example, relative, material vajras are also said to have four vajra pledges, but they could never be thrown as hand implements of gods such as Brahmā and Indra. If they were thrown, they would never hit their target, and even if they did, they would never cut through it. While anything that can be severed cannot possibly be immortal, the ultimate, indestructible vajra is indeed imbued with four pledges.[103] What are they? (1) Realization of the ultimate nature of existence and all modes of being depends on whether fortunate beings have suitable prayers from the past conjoined with karmic momentum. Without them, it is impossible for any kind of sentient being to realize the meaning of this. (2) Once it has been realized and put into practice, it is impossible for you not to acquire indwelling confidence in saṃsāra and nirvāṇa as displays of the equality [of the ground]. (3) When you acquire the degree of warmth of the four kinds of confidence, it is impossible for you not to be liberated in the absolute space of equality of the three kāyas. (4) As for the extent of your liberation, it is impossible for you not to become enlightened as the inwardly illuminated youthful vase *kāya*. Thus, since it is imbued with these four vajra pledges, it is called the *immutable vajrakāya*.[104]

In reality, teachings about these five kāyas as being naturally present [222] as nothing but the ground are ultimate, while discussions of them as existing separately somewhere else as kāyas, pure realms, and so on are relative, provisional meanings that constitute paths of skillful means.

> **"In accordance with beings' obsessions with families, here is the basis for speaking of the families of deities: Since the ground of being is such that the defilements of habitual propensities are cleansed in absolute space, it is said to be *cleansed*. Since the facets of primordial consciousness and sublime qualities are naturally fulfilled, it is said to be *fulfilled*. Since it is imbued with the seven vajra qualities, it is called the *vajra family*. Since it is the origin of all kāyas and facets of primordial**

103. Tib. *dam bca' bzhi.* See also VE 189.

104. This etymologizes "immutable vajrakāya" (Tib. *mi 'gyur rdo rje sku*): immutable (*mi 'gyur*) vajra (*rdo rje*) kāya (*sku*).

> **consciousness, it is called the *jewel family*. Since it is not sullied by faults or defilements, it is called the *lotus family*. Since it thoroughly accomplishes enlightened activities, it is called the *karma family*. The term *family* refers to the respective associations embraced by each one."**

[The following explanations are given] due to people's obsessions with castes: A lord of one hundred thousand cities or more is said to be of a royal caste. A lord of ten thousand cities or more is said to be of a noble caste. Those who belong to worker families are said to be of a commoner caste. Those who engage in pure conduct, eat pure food, and have virtuous attitudes are said to be of a priestly caste. Those who live on flesh and blood and engage in negative conduct are said to be of an untouchable caste. Discussions of families regarding deities are presented to guide people by turning them away from their obsessions with those five castes.

In the essential nature of the ground of being, since the defilements of habitual propensities of ignorance of the great absolute space of the one taste of the nonduality of all the jinas of the three times are cleansed in absolute space, [the ground] is said to be *cleansed*. Since the facets of primordial consciousness and sublime qualities are naturally fulfilled, it is said to be *fulfilled*. The various displays of emanations from its essential nature are called *family*.[105] Likewise, since the ground of being is imbued with the seven vajra qualities, [223] which cannot be destroyed by anything, it is called *vajra*. The various displays of emanations from its indestructible, vajra-like nature are called the *vajra family*.[106]

As for the jewel family, just as a wish-fulfilling jewel is priceless due to its granting one's every desire, so all the kāyas, facets of primordial consciousness, and sublime qualities of the path and fruition of the ground sugatagarbha, the source of the unimaginable array of entrances to the path, are presented in accordance with the mentalities of individual disciples. This is why it is called the *jewel family*.[107]

Likewise, just as a lotus flower grows from the mud without being fouled by it, the ground sugatagarbha is uncontaminated by the defilements of the

105. This etymologizes "buddha family" (Tib. *sangs rgyas rigs*): cleansed (*sangs*), fulfilled (*rgyas*) family (*rigs*).

106. This etymologizes "vajra family" (Tib. *rdo rje'i rigs*): vajra (*rdo rje*) family (*rigs*).

107. This etymologizes "jewel family" (Tib. *rin chen rigs*): jewel (*rin chen*) family (*rigs*).

three worlds, so it is called the *lotus family*.[108] In the very nature of the ground sugatagarbha, all actions are accomplished without anything being done and without effort, so it is called the *karma family*.[109] Thus, teachings on the natural perfection of all the families without their being separate from the ground are ultimate, and teachings on their being fabricated as various families are relative and provisional.

The word *family* refers to everyone who comes under the jurisdiction of one who is called a great king, [224] and to everyone who belongs to a family bloodline.

> **"The following are teachings on the five buddhafields, presented in accordance with people's obsessions with land: Ghanavyūha [Compact Display] is so called because of the spontaneously actualized, compact density of sublime qualities in the absolute space of the ground. Abhirati [Higher Joy] is so called because it is imbued with great joy that is not created by any object, condition, or agent. Śrīmat [Endowed with Glory] is so called because it is imbued with a glorious bounty of facets of primordial consciousness and sublime qualities. Sukhāvatī [Land of Bliss] is so called because it is imbued with the taintless primordial consciousness of bliss and emptiness. Karmaprasiddhi [Perfection of Excellent Deeds] is so called because it brings to perfection all actions of purification and liberation.**
>
> **"The term *field* refers to absolute space, and the term *realm* indicates that it is none other than that absolute space."**

Likewise, in order to counteract people's obsessions with land and to guide them, these are teachings on the five buddhafields of the deities. The buddhafield of Ghanavyūha[110] is so called because of the spontaneously actualized, compact density and the innumerable and limitless sublime qualities in the absolute space of the ground sugatagarbha. The buddhafield of Abhirati[111] is so called because in the lucid, luminous absolute space of the ground, free of

108. This etymologizes "lotus family" (Tib. *pad ma rigs*): lotus (*padma*) family (*rigs*).

109. This etymologizes "karma family" (Tib. *las rigs*): karma (*las*) family (*rigs*).

110. Tib. *stug po bkod pa*. Lit. "Compact Display," this is the buddhafield of Vairocana in the central direction.

111. Tib. *mngon par dga' ba*. Lit. "Higher Joy," this is the buddhafield of Akṣobhya in the eastern direction.

contamination, it is imbued with great joy that is not created by any object, condition, or agent. The buddhafield of Śrīmat[112] is so called because it is imbued with a glorious bounty of all facets of primordial consciousness, sublime qualities, and Dharmas of the path and fruition, which are naturally present in the ground. The buddhafield of Sukhāvatī[113] is so called because ultimate reality, the absolute space of the ground, is of the nature of great bliss and is imbued with the taintless primordial consciousness of bliss and emptiness. The buddhafield of Karmaprasiddhi[114] is so called because of the primordial consciousness of purification and liberation in the ground itself, [225] and because it effortlessly and spontaneously brings to perfection all virtuous actions.

The term *field* refers to pristine absolute space, and the term *realm* refers to all facets of primordial consciousness and sublime qualities that are none other than absolute space.[115]

In order to counteract people's obsessions with houses and to guide them, the following are teachings concerning the deities having palaces.

> **"Since the sublime qualities of the ground cannot be measured, it is called *immeasurable*, and since it fills all of saṃsāra and nirvāṇa, it is called a *palace*."**

Since the facets of primordial consciousness and sublime qualities of the ground cannot be measured, and since it is beyond the scope of the intellect, it is said to be *immeasurable*. Since the ground fills and pervades all of saṃsāra and nirvāṇa, it is called a *palace*.[116] In order to counteract people's obsessions with the male gender and to guide them, the deities are also said to have male gender.

> **"When the natural glow of the omnipresent absolute space of the ground is made manifest by all-pervasive great wisdom, all**

112. Tib. *dpal dang ldan pa*. Lit. "Endowed with Glory," this is the buddhafield of Ratnasaṃbhava in the southern direction.

113. Tib. *bde ba can*. Lit. "Land of Bliss," this is the buddhafield of Amitābha in the western direction.

114. Tib. *las rab rdzogs pa*. Lit. "Perfection of Excellent Deeds," this is the buddhafield of Amoghasiddhi in the northern direction.

115. This etymologizes "buddhafield" (Tib. *zhing khams*): field (*zhing*), realm (*khams*).

116. This etymologizes "immeasurable [or celestial] palace" (Tib. *gzhal yas khang*): immeasurable (*gzhal yas*) palace (*khang*).

> **the facets of primordial consciousness and sublime qualities of the domain of the ground sugatagarbha are illuminated. Because [the ground] is imbued with the seven indestructible vajra qualities and is free of wavering and movement throughout the three times, it is an immutable vajra. Because it is the source of all the dharmas of the path and fruition, and because it is imbued with a bounty of sublime qualities, it is called a source of jewels. The illumination of the ground is limitless, so it is boundless illumination. Since all authentic aims naturally emerge within it, it is said to accomplish aims."**

When the hidden, natural glow and all the kāyas, facets of primordial consciousness, and sublime qualities of the omnipresent absolute space of the ground are made manifest by pervasive, all-seeing great wisdom, all the aspects of the facets of primordial consciousness and sublime qualities of the domain of the ground sugatagarbha are *illuminated*, so it is known as Vairocana.[117]

Because the ground itself is a great reality imbued with the seven indestructible vajra qualities and [226] is free of wavering and *immovable* in the three times of the past, present, and future, it is called Akṣobhyavajra.[118]

Likewise, ultimately, the absolute space of the ground, the great treasure expanse of precious, spontaneously actualized kāyas and facets of primordial consciousness, is called *ratna* [jewel]. Because it is the *source* of all the dharmas of the kāyas, primordial consciousness, and the path and fruition, and because it is imbued with a bounty of sublime qualities, it is called Ratnasaṃbhava.[119]

The immeasurable and *boundless* light of the ground *illuminates* the displays of the kāyas and facets of primordial consciousness and is therefore called Amitābha.[120]

Likewise, since the meaning of all authentic dharmas is naturally present in

117. This etymologizes "Vairocana" (Tib. *rnam par snang mdzad*): illuminator (*rnam par snang mdzad*).

118. This etymologizes "Akṣobhyavajra" (Tib. *mi bskyod rdo rje*): immovable (*mi bskyod*) vajra (*rdo rje*).

119. This etymologizes "Ratnasaṃbhava" (Tib. *rin chen 'byung gnas*): jewel (*rin chen*) source (*'byung gnas*).

120. This etymologizes "Amitābha" (Tib. *snang ba mtha' yas*): illumination (*snang ba*), boundless (*mtha' yas*).

the absolute space of the ground, it is imbued with *meaning*; and since it thoroughly *accomplishes* all enlightened activities, it is called Amoghasiddhi.[121]

In order to counteract people's obsessions with the female gender and to guide them, the deities are also presented as ḍākinīs as follows:

> **"Since all phenomena of saṃsāra and nirvāṇa appear in the manner of coming and going in the true vajra, the space of emptiness, this is called Vajraḍākinī. The self-emergent aspect of all the facets of primordial consciousness and sublime qualities, which are like a treasury of jewels, is Ratnaḍākinī. The aspect of freedom from all attachments is Padmaḍākinī. The self-emergence of actions of the spontaneously actualized kāyas and facets of primordial consciousness—not performed with deeds or accomplished with effort—is Karmaḍākinī. Since the afflictive and cognitive obscurations are cleansed in the absolute space of phenomena, and the facets of primordial consciousness and sublime qualities are naturally brought to fulfillment, it is called Buddha; and since all phenomena of saṃsāra and nirvāṇa appear in the aspects of coming and going in the expanse of the space of great emptiness, it is called ḍākinī."**

Since the great absolute space of ultimate emptiness is imbued with the seven indestructible vajra qualities, it is called vajra; and since all phenomena of saṃsāra and nirvāṇa appear as if they were expressions of going and coming in the space of the great uniform pervasiveness of ultimate reality, it is called Vajraḍākinī. For example, just as all of one's many desires [227] are naturally fulfilled by a treasury of jewels, so Ratnaḍākinī is the self-emergent, effortless aspect of the spontaneously actualized kāyas, facets of primordial consciousness, and sublime qualities in the absolute space of the great uniform pervasiveness of the ground. Just as a lotus flower is unstained by mud, so the ground sugatagarbha is untainted by the qualities of attachment and is free of all faults. This aspect is called Padma, and since it appears as many entrances of skillful means from the power of compassion in the space of ultimate reality, it is called Padmaḍākinī. All sublime qualities of the ground, spontaneously actualized kāyas, facets of primordial consciousness, and so on primordially emerge of themselves in the ultimate reality of the ground of being itself, without needing to be performed with deeds or accomplished with

121. This etymologizes "Amoghasiddhi" (Tib. *don yod grub pa*): meaning (*don yod*) accomplishes (*grub pa*).

effort. This aspect is Karmaḍākinī. In the nature of the ground sugatagarbha, the stains of afflictive and cognitive obscurations are cleansed in absolute space without its ever being defiled by them, so it is called *cleansed*; and the natural fulfillment of all the kāyas, facets of primordial consciousness, and sublime qualities is called *fulfilled*. Since all the phenomena of saṃsāra and nirvāṇa appear in the aspects of going and coming in emptiness, the expanse of the space of Buddhaḍākinī, it is called Buddhaḍākinī.

Therefore, references to the bodily aspects of faces, arms, body colors, and individual locations in the center and cardinal directions [228] are relative, provisional meanings. Like fire and heat, water and moisture, air and coolness, and gold and its sheen, the kāyas and facets of primordial consciousness are complete in the ground of being itself. Nevertheless, discussions of the dharmakāya being present as the great sole bindu, devoid of the symbols of faces and arms, constitute the ultimate, definitive meaning. Moreover, all the sublime qualities that appear in sets of five are merely nominally expressed in words, but their lack of real existence is ultimate. The appearance of space as the nature of space constitutes skillful means and relative truth, while the experience of space as inherently unreal is ultimate and is wisdom.

Then, to summarize skillful means and wisdom:

> **"Thus, the manifestation of the ground dharmakāya, the sugatagarbha, the great reality that totally pervades saṃsāra and nirvāṇa, is the ground pristine awareness, which is the great freedom from extremes; and all ultimate sādhanas are synthesized as follows:"**

Ultimate truth is the realization of pristine awareness, the sugatagarbha; and apart from this, faces and arms are not established as having their own defining characteristics, their names have no referents, and the dharmakāya is devoid of signs. The realization of its nature alone subsumes all the ultimate *sādhanas*, which are perfected here. Nevertheless, as skillful means to lead disciples who grasp at the permanence of the absolute space of ultimate reality—which is free of conceptual elaboration—by following relative, effortful paths in accordance with the ways of saṃsāra, [229] teachings are given that present the displays of the supporting maṇḍalas and the beings who are supported by them as if their names and existence were real.

First of all, going for refuge is as follows:

> **"Self-mastery—through your conviction that the ground pristine awareness is the synthesis of all the [Three] Jewels—is the**

> **ultimate, unsurpassed, real taking of refuge in the nature of existence."**

Ultimately, at the culmination of accurately knowing and realizing all the modes of existence and the nature of being of the primordial ground sugatagarbha, you come to a firm conviction within yourself that your own pristine awareness has never been anything other than a display of the kāyas and facets of primordial consciousness. This pristine awareness of gaining mastery over the ground of being is the essential nature that synthesizes all the Jewels. How so? The empty essential nature of pristine awareness is the dharmakāya, its luminous nature is the saṃbhogakāya, and its all-pervasive compassion is the nirmāṇakāya. Therefore, it is the synthesis of all the three kāyas.

It has never been defiled by any karma, mental afflictions, or habitual propensities, so it is awakened. All the kāyas, facets of primordial consciousness, and sublime qualities are naturally present in it, so it is full. Hence it is Buddha. The natural radiance of pristine awareness as the kāyas and spontaneously actualized displays is the Dharma, and the aspiration for the indivisibility of the spontaneously actualized displays and the sugatagarbha is the Saṅgha. So all the [Three] Jewels are synthesized.

The guru is so called due to being the basis for establishing saṃsāra and nirvāṇa [230] and being the culmination of all phenomena to be realized. Your conviction that the ground of being is none other than the nature [of the guru] is your personal deity. The presence of all of saṃsāra and nirvāṇa in the space of ultimate reality, without going or coming, is the ḍākinī. So this is the synthesis of the Three Roots. As it is written:

> The mind that is devoid of achieving purity is Buddha,
> immutable stainlessness is Dharma,
> and the spontaneous perfection of sublime qualities is the
> Saṅgha;
> so the ultimate nature of your own mind is supreme.

Vidyādhara Jikmé Lingpa wrote:

> This unmodified, self-emergent pristine awareness
> is unrecognized as the essential nature of all the objects of refuge.

Never letting such pristine awareness be separated, even for an instant, from the nature of primordial consciousness is said to be the unsurpassed, real going for refuge in the nature of existence. It is free of anyone who goes for refuge and from all that provides refuge. In place of that, in accordance with the ways of saṃsāra, once you have taken refuge with a king, wherever you stay in his kingdom, no one is allowed to harm you. Likewise, once you have gone for refuge in the Three Jewels, obstructive beings and interferences will not arise.

Thus, at the outset visualize in the space in front of you the glorious Youthful Vajra surrounded by jinas and *jinaputras*. [231] Light emanates from his three places, inviting deities like himself from absolute space, who then dissolve into him. Imagine yourself being surrounded by all sentient beings, principally your own parents, malevolent spirits, obstructive beings, and so forth. Assemblies of deities face all these sentient beings, including yourself; they witness you with their eyes and hold you in mind with great affection, and you ask them to remain. Visualizing them in front of you, you and all sentient beings bow to them reverently with your bodies, reverently chant the words of going for refuge with your voices, and with your minds reverently go for refuge with a sense of utter trust in their total awareness of all you do. This is merely relative.

Regarding the generation of bodhicitta:

> **"Throughout the course of beginningless lifetimes, you have grasped at true existence and have fixated on objects, causing you to become very small minded. Now, having come to a decisive understanding of saṃsāra and nirvāṇa as continuous displays of the one pristine awareness, the scope of your mind is expanded. This is the most sublime of all methods for generating bodhicitta."**

Ultimately, over the course of beginningless lifetimes, that which is called your *mind* has focused on yourself alone. Due to grasping at the "I," you have deceived yourself by reifying the distinction between yourself and others and fixating on objects, deluding yourself about them. As a result of such reification, you have become very small minded, and under the influence of minor circumstances you have clung to all manner of joys, miseries, and indifferent feelings. This continuous stream of desires and cravings is called the *mind*. When you realize ungenerated, [232] precious bodhicitta of the nature of being, which is the dharmakāya, pristine awareness that is present in the ground, you will realize all of saṃsāra and nirvāṇa as continuous displays of the one pristine awareness, and you will experience absolute space that is devoid of activity and free of conceptual elaboration. Having come to a decisive recognition of all that appears as displays of the dharmakāya, the scope of your mind is expanded, such that all of saṃsāra and nirvāṇa arises as great displays of bodhicitta. This is the fruition of all methods for generating bodhicitta, and it is the most sublime of all dharmas.

At the outset, determining with discerning wisdom the nature of being of all of saṃsāra and nirvāṇa is *aspirational bodhicitta*, and in the end, the realization of saṃsāra and nirvāṇa as displays of perfection is called *engaged bodhicitta*. In the place of that, the pledge to serve the needs of sentient beings by aspiring to free all beings of the three realms from the ocean of suffering of conditioned existence with compassion, loving-kindness, empathetic joy, equanimity, and so forth is *aspirational bodhicitta*. Focusing on the welfare of all sentient beings and then applying yourself to the six perfections and to steadfastly practicing the profound methods of meditating on deities and reciting mantras [233] is called the *cultivation of engaged bodhicitta*.

Regarding expelling obstructive beings:

> **"The dualistic mind that grasps at the apprehender and the apprehended is the great demon of conditioned existence that causes you to wander among the three realms of saṃsāra. With discerning wisdom, expel this into emptiness devoid of objects."**

The malevolent, obstructive spirit that obscures your own face of ultimate reality, or suchness, is the great demon of grasping at the "I" throughout the three realms of saṃsāra. All the positive thoughts that derive from this are the divine spirits of the positive side of conditioned existence, and all the negative thoughts are the vicious, demonic spirits of the negative side of existence. Subtle configurations of discursive thoughts move about like obstructive beings who are masters and mistresses of adversity. Determine with discerning wisdom that great, middling, and minor demonic spirits have no real existence apart from such thoughts, and then expel them into emptiness devoid of objects. This is ultimate.

In place of that, imagine emanating tormas as ransom to the assemblies of obstructive spirits who interfere with your achieving enlightenment. With the samādhi of displaying apparitions of ultimate reality, visualize these tormas as an inconceivable bounty of pleasures of the victorious gods of Tuṣita; and imagine the obstructive spirits being satisfied with your offering and returning to their own abodes. As for all those spirits who still do not obey your command, imagine yourself in the form of the Great Glorious One [Heruka], emanating many ferocious weapons and flames from your body

[234] and expelling the spirits into the darkness of a realm on the far side of the great ocean. Imagining that their own appearances shift and that they are all in their own abodes is merely relative.

Regarding the protective tent:

> **"The experience of the wisdom that realizes identitylessness is the wheel of protection of bodhicitta, which cannot be vanquished or destroyed."**

Ultimately, as a result of experiencing the wisdom that realizes identitylessness and of recognizing all of saṃsāra and nirvāṇa as the play of bodhicitta, you decisively understand that all who inflict harm and all who are harmed have never been established as real. This is the wheel of protection of bodhicitta, which cannot be vanquished or destroyed, and it is the ultimate, primordial protective tent. All inflictors of harm are released right where they are, and are banished into nonobjectivity.

In place of that, withdraw all the ferocious weapons and flames that had been emanated outward and transform them into a wheel of protection, including vajras, wheels, jewels, lotuses, swastikas, volcanoes, and so forth. Visualize yourself and others to be protected as deities inside the wheel, and imagine that no demonic or obstructive beings can harm you. This is merely relative.

Regarding the descent of blessings:

> **"The descent of the great blessing of primordial consciousness, pristine awareness, into the darkness of ignorance constitutes the actual descent of blessings."**

Once you have determined the nature of all impure, delusive appearances and mindsets [235] and have experienced the nature of existence and mode of being of the ground, the darkness of ignorance is dispelled regarding the ground of being, and you gain mastery over great primordial consciousness, pristine awareness. This constitutes the actual descent of blessings.

In place of that, with heartfelt faith and reverence imagine rays of light emitted from your heart, arousing the mindstreams of the jinas and jinaputras and drawing forth their physical kāyas from the absolute space of phenomena. All empowerments, blessings, and siddhis appear as subtle symbols of their bodies manifesting as five-colored mounds of light, like a mass of clouds and rainbows. Their speech appears as various seed syllables, and their minds take on the aspects of various hand implements. They all dissolve into the practice substances and life necessities of your own abode, which you visualize as the actual, self-appearing, great Akaniṣṭha. Imagine your dwelling as a palace composed of the five facets of primordial consciousness, your practice substances as the ambrosia of primordial consciousness, and the body, speech, and mind of the practitioners as being blessed as the nature of the three vajras. This is merely relative.

Regarding the blessing of the offering substances:

> **"With the realization of how appearances arise as ornaments of pristine awareness, the arrays of naturally occurring sensory experiences become offerings."**

The ultimate is the self-emergent manifestation of the spontaneously actualized dharmakāya, absolute space, free of the extremes of conceptual elaboration, arising as displays of the kāyas and facets of primordial consciousness. [236] With the authentic realization of how all phenomena arise as ornaments of pristine awareness, great primordial consciousness, you recognize the appearances of all self-emergent sensory experiences as uncreated, primordially presented offerings.

In place of that, with the great primordial consciousness of the three kāyas, seal the self-emergent appearances of sensory experiences arising as sensory objects of deluded sentient beings. Then, in all the maṇḍalas of self-appearing primordial consciousness, emanate great clouds and oceans of offerings of the seven outer offerings, the five inner offerings of sensory objects, the secret offerings of medicine, tormas, and blood, and the very secret offerings of union and liberation, as well as the offering of suchness. Imagining the emanation of inexhaustible sensory objects as an unimpeded flow of displays of ornamental wheels of the nature of the elements is relative.

First, the main practice of generating deities is as follows:

> **"The transformation of the substrate into the dharmakāya is the enlightenment of the primordial ground of being. The actualization of the wisdom that knows the nature of existence [of that ground] just as it is, along with the all-knowing and all-illuminating wisdom that perceives the full range [of phenomena], is the synthesis of the mysteries of all the jinas and jinaputras.**
>
> **"The assembly of haughty guardians of the teachings represents the path of skillful means for your initial realization; the array of bodhisattvas represents the path of skillful means for the mastery of the eighth bodhisattva ground and higher;**

and the array of buddhas and buddhafields represents the path of skillful means for manifest buddhahood.

"Explanations of the ignorance of the substrate as Maheśvara and of all the configurations of thoughts that arise from it as the eight classes of guardians of the teachings, dharmapālas, gods, and demons are expressions of skillful means.

"The appearances of creative expressions of great primordial consciousness emerging of themselves from the manifestation of the dharmakāya, the primordial ground of being, are classified and presented as paths of skillful means, and the manifestation of ultimate buddhahood is the sādhana. All sādhanas and maṇḍalas are synthesized and perfected in this."

Having transformed the substrate into the dharmakāya, the authentic actualization of the Buddha Samantabhadra—who is of the nature of the four kāyas and the five facets of primordial consciousness—is the wisdom that knows reality as it is. The unimpeded knowledge of all-illuminating, unimpeded consciousness that is [237] all-knowing and all-cognizing is the great wisdom that perceives the full range of phenomena. The experience of the great primordial consciousness that knows reality as it is and perceives the full range of phenomena is the synthesis of the mysteries of all the jinas and jinaputras, and this is the real, profound sādhana.

Not realizing that, sentient beings reify the delusive appearances of thoughts as autonomously existent objects that arise in the aspects of apparitions of the three kinds of vicious grahas, demons, and *rākṣasas*.[122] They also become deluded by grasping at other assemblies of haughty guardians of the teachings as being autonomously existent. Individuals who have slightly identified and realized pristine awareness know and realize that the apparitions of the three kinds of vicious grahas and their attendants are merely creative expressions of their own three poisons and have no autonomous existence of their own. They know that the guardians of the teachings and dharmapālas are nothing other than creative expressions of pristine awareness; and due to seeing how the basis of accomplishment is completely present in themselves, they do not go astray by regarding it as autonomously existent.

Simply by reaching the eighth bodhisattva ground, you achieve extraordinary, sublime qualities through the transformation of your faculties: impure appearances cease by themselves, all appearing objects are perceived as buddhafields, and all appearing forms are perceived to be of the nature of [238] male and female bodhisattvas. From the time that you gain mastery of the

122. Tib. *srin po*. Wrathful emanations of good thoughts induced by ego-grasping.

three pure bodhisattva grounds, there is the distinction that the eight groups of [conceptualizations arising from] the substrate appear as sublime qualities that are transmuted into primordial consciousness. At the end of the continuum of the tenth bodhisattva ground, the obscurations of habitual propensities are overcome by the antidote of the vajra-like samādhi, and you become enlightened in the eleventh ground of Omnipresent Light. Then, on the twelfth ground of the Lotus of Detachment, the thirteenth ground of the Holder of the Vajra, and so on, the experiences of the sublime qualities of enlightenment are said to be the state of buddhahood. Moreover, teachings that the arrays of pure lands and buddhafields appear to be adorned with the signs and symbols of a buddha's body and teachings that the teacher and his circle of disciples exist as different from each other represent the path of skillful means.

To explain this in a little more detail, the assemblies of nāgas, grahas, and kṣamāpatis emerge from the creative power of delusion. The assemblies of male grahas and pārthivas emerge from the creative power of hatred. The assemblies of female grahas and female demonesses emerge from the creative power of attachment. The ancient, primal demons, including the eighteen great principal grahas, the fifteen great minor grahas, the mother hāriṇī and her five hundred sons, [239] and so on, emerge from the creative power of the 84,000 mental afflictions in the forms of adventitiously assembled minor demons.

Likewise, regarding the dharmapālas, teachings about the appearances of displays of principal deities and their retinues—including Maheśvara as the nature of ignorance of the substrate, the emptiness and luminosity of the substrate consciousness as the assembly of the female lineages, the eight collections [of consciousness] as the eight classes [of guardians of the teachings], afflictive mentation as the planets, and mentation as yakṣas—are just expressions of skillful means, for they all lack autonomous existence. Thus, by practicing such that the basis of accomplishment is present within yourself, accomplishments also arise due to this vital point.

Here is how there is no contradiction in the bodhisattvas being merely nominally imputed, while having no autonomous, objective existence. Regarding the name Mañjughoṣa, since the ground sugatagarbha is free of all the roughness of mental afflictions, it is called *gentle*; since it is imbued with the glory of the spontaneously actualized kāyas and facets of primordial consciousness, it is called *glorious*; and since enlightened speech is imbued with sixty qualities, it is called *melody*.[123] Likewise, regarding Avalokiteśvara, because of the manifestation of omniscient primordial consciousness, it is

123. This etymologizes "Mañjughoṣa" (Tib. *'jam dpal dbyangs*): gentle (*'jam*), glorious (*dpal*) melody (*dbyangs*).

called *eye*; because great, all-seeing primordial consciousness is devoid of partiality and because it luminously perceives all phenomena without attachment, obstruction, or confusion, it is called *seeing*.[124] [240] Likewise, because one has achieved *great power*, *holding* the power of liberating all impure appearances and mindsets into pure states is called Mahāsthāmaprāpta.[125] Such expressions are ultimate, and references to them as existing otherwise are relative expressions of skillful means.

In short, classifications of appearances as creative expressions of the great, self-emergent primordial consciousness of the buddhas, who actualize the great dharmakāya of the primordial ground, are merely artificial expressions of the path of skillful means. Ultimately, by recognizing the nature of existence and mode of being of the ground, you finally come to a conviction within yourself, and you do not digress from this manifest state. This is the actual, profound sādhana, and all sādhanas and maṇḍalas are synthesized and perfected in it.

Now, instead of those, for the main practice, before meditating on the supporting buddhafield and palace and on the deities who reside there, the impure karmic eon must be dissolved into absolute space and brought forth as pure appearances of primordial consciousness deities. For example, dream appearances and waking appearances do not both appear simultaneously, nor can the human realm and hell realm possibly manifest at the same time. Likewise, [241] the impure appearances of saṃsāra and the buddhafields of primordial consciousness deities cannot possibly exist simultaneously.

So first, imagine that the phenomenal physical worlds, the animate sentient beings who inhabit them, and the appearances of the five sensory objects all dissolve into absolute space as illusory apparitions dissolving into the nature of emptiness. The manifestation of this mode of existence of suchness, ultimate reality, is called the *samādhi of suchness*. Those who do not know the nature and mode of being of emptiness merely impose some kind of emptiness upon that which is not empty, and they do not directly experience the samādhi of suchness. The actual samādhi of suchness is experienced only by yogins who have realized the view of emptiness.

Once again, with the manifestation of the mode of being of the ground—great, all-pervasive primordial consciousness—all the phenomena of saṃsāra and nirvāṇa manifest as displays of great spontaneous actualization, like planets and stars in the ocean. This manifestation of everything

124. This etymologizes "Avalokiteśvara" (Tib. *spyan ras gzigs*): eye (*spyan*) seeing (*gzigs*).

125. This etymologizes "Mahāsthāmaprāpta" (Tib. *mthu chen thob*): great power (*mthu chen*) holding (*thob*).

is called the *all-illuminating samādhi*. This is in the realm of experience only of those yogins who have identified the dharmakāya, pristine awareness that is present in the ground, [242] and of no one else. Others' cultivation of compassion with sentient beings as the object or with no object by means of the intellect and mentation entails an object and cogitation, and the all-illuminating samādhi does not manifest. So recognize that one is merely a substitute for the other.

Regarding the *causal samādhi*, in an instant, like rainbows suddenly appearing in the sky where none existed previously, and like planets and stars suddenly appearing in a pool of water where none existed before, from the absolute space of all-pervasive ultimate reality, free of conceptual elaboration, visualize your awareness as the causal syllable *Oṃ*, white and blazing with light and rays of light. This is the cause for the emanation of the nature of all foundational [maṇḍalas] and those who reside in them.

Thus, the authentic revelation of the samādhi of suchness and the all-illuminating samādhi transcends the intellect, mentation, and conceptual objects, and it is the primordial consciousness of emptiness and of pristine awareness. Causal samādhi consists of apparitions involving objects [the five elements] and luminosity [of their seed syllables].[126]

From the visualized causal, dark-blue syllable *Hūṃ*, the syllables *Eḥ*, *Yaṃḥ*, *Baṃḥ*, *Laṃḥ*, and *Raṃḥ* are emitted, symbolizing the five purified elements. *Eḥ* totally transforms into lucid, clear space, from which anything can appear. *Yaṃḥ* transforms into [243] air in the form of a black mountain with the shape of a crossed vajra in the realm of baseless emptiness. *Baṃḥ* transforms into a serene, clear, pure ocean in the form of a spherical, swirling water maṇḍala. *Laṃḥ* transforms into a powerful, golden, rectangular ground. *Raṃḥ* transforms into the nature of fire, of the nature of them all, in a warm, crescent-shaped form.

As a symbol of victory over the three realms, *Keṃḥ* transforms into a three-tiered mountain of bones as vast as absolute space. On it is a variegated lower foundation upon which a causal syllable in the center of a vajra emanates a syllable *Bhrūṃ*. It totally transforms into a palace imagined outwardly as peaceful and inwardly as wrathful, in order to block impurities and thoughts. The exterior of the spontaneously actualized palace of great bliss consists of a five-layered wall symbolizing the five facets of primordial consciousness. The exterior is rectangular, symbolizing the four kāyas. Its four sides, symbolizing four facets of primordial consciousness, blaze white to the east, yellow to the south, red to the west, and green to the north. The sidelights to the left and right, radiant like the stars during the interval between the sun and moon,

126. These five paragraphs compare with VE 213–15.

symbolize the skillful means of great bliss and the wisdom of emptiness. The four doors in the shapes of the four enlightened activities symbolize the four immeasurables. [244] The steps composed of various precious substances and the paintings and sculptures at the corners in four beautiful colors symbolize the unimpeded luminosity of primordial consciousness. The ledge[127] at the base of the walls symbolizes the principle that attractive appearances to the senses are not to be rejected but rather arise as ornaments. The beautiful, lovely borders, pendants, cornices, balustrades, and so on symbolize the transformation of the appearances of the ground into the spontaneous actualization [of pristine awareness]. The lapis-lazuli[128] roof symbolizes the primordial consciousness of the absolute space of phenomena, and the vases and awnings are symbols of immutable bliss and emptiness. The Dharma wheels and parasols symbolize the unified perfection of all the stages of the grounds and paths. The beautiful top ornaments of the sun, moon, and jewels symbolize the completion of the three *ati* yānas. The eight portals above the four entrances—shaped like a horse's hoof, a lotus, a chest, cross-hatched lines, a garland of flowers, tassels and garlands, a cornice, and the edge of a roof—are symbols of phenomena arising as displays in the expanse of ultimate reality. Above them, the roof is adorned with deer listening to the Dharma, lotuses, Dharma wheels, parasols, and so on; and to symbolize the purification of the assemblies of thoughts, beneath the four stūpas on each of the four corners, streams of blood trickle from the mouths of four water dragons. Between them, mouths adorned with human heads are adorned with bone lattices and pendants. [245] The fire and wind at the end of the eon blazes fiercely, symbolizing the destruction of the six realms of saṃsāra in absolute space. In order to overcome the impure, delusive cycle [of existence], spiritual messengers, weapons, and so on terrifyingly swirl about like a blizzard. The entire display of charnel grounds is symbolic of the purification of the objects of the senses; imagine that this is all gradually surrounded by a protection wheel established as a self-appearance of primordial consciousness.

In the center of all of this is a wrathful palace, which is triangular inside and dark blue in color, manifested to subdue the assemblies of vicious beings who lead others astray. Its foundation is composed of dried human heads symbolizing the three kāyas, its walls are composed of moist heads, and the eaves are composed of old heads. The meteorite nails driven into it symbolize bodhicitta; and devas, nāgas, planets, directional protectors, and constellations are represented by pillars and rafters.

127. Tib. *'dod yon gyi snam bu*. A "desirables" ledge surrounding the palace where goddesses face outward, making offerings.

128. Skt. *vaiḍūrya*.

Visualize in the center of the entire display of the wrathful palace the spokes of a wheel symbolizing the purification of the eight sensory objects. Eight lions symbolize the purification of the eight types of consciousness, [246] the jeweled throne represents the transcendence of mundane existence, the lotus represents detachment toward saṃsāra, the moon represents a lack of contamination by faults, and the sun represents freedom from all faults. The māras of the aggregates and the mental afflictions lie face down on the right, symbolizing the slaying of self-concepts in absolute space and the pervasive realization of identitylessness. The māras of the devas and the Lord of Death lie face up on the left. The causal awareness syllable *Hūṃ* descends and is seated upon them, and from it rays of light are emanated upward, making offerings pleasing to all the jinas and jinaputras of the three times. Arousing the mindstreams of the personal deities, all the ornamental wheels of their enlightened body, speech, mind, qualities, and activities converge in the form of light rays and dissolve into the *Hūṃ*. Rays of light are then emitted downward, utterly purifying all the vices, obscurations, habitual propensities, karma, mental afflictions, and suffering of all sentient beings. Then, as if forcefully arousing them from sleep, they are all liberated in absolute space, with no vestige of delusion. The light rays retract [back into the *Hūṃ*, and] simultaneously all the vitality, merit, brilliance, and majesty of the five elements [247] of all sentient beings dissolves into the *Hūṃ* in the form of five-colored rays of light.

The syllable *Hūṃ* then transforms into you as the glorious Youthful Vajra, the dharmakāya, indigo in color, symbolizing freedom from conceptual elaboration. Your three heads symbolize the three kāyas; your central eye symbolizes the primordial consciousness of the essential nature of emptiness; your right eye symbolizes the primordial consciousness of the nature of luminosity; and your left eye symbolizes the primordial consciousness of all-pervasive compassion. Your two ears represent the union of the two truths; your two nostrils represent the fulfillment of the two concerns [your own and others']; the symmetry of your face represents great bliss; your tongue is a symbol of the equal liberation of saṃsāra and nirvāṇa; your orange hair streaming upward represents primordial freedom from delusion; your sun and moon earrings symbolize skillful means and wisdom; your six arms symbolize the six facets of primordial consciousness;[129] the nine-pointed vajra symbolizes the nine grounds; the five-pointed vajra symbolizes the five kāyas and the five

129. These include the five well-known facets of primordial consciousness along with the primordial consciousness of knowing all aspects of reality (Tib. *rnam pa thams cad mkhyen pa'i ye shes*).

facets of primordial consciousness; the three-pointed khaṭvāṅga symbolizes the release of the three poisons into absolute space; the mass of fire symbolizes the incineration of karma, mental afflictions, and habitual propensities; the Mount Meru kīla represents the release of the four māras into absolute space; and your four legs represent the four bases of miraculous power.[130] [248] The complete array of accoutrements and wrathful clothing of the charnel ground symbolizes the objects of the senses arising as ornaments. You dwell within a mass of fire, symbolizing the incineration of mistaken, ignorant thoughts.

A wheel of consorts synthesized in the form of the consort Gyedepma symbolizes the nonduality of appearances and emptiness. Vajrakīla is of the nature of mirror-like primordial consciousness; Ratnakīla is of the nature of the primordial consciousness of equality; Padmakīla is of the nature of discerning primordial consciousness; and Karmakīla is of the nature of the primordial consciousness of accomplishment. The purification of configurations of thoughts is symbolized by the ten wrathful beings, together with their consorts and all their retinues and gatekeepers; all these appear but are devoid of inherent nature, like rainbows; and being luminous but without conceptual grasping, they are generated like reflections in a mirror.

Visualize the face and form that you have imagined in your self-generation as appearing instantaneously in front of you, like a reflection appearing in a mirror. At the three places in yourself and in the being visualized in front of you, visualize the three seed syllables, from which light emanates, arousing the mindstreams of the jinas and inviting the empowering deities in the form of the five buddha families. They bestow the empowerments for the five facets of primordial consciousness, purifying the contaminations of afflictive and cognitive obscurations and transforming your five aggregates into themselves, the five buddha families. [249] You are enthroned as a regent of the jinas, and you are invigorated in the great, universal splendor of saṃsāra and nirvāṇa. Imagine that the remaining water solidifies on the crown of your head, transforming into an ornamental half-vajra as a sign of your empowerment, and that you dwell as the principal deity of the family, with your head adorned by the five families.

Again visualize at your three places, upon a wheel, lotus, and sun [disc], a white syllable *Oṃ*, red *Āḥ*, and indigo *Hūṃ*, from which lights are emanated. All the jinas appear in the form of the three seed syllables and dissolve into

130. The four bases of miraculous power (Tib. *rdzu 'phrul gyi rkang pa bzhi*; Skt. *catvāro ṛddhipādāḥ*) are the samādhis of aspiration (Tib. *'dun pa*), enthusiasm (Tib. *brtson 'grus*), intention (Tib. *sems pa*), and analysis (Tib. *dpyod pa*).

you, sealing the deities of your body, speech, and mind. Imagine that you actualize the three innate, indestructible vajras.

The invitation is as follows:

> **"The invitation consists of manifesting the essential nature by transforming all phenomena of the three realms of saṃsāra into displays of the one great ultimate reality."**

Ultimately, when the nature of existence of the ground pristine awareness, the great freedom from extremes, manifests, everything that appears as phenomena of the three realms of saṃsāra is purified in the nature of the three vajras of the body, speech, and mind of the jinas. They are of one taste in the absolute space of the great uniform pervasiveness of ultimate reality, and the invitation consists of manifesting naturally present great primordial consciousness by transforming saṃsāra and nirvāṇa into displays of the ground of being.

In place of that, by emanating white, red, and indigo rays of light from your three places, [250] from the absolute space of the treasury of ultimate reality, invite all the jinas and jinaputras of the ten directions and the four times as displays of the supporting maṇḍala and supported deities, like a swirling blizzard. Imagine that they come to you and to the practice substances, dissolving into you and the deities in front of you as well as into the practice substances. This is merely relative.

The request to remain is as follows:

> **"Holding your own ground within yourself, without movement or change within the three times, is the request to remain."**

Ultimately, identifying pristine awareness that is present in the ground of being, free of movement and change within the three times, and holding your own ground within yourself and stabilizing this within your mindstream is the request to remain. In place of that, in accordance with the ways of saṃsāra, you offer thrones that are pleasing to the jinas and request them to remain. As you do so, you imagine placing them on the thrones, and this is merely relative.

The homage is as follows:

> **"When you encounter your own face as the dharmakāya—the primordial ground of being, the sovereign view—your experience of great wonder is the homage of engaging with the view."**

Ultimately, when you determine pristine awareness as the absolute space of the three kāyas by way of the view and encounter your own face as the dharmakāya—the primordial ground of being, uniform pervasiveness free of elaboration—you experience great wonder at the perfection of the spontaneous actualization of all the kāyas and facets of primordial consciousness. This is simply an expression of the sounds of homage of engaging with the view. [251]

In place of that, in accordance with the ways of saṃsāra, as if you were paying homage and bowing to lords of men, such as kings, you visualize yourself as a deity and imagine emanating from your body as many ordinary sentient beings as there are particles of dust on the earth. By recalling the sublime qualities of the assemblies of deities of the maṇḍala, you pay homage, and this is merely relative.

The offering is as follows:

> **"The display of phenomena as ultimate reality is the great offering."**

Ultimately, when you truly perceive the mode of existence of pristine awareness that is present in the ground, all desirable things that are grasped as phenomena having their own characteristics arise as ornamental displays of ultimate reality, the sugatagarbha, and this is the great offering.

In place of that, in accordance with the ways of saṃsāra, recognize all possible desirable phenomena as unprepared, self-emergent offerings, and offer them up. Regard prepared substances as if they were illusory substances, regard enriching mantras as if they were mantras of illusory substances, and regard mentally emanated offerings as if they were illusory objects. Emanate bountiful offerings as apparitions presented to the senses of deities who appear as if they were the audience, and offer all of these. Offer the seven outer offerings and the inner offerings of visual form, sound, smell, taste, tactile sensations, and so forth. [252] For the secret offerings, transform the three realms into the ambrosia of enlightened body, speech, and mind, and offer it. Imagine saṃsāra as *rakta* displayed as blood, and the world of appearances as a torma that synthesizes the vital essence. By unifying appearances and emptiness, all phenomena encompassed by dualistic grasping melt into white and red bodhicitta, and offering this to the deities constitutes the offering of union. With the objects of ultimate reality and the vajra of skillful means of the swift realization of ultimate reality,[131] transform the three realms into

131. Tib. *'phral rtogs.*

flesh, blood, and bone, which liberates the *rūdra*[132] of the reified view of the self into selflessness, and offer that. Then, releasing all appearing phenomena into great ultimate reality that transcends the intellect is the offering of liberation, and this is merely relative.

The praise is as follows:

> **"The wonder and confidence upon truly perceiving the mode of existence of the Great Perfection of saṃsāra and nirvāṇa is the actual praise."**

Ultimately, when the pristine awareness that is present in the ground, dharmakāya, is actualized, you recognize and realize all the phenomena of saṃsāra and nirvāṇa as displays of the one great emptiness. This is the true perception of all the modes of existence and nature of being of the Great Perfection. So the wonder and enduring delight at this—and the certainty of it due to perceiving the meaning of the primordial perfection of the fruitional kāyas and all the sublime qualities of primordial consciousness as the ultimate reality of the ground—constitute the real praise. [253]

In place of that, imagine emanating from yourself countless vīras and ḍākinīs who praise the body, speech, and mind of the assembly of deities with an unimaginable variety of musical instruments and pleasing songs. This is merely relative.

> **"The individual, distinct appearances of various phenomena are arrays of the enlightened body. Their spontaneous perfection and actualization is the display of the enlightened speech. Primordially pure absolute space, free of the extremes of conceptual elaboration, is the display of the enlightened mind."**

In short, the individual, distinct illuminations of various appearances are pure by way of the eight gateways of spontaneous actualization, and they are nondual from the enlightened body, speech, and mind: (1) By appearing as kāyas, the displays of buddhafields and palaces are self-appearing. (2) By arising as lights, the five individual, distinct lights clearly manifest. (3) By appearing as compassion, the primordial consciousness of wisdom and heartfelt compassion are unimpeded. (4) By appearing as nondual, pristine awareness arises like that, so it is undifferentiated and nondual. (5) By appearing as being free of extremes, [pristine awareness] does not fall to the extremes of existence

132. Tib. *ru dra*. A demon that personifies clinging to true existence.

or nonexistence. (6) By appearing as primordial consciousness, the stages of the ground, path, and fruition are also known to not be separate but to be of one taste with the ultimate nature. (7) By appearing as impure expressions of saṃsāra, all the appearances of the physical world and its sentient inhabitants appear to exist even though they do not, and thus they arise like apparitions. (8) By appearing as pure expressions of nirvāṇa, [254] the self-appearing pure experiences of great primordial consciousness are perfected as the wheel of limitless ultimate reality.

Thus, the individual, distinct appearances of various phenomena are arrays of the enlightened body. They are not newly produced by fresh causes and conditions but are spontaneously actualized as displays of the five energies of pure primordial consciousness, and their primordial perfection as the radiance and mantras of these energies is the wheel of the enlightened speech. Although appearances arise as the enlightened body and sounds arise as displays of mantras, they do not move beyond primordially pure absolute space itself, free of the extremes of conceptual elaboration. So they are displays of the enlightened mind. As the omniscient guru [Longchenpa] states:

> Thus, all that appears as form
> arises as ornaments of absolute space, the wheel of the enlightened body.
> All sound and speech without exception
> arises as ornaments of absolute space, the wheel of the enlightened speech.
> And the inconceivable array of discursive thoughts, movements, and dispersions of the mind
> arises as ornaments of absolute space, the wheel of the enlightened mind.
> The six kinds of sentient beings, with their four modes of birth,
> do not move beyond the absolute space of phenomena, even the slightest bit.

> **"The qualities of realizing how the displays of the kāyas and facets of primordial consciousness are spontaneously actualized, without being sought after, include mastery over the four kinds of enlightened activity; and these are characteristics of the pristine awareness of the Great Perfection."**

Truly recognizing and realizing the nature of the kāyas and the facets of primordial consciousness [255] has the quality of perfecting the spontaneous actualization of your own and others' well-being, just as seeing the characteristics of a wish-fulfilling jewel naturally fulfills all your desires. Temporally speaking, you gain mastery over the four kinds of enlightened activity, and the effortless occurrence of all activities and siddhis constitutes such enlightened activity. These are characteristics of the pristine awareness of the Great Perfection.

> **"Know that the four empowerments are likewise simultaneously perfected in the enlightened body, speech, mind, qualities, and activities within yourself."**

If you know and realize this, the four empowerments are also primordially perfected in the ground of being, without receiving initiation. By determining the nature of saṃsāra and nirvāṇa as great emptiness, the appearances of the enlightened body are perfected; and by realizing the emptiness of the nature of great, unobstructed pristine awareness as the great bliss that dwells within, appearances and emptiness manifest as primordial consciousness, so the vase empowerment of the enlightened body is perfected.

Moreover, all the appearances of the spontaneous displays of the five pure lights as all the appearances of the physical world and its sentient inhabitants are none other than the essence of the energies of primordial consciousness. From the luminous aspect of these energies emerge all apprehended and nonapprehended sounds. From the empty aspect of their essential nature, the inconceivable secrets of the enlightened speech are primordially purified as the natural sound of the ineffable *nāda*; and this brings forth the meaning of the indivisibility of luminosity and emptiness, thereby perfecting the secret empowerment of enlightened speech. [256]

All movements subsumed by the mind are in reality none other than the essential nature of nonconceptual awareness and emptiness, and they arise solely as emergent appearances of the primordial consciousness of great bliss. By simply resting in meditative equipoise in the nature of ultimate reality—the nonduality of bliss and emptiness, free of conceptual elaboration—the great primordial consciousness that dwells within is actualized. So this perfects the wisdom–primordial-consciousness empowerment.

Thus, when mastery is gained over the ground of being—great ultimate reality—and the spontaneously actualized wheels of appearances of the path, then you experience the nature of existence of awareness and emptiness, which is primordial consciousness, inexpressible by speech or thought. So this perfects the originally pure word empowerment.

For these reasons, the aggregates are liberated as a body of light; with the entrance of the power of speech, mastery is gained over the nature of existence of phenomena; with the transference of the mind to the dharmakāya, the continuum of delusive appearances is terminated; and once you have awakened within yourself, you achieve actual buddhahood as the luminous youthful vase kāya.

Now, in order to guide others, there are many ways of revealing empowerments, but by realizing the meaning for yourself, you gain the experience of yogins who have liberated themselves. Apart from that, talking about guiding others without having liberated yourself [257] is as futile as trying to squeeze butter out of sand. This is like an unanointed king commanding that someone else's kingdom should be given to beggars—nothing whatsoever comes from it!

Therefore, yogins who have decisive understanding—that all the peaceful and wrathful maṇḍalas are none other than creative expressions of their own pristine awareness—visualize their disciples as deities and bless them. While the guru chants the liturgy of empowerment, the disciples also imagine that from the heart of the guru and the deity visualized in front of them, a second deity separates off and dissolves into their sacred places. In this way, they imagine that the glories and sublime qualities of each of the deities are perfected; and if they harbor no doubts about this, they receive the empowerment. This is like a king endowed with the status of his station and with sovereignty over his kingdom granting property and wealth to others—they actually receive it.

"Thus, truly knowing and realizing the nature of perfection is certainly the Great Perfection. As a result of failing to know this, you have wandered in saṃsāra in the past. Although perfection is primordial, it has been obscured by ignorance. This is like water that is naturally liquid freezing into a solid, and like having no relief from poverty due to failing to recognize gold and jewels.

"Ultimately, the facets of primordial consciousness and sublime qualities of the ground sugatagarbha are perfected as creative displays of this ground. Explanations of them as individual supporting maṇḍalas and supported deities are presented as skillful means to guide disciples who grasp at things as permanent in ultimate, effortless absolute space, and they depend on relative paths entailing effort. Therefore, using the three essential points of luminosity, purity, and emptiness, those disciples are led to the fruition of supreme absolute space."

With these words, he disappeared.

Thus, truly recognizing how all phenomena—including the kāyas, facets of primordial consciousness, path, and fruition—are primordially perfect in the ground of being and realizing their mode of existence and nature of being are certainly the view and tenet system of the Great Perfection. As a result of failing to correctly perceive and realize the definitive mode of existence and nature of being and so forth, [258] you have wandered in saṃsāra in the past, and you will still not transcend saṃsāra. Why? Because absolute space, in which the purity and equality of the three kāyas is primordially perfect in the ground of being, has been obscured by ignorance. Failing to perceive your own face as the ground of being is like water that is naturally liquid freezing into a solid due to a cold wind; and it is like gold and jewels in the home of a beggar who, because he doesn't recognize them, has no relief from poverty. Likewise, by failing to recognize the nature of being and mode of existence of the ground, you can do nothing more than merely accumulate merit within saṃsāra, reaching the three higher states of existence by mere physical and verbal virtues, and descending to the three miserable states of existence as a result of nonvirtues.

Ultimately, all the facets of primordial consciousness and sublime qualities of the ground sugatagarbha are perfected as creative displays of this ground. Explanations of them as individual maṇḍalas of supporting palaces and supported deities are presented as skillful means for guiding disciples who grasp at things as permanent in ultimate, effortless absolute space, and [such people] depend on relative paths entailing effort. [259]

Therefore, using the pith instructions, life force, vows, and nails of the three essential points of luminosity, purity, and emptiness, disciples are led to the fruition of supreme absolute space. In this regard, there are the nail of luminous deities, the nail of samādhi, the nail of the view of ultimate reality, and the nail of enlightened activities of emanation and reabsorption.

Within this category, first, the nail of luminous deities is to counteract ordinary fixations by vividly imagining as mental objects all the bodily colors, hand implements, ornaments, and garments of your personal deity. If you do so with pure recollection, this prevents the stage of generation from degenerating into reification.

Second, the nail of samādhi is to stabilize the pride of regarding yourself as the deity. Until now, the latent consciousness that grasps at appearances of sentient beings' bodies as "I" while roaming about within saṃsāra has been self-grasping. This is the creator of all appearances and mindsets. To remedy it, visualize your body as the deity and stabilize the pride of the unimpeded sense of being the deity. When a clear appearance emerges, finally eight measures of clarity and stability fully expand, and you definitely gain the power of directly seeing and touching this appearance. As Vajradhara proclaims, [260] "With the passing of six months of unwavering admiration and reverence, the state of Vajradhara will be achieved." You must practice without contamination by human speech, without letting the warmth of your meditation cushion dissipate, and without letting your mind wander elsewhere. As a tantra states, "Regarding the nail of samādhi, single-pointedly sustain your attention, without wavering, on the kāya above." Practicing without laziness is the nail of samādhi.

Third, regarding the nail of the view, from the dharmakāya Samantabhadra above down to the insects in the grass below, you must decisively understand that they are none other than displays of the one sugatagarbha. Those who fail to realize this may actualize the primordial-consciousness beings, but due to reifying them, such people remain as mere worldly beings, with no possibility of truly realizing the primordial-consciousness beings, just as there is no medicine in poison. This is due to failing to realize emptiness. If you truly realize emptiness, you may become like a yogin in the past who effortlessly achieved the four kinds of siddhis of enlightened activity by actualizing a *theurang*.[133] If you don't realize emptiness, even if you actualize Samantabhadra, he will be established as a worldly being. By actualizing a peaceful deity, you will be reborn as a god of the form realm, and by actualizing a wrathful deity, [261] you will become a māra, a rūdra, and so on. A tantra explains this:

> If you lack the nail of immutable enlightened view,
> even if you actualize the Great Glorious One, you will remain ordinary,
> and without achieving the supreme siddhi, you will degenerate into a rūdra.

Therefore, even though everything in the world of appearances of saṃsāra and nirvāṇa consists of displays of your own appearances, a single cognition that reifies their existence causes all physical worlds, their sentient inhabitants, and all sensory objects to appear as if they were truly existent. Due to dualistic grasping, you become deluded by regarding as existent that which does not exist, like Geshé Druldowa and the *tīrthika* Drakgompa. In the past, a son of the gods asked Mañjuśrī whence arose the physical world and its sentient inhabitants, including Mount Meru, the sun, and the moon, and he replied that they arose from the thoughts of a single sentient being. The

133. Tib. *the'u rang.* A type of preta.

son of the gods then asked how they could arise just from thoughts, and he responded by telling the account of an old Vārāṇasī woman long ago who visualized her body as a tiger during the early part of her life; during the latter part, her body actually appeared as a tiger, and she killed many people in the city. Since beginningless time, if you reify things, of course such things will happen, he concluded. This illustrates the necessity of knowing the manner in which all phenomena are empty. [262]

Therefore, once you have decisively recognized the physical world and its sentient inhabitants as your own appearances, you should unwaveringly rest in that awareness. As Machik Lapdrön states, "If there is no activity in the mind, there are no obstructive beings or pitfalls."

Intellectuals retort that resting in your own nature without doing anything is the view of Hashang,[134] but no one knows how to characterize him,[135] for the Buddha's teachings in the second turning of the wheel of Dharma are able to explain to the intellect phenomena without characteristics. When the extraordinarily brilliant master Kamalaśīla symbolically asked, by whirling his staff around his head, "What is the root of the three realms of saṃsāra?" [Hashang] responded by slapping together his two sleeves, indicating that it is dualistic grasping. Both the symbolic question and the symbolic answer illustrated their sharpness of understanding. As it is said, this is comprehended only by the omniscient mind of the Buddha, and no one else can decide it. No one can know the level of Hashang's mindstream.

In general, if you maintain that the physical world and its sentient inhabitants exist autonomously, they would not be emptiness; and even if you maintain that they are empty, if you assert nothing more than their mere emptiness from their own side, there are many kinds of emptiness, such as a hole left by removing a stake from the ground. [263] This is merely naming that which is not empty as being empty, and it is not authentic. If you assert that there is one basis for saṃsāra and nirvāṇa, you would have to agree that when one sentient being achieves enlightenment, all sentient beings would achieve enlightenment simultaneously. If you say that although there is only one basis, they don't all achieve enlightenment at once, then even if one part of the basis achieved enlightenment, since that being would finally be merged in the basis of sentient beings, he would become deluded all over again. What is the use of asserting that sentient beings exist autonomously? By recognizing

134. Hashang Mahāyāna, an eighth-century monk associated with the northern school of Chan Buddhism.

135. The meaning here is that no one can determine whether he was a Buddhist or non-Buddhist.

that sentient beings have no autonomous existence, what harm is there? This is a pointless dispute. Since beginningless time, due to reifying existence, the six kinds of sentient beings appear and are deluded; so recognizing that all phenomena have always been empty and identityless is a crucial point.

Nowadays since many people fail to realize this, even though they all debate about it, if they don't gain decisive understanding of their own view and meditation from within, they are in danger of going astray. So once you truly know the nature of being of the view, you don't need to cut through others' misconceptions. This is very important. [264] As the perfect Buddha declared:

> Monks, just as the wise accept gold after testing it
> by melting (red), cutting (white), and rubbing it (yellow),
> so are my words to be accepted after examining them,
> but not just out of respect for me.

Thus, not mistaking the cause [of saṃsāra] is the defining characteristic of the view, and realization is the nail of immutable wisdom.

Fourth, the nail of enlightened activities of emanation and reabsorption consists of four kinds of recitations and visualizations. First, the display of recitations, like the moon and a garland of stars, is as follows: Visualize yourself as your personal deity, luminous yet empty, as a body of light like an inflated balloon. On a lotus and sun seat at the level of your heart is the *jñānasattva* Akṣobhya, one inch in height, dark blue, and holding a vajra and bell crossed at his heart. Imbued with great peace, he sits in the *vajrāsana* in a haloed expanse of the light of the five facets of primordial consciousness. At his heart is a sun seat, no larger than a flattened pea, on the center of which stands upright a nine-pointed meteorite vajra, the size of a seed. Within its center are a wisdom sun maṇḍala and a skillful-means moon maṇḍala, both of them white on top and red on the bottom. They are in the shape of an amulet box the size of a grain of mustard, within which is the dark blue *samādhisattva* syllable *Hūṃ*, as fine as if it were drawn with a single hair. [265] It faces forward, and there is a *visarga* behind it. Imagine this as the essential nature of the life force of all of saṃsāra and nirvāṇa, concentrated in Akṣobhya's heart. Inside the bindu visualize the guru; on the crescent, the personal deity; on the top line of the syllable, the ḍākinī; and inside the *Ha* syllable, all the dharmapālas. Inside the *u* vowel sign visualize the life-force mantras of the eight classes of gods and spirits, facing downward. On the right side of the *Ha* syllable visualize the male guardians, and on the left side, the female guardians. In front of it visualize disciples, and behind it, the circle of attendants with their favorite enjoyments. The general guardians are hidden within the ranks of the gods, but they are not to be hidden in the heart of the life force. Men should visualize the *Hūṃ* syllable being circled by the mantra garland in a counterclockwise direction and the retinue in a clockwise direction, while women should visualize the *Hūṃ* syllable being circled by the mantra garland in a clockwise direction and the retinue in a counterclockwise direction.

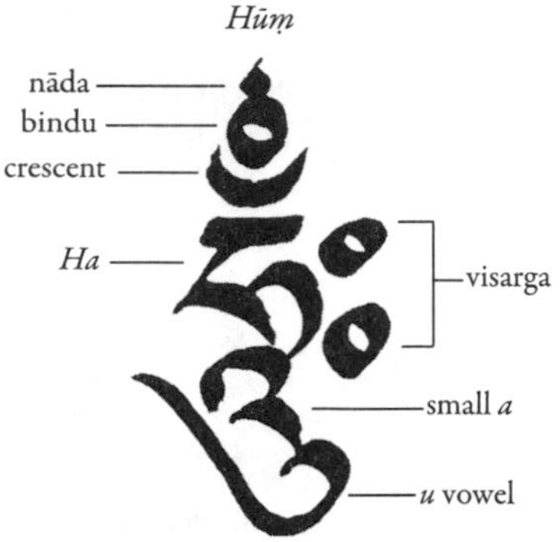

Immeasurable rays of white light are emanated from the nāda and bindu of the *Hūṃ*, making offerings pleasing to the body, speech, and mind of all the jinas and jinaputras of the ten directions. All their compassionate blessings, glory, power, and siddhis [266] dissolve into your heart in the form of a mass of white light. Imagine that all impure appearances and mindsets are forcefully purified, and that your body, speech, and mind are enlightened in the nature of the three vajras. With your attention single-pointedly focused on the kāya, mantra garland, mind, life force, syllable *Hūṃ*, and so on, the entwining of [samādhi and] the mantra recitation constitutes the worship of the deity.

The mantra garland then rises up above the seat and circles clockwise at the midsection of the *Hūṃ* like a firebrand, emanating rays of light and goddesses bearing offerings, which are offered to the jinas and jinaputras, pleasing and satisfying their minds. In this way the two accumulations are perfected. All the blessings of compassion emerge in the form of light rays and dissolve into you, completely purifying the stains and habitual propensities of mental afflictions and obscurations. Then imagine that the body, speech, and mind of the deity become nondual with your own. This constitutes the close worship of the deity.

Once again the mantras stand on the seat, enunciating their respective sounds and circling in a clockwise direction. A second mantra garland separates from the first, like a second candle being lit from the first, and it enters through the *u* vowel sign of the *Hūṃ*, emerges from the nāda, and then moves from your mouth to that of the consort. [267] Imagine that the form of the kāya is transmitted from the lotus of the consort into the opening of your own vajra and then dissolves into the *u* vowel sign of the *Hūṃ*. From the life force at your heart, red light rays are emitted, making offerings to all the jinas. Imagine that all the blessings of compassion, splendor, power, and siddhis in the form of a mass of red light dissolve into the practice substances actualized in front of you, and that you achieve all the supreme and common siddhis. This is the visualization for gathering blessings for your own sake.

Between yourself and the deity visualized in front of you, a circling mantra garland emerges from your mouth and enters the mouth of the principal deity generated in front of you. The form of the kāya is transmitted from the deity's vajra into the consort's lotus, and then moves from the consort's mouth into the mouth of your own consort. Immersing yourself single-pointedly in this continuous cycle like before constitutes the accomplishment.

From the mantra garland, five-colored rays of light are emitted, making offerings pleasing to the body, speech, and mind of the jinas. Imagine that all the blessings of compassion, splendor, power, and siddhis are invited in the form of five-colored lights and dissolve into yourself and the deity visualized in front of you, and that you achieve all siddhis. [268] As light rays are emanated downward, all the karma, mental afflictions, vices, obscurations, and habitual propensities of all sentient beings of the three realms are completely purified, like sunlight striking hoarfrost. All appearances transform into a buddhafield and celestial palace, and all beings transform into the nature of gods and goddesses. Imagine that they all loudly recite the sounds of the mantras with one voice and one mind, like bees when their hive is being destroyed, such that all realms of the world of appearances move, shake, and tremble. This is the great accomplishment.

Although there are many kinds of activities, in general there are visualizations for four activities. In the morning, visualize that immeasurable rays of light are emitted from your heart and that of the deity in front of you, spreading out to the ten directions and making offerings pleasing to the jinas and jinaputras. Strongly arousing the mindstream of your personal deity, all the power, blessings, siddhis, facets of primordial consciousness, and sublime qualities of the inexhaustible ornamental wheels of his enlightened body, speech, mind, qualities, and activities are drawn inward in the form of a mass of white light, and they dissolve into yourself and the deity in front of you. Then imagine that you have received all the power and might of peaceful activity. [269] Again a mass of white light is emitted, striking all the sentient beings of the six classes and three realms, completely purifying all their vices, obscurations, habitual propensities, karma, mental afflictions, and suffering; and imagine that they all transform into kāyas of jñānasattvas.

The visualization for enriching activity is as follows: At noon, visualize immeasurable rays of yellow light being emitted from your heart and that of the deity in front of you, causing all the enlightened body, speech, mind, qualities, and activities of the jinas and jinaputras, the vital force and merit of all the devas, *ṛṣis*, and vidyādharas, the quintessence and vital essence of the five elements, and all the life force, merit, splendor, and wealth of all sentient beings of the three realms to manifest in the form of a mass of yellow light, which dissolves into yourself and the deity in front of you. Thus imagine that your life force, merit, wealth, facets of primordial consciousness, and sublime qualities all increase.

The visualization for powerful activity is as follows: In the evening, imagine immeasurable rays of light, red like the color of rubies, being emitted and drawing in all the jinas and jinaputras of the ten directions in the form of a mass of red light. As they dissolve into you, imagine that all their power, blessings, and siddhis [270] are perfected. Once again, immeasurable rays of red light in the form of hooks are emitted, drawing into your power sentient beings of the three realms, including all the gods, spirits, and humans of the world of appearances. As soon as they arrive in front of you, imagine that their hearts gush forth from their mouths and dissolve into the soles of your feet, so that they are helplessly captured as your servants. Onto the crowns of the heads of all those who harbor harmful, rough attitudes, a red mass of light descends from your heart, transforming into a meteorite vajra. For those who abide by their samayas, this serves as a support for their samayas, but for those who allow their samayas to degenerate, it transforms into an iron scorpion that destroys their hearts' blood. Once you have conquered all their strength and glory, imagine that they enter your service and abide by their samayas.

The visualization for wrathful activity is as follows: At night, visualize yourself as the deity, and from your body emanate [a flurry of] weapons, articles for sorcery, hail, and thunderbolts, like a violent dust storm, pulverizing all enemies, obstructive beings, and malevolent beings, like water extinguishing sparks or hail striking mushrooms. Emanate countless small, wrathful beings, iron scorpions, and garuḍas, [271] who completely devour mounds of [the enemies'] blood, flesh, and bones. Imagine that they are incinerated in a blazing ball of fire and that their remains are scattered by a gale of razors, so that not even a trace remains. Imagine repeatedly that their consciousnesses are liberated in the absolute space of phenomena, where there is no delusion.

By visualizing your body as a deity, you receive the vase empowerment of the body. By verbally reciting mantras, you receive the secret empowerment of speech. By not allowing your mind to be separated from the radiance of primordial consciousness, you receive the wisdom–primordial-consciousness empowerment of the mind. By realizing the nonduality of the deity and your own appearances, you receive the precious word empowerment. Thus the four empowerments are perfected simultaneously.

In general, you must keep secret the place, time, companions, substances, mantras, and ritual articles for your practice. If secrecy is not kept, siddhis won't occur, and there is the danger that obstacles will arise, so it is said that extreme secrecy is of the utmost importance. Finally, when you are about to settle into your session, emanate from all your vital places countless offering goddesses, who make offerings and utter praise as before. Afterward, the sequence of activities for the *gaṇacakra* offering can be learned in the *Vajra Essence*.[136]

Then, [272] regarding receiving siddhis, powers, and blessings—the siddhis of the enlightened body, speech, mind, qualities, and activities of all the deities generated in front of you arise in the form of *Oṃ*, *Āḥ*, *Hūṃ*, and five-colored rays of light, and they dissolve into your three places. Imagine that you achieve the supreme siddhi, the four grounds of vidyādharas, the eight mundane siddhis, and so forth.

Regarding the dedication, imagine unifying all the virtues and collections of virtues you accumulate in the three times, and just as all the jinas of the three times have dedicated and will dedicate their virtues, likewise dedicate them so that all sentient beings—whether near or far, without bias or discrimination in terms of time—may achieve the state of perfect, omniscient enlightenment.

Regarding prayer, pray that all sentient beings may achieve the omniscient state of enlightenment.

Regarding reabsorption and reemergence as the deity, by reversing the order in which the primordial consciousness deities previously emerged from the causal syllable, now reabsorb them back into the nature of ultimate reality. All the displays of buddhafields reabsorb into the celestial palace, the palace reabsorbs into the assembly of deities, the assembly of deities reabsorbs into the principal deity and consort, the consort reabsorbs into the principal deity, [273] the principal deity reabsorbs into the jñānasattva, the jñānasattva reabsorbs into the mantra circle, the mantra circle reabsorbs into the form of the samādhisattva syllable *Hūṃ*, the *u* vowel sign reabsorbs into the small *a*, the small *a* reabsorbs into the main body of the *Ha*, the main body of the *Ha* reabsorbs into its top line, the top line reabsorbs into the crescent, the crescent reabsorbs into the bindu, the bindu reabsorbs into the nāda, and the nāda reabsorbs into the absolute space of phenomena.

Then, by releasing yourself into uniform pervasiveness in the nature of ultimate reality, free of conceptual elaboration, and remaining in meditative equipoise for as long as you can, the extreme of permanence is dispelled. By again uttering the root mantra from the nature of this luminosity, you

136. See VE 250–64, 338.

suddenly appear as the body of your personal deity, like a fish surfacing from water. By generating the physical world and its sentient inhabitants as the circle of deities, the extreme of nihilism is dispelled, and you enter into stream-like conduct.

As for auspiciousness, generate from the absolute space of phenomena all the jinas and jinaputras of the ten directions as *rūpakāya*s, who then perform auspicious dances in the sky and verbally chant auspicious verses and melodies of Brahmā; and mentally imagine them granting the glories of compassionate benefits and joys to sentient beings. From their hands falls a great rain of various auspicious flowers, [274] which overcomes all unwelcome adversities, while increasing all virtues, goodness, and sublime qualities, like a waxing moon. Imagine that they enjoy the glories of the first eon of perfection[137] and chant auspicious verses.

If you do not truly fathom the purity of the visualization of the nail of the deities,[138] the generation practice will degenerate into reification. Therefore, all the distinct appearances of their bodies and ornaments, the principal deities and their retinues, and the sublime qualities of the great, naturally present primordial consciousness of the ground of being manifest as extraordinary skillful means in the luminous external forms of the deities' bodies. You must correctly fathom this view and conduct.

The visualization of deities constitutes the aspect of appearances, and the aspect of emptiness is their absence of inherent existence, never wavering from the nature of great ultimate reality and free of elaboration, like a reflection of the moon in water. This must be visualized without grasping, like a rainbow in the sky. With these crucial points, by perfecting the assembly of thoughts as the circle of deities, the ten bodhisattva grounds will be gradually reached, and the three fruitional grounds will be simultaneously perfected, such that you become enlightened on the unsurpassed thirteenth ground of Vajradhara. [275]

With these words, he disappeared.

The purpose of teaching the stage of generation as an entrance of relative skillful means is as follows:

137. Tib. *rdzogs ldan gyi dus*; Skt. *kṛtayuga*. This was the eon of virtuous "completeness," when people maintained great beauty, merit, long life, and wealth.

138. See the nail of luminous deities at GD 259.

Teachings of the Lake-Born Vajra of Orgyen

On yet another occasion, I met the glorious Lake-Born Vajra and asked him, "O Omnipresent Lord and Primordial Protector, why are there teachings on the generation and accomplishment of buddhafields, celestial palaces, and deities?"

He replied, "These worlds that extend throughout space are the outer rūdra of the reified view of the self. The remedy for it is the purification of buddhafields created from emanated light. Inwardly, grasping at your dwelling place, possessions, and body is the inner rūdra of the reified view of the self. The remedy for it is meditation on celestial palaces and deities. At all times and in all circumstances, the cohesive, uninterrupted latent consciousness of that which appears as a self called 'I' is the secret rūdra of the reified view of the self. This is the common thread running through all appearances and mindsets of saṃsāra. The remedy for it is firmly holding to divine pride."

ON YET ANOTHER occasion I met the glorious Lake-Born Vajra, the illusory body of primordial consciousness, and asked him, "O Omnipresent Lord and Primordial Protector, why are there teachings on the generation and accomplishment of buddhafields, celestial palaces, and deities?"

The teacher replied, "Those three stages of generation are taught as remedies for the three rūdras. The ground of being, the uniform pervasiveness of the panoramic sweep of space, is obscured due to not knowing that the nature of your own face is the nature of the kāyas and facets of primordial consciousness, and this leads to reification of things as being truly existent. The sugatagarbha appears as earth, water, fire, and air. The appearance of flesh as the earth element, blood as the water element, warmth as the fire element, breath as the air element, the mind as the space element, the white and red elements as the sun and moon, the channels as Rāhula, and the configurations of thoughts as the planets, stars, and so on is the outer rūdra of the reified view of the self. The remedy for it is the purification of appearances as buddhafields.

"Inwardly, grasping at your dwelling place, possessions, and body [276] is the inner rūdra of the reified view of the self. The remedy for it is meditation on celestial palaces and deities.

"At all times and in all circumstances, the cohesive, uninterrupted latent consciousness of the 'I' appearing as the self is the secret rūdra of the reified view of the self. This is the common thread running through all appearances and mindsets of saṃsāra. The remedy for it is firmly holding the pride of being the deity."

In terms of relative truth, in the rākṣasa region known as Laṅkapuri lived a courtesan named Kuntugyu who gave birth to a son who personified the three qualities of a god, a demon, and a rākṣasa. This devil, named Matraṃ Rūdra, was an uncouth being with three heads, six arms, four legs, and two wings. As soon as he was born, he killed and devoured his mother, and after forty-nine days he grew to adulthood and gained mastery over the desire realm. Killing men whenever he saw them and raping women whenever he saw them, he set out to destroy the Buddha's teachings. At that time, according to one version, the teachings of all the jinas and the enlightened activities of the sugatas of the three times were simultaneously unified and generated as the deity Hayagrīva and his consort Vajravārāhī, who liberated Rūdra; or according to a second version, he was liberated by the great Heruka.

Be that as it may, ultimately, [277] the ground sugatagarbha, the source of all of saṃsāra and nirvāṇa, is represented as the mother. The son, known as the rūdra of the reified view of the self, who is an appearance contributing to three kinds of ignorance,[139] arises as the rūdra of grasping at the "I." The statement that he devours his mother means that this obscures your own face as the ground of being. His three heads represent the three poisons. His six arms represent the five poisons and avarice. His four legs represent the four modes of birth. His two wings represent dualistic grasping. The statement that he gained mastery over the desire realm means that you revolve within the three realms of saṃsāra and rove about without obstruction. The assertion that he was finally liberated by Heruka means that when nonconceptual primordial consciousness of ultimate reality manifests as Heruka—the kāya of pristine awareness—ignorance is liberated into nonobjectivity. In short, the whole of the world of appearances of saṃsāra and nirvāṇa consists of the appearances manifesting to one individual. Therefore, when a yogin inserts

139. The three kinds of ignorance are (1) ignorance of yourself alone, (2) connate ignorance, and (3) speculative ignorance. The first acts as the primary cause of the latter two.

his energy-mind into the central channel, as outer signs of this, the sun and moon are simultaneously inserted into the mouth of Rāhula, and there are six kinds of earthquakes, five kinds of sounds, and two expansions of halos. These are some of the actually occurring signs of becoming enlightened.

As for the inner signs, [278] ten signs of appearances of clear light occur; and when your body passes into nirvāṇa, the outer signs of the movements of sounds, light, and light rays occur like before. As for inner signs, various relics occur, and these are signs of the union of the outer and inner, so it is important to know this.

> **"If they do not know these vital points, some people disregard the visualizations of the stage of generation and the maintenance of divine pride and apply themselves to verbal recitations alone. Some people practice while reifying the deities and buddhafields. But since it is impossible to achieve enlightenment in those ways, recognize these vital points."**
>
> **With these words, he disappeared.**

Some people, not knowing these secret, vital points, disregard the visualizations of the stage of generation and the stability of divine pride and apply themselves to verbal recitations alone, but by so doing they will never achieve enlightenment. As the great Orgyen states:

> Perform the recitations with unwavering samādhi,
> for if you are distracted elsewhere,
> results will not arise, even if you recite for an eon.

Thus, this samādhi is extremely important.

Some people reify the deities and buddhafields as being autonomously and truly existent, and if they actualize peaceful deities, they are led astray to the form realm; if they actualize wrathful deities, they are led astray to rebirth as māras, matraṃ rūdras, and so forth. Thus, it is impossible for a so-called deity to be autonomously existent. Deities are generated from your own single-pointed consciousness, and if they are assiduously actualized, they are realized, since the basis of realization is already within you.

With these words, he disappeared. [279]

Teachings of Ekajaṭī

The Perfection of the Greatness of the Names of This Yāna

THE PERFECTION of the greatness of the names of this yāna is as follows:

> **On yet another occasion, when I had a vision of the Lady of Absolute Space, Ekajaṭī, I asked, "O sole grandmother of saṃsāra and nirvāṇa, what is the name of this yāna that is displayed in the secret space of the Lady of Absolute Space, the great emptiness of saṃsāra and nirvāṇa?"**
>
> **She replied, "O mother's little boy, I have fully granted you the Enlightened View Lineage of the Buddhas, which is like providing you with a body. I have reared you, as though suckling you with mother's milk, with the Symbolic Lineage [of the Vidyādharas]. I have fostered your wisdom by providing you with the heartfelt advice of the Aural Lineage [of Ordinary Individuals]. Revealing this to all those fortunate disciples who are connected to it by way of their karma and prayers is meaningful.**
>
> **"My name is given to the king of all yānas. All sounds express my name. The essential secret—this perfected display as the unsurpassed space of the mother ḍākinī—has numerous synonyms, but I say they are included in seven names."**

On yet another occasion, when I had a vision of the Lady of Absolute Space, Ekajaṭī, I asked, "O sole grandmother of saṃsāra and nirvāṇa, what is the name of this yāna that is displayed in the secret space of the Lady of Absolute Space, the great emptiness of saṃsāra and nirvāṇa?"

She replied, "O mother's little boy, the marvelous, sovereign view is directly seeing within yourself the pristine awareness that is present in the ground of being, not leaving it as an assumption. It is of the great nature of the absolute space of the four kāyas and the five facets of primordial consciousness, which is of one taste in the absolute space of the one ultimate reality, the [Lineage] of the Enlightened View from the dharmakāya Samantabhadra to your root guru. This is the meaning of the renowned Lineage of the Enlightened View of the Buddhas, so it is synonymous with identifying, or perfecting, [pristine awareness] in a physical way. The Symbolic Lineage [of the Vidyādharas] is the understanding by way of the signs and symbols of the ḍākinīs of the three places, who do not rely on the conditions of practice or training, and the understanding by way of symbolic communication from the assemblies of vidyādhara gurus. They are reared as if suckled on mother's milk. [280] The Aural Lineage [of Ordinary Individuals] occurs as teachings by assemblies of ḍākinīs with the simultaneous power of transmission and prayers, like speech among humans. This is to be taught to intelligent individuals as heartfelt advice. Now this is revealed to fortunate disciples with whom there is a connection of karma and prayers, and it has the power to lead all those for whom this is meaningful to the state of liberation.

"Thus, the king of all yānas, which synthesizes the lineages having these three characteristics, is an inconceivable synonym for my name. All sounds express me, all names refer to my name, and all forms are appearances of my primordial consciousness. In short, the outer physical world and its sentient inhabitants consisting of the five elements—earth, water, fire, air, and space—the inner aggregates and elements, and all the secret assemblies of objects are none other than my nature. The essential secret, this perfected display as the unsurpassed space of the mother ḍākinī, has numerous synonyms, but I say they are included in seven names."

> **"Since this Dharma involves two great kinds of secrecy, it is called *secret.* Since it protects you from the dangers of concepts of the self and engaging with its characteristics, it is called *mantra.* It is called the ultimate, indestructible *vajra.* Since the sublime qualities of all paths are distilled in it, it is called *yāna.***
>
> **"Since it is present as the ultimate mode of being of all phenomena, it is called *reality.* Since it is the foremost of all that is to be realized, it is called *ultimate.* Since it is purified of all faults and stains, it is called *pure.* Since it fully embraces all kāyas, facets of primordial consciousness, and sublime qualities of the path and fruition, it is called *full.* Since it is the basis for the emergence of everything appearing as various displays of purity and equality, and since it is present as the sole life force of the three vajras, it is called *citta,* or heart—that is, mind.**
>
> **"It is the *perfection* of saṃsāra and nirvāṇa. Since it synthe-**

sizes and unifies all the yānas, it is the universal basis of all yānas and is therefore called *great*.

"Since it transcends all the edges and corners of concepts, it is called *bindu*. Since saṃsāra and nirvāṇa are of one taste in bodhicitta, it is called *sole*.

"Since the nature of pristine awareness, the sugatagarbha, is lucid, luminous, and free of contamination, it is called *clear light*. Since it is imbued with the seven indestructible vajra qualities, it is called *vajra*. Since it abides as the distilled essence of all phenomena of saṃsāra and nirvāṇa, it is called *essence*.

"Since all phenomena of *saṃsāra and nirvāṇa* are fully *embraced* and *consummated* in the nature of the sugatagarbha, it is called the *complete consummation of saṃsāra and nirvāṇa*.

"Since it is free of birth, death, aging, and degeneration, it is called *youthful*. Since it does not breach the periphery of spontaneous actualization, it is called *vase*. Since it is like an accumulation and compilation of all facets of primordial consciousness and sublime qualities, it is called *kāya*."

With these words, she disappeared.

With that general explanation having been presented, I shall give a more specific account of the manner in which all sublime qualities of the paths of the nine stages of yānas are perfected.

Śrāvakas are so called because they see that everything that appears as a self, which is the basis of grasping at "I" and "self," is devoid of inherent nature. Pratyekabuddhas are so called because they realize all outer and inner things solely as dependently related illusory appearances. Bodhisattvas are so called because for them, the power of realizing emptiness arises in the nature of compassion, effortlessly subsuming all aspects of skillful means and wisdom.

The sublime qualities of these three yānas that lead you away from the origins of suffering are perfect, such that the higher approaches subsume the lower ones.

In kriyā tantra, you please the deity by means of austerities and ritual purifications. In upāya tantra, you achieve siddhis by oral recitations and samādhi. In yoga tantra, there is the yoga of śamatha and vipaśyanā in which you witness the blessings of absolute space, devoid of characteristics, within the great maṇḍala of the vajra, absolute space.

All the sublime qualities and functions of these three yānas

that evoke pristine awareness by means of austerities are perfect and complete within the single, coemergent absolute space of your own inexpressible mind, the essence of siddhis.

All the qualities of the father tantra, mahāyoga, are pure from the very beginning in the supreme dharmakāya, ultimate reality endowed with seven attributes, or the indivisibility of the two higher levels of truth.

In orally transmitted anuyoga, the son of the union of primordial being and the maṇḍala of spontaneously actualized primordial consciousness is great bliss, in which appearing phenomena are perfected in great purity and equality in the maṇḍala of bodhicitta.

The nature of existence of the Great Perfection is clear light, in which the precious, spontaneously actualized appearances of the ground of being and phenomena naturally arise without bias or partiality in the one absolute space, which has no periphery or center. All such appearances, undifferentiated like gold and its glow, are simultaneously subsumed in the dharmakāya—unchanging pristine awareness, the great freedom from extremes—and the absolute space of the ground of being, the sugatagarbha. These individual accounts are presented simply for the sake of leading disciples stage by stage.

The [seven synonyms are] secret mantra Vajrayāna, ultimate bodhicitta, [281] the Great Perfection, the sole bindu, the clear-light vajra essence, the complete consummation of saṃsāra and nirvāṇa, and the youthful vase kāya.

Regarding the first, secret mantra, Vajrayāna, this is the most secret of the secret teachings, the synthesized secret of the mind of all the jinas. Thus it is called *secret*. This path is imbued with two great secrets. The concealed secret is the pervasion of the mindstreams of all sentient beings by the ground sugatagarbha, which saturates them like oil saturates sesame seeds. This is like a poor person not knowing about the presence of a treasure of jewels beneath the floor of his house. The hidden secret refers to the fact that it is not to be discussed in inappropriate places, at inappropriate times, or with unsuitable people, for the listeners may then abuse and revile the teachings. Why? Because those who are unsuitable listeners may develop false views about the Dharma that transcends cause and effect, which may finally hurl them into hell, so this must be kept secret from them. As it is said:

> The secret mantra is not faulty,
> but for the sake of sentient beings, it should be kept secret.

On the other hand, those with faith should teach it to those with violent karma and to those of good fortune. [282] All the appearances and mindsets of the three realms of saṃsāra and all the intellectual, philosophical systems of the eight yānas are vanquished in the nature of ultimate reality devoid of signs. So it is called *mantra*. The dharmakāya, pristine awareness that is present in the ground of being, is imbued with the seven vajra qualities, so it is called *vajra*. When sentient beings are deluded, it is not degraded by vices, obscurations, or suffering; and when buddhas become enlightened, it is not improved or altered by all the facets of primordial consciousness and sublime qualities of the path. It holds all good and evil, so it is called *yāna*.[140]

Second, regarding ultimate bodhicitta, all authentic realities are included in bodhicitta, so it is called *reality*. Just as the source of all rivers and streams is determined to be the ocean, the source of all Dharmas is determined to be bodhicitta, so it is called *ultimate*. It is free of all faults and stains, so it is called *pure*. Since it fully embraces all kāyas, facets of primordial consciousness, and sublime qualities, it is called *full*. Both saṃsāra and nirvāṇa are equally displayed in the dharmakāya, the absolute space that is present in the ground of being, so it is the great, inconceivable *mind* and is thus called the *ultimate nature of the mind*.[141]

Third, regarding the Great Perfection, all the phenomena of saṃsāra and nirvāṇa are perfect in the ground of being itself, [283] so it is called *perfection*. How are the nine yānas perfected in the originally pure ground of being, the Great Perfection? All phenomena of the ground, path, and fruition are perfect in the one spontaneously actualized Great Perfection. Thus, due to subtle self-grasping suppressing the appearances of the ground, the great appearances of the five spontaneously actualized lights, kāyas, and facets of primordial consciousness subside into the inner glow. Their outer radiance is perfected as the appearances of the three realms, with their apparitional impurities, and the appearances and mindsets of saṃsāra. The minds of sentient beings are empty and luminous by nature; and the empty and luminous dharmakāya, pristine awareness that is present in the ground, is devoid of grasping. The extreme of nihilism results from freedom from reification of the mode of existence of the ground, great emptiness that is devoid of the eight extremes. The extreme of permanence results from the unimpeded radiance of the spontaneously actualized nature of reality. So the extremist views of seeking the path are perfected.

140. This etymologizes "secret mantra Vajrayāna" (Tib. *gsang sngags rdo rje'i theg pa*): secret (*gsang*) mantra (*sngags*) vajra (*rdo rje*) yāna (*theg pa*).

141. This is etymologizes "ultimate bodhicitta" (Tib. *don dam byang chub kyi sems*): reality (*don*) ultimate (*dam pa*), pure, full (*byang chub*) mind (*citta*; *sems*).

As for the nine yānas of the path, there are the outer yāna of philosophical analysis, the inner yāna of the secret mantra, and the unsurpassed fruition; and by dividing each of these into three, there are nine. Associated with the first are the śrāvakas, pratyekabuddhas, and bodhisattvas. Regarding the two kinds of identitylessness, the śrāvakas realize that an individual does not exist from his own side, [284] and given their view of phenomena as being autonomously existent, they assert [only] the identitylessness of persons. With the Great Perfection, you realize the two kinds of identitylessness [of persons and of phenomena] as not truly existent. The pratyekabuddhas view things as unreal simply by way of seeing all phenomena as the twelve links of dependent origination in forward and reverse order. With the Great Perfection, you view all dependently related phenomena as primordially empty of inherent nature. Among bodhisattvas there are Cittamātrins and Mādhyamikas. Cittamātrins assert that all appearances are the mind, while Mādhyamikas assert the unity of the two truths. According to the Great Perfection, appearances are not the mind, nor are they other than the mind. The great Madhyamaka of empty awareness is the realization of the indivisibility of the two truths.

Secondly, among the inner tantras, the kriyā tantra primarily emphasizes bathing and cleanliness, and it asserts that fruition is achieved by means of accomplishing bountiful causes. The Great Perfection purifies causes and conditions, so results are perfected naturally. Although its view is regarded as yoga tantra, in terms of conduct, the upāya tantra primarily teaches in accordance with the kriyā tantra. With the Great Perfection, you fully comprehend the nonduality of the view and conduct. The yoga tantra primarily emphasizes the view and teaches only a little about conduct. [285] The Great Perfection asserts that you should dwell in the view continually and naturally.

Third, regarding the unsurpassed secret [tantras], with mahāyoga you actualize appearances, sounds, and awareness as the three maṇḍalas, and indivisibly unite the *samayasattva*s and jñānasattvas. With the Great Perfection, you realize the indivisibility of the deities and primordial consciousness. The anuyoga asserts that you actualize the channels, bindus, and vital energies as the three kāyas. The Great Perfection asserts the indivisibility of absolute space and primordial consciousness. Within atiyoga, the outer mind division takes the aspects of the mind as the path, the inner expanse division is said to indivisibly unify absolute space and pristine awareness, and the secret pith instruction division nakedly determines originally pure, unobstructed, empty awareness. This secret pith instruction division is the source of all paths, so it is the general atiyoga. It is also so called because it is the foremost of all the yānas, for it simultaneously perfects all grounds and paths. It synthesizes all yānas and accomplishes them as one point. It is the *great* unification of them in one essence, so it is called the supreme yāna of the Great Perfection.[142]

Fourth, regarding the sole bindu, the nature of existence and mode of being of the dharmakāya, pristine awareness that is present in the ground, [286] which cannot be penetrated by the intellect or analyzed by mentation, and which is beyond articulation, is the bindu that totally encompasses all boundaries. It is called the bindu that transcends the edges and corners of the intellect, mentation, and concepts, for the great *bindu* has no edges or corners. Although there are many explanations of the specific aspects of saṃsāra and nirvāṇa, in reality they are of one taste in the great, original, primordial ground. For this reason it is called *sole*.[143]

Fifth, regarding the clear-light vajra essence, the nature of the mind is primordial clear light, the lucid luminosity that manifests as appearances during the waking state, the dream state, the intermediate period, and so on. Identifying this for yourself is decisively fathoming saṃsāra and nirvāṇa as displays of clear light, so it is called *clear light*. Because it is imbued with the seven indestructible vajra qualities and the four vajra pledges,[144] it is called the ultimate, indestructible *vajra*. Because it synthesizes the essence of all phenomena of saṃsāra and nirvāṇa, just as gold is the essence of earth, it is called *essence*.[145]

Sixth, regarding the complete consummation of saṃsāra and nirvāṇa, the impure three realms revolve in a stream of ignorance, karma, and mental afflictions, so it is called *saṃsāra*; and because it transcends suffering, karma, mental afflictions, and habitual propensities, it is called *nirvāṇa*. Because it completely encompasses all phenomena included in saṃsāra and nirvāṇa in the expanse of the one pristine awareness, [287] it is called *complete*. Because it completely perfects saṃsāra and nirvāṇa, the three paths, and causality in

142. This etymologizes "Great Perfection" (Tib. *rdzogs pa chen po*): perfection (*rdzogs pa*), great (*chen po*).

143. This etymologizes "sole bindu" (Tib. *thig le nyag gcig*): bindu (*thig le*), sole (*nyag gcig*).

144. The four vajra pledges (Tib. *dam bca' bzhi*) are that (1) one without the necessary karmic propensities cannot realize the sugatagarbha, (2) one who realizes it cannot but achieve confidence, (3) one who achieves confidence cannot but become liberated, and (4) one who is liberated cannot but become enlightened. See GD 221, VE 189.

145. This etymologizes "clear light vajra essence" (Tib. *'od gsal rdo rje'i snying po*): clear light (*'od gsal*) vajra (*rdo rje*) essence (*snying po*).

the expanse of the dharmakāya, the sugatagarbha, the ground pristine awareness, the great freedom from limitations, it is called *consummation*.[146]

Seventh, regarding the youthful vase kāya, because it does not fall to the extreme of any aspect of birth, death, aging, or degeneration, and is free of them, it is called *youthful*. Because all phenomena of saṃsāra and nirvāṇa, without breaching the outer periphery of displays of spontaneous actualization, are the great inner luminosity, it is called a vase. Just as all the reflections of planets and stars do not exist apart from the expanse of the ocean, all physical worlds and their sentient inhabitants do not exist apart from the expanse of space. Thus it is called *vase*. Because it is like an accumulation and compilation of all the sublime qualities of the kāyas, facets of primordial consciousness, path, and fruition, it is called a *kāya*.[147]

In general, the Great Perfection is the great absolute space that perfects saṃsāra and nirvāṇa and the three paths. Its nature of being is accurately determined by way of the two kinds of identitylessness. All yānas are similarly determined in this way. Some people determine this by asserting that the self alone does not exist from its own side, while regarding every other phenomenon as autonomously existent. [288] Others assert this only as dependent origination, and yet others assert the intellect that apprehends emptiness, while saying that the kāyas and facets of primordial consciousness must be approached in some other way, and so on. However, according to our tradition, all sublime qualities of the kāyas, facets of primordial consciousness, path, and fruition are from the very outset primordially, naturally, and perfectly present in the ground of being itself. Truly knowing this is ascertained as the view and tenet system of the Great Perfection.

All that has been said thus far presents the view of determining the ground—self-emergent primordial consciousness—and this completes the presentation of enlightened awareness of the great freedom from extremes.

146. This etymologizes "complete consummation of saṃsāra and nirvāṇa" (Tib. *'khor 'das 'ub chub*): saṃsāra (*'khor*), nirvāṇa (*'das*), complete (*'ub*) consummation (*chub*).

147. This etymologizes "youthful vase kāya" (Tib. *gzhon nu bum pa'i sku*): youthful (*gzhon nu*) vase (*bum pa*) kāya (*sku*).

Teachings of Śrī Siṃha

2. The Practice of Cultivating the Path

> **On another occasion when I encountered the king of vidyādharas, Śrī Siṃha, I asked, "O Teacher, please show me the path of the Great Perfection."**
>
> **He replied, "The Great Perfection is the great, universal basis of saṃsāra and nirvāṇa, the great absolute space in which saṃsāra, nirvāṇa, and the path are perfect and complete. Knowing its mode of being is the view. Gaining mastery over this great, original, primordial ground, you awaken and expand within yourself, which is meditation that is devoid of a referent. This is like a drop of water merging with the ocean, becoming the ocean without modifying it. It is like the space inside a vase merging with the space outside it, such that it expands infinitely into space without modifying it.**
>
> **"Although there is no outer or inner with respect to the ground of being and the mind, self-grasping superimposes boundaries between outer and inner. Just as water in its naturally fluid state freezes solid due to currents of cold wind, likewise the naturally fluid ground of being is thoroughly established as saṃsāra by cords of self-grasping."**

IN THE EXPLANATION of how to practice cultivating the path there are (a) the concise teachings of pith instructions on the vital points of methods for placing the mind, (b) the four methods of liberation of the radiance, and (c) the specific teachings of the four kinds of open presence.

a. The Concise Teachings of Pith Instructions on the Vital Points of Methods for Placing the Mind

Like oil saturating sesame seeds, the primordial ground sugatagarbha abides as great spontaneous actualization, eternally pervading the mindstreams of all sentient beings. However, with grasping at external objects serving as the cause, and grasping at the internal mind serving as the contributing condition, you have become deluded under the influence of ignorance. [289]

First you determine by way of the view how all phenomena included in saṃsāra and nirvāṇa are not inherently existent. Then you decisively ascertain your own awareness as being groundless, rootless, and of the great all-pervasive nature of saṃsāra and nirvāṇa—which consists of displays of pristine awareness, self-emergent primordial consciousness. Do not follow after past thoughts, do not anticipate future thoughts, and do not fall under the influence of present thoughts. Rather, rest in meditative equipoise in the naturally settled, great clear light. You must recognize that there is nothing else for you to meditate upon. Regarding the indubitability of this, even if Lord Buddha were to actually come to you, you must not be ambivalent or uncertain. If you do not realize this, even though you may give lip service to identitylessness, in reality you will be unable to endure misfortune and will have no inner fortitude, and this will be the reason why.

Therefore, it is important to correctly know how to perform the outer purification and, specifically, [how to purify] the eight collections [of consciousness] in forward and reverse order. If you do not know this, it is said that your meditation will not rise above an ethically neutral ground and will therefore not lead to the path. Due to not experiencing the nature of existence of the sugatagarbha, you become deluded; [290] but when you actualize the nature of all-pervasive great wisdom, you are liberated within yourself. For this, you must decisively ascertain that all of saṃsāra and nirvāṇa consists of nothing but your own appearances.

In general, the minds of sentient beings are an expanse of emptiness and luminosity, in which all kinds of thoughts can arise. So as you let your mind illuminate them like a candle, the appearances of various thoughts emerge from the domain of afflictive mentation, like sparks emerging from fire. When waves emerge from water, even though the water and the waves appear to be separate, they are of one taste in the nature of water, without one being worse or better than the other. Likewise, from the very moment that thoughts arise, the ground of their arising is the absolute space of ultimate reality; and the thoughts and the one to whom they appear are not really different, but are rather of the same taste. You must know how this is so. On the other hand, if you foster thoughts and block them by applying antidotes and so on—like blocking the mouth of a great river, resulting in the land being destroyed by water—karmic energies will enter your life-force channel and you will certainly go mad.

With respect to viewing your own creative power as a problem and then blocking it and so forth, the unimpeded radiance of the dharmakāya is the wisdom that perceives the full range of phenomena. [291] So if you abandon this, you will certainly not become a buddha by divorcing yourself from the primordial consciousness that knows [reality as it is] and perceives [the full range of phenomena]. In general, in one twenty-four hour period there are movements of 21,600 thoughts, so—no matter what—they fade away, whether or not they are inhibited or sustained. And the subsequent consciousness is none other than the primordial consciousness of the dharmakāya. For this reason, gurus of the past have stated that however many thoughts proliferate, to the same extent the dharmakāya proliferates, just as a mass of fire flares up in accordance with the amount of fuel. Just as kindling burns itself up, so do thoughts release themselves, resulting in their infinite dispersion exclusively into the primordial consciousness of the dharmakāya. Therefore, it is said that as long as you meditate by blocking thoughts, enlightenment will not be achieved.

So-called meditation is not searching for something. Without falling into an ethically neutral, nonmeditative state, dwell in the great, natural settling in ultimate reality, as Ācārya Koṭali taught:

> Mental meditation is not meditation;
> not meditating is also not meditation.
> Transcending meditation and the meditator,
> having nothing in mind is Mahāmudrā.

You might think there is no difference between this and an ordinary sentient being, but there is a difference: [292] Sentient beings do not know the characteristic of the noninherent nature of all appearances of phenomena, so they reify all appearances; and their minds descend, as it were, into darkness.

Just as water, which is naturally liquid, solidifies when it freezes, you are deluded by being bound up with the cords of dualistic grasping, and your own nature is solidified. Yogins' realization of how all the phenomena of saṃsāra and nirvāṇa are not inherently existent is like the breaking of the dawn and the rising of the sun. Until this occurs, apart from applying yourself to actualizing the naturally settled clear light, there is nothing whatsoever to meditate upon. Just as there is nothing more to open once you have opened one eye and can see, apart from simply seeing space with your eyes, there is no other object of focus or act of focusing.

You might think that there is no difference between this and ordinary sentient beings or even animals seeing space, but it is not so. Sentient beings do not know the nature of being of the ground, so they see nothing more than the immateriality of space. Therefore, this is like seeing a striped rope as a snake or mistaking a pile of stones for a man. [293] In reality, there is a difference between being aware and not being aware and between knowing and not knowing, just as there is a difference between gold and stone.

Some people claim that without knowing the nature of emptiness, simply by the power of enduring the hardships of ordinary life one must gain knowledge, and apart from this, there is no difference between seeing and not seeing the nature of emptiness. Well, if that were the case, then the teachings of the perfect Buddha, the Bhagavān, in the second turning of the wheel—which demonstrates the absence of intrinsic characteristics and the emptiness of all phenomena from visual form up to the omniscient mind—would be pointless. Even though you resolutely withstand hardships throughout lifetimes in beginningless saṃsāra until now, while you may be lifted up, there will not be even the slightest bit of progress, so there will still be no occasion for realization. Realization occurs in reliance upon the teachings of the jinas, the transmission of the gurus, and the valid cognition of your own awareness. This is a crucial point.

From the time that you identify nonconceptual space—the secret absolute space of the equality of the three kāyas—and apply yourself to this experience, there is nothing else whatsoever to meditate upon. Ācārya Bagompa stated:

> Fathom this space! [294] If it is realized as objectless, the great nail of nonmeditation is struck.

And:

> The nature of the mind is the great sky of absolute space.

As Saraha declared:

> Everything without exception is of the nature of space,
> and never is there any wavering [from it].
> Even though I exclaim, "Space, space,"
> the essential nature of space is not established as anything.
> It is not existent or nonexistent, nor is it a nonentity or a non-nonentity,[148]

148. Emending *yod dang med yod min med min yin* ("It is existent and nonexistent, and it is a nonentity and a non-nonentity") to *yod dang med yod min med min mi* ("It is not existent or nonexistent, nor is it a nonentity or a non-nonentity").

and it is beyond the scope of any other demonstrable object.
Thus, the mind, space, and ultimate reality
are not the slightest bit different.

In reality, there is no object of meditation or agent who meditates, no object of application or agent who applies, no entity upon which you focus or agent of attention, and nothing to be unified or agent who unifies. So settle in the great place of rest, ultimate reality, which is inexpressible by speech or thought.

b. The Four Methods of Liberation of the Radiance

These four are: (1) perceiving the vital point of primordial immutability within the three times, which is like primordially liberated space; (2) the natural liberation of thoughts releasing themselves without reliance on other remedies, which is like the knots in a snake unraveling themselves; (3) the arising of the absolute space of ultimate reality and the originally pure perception of this arising as primordial consciousness, which is like the arising and release of waves; and [295] (4) appearances not being able to be grasped by the intellect from the moment they arise, and being liberated right where they are, without being bound by grasping. This naked, instantaneous liberation is like snow falling on heated rocks. The four methods of liberation of the radiance are implicitly perfected.

c. The Four Kinds of Open Presence

(1) Regarding the view of open presence, the great uniform pervasiveness of the view transcends intellectual grasping at signs, does not succumb to bias or extremes, and realizes unconditioned reality, which is like space. (2) Regarding the meditation of open presence, just as the water of the great ocean is unfathomable, whatever arises is none other than the nature of ultimate reality. Just as water is permeated by lucid luminosity, in ultimate reality there is no saṃsāra or nirvāṇa, no joy or sorrow, and so forth, for you realize that everything dissolves into uniform pervasiveness as displays of clear light. (3) Regarding the pristine awareness of open presence, just as the supreme mountain in the center of this world system is unmovable, pristine awareness transcends time, without wavering even for an instant from the nature of its own great luminosity. (4) Regarding the appearances and mindsets of open presence, all appearing phenomena are naturally empty and self-illuminating. They are not apprehended by the intellect, not grasped by the mind, and not modified by awareness. Rather, they dissolve into great uniform pervasiveness, [296] so they are liberated with no basis for acceptance or rejection, no distinction between luminosity and emptiness, and no ambivalence.

To summarize all these points, the Great Perfection of ultimate reality is the great universal basis of saṃsāra, nirvāṇa, and the path, as well as the great absolute space that encompasses saṃsāra, nirvāṇa, and the path. Truly perceiving its character and nature of being is the view; and when you see your own nature, you gain mastery over the great, original, primordial ground of being. By holding your own ground within yourself, pristine awareness awakens to its own nature; and meditation—without wavering from great uniform pervasiveness, free of conceptual elaboration—is devoid of any objective referent. When a water drop merges with the ocean, it is indivisible from the ocean; and the one space on the outside and inside of a broken vase cannot be differentiated, but extends into a single, all-pervasive space. Likewise, in the identification within yourself of the dharmakāya, pristine awareness that is present in the ground, there is nothing to be altered and nothing else with which to engage.

Without knowing this, under the influence of self-grasping—despite the fact that there is no distinction of outer and inner regarding the ground of being and the mind—the self is demarcated as being over here, and the ground of being is demarcated as being over there, thus bifurcating inner and outer. Just as water in its naturally liquid state freezes solid [297] due to currents of cold wind, the ground of being of the naturally liberated state is bound up by cords of self-grasping, and the whole of saṃsāra appears and is established as real.

> **"Recognizing how that is so, relinquish good, bad, and neutral bodily activities, and remain like a corpse in a charnel ground, doing nothing. Likewise, relinquish the three kinds of verbal activity and remain like a mute; and also relinquish the three kinds of mental activity and rest without modification, like the autumn sky free of the three contaminating conditions. This is called *meditative equipoise*. It is also called *transcendence of the intellect*, for by relinquishing the nine kinds of activity, activities are released without doing anything, and nothing is modified by the intellect. In the context of this vital point, you will acquire great confidence within yourself.**
>
> **"Moreover, at all times while moving about, sitting, shifting positions, and engaging in oral recitations and mental activities, without losing the perspective of the view, regard appearing phenomena as being like illusions. Without losing the confidence of meditation, be consciously aware of the nature of phenomena. Without allowing your conduct to become**

> **careless, properly devote yourself to the four kinds of activity. This is the natural liberation of meditation that transcends the intellect."**

Once you truly know and realize that, relinquish outer activities of the body, such as walking, sitting, and moving about; inner activities of prostrations and circumambulations; and secret activities of ritual dancing, performing mudrās, and so on. Resting in inactivity, with a great sense of release, remain like a corpse in a charnel ground. Relinquish outer activities of speech, such as all kinds of delusional chatter, inner activities such as reciting liturgies, and secret activities such as counting propitiatory mantras of your personal deity. Remain in silence, as if you were mute. Relinquish outer activities of the mind, such as thoughts aroused by the five poisons and the three poisons, inner activities of mind training and cultivating positive thoughts, and [the secret activity of] dwelling in mundane states of dhyāna. Not wavering from uncontrived, naturally settled clear light, like the early morning sky in autumn, uncontaminated by dust, mist, or darkness,[149] [298] is called *meditative equipoise*. By utterly relinquishing all activities in this way, you achieve the state of great inactivity, and by not modifying this with the intellect, it is said that the intellect is transcended. You will then acquire confidence within yourself in these vital points, and when you experience your own ground as Samantabhadra, you will see that there is no buddha apart from your own awareness. Consequently, you will acquire confidence such that even if you saw the whole sky filled with buddhas, this would not arouse even the slightest bit of faith. By decisively understanding saṃsāra and nirvāṇa as your own appearances, you will acquire the confidence of achieving enlightenment within yourself, without looking to any other causes or effects. By coming to rest in your own ground as Samantabhadra within yourself, even if you were surrounded by a hundred assassins, you would have confidence free of even the slightest fear. By realizing saṃsāra as nameless, you acquire the confidence of fearlessness regarding saṃsāra and the miserable states of existence.

This is the vital point of meditative equipoise, and until you achieve it, it is crucial that you know how misery arises from nonvirtue and how happiness arises from virtue. Therefore, even during postmeditative periods, do not lose this way of viewing reality, but sustain the subsequent flow of awareness of decisively knowing the nondual displays of saṃsāra and nirvāṇa. [299] Do not lose the confidence of meditation, which means that by remaining in the presence of the lucidity and luminosity of space, you do not depart from the

149. Dust, mist, and darkness are the "three contaminating conditions" in the root text.

great glow of the actualization of the radiance of awareness free of activity. Do not stray into careless behavior, but avoid negative, nonvirtuous actions as if they were poison. When you are eating, resting, walking, and sitting, engage in these activities in a gentle and relaxed way, without ever becoming careless, even for an instant. Wherever you are, let your perception be vast and spacious. Whomever you accompany, be of good cheer. These two points are to be cultivated until the end of your life. If they are not cultivated, it is not enough merely to identify [pristine awareness], which would be like having food but not eating it, or having clothing but not wearing it. Even if you have an ocean of learning, if you do not meditate, you will fall into delusion; and when you face death you will certainly do so as an ordinary being. Jikmé Lingpa stated:

> Even if you identify your own nature, if you do not familiarize yourself with it,
> you will be carried away by malevolent thoughts, like a child in battle.

If you meditate with a sense of fortitude, you will disappear as a rainbow body, like the eighty realized adepts of Yerpa and so forth. [300] Nowadays, some people speak in exalted ways and put on a good show, but when they face death, there's no difference between them and ordinary people; and this is because they can't meditate due to their weak fortitude.

Therefore, now, while you are young, you should know how to practice Dharma and apply yourself while you can. Otherwise, when you are struck down by a terminal disease for which neither medical treatment nor religious services are of any help, and your respiration grows fainter, you will remember all the nonvirtuous deeds you have done in the past and will be terrified of the results. Overcome by remorse at not having applied yourself to the sublime Dharma, your heart will burst—but it will be too late. The great Orgyen declared:

> Even if an old sinner feels remorse when facing death, it is too late.

So now you must swiftly enter the path of Dharma and abandon the sense that you are going to be here for long. As Padampa Sangyé commented:

> When you are mindful, your progress is swift, people of Dingri.

Do not turn your mind to your father for advice, do not seek counsel from your mother, and do not try to decide for yourself, but entrust your mind to your guru and to the Three Jewels. You should diligently apply yourself to the Dharma, as Jikmé Lingpa said:

> As for your training, at the outset trust no one but a qualified guru as your teacher, and do not listen to just anyone. Do not procrastinate when it comes to the Dharma, but swiftly strive diligently. [301]

This is the natural liberation of meditation that transcends the intellect.

3. The Accompanying Conduct for Those Two [View and Meditation]

> **"As for the vital point of conduct, do not go astray in your conduct due to your view, thinking that 'Everything is emptiness, so however I behave, I will not be contaminated by faults.' Avoid nonvirtues of the body, speech, and mind as if they were poison. Serene, subdued, and conscientious, behave as if you were entering the presence of a supreme judge.**
>
> **"On the other hand, if you fixate on other virtues of the body, speech, and mind as if they were of the utmost importance, this will overwhelm the authentic view and meditation. If you spend your whole life merely accumulating merit within saṃsāra, it will be as if you were bound with chains of gold. Without overemphasizing proper conduct at the expense of the view, be like an unconquerable snow lion standing proudly in the snow.**
>
> **"Furthermore, if you follow after those who say that you must cultivate compassion in some other way, even though you have realized the view of emptiness, this will be like someone who has water but seeks moisture elsewhere, like someone who has fire but seeks warmth elsewhere, or like someone who has wind but says coolness must come from somewhere else.**
>
> **"The decisive ascertainment of saṃsāra and nirvāṇa as great emptiness is the unsurpassed bodhicitta—the compassion of viewing saṃsāra and nirvāṇa as displays of purity and equality."**

Do not let the view lead you into improper behavior, but rather avoid the ten nonvirtues like poison and conduct yourself in a serene, subdued, conscientious fashion, as if you were entering the presence of a supreme judge. If you let the view lead you into improper behavior, this will result in careless behavior, and by becoming addicted to mundane affairs, you will become caught up in an ongoing flow of negative actions. Developing false views regarding the Three Jewels, you may dismiss the laws of karma. As a result of laughing and frolicking and not practicing the ultimate view and meditation, you will not even begin to accumulate the merit for taking rebirth as a god or a human. So if you spend your time in negative, idle chatter, this acts as a cause for such rebirths as a māra or rūdra. This would be like seeking a healing medicine but instead encountering a plant that is poisonous to the touch.

In general, the antidote for unawareness [ignorance] is awareness and the antidote for saṃsāra is emptiness; but if this is misunderstood, your mindstream will be filled with false views [302] and you will behave in various ways that are incompatible with the Dharma. There are a number of instances in which this has evidently occurred, and it is due to misunderstanding emptiness.

To return to the analogy of entering the presence of a supreme judge, when coming into the presence of a very strict judge, if you do not bow, behave courteously, walk and conduct yourself slowly, speak with dignity, mentally examine things with care, and so forth, your life may be endangered. Likewise, without letting the view lead you into improper behavior, you should investigate carefully and behave with restraint, physically and verbally. The Lord of Death is even more strict, and if you cut the life-force channel of liberation, it is crucial that you mend your mindstream. Until you reach the intellect-transcending extinction into ultimate reality, you must behave appropriately concerning even the subtlest causes and effects. As the great Orgyen declared:

> Although my view is higher than the sky,
> my conduct regarding cause and effect is finer than barley flour.

Do not let behavior lead you into false views. You should be like an unconquerable snow lion with a rich mane, the king of beasts, standing proudly in the snow. If you become overly preoccupied with other virtues of the body, speech, and mind, [303] this will overwhelm the view and meditation. If you spend your life merely accumulating merit within saṃsāra, it is like being bound with chains of gold. If your efforts in Dharma practice are like plucking flowers in the summertime, each one prettier than the last, you will dispense with the practice of the profound view and meditation; and you will inevitably face death as an ordinary person and thereby perpetuate saṃsāra.

Apart from aspiring for the merely temporary joys of gods and humans, you will not achieve the fruition of liberation, and this is what binds you.

You must achieve firm conviction in the qualities of the profound view and meditation, such that even if you see or hear of the qualities of other Dharmas, this will not overwhelm your view and meditation. In particular, there are people who say that even if you have realized the view of emptiness, you must strive to cultivate compassion by some other means. However, such compassion that distinguishes between self and others is not free of the mentality of attachment and aversion, so such generation of bodhicitta is merely an aspiration but is not engaged. If you adhere to this notion, you will definitely be like a person who has water but says that moisture must come from elsewhere, like someone who has fire but seeks warmth elsewhere, or like one who has wind but hopes to find coolness elsewhere. [304] Once you have recognized and realized the nature of the one great emptiness of saṃsāra and nirvāṇa, the decisive understanding resulting from this is the compassion of viewing saṃsāra and nirvāṇa as displays of purity and equality. There is nothing called compassion or bodhicitta apart from this.

> **"Even though you have correctly identified and recognized the vital points and nature of the view and meditation, if you decide that this alone is sufficient and then fixate on mundane activities, it will result in wasting your life in various activities of attachment and aversion. By so doing, all your view and meditation will be overwhelmed by delusive activities of saṃsāra."**

By relying upon the pith instructions of the guru in that way, even though you correctly identify the nature of the view of the ground of being—without familiarizing yourself with it, but rather having confidence in mere intellectual understanding, thinking that this is enough, and deciding on just this—you will become fixated on mundane activities like before. You will segregate some people as your enemies and feel aversion toward them, while partitioning off those you regard as your friends and feeling attachment toward them. By coming under the domination of such delusive mental afflictions, you will set in motion all manner of negative, nonvirtuous actions. By failing to acquire confidence and stability in a lifelong practice that is a useless waste, all views and meditations will be overwhelmed by delusion and the affairs of saṃsāra. This is due to failing to familiarize yourself with the view, even though you have identified it.

On the other hand, if you ascertain saṃsāra and nirvāṇa as displays of equality without losing the perspective of the profound view, you will not lose the confidence of meditation. [305] Just as the ocean is imbued with lucidity and clarity, so will you gently dwell in the actualization of the radiance of pristine awareness. Until phenomena dissolve into ultimate reality, do not let your behavior degenerate due to your view, but rather regulate your expressions of body, speech, and mind, while rejecting nonvirtue as if it were poison.

Not letting your view be led astray by behavior is like a snow lion with a turquoise mane, unconquerable by other creatures, overpowering all other beasts simply by standing proudly in the snow, with no creature daring to approach it. Likewise, a yogin who has perfected in his body the three creative expressions of the profound view and meditation masters and overpowers all outer appearances. So you must not be misled by effortful paths.

An Explanation of Three Pitfalls of Meditative Experiences

> **"Appearances of meditative experiences occur when your mind and consciousness shift in unprecedented ways. Pleasurable, soothing experiences of bliss propel you to rebirth as a god of the desire realm. Vivid experiences of luminosity propel you to rebirth as a god of the form realm. A nonconceptual sense of vacuity, in which awareness is withdrawn in an unconscious, blank, unmindful state like deep sleep, propels you to rebirth in the four dimensions of the formless realm. Lacking any knowledge of the view of emptiness, you may determine that the mind is empty merely in the sense that it is not established as something substantial. Resting the mind single-pointedly in this state of vacuity is a view that propels you to the peak of mundane existence and to rebirth as a god who lacks discernment."**

As for appearances of meditative experiences, an unprecedented, soothing sense of bliss may arise from which you never want to be separated; and if you cling to this and achieve stability in it, this will propel you to rebirth as a god of the desire realm. An unprecedented sense of vivid luminosity may arise that will propel you to the form realm, and you may also experience subtle kinds of extrasensory perception. [306] If you cling to this, it will propel you to the form realm. You may experience a nonconceptual sense of vacuity that propels you to the four dimensions of the formless realm. This is a mindless, unconscious experience of inner vacuity in which grasping becomes subtle and dormant, as if you were deep asleep. With no knowledge of the view of emptiness, the mind decisively settles on the nature of emptiness as the mere absence of substantiality. If you single-pointedly focus on such vacuity, this will propel you to the peak of mundane existence and to rebirth as a god who lacks discernment. By recognizing this view, you must not fall under such influences. Rather, whichever of these occur, know them to be patterns of meditative experiences that are devoid of true existence, while securing the stronghold of pristine awareness.

> **"Moreover, outer upheavals include various apparitions appearing to your senses, such as visions of gods and demons arising as bad omens. Inner upheavals include the occurrence of various illnesses and pains in the body. Secret upheavals include random mood swings. If you are aware of the deceptive flaws of all of these and come to a decisive understanding of them, they will vanish of their own accord. If you cling to their true existence and obsessively fixate on hopes and fears, they can become life threatening, resulting in psychotic episodes, fits, seizures, and so on. Succumbing to fixating on them as divine and demonic appearances causes meditative adepts to degenerate into being merely ordinary."**
>
> **With these words, he disappeared.**

Furthermore, as for outer upheavals, these are various: there are apparitions of gods and demons arising to your senses as bad omens and so on; appearances of various inauspicious forms of gods and demons; various disagreeable mental experiences arising due to waking up in a panic from seeing unpleasant forms in your dreams; illnesses arising due to food, lodging, and trauma; illnesses difficult to heal arising merely from coming in contact with earth, stone, wood, and weapons; [307] and the mysterious occurrences of wounds, leprosy, ulcers, and so on.

As for inner upheavals, any of the 404 types of imbalances of wind, bile, phlegm, and combinations of them may arise in the body, and—as if the entire might and strength of your mind had seeped away into them—inexpressible suffering and various pains may occur.

Secret upheavals include experiences of joys and sorrows, unpleasant attachment, hatred, craving, unbearable suffering, delight, depression, and clinging to experiences of emptiness and luminosity; a sense of sheer vacuity, in which appearances and mindsets are impeded; paranoia, in which everything you see or feel is out to harm you; disturbing the minds of others due to your own anger and malice, and afterward feeling remorse; having the pride of thinking that "There is no yogin on earth who has a view and meditation like mine"; and feeling that everything you have done is wonderful, and consequently feeling free to do whatever you like. Such unpredictable joys and sorrows will certainly arise.

If you reify and fixate on such experiences and fortify them with hopes and fears, [308] these meditative experiences will turn into illnesses. You may then reinforce them by apprehending them as demonic influences. Even though you apply yourself to medical treatments and magic rituals to dispel obstacles, you will not receive even the slightest benefit. If the sentry that identifies meditative experiences is lost, this might cause you to go insane, pass out, faint, and so on, leading to your own death; or you might become as stupid as an animal, and so forth. Fixating on mere meditative experiences of clear visions due to *śamatha* as apparitions of gods or demons, clairvoyant knowledge of others' minds, and so on leads contemplatives to fall to ordinary states.

You must practice so that you know and decisively recognize that all such sensations are deceptive experiences of your own flaws, and they will naturally disappear. Whenever any patterns of joyful and miserable experiences arise, recognize them as being not truly existent, and neither block nor affirm discursive thoughts. Rather, by recognizing their nature as deceptive meditative experiences, the appearances of these experiences will vanish by themselves, like mist fading into the sky. As the Great Perfection states, "Meditative experiences are like mist that fades away."

If you block these discursive thoughts, it will be like blocking the mouth of a great river, as Padampa Sangyé said: [309]

> Avoid blocking thoughts, for they are like bubbles that burst of
> their own accord.
> They will not be stopped by blocking them, people of Dingri.

The great Orgyen said:

> There are many who know how to build up meditation,
> but only I know how to break it down.

Casting aside all conceptual elaboration of mental activity and resting without a mental object and without grasping is a sublime, crucial point.

With these words, he disappeared from sight.

Teachings of Zurchung Sherap Drakpa

Further Teachings on Authentic Conduct

On yet another occasion, when I encountered Zurchung Sherap Drakpa in the Blazing Volcano Charnel Ground in the self-appearing, actual Akaniṣṭha, I asked, "O guru, please grant me practical instructions that are your heart essence expressed with few words but comprehensive meaning."

He replied, "O you who have assembled accumulations, prayers, and karmic momentum for incalculable eons, listen! If you wish to ascend to the state of omniscient buddhahood, please your guru, with constant admiration and reverence, in all your activities. Continuously cultivate affection and pure perception regarding your friends. With heartfelt compassion for sentient beings, strive for liberation and the state of omniscience. Constantly bearing in mind the impermanence of all composite phenomena, abandon mundane activities and dwell in a state of inactivity. This is the unsurpassed quintessence of all Dharmas.

"Three vital points are offering service to the sublime guru by not squandering his practical instructions; honoring your samayas without hypocrisy, as the life-principle stone of the gods and guardians; and devoting your whole life to the Dharma, so that you know there is nothing left unfinished at the time of death.

"Guarding your samayas and vows as if they were your own life force is the vital point to prevent contemplatives from degenerating into ordinary people. Cultivating contentment with regard to sensory pleasures is how to not get caught up in negative objects. Recognizing that saṃsāra has no essence is how to cut through the fixations of attachment and aversion. Recognizing that mundane activities are never finished and

accomplished, that they are like lines of smoke from an incense clock, is the pith instruction for bringing activities to a close."

ON YET ANOTHER occasion, when I encountered Zurchung Sherap Drakpa in the Blazing Volcano Charnel Ground in the self-appearing, actual Akaniṣṭha, I asked, "O guru, please grant me practical instructions that are your heart essence expressed with few words but comprehensive meaning."

He replied, "O you who have assembled accumulations, prayers, and karmic momentum for incalculable eons, if you wish to ascend to the state of omniscient buddhahood, (1) at all times and on all occasions have admiration and reverence for your guru; (2) cultivate affection and pure perception regarding your [vajra] siblings and friends; (3) strive for liberation and the state of omniscience with compassion for sentient beings; and [310] (4) meditate on the impermanence of life." These four are indispensable:

(1) First, you must embrace the essence by devoting yourself solely to a spiritual mentor, who is the root of the path. The *Condensed Perfection of Wisdom* states:

> Always devote yourself to wise gurus.
> Why? Because qualities of wisdom arise from them.
> Just as you devote yourself to a doctor to heal your illnesses,
> diligently devote yourself to a spiritual mentor.

As for the guru to whom to devote yourself, whatever Dharma he teaches, he should have in mind, reveal, and elucidate only the absolute space of phenomena, ultimate truth. In this way, the spiritual mentor should guide you along a straight path. Regarding his specific qualities, the *Clear Elucidation of Samayas* states:

> There are six kinds of *ācāryas*: general ācāryas, ācārya guides,
> ācāryas for samayas and empowerments, ācāryas for restoring
> broken commitments,
> ācāryas for liberating the mind, and ācāryas for pith instructions
> and oral transmissions.

One who is a master of the general teachings, who is revered by everyone, and who receives modest gratitude is a general ācārya. A master who leads you to the entrance of the Dharma, by granting monastic ordination for example, is an ācārya guide. One who grants samayas and bestows empowerments is an ācārya for samayas and empowerments. One to whom you confess faults and downfalls [311] is an ācārya for restoring broken commitments. One who teaches Dharma, for instance, is an ācārya for liberating the mind. One who offers pith instructions and grants oral transmissions is an ācārya for pith instructions and oral transmissions.

Among these kinds, the teacher who clearly reveals the inner meaning of real primordial consciousness by bestowing empowerments that ripen and guidance that liberates, together with providing pith instructions and oral transmissions, embodies the essential nature of all gurus and perfectly synthesizes them in one lineage. So correctly devote yourself to all the teachings in the tantras and scriptures. Without pretense, devote your body, speech, and mind to whatever is pleasing to the guru. It is important that you constantly behave with admiration and reverence. With heartfelt admiration and reverence for such a guru who is imbued with those three kindnesses, think of him as actually being the great Orgyen. Then, when you are sitting, imagine him on the crown of your head; when walking, imagine him above your right shoulder; when lying down, imagine him at your heart; and when eating and drinking, imagine him at your throat. By so doing, look upon him as the foundation of your supplications, the object of your circumambulations, the essential nature of your own clear-light awareness, and the field by which you accumulate merit and knowledge. By serving and seeking refuge in him without being separated from the four kinds of knowledge, [312] the nonconceptual primordial consciousness of the guru's mindstream will be powerfully transferred to you. Drikung Kyobpa Rinpoché stated:

> If the sun of admiration and reverence does not rise
> on the snow mountain of the four kāyas of the guru,
> the stream of blessings will not flow.
> So earnestly devote your mind to admiration and reverence
> for him.

Thus, meditating on the sublime vajra guru, offering prayers of supplication, receiving empowerments, merging your mind with his, and so on, ripen you along all the paths of the stages of generation and completion. This is the profound, marvelous, swift path to achieving all supreme and mundane siddhis simultaneously. The *Great Presentation of Ati* states:

> It is better for the guru to appear in the maṇḍala of your mind
> than to visualize a hundred thousand kāyas of deities.

And:

> Worshiping the buddhas of the three times
> is not equivalent to one one-hundredth of worshiping the guru.

In summary, do not do anything to displease your guru for even an instant, but rather please him with your body, speech, and mind, and listen to whatever he says. If you please him by all that you do, this will purify all your previous karma, mental afflictions, and habitual propensities, and you will instantly accomplish an ocean of accumulations of merit and knowledge. [313]

The best [form of service] is to establish the teachings of the practice lineage through rendering service by way of your spiritual practice. Middling is to render service with your body and speech, which can merely purify obscurations of the body, speech, and mind. And the least form of service is to please the guru with material goods, which adds to your accumulations of the two kinds. The *Tantra of the Supreme Samaya* states:

> Faithful ones who desire siddhis:
> siddhis arise from pleasing the guru.

The disadvantages of displeasing the guru are stated in the *Illusory Matrix*:

> The disadvantage of disparaging the guru
> and disturbing his mind
> is that suffering is experienced for the duration it would take
> to scoop out all the water
> in the great, outer ocean with a hair:
> this is known as Vajra Hell.

The way to confess that is stated in the *Self-Arising Pristine Awareness Tantra*:

> If your samayas degenerate regarding your teacher,
> create a great maṇḍala of gaṇacakra offerings,
> and do the same for your vajra siblings;
> make offerings of goods that please your teacher,
> and offer whatever you have to the ārya.

Therefore, please your guru by preparing and offering a maṇḍala of gaṇacakra offerings, butter lamps, and so forth, and by confessing your faults. If the fault is by way of your body, purify it by placing your body in the service of the guru. [314] If the fault is by way of your speech, proclaim the virtues of the guru to the ten directions. If the fault is by way of your mind, you should primarily focus your attention on the cultivation of admiration, reverence, and the guru's positive qualities. As for the measure of having confessed the fault, by confessing perverse aspirations and contempt seven or ten times, they will be purified; but if [three] years pass by, they will not. The *Presentation of Samayas* states:

> If someone who commits a misdeed toward the guru
> feels remorse about it and confesses it seven or ten times,
> the misdeed will be purified.
> But if [three] years pass, Vajrasattva will not allow it.

At all times, do not dwell on the guru's errors but recall his positive qualities. Like a patient devoting himself to a doctor, reverently and sincerely devote your body, speech, and mind in honor and service for the sake of gaining liberation from the chronic disease of saṃsāra. Just as one who wants a boat ride relies on the boatman, in order to cross the river of suffering of saṃsāra you should always bear in mind whatever the guru says. Just as a merchant relies on the caravan leader, one seeking liberation should adhere to the mind of the guru who reveals the authentic path. Free of deception, you should know the nature of the precious ninefold assembly[150] and devote yourself to it with immutable faith. [315] The *Great Reverberation of Sound Root Tantra* states:

> The advantages of devoting [yourself to the guru] are
> immeasurably greater than the advantages of a wish-fulfilling tree,
> a wish-fulfilling jewel, and a wish-fulfilling cow.
> Bearing this in mind, devote yourself to the guru,
> and this will turn the battle of saṃsāra.

(2) Second, as for the cultivation of affection and pure perception regarding your [vajra] siblings and friends, these are the kinds of vajra siblings: *general* siblings who are pervaded by the sugatagarbha, *distant* siblings who are devoted to the Buddha's teachings, *close* siblings who have entered the gateway of Vajrayāna, those who are like siblings of the same father guru, and

150. Tib. *dgu sprug*. The ninefold assembly comprises the Three Roots (guru, personal deity, and ḍākinī), the Three Jewels (Buddha, Dharma, and Saṅgha), and the three kāyas (dharmakāya, saṃbhogakāya, and nirmāṇakāya).

those who are like siblings belonging to the same mother maṇḍala. Those who depend on the same guru and maṇḍala are like twin brothers and sisters.

You must never part from a sense of affection and love for them all, and always act with pure altruism toward them. Since you must accompany them until you ultimately achieve enlightenment, if your affection and samayas degenerate, you will wander in regions where the Dharma is nowhere to be found. Therefore, you must arouse affection and keep your samayas, and continually cultivate faith and pure perception toward them as being of the nature of vīras and ḍākinīs. [316]

(3) Third, regarding the cultivation of compassion for sentient beings, there is not even one sentient being within the three realms of existence who has never been your parent, and beings are all constantly tormented by suffering in a unbearable prison of misery, without even a moment of happiness. So out of heartfelt, earnest compassion you must strive for and accomplish the state of liberation and omniscience. Therefore, nowhere is it said that even though you are devoid of loving-kindness, compassion, and bodhicitta, you can achieve buddhahood by following some other profound path. Recognizing that these three are the core of all paths, you must practice them correctly.

(4) Fourth, regarding the meditation on the impermanence of composite phenomena, by constantly reflecting on the ways in which all composite phenomena are impermanent, you see that no one who is born is immortal. Moreover, by considering the various aspects of impermanence, such as the uncertainty of the time of death and the unpredictability of the causes of death, you must bear death in mind and always diligently apply your body, speech, and mind to the Dharma, without falling under the influence of distraction and laziness for even an instant. [317]

Now you have the freedom to practice the Dharma, and you have the eyes with which to distinguish what to adopt and what to avoid. If you are incapable of practicing the authentic Dharma on this occasion, then when you eventually contract a terminal illness, there's no way you will be able to practice in the face of death. So by recognizing this, dispense with mundane activities and dwell in inactivity. This is the unsurpassed quintessence of all sublime Dharmas. Three vital points are offering service to your guru by not squandering his practical instructions; honoring your samayas without hypocrisy, as the life-principle stone of the gods and guardians; and devoting your whole life to the Dharma, so that you know there is nothing left unfinished at the time of death.

Guarding your samayas and vows like your own life force is the vital point that prevents contemplatives from reverting to ordinary states. Recognizing that all pleasures that appear to the five senses are like last night's dream, be content with just enough food to sustain your life and with clothing that is merely adequate to protect you from the wind. This is advice that will protect you from being led astray to negative things. Recognizing that mundane activities are utterly devoid of any essence, cut off the addictions of attachment and anger, such as [activities of] subduing your enemies and protecting your friends. [318]

Recognizing that mundane activities are never finished and accomplished, that they are endless like lines of smoke from an incense clock, strictly control your mind without wasting your life thinking that you will practice the Dharma tomorrow or the next day. Swiftly applying yourself to essential practice is the pith instruction for bringing an end to harmful conduct. Planning to practice Dharma after your mundane tasks are finished and so on is the way to become a māra by not practicing Dharma. Avoiding that, from the time that you enter the door of Dharma until you die, assiduously and single-pointedly devote yourself day and night to the practice of original purity and spontaneous actualization, without letting your body, speech, and mind fall under the influence of unconscientious conduct that is contrary to the Dharma even for an instant. It is very important that you maintain a firm practice and generate courage and fortitude.

Thus, if you can devote your entire life to the Dharma, that is best. If you devote half your life to the Dharma, that is middling. At the very least you should meditate for a few months. Those who don't meditate even that much are brainless, meritless people with no essence who are imprudent regarding both this life and the hereafter. Just look at how you have wasted your life until now. Now for the remainder of your life, which is like a fleeting ray of sunlight, if you fail to take a step on the path to liberation, you will not gain a human life of leisure and opportunity repeatedly, [319] it will be difficult for you to meet with qualified gurus, and it will be hard to find practical instructions on the sublime Dharma. Consider this very carefully. By not disregarding his practical instructions, you must not be shamed by your guru; by not being devious regarding your samayas, you must not be shamed by the gods and guardians; and by devoting your entire life to the Dharma and having no regrets when you die, you must not be shamed by yourself. Now, from whichever of two points of view [mundane and spiritual] and whatever fame, power, and wealth you may have, overcome your pride and take the lowest place, as if you were a leper. When you encounter hostile environments and adversities, whatever suffering comes your way, do not lose your courage, but be like a wild lunatic who recognizes everything as being like an illusion and a dream.

Some people leave their little home and move elsewhere, and then claim to be hermits. With lies and deceit they mislead others, and clinging to their greater home, they spend their time in inappropriate, mundane activities. This is a disaster. The venerable Milarepa declared, "If Dharma practitioners do not remain in retreat, there is no greater disaster than that." [320] Others appear as old monks and pompously claim that they can guide the dead and protect the living. Making their living from wages demanded as repayment for the corpses and so on, they squander their lives while arrogantly viewing this as virtue. Gurus who take money by wielding their authority and bandits who take money by [violent] means are similar in their intentions and conduct, so they are objects worthy of great compassion. Therefore, you must take stock of yourself and swiftly accomplish something very meaningful for the hereafter.

4. How to Finally Progress on the Grounds Leading to the Ultimate Fruition of Eternal Liberation

> **"First you gain knowledge in reliance upon training. Then you gain experience in your own mindstream and realization by means of investigation and analysis. But liberation is not achieved merely by such knowledge and realization, just as hunger is not satisfied if you have food but don't eat it. Just as darkness does not appear once dawn has broken, when you have given up the nine kinds of activity, you acquire stability within yourself due to the power of meditation. When there is no fragmentation of the panoramic sweep of pristine awareness, indwelling confidence is acquired within your own pristine awareness.**
>
> **"Still, that by itself will not bring you to enlightenment. When phenomenal appearances have been extinguished into ultimate reality, there is an infinite expansion into the great, all-encompassing sphere of the absolute space of phenomena, devoid of even a trace of the appearances and mindsets of saṃsāra. You have then reached the state of liberation.**
>
> **"Within this experience, even the subtlest of cognitive obscurations have been utterly cleared away, and mastery is gained over great primordial consciousness that knows reality as it is and perceives the full range of phenomena. So you achieve buddhahood in the dharmakāya, which is like space, and the three kāyas arise as displays of uniform pervasiveness."**

First, by devoting yourself to a sublime, qualified vajra guru, and in reliance upon unmistaken training in whatever is to be practiced, you gain knowledge by way of the wisdom gained through listening to teachings. Next, as a result of investigation and analysis, experiences arise within your mindstream, and realization is gained by way of the wisdom gained through reflection. Finally, you should become deeply familiar with that which has been realized until this culminates in the freedom of the four kinds of unshakable confidence. Without it, liberation will not be gained due to such knowledge and realization alone, just as hunger is not satisfied if you have a mountain of food but don't eat it. [321] Once you have given up the nine kinds of activity, the stability acquired within yourself as a result of the power of the wisdom of meditation is like darkness being banished once dawn has broken. When there is no fragmentation of the panoramic sweep of pristine awareness, indwelling confidence is acquired within your own pristine awareness.

That by itself will not bring you to enlightenment. Thus, once phenomenal appearances have transformed into the nature of ultimate reality, the fundamental basis of saṃsāra is voided, dualistic fixations are immediately released, and appearances of self and others dissolve into the absolute space of phenomena. Grasping at attachments, aversions, hopes, and fears is then vanquished, ignorance is dispelled in the ground of being, and you gain the vision of ultimate reality. By cutting the root of self-grasping, the grasping mind is extinguished. By severing the bonds of dualistic grasping from your heart, grasped objects are extinguished, and with the extinction of dualistic concepts, you expand into the purity and equality of saṃsāra and nirvāṇa.

At this time, with your body like a corpse lying in a charnel ground, even if you were surrounded by a hundred assassins, there would be no fear or trepidation. With your speech repeating after others like an echo, the movement of the vital energy of your speech is naturally released in its own place of rest. With your mind like a rainbow disappearing into the sky, [322] phenomenal appearances are extinguished into ultimate reality; and there is an infinite expansion into the great, all-encompassing sphere of the absolute space of phenomena, original purity, free of conceptual elaboration and devoid of even a trace of the appearances and mindsets of saṃsāra. You have then reached the state of liberation.

At this time there are three levels: Optimally, dreams are purified in the clear light, which uninterruptedly pervades all your experiences throughout the day and night. Next best is to recognize the dream state for what it is, leading to such abilities as emanating within and transforming dreams. At the very least, bad dreams cease altogether and you have only good dreams, such as dreams of seeing deities and buddhafields, drawing maṇḍalas, bestowing empowerments upon others, and teaching the Dharma; for negative habitual propensities have been extinguished.

Some people claim to have extinguished phenomena into ultimate reality, but in doing so, they are subjects, revealing the fault that such extinction into ultimate reality has not occurred. Others claim that they are pretending to have attachment and clinging even though they have no such grasping, but such frauds—who pretend to have what they lack—have not gained such extinction. So accomplished scholars rebuke them by way of scriptures and reasoning.

Even when you reach the immutable nature of reality—like briefly glimpsing your own fingers during an occasional flash of lightning—due to your very subtle, lingering cognitive obscurations, [323] you return to talking and so on, as you did in the past.

Then, for those with superior faculties, even the subtlest cognitive obscurations are completely cleared away within seven days; for those with middling faculties, six months; and for those with inferior faculties, within one year. Then you gain mastery over the ground of being by means of the primordial consciousness that knows reality as it is. Due to gaining mastery over the path by means of the primordial consciousness that perceives the full range of phenomena, your dharmakāya is the essential nature of emptiness, your saṃbhogakāya is the unimpeded nature of spontaneous actualization, and your nirmāṇakāya manifests as unimpeded displays of omnipresent compassion. For your own sake, you realize the state of the dharmakāya in the great expanse of the uniformly pervasive three kāyas, and you become a buddha.

For the sake of others, by means of the rūpakāyas, you arise as the great saṃbhogakāya of absolute space until the three realms of saṃsāra are empty. Emerging from this are the nirmāṇakāyas and saṃbhogakāyas, the six sages who subdue living beings, and one who reveals the ways of the buddhas, such as Śākyamuni, by way of the twelve enlightened deeds of a supreme nirmāṇakāya. In addition you reveal created nirmāṇakāyas, living-being nirmāṇakāyas, material nirmāṇakāyas, and so on, manifesting in whatever ways are needed to train sentient beings. In these ways you manifestly perform the deeds of a buddha, in which your own well-being and that of others are perfected in the vast ability to serve the needs of the world. [324]

When such yogins pass away, there appear the external signs of enlightenment, such as their being enveloped in two kinds of light, the sun and moon being inserted into the mouth of Rāhula, the earth quaking in six ways, and the roaring of five kinds of sounds. Inner signs include the emergence of bone relics, granular relics, and the two kinds of [peaceful and wrathful] kāyas. When all the signs of buddhahood occur, one has manifestly achieved perfect enlightenment. The *Blazing Bone Relics* states:

For a person of superior mental faculties,
in this delusive appearance,
the elements dissolve away, right where they are.
In the fruition of the ultimate nature of reality,
the defiled aggregates vanish,
and one achieves the fruition of one's own enlightenment.
The external signs
of an individual achieving nirvāṇa
are the emergence of [peaceful and wrathful] kāyas and bone relics,
lights and sounds,
and the quaking of the earth.

The *Mirror of the Heart of Vajrasattva* states:

One who achieves perfect buddhahood
becomes enlightened without leaving any aggregates behind.
With the manifest achievement of perfect buddhahood,
lights, sounds, [peaceful and wrathful] kāyas, bone relics,
earthquakes, and so on occur.

Then, key distinctions [325] are to be made between (a) the mind and pristine awareness, (b) mentation and wisdom, (c) conditioned consciousness and primordial consciousness, and (d) the substrate and dharmakāya.

a. The Distinction between the Mind and Pristine Awareness

"Son of the family, the defining characteristic of the mind is ignorance of the ground of being, with concepts subject to origination and cessation emerging as its creative displays. The defining characteristic of pristine awareness is the realization of the ground of being, with a great, atemporal state of relaxation as its creative display. The ground pristine awareness is knowing the mode of existence of the ground of being. The path pristine awareness is lucid, clear consciousness, free of contamination, by which you experience ultimate reality. All-pervasive pristine awareness, in which these two aspects are simultaneously conjoined, is the Great Perfection."

The mind is subdivided into the mind that clings to delusive appearances, the mind that seeks the path by way of affirmation and negation, and the mind that sees naked consciousness. The first refers to the minds of ordinary sentient beings who seek the path but do not perceive the entrance to the actual path. The second refers to the mind observing the mind, thoughts observing thoughts, consciousness observing thoughts, modifications by the intellect and mentation, rejecting [vices], nurturing [virtues], and merely arousing joys and sorrows. Because you are seeking the path, this is called *taking the mind as the path*. The third refers to the actualization of unimpeded conditioned consciousness, which is the ground of the mind. Because it does not realize the view, outer appearances are reduced to an ethically neutral state; and since appearances are grasped as things, reification is not averted. Inwardly, your own body is ethically neutral, so reified fixation upon the body is not averted. Since both are grasped as ethically neutral and autonomously existent, [326] the mind is not transcended; therefore, this too is called the *mind*.

In summary, the mind is of the nature of confusion, involving ignorance of the mode of existence of the ground of being and not knowing its characteristics, with various concepts emerging from it as its creative displays, together with the creation and cessation of mental processes and roving thoughts that grasp at objects and come under their domination. These are the defining characteristics of the mind. Its essential nature is ignorance. Its creative expressions are thoughts, the eight kinds of consciousness, and the primary mind and mental factors; and the appearance of its radiance and its displays are relative.

Pristine awareness realizes the essential nature of the ground of being—the absolute space of the purity and equality of the three kāyas. The creative power of pristine awareness is transformed into great primordial consciousness. These are the defining characteristics of pristine awareness. Such pristine awareness that is present in the ground dharmakāya, free of extremes, is the mode of existence of the great, vast expanse, free of conceptual elaboration. The ground pristine awareness is the total, authentic comprehension of the nature of being of the kāyas and great primordial consciousness. In dependence upon the pith instructions of a sublime guru, the characteristics and nature of being of the ultimate reality of the ground, which is empty, luminous, unconditioned, spontaneously actualized, lucid, clear, and devoid of contamination, are realized. This realization of the nature of the great clear light of awareness [327] is the path pristine awareness.

Once you have experienced the ground pristine awareness and have come to the culmination of the path, the all-pervasive awareness in which these creative displays are simultaneously conjoined and perfected is called the Great Perfection, and this is the fruitional pristine awareness. Its essential nature is the dharmakāya, its creative power is primordial consciousness, and its displays are ultimate.

b. The Distinction between Mentation and Wisdom

> **"The term *mentation* refers to the consciousness that experiences all appearances that emerge as apparitions of thoughts. The term *mental consciousness* refers to the unimpeded avenue for the six objects that emerge as appearances. The *ground wisdom* correctly knows the nature of saṃsāra and nirvāṇa to be great emptiness. The *path wisdom* is the identification of unadulterated, open, unimpeded consciousness. The simultaneous conjunction of these two is called *pervasive wisdom*."**

Mentation is the clear-light nature of the mind and the basis for the emergence of various apparitions of thoughts, and it is the unimpeded basis for experiencing all appearances of the outer physical world and its inner sentient inhabitants. The six objects unimpededly emerge as appearances that are seen, heard, smelled, tasted, and felt within its expanse, and all appearing objects are apprehended distinctly. This is called *mental consciousness*.

Ground wisdom comprehends all of saṃsāra and nirvāṇa in the expanse of the one great emptiness, and it correctly knows and is aware of how this is completely perfect. Path wisdom identifies the mode of existence of the dharmakāya, the sugatagarbha, and finally realizes unadulterated, open pristine awareness, uncontaminated by intellectual concepts, luminous and empty, [328] free of grasping, the unimpeded avenue of self-illuminating primordial consciousness. The great, omnipresent primordial consciousness that emerges with the simultaneous, uniformly pervasive union [of the ground wisdom and path wisdom] is called *pervasive wisdom*.

c. The Distinction between Conditioned Consciousness and Primordial Consciousness

> **"The unimpeded avenue for appearing objects that emerge as sensory appearances is called *conditioned consciousness*. Thoughts that reify these appearances as things are called *karmic energies*. With the conjunction of these subtle and coarse aspects of mental consciousness, saṃsāra is thoroughly established. The *primordial consciousness that knows reality as it is* correctly knows the nature of ultimate reality, the sugatagarbha. When the mode of existence of suchness, ultimate reality, is actualized, unimpeded, all-knowing, all-cognizing awareness is the *primordial consciousness that perceives the full range***

> ***of phenomena.* The uniform pervasiveness [of these two] is called the *originally pure primordial consciousness of equality*."**

Conditioned consciousness is the naturally present lucidity and luminosity that allows for the emergence of sensory appearances, which manifest as appearing objects in the expanse of mentation. As consciousness enters into the paths of the individual sensory channels, it encounters objects and nonconceptually apprehends them. The five kinds of sensory consciousness are the emergences of appearances of forms, sounds, smells, tastes, and tactile sensations, for they look outward by way of the individual senses. The apprehension of appearances as distinct things is mounted upon karmic energies, and their subsequent naming and the reification of their referents is *mental consciousness*. With the conjunction of the subtle and coarse aspects of former and subsequent consciousness, saṃsāra is thoroughly established.

The *primordial consciousness that knows reality as it is* correctly knows the nature of ultimate reality, the sugatagarbha, the natural radiance of the great, uniformly pervasive absolute space of the three kāyas; it knows the nature of all the kāyas, facets of primordial consciousness, path, and fruition; [329] and it perceives the mode of existence of the ground of being.

When the entire mode of existence and nature of being of suchness, ultimate reality, is experienced without being reduced to an assumption, such that pristine awareness is perfected in its own essential nature and the path is actualized, one knows the characteristics of all phenomena. The unimpeded avenue of clear light, by which all the phenomena of saṃsāra and nirvāṇa are realized as self-emergent displays of pristine awareness, is called the *primordial consciousness that perceives the full range of phenomena*. The essential nature of such primordial consciousness that knows [reality as it is] and perceives [the full range of phenomena] is originally pure; and due to the displays of saṃsāra and nirvāṇa as purity and equality in the absolute space of phenomena, free of conceptual elaboration, there is the *originally pure primordial consciousness of equality*.

d. The Distinction between the Substrate and Dharmakāya

> **"An ethically neutral state results from the influence of ignorance of the ground of being. Various karmic energies move within the space of the substrate, like various dreams appearing during sleep, and this is the basis and root of the whole of saṃsāra. Within the wide-open clarity of ultimate reality, free of the extremes of conceptual elaboration—the great purity and**

> **equality of saṃsāra and nirvāṇa—all appearing phenomena are the spacious dharmakāya, Samantabhadra."**

In the substrate, the inner glow of the ground absolute space, the great dharmakāya, does not manifest, and due to the ground being veiled by ignorance, the ground is reduced to an ethically neutral state. The substrate of descent is like being thoroughly immersed in a state in which the creative power of the inner glow is impeded, as when you are deep asleep. The temporarily luminous substrate [330] is the luminosity and nonconceptuality of the substrate consciousness. Just as various dream appearances emerge from the domain of this substrate, so do karmic energies move from the space of the substrate, serving as the basis for the emergence of all manner of appearances; and this is the essential nature, basis, and root of all of saṃsāra. The essential nature of the substrate is ignorance, appearances are its radiance, mental factors are its creative expressions, and all phenomena are included in its relative displays.

The dharmakāya knows the characteristics of the ground sugatagarbha, the nature of the three kāyas, and the five facets of primordial consciousness, and it realizes the empty, identityless nature of all phenomena in the great, omnipresent nature of all of saṃsāra and nirvāṇa. Recognizing all reified appearances as ultimate reality, free of conceptual elaboration, the great purity and equality of saṃsāra and nirvāṇa, it is uncontaminated by the mental defilements of reification. Never wavering from the nature of wide-open, spacious clarity, it is called the *dharmakāya, Samantabhadra.* Unchanged by any kind of fault or positive quality and immutable throughout the three times, it is called the *dharmakāya.*

To summarize the vital points of the ultimate and the relative: [331]

> **"Son of the family, all reflections of the moon and other things in water are displays of the water and are none other than water. All unmoving and moving things in the physical world and its sentient inhabitants are displays of space and are none other than space. All of saṃsāra and nirvāṇa consists of displays of the one ultimate reality and is none other than ultimate reality.**
>
> **"Thus, when the great depth and luminosity of the ground dharmakāya is actualized, its essential nature is the dharmakāya, the purity and equality of saṃsāra and nirvāṇa; its manifest nature is the saṃbhogakāya, replete with the facets of primordial consciousness and sublime qualities; and the nirmāṇakāya is self-illuminating compassion, free of obscuring veils. Its displays are called *ultimate.***

> **"Ignorance of the essential nature of the originally pure ground of being is the substrate. Appearances arise from its radiance and displays of mental factors arise as its creative expressions, and they are called *relative*."**

Son of the family, all appearances of planets, stars, and other reflections in the lucid clarity of water are displays of the water and are none other than water. All appearances of the physical world and its sentient inhabitants, however vast and numerous they may be, are displays of space and are none other than space. Likewise, all phenomena within saṃsāra and nirvāṇa, however vast and numerous they may be, are displays of the ultimate nature of the mind, the one sugatagarbha, and are none other than that. In the ground of being they are of one taste, and they are none other than the ultimate nature of the ground.

Thus, when the great depth and luminosity of the ground dharmakāya is actualized, its essential nature is the dharmakāya, the purity and equality of saṃsāra and nirvāṇa; its manifest nature is the saṃbhogakāya, replete with the facets of primordial consciousness that knows reality as it is and perceives the full range of phenomena; and the nirmāṇakāya is self-illuminating compassion, free of obscuring veils. This abides as the two avenues of the luminous, unimpeded nature of the ground, manifesting in six ways. The dharmakāya is its essential nature, wisdom is its radiance, the facets of primordial consciousness are its creative expressions, and its displays are called *ultimate*.

The substrate is the ethically neutral state [332] of ignorance of the essential nature and character of the originally pure ground of being. Ignorance is its essential nature, appearances are its radiance, mental factors are its creative expressions, and its displays are said to be *relative*.

As for the manner in which saṃsāra and nirvāṇa are finally encompassed by great ultimate reality:

> **"Having recognized in this way the nature of all displays, encompassments, and uniform pervasiveness, you simply rest in ultimate reality and come to certainty in the natural abiding of great, intellect-transcending, spacious, vacuous, ineffable ultimate reality. Until great, omniscient primordial consciousness is attained, practice with intense, unflagging enthusiasm. Adhere to this supreme vital point!"**
>
> **With these words, he expanded into the absolute space of ultimate reality.**

Regarding encompassments, all reflections of the planets and stars in water are encompassed by the water. All these inanimate things and animate beings are encompassed by space. All appearances of saṃsāra and nirvāṇa, however vast and numerous, are encompassed by the one ultimate reality of the ground of being. The *Perfection of the Lion's Creative Power* states:

> In the vast expanse of Samantabhadrī's bhaga,
> the five elements of the world of appearances of saṃsāra and
> nirvāṇa are perfected.

The *All-Creating Sovereign* states:

> Thus, there is nothing in the entire appearing world
> of all of saṃsāra and nirvāṇa that does not dwell in space;
> likewise, all buddhas, sentient beings, physical worlds, and
> inhabitants
> are encompassed by the great, vast expanse of bodhicitta.

Regarding displays, just as reflections of the planets and stars are displays of the ocean, and the physical world and its sentient inhabitants are displays of space, so are saṃsāra and nirvāṇa displays of ultimate reality.

Regarding uniform pervasiveness, just as the physical world and its sentient inhabitants are pervaded by space and reflections of the planets and stars are pervaded by the ocean, so are saṃsāra and nirvāṇa pervaded and permeated by the ground of being. [333] Having correctly recognized their nature as the mode of existence and nature of being of the ground, pervaded by ultimate reality, you simply rest in the nature of ultimate reality, without modifying anything. Utterly resting in that state is the great settling in the essential nature. This is the great transcendence of the intellect, for it is free of the intellect's grasping and striving. This is the great spaciousness, for it is the great, unmodified release into your own nature. In summary, there is nothing to be apprehended such that you can say, "It's like this." You must come to certainty in the nature of great, vacuous, ineffable ultimate reality, devoid of the ways of signs and words. As the *Treasury of the Mode of Existence* states:

> In the great expanse that is nameless and free of conceptual
> elaboration,
> come to certainty concerning phenomena of the world of
> appearances of saṃsāra and nirvāṇa.

Come to certainty regarding all phenomena of saṃsāra and nirvāṇa that arise from the nature of pristine awareness, primordially free of conceptual elaboration. As the *Great Reverberation of Sound Root Tantra* states, "The place of liberation is the very beginning." Therefore, until great, omniscient primordial consciousness is attained, practice with intense, unflagging enthusiasm. Take a rocky cave as your cap, the primordial consciousness of pristine awareness as your companion, and nettles and leaves as your food. [334] Entrust your innermost heart to the Dharma. Entrust your innermost Dharma to poverty. Entrust your innermost poverty to death. Entrust your death to an empty cave. Adhere to single-pointed practice as the supreme vital point!

With these words, he expanded into the absolute space of ultimate reality.

C. The Virtuous Conclusion

This text was written in response to heartfelt requests by Pema Lungtok Gyatso and Khyenrap Gyatso, two tulkus who have been connected to me over many lifetimes by their karma and prayers. I, Traktung Düdjom Dorjé Trolö Tsal, codified this from the treasury of the vast expanse of apparitional displays. The ḍākinīs prophesied that sixty-eight sublime individuals would serve as custodians of this Dharma. By the command of the great Orgyen, this was the first occasion on which auspicious circumstances came about [for these teachings to be written down]. My own sublime son, the outstanding scholar Sönam Tenzin (Dodrup Rinpoché), carefully edited the manuscript.

For this Dharma, there is virtue at the beginning due to the power of the teachings, virtue in between due to swift blessings, and virtue at the end due to auspiciousness. Living beings, including the gods, honor and revere these teachings with the words "Well done!" Wherever and whenever this Dharma spreads, may there be auspiciousness: *maṅgalam*!

Among the limitless, profound, secret, essential teachings,
the foremost of them all are the pith instructions on the Great Perfection.
This uncommon path to achieving enlightenment in one life,
this profound entrance to the profound, essential meaning,
the way of teaching of the oral traditions of vidyādhara gurus,
is synthesized in this essential ambrosia of secret teachings

of the protector, the incomparable, great treasure of the master
guru. [335]
May they beautifully arise in the glorious lotus of my mind!
With the reverent, sublime intention of a healer for the
teachings and the world,
I have synthesized the vital essence of the authoritative words of
advice of the oral lineage
into essential points for practice, and have written them down
with clarity.
If fortunate ones embrace this as their crown jewel,
they will be liberated in this life, without needing to strive for
eons.
May those fortunate beings instantly achieve perfect
enlightenment
by the power of this profound path!
May the omniscient sovereign Sang Ngak Lingpa [Drimé Özer]
fully preserve the teachings of the mind of Samantabhadra,
may the all-illuminating light totally dispel the darkness of
delusion of living beings,
may everyone be led to the lotus light,
may we be among his initial circle of disciples,
and may the awareness of the teacher and disciples become
indivisible!
May the teachings of the jinas spread in all ten directions,
may those who uphold the jinas' teachings enjoy long lives,
and may the essential Dharma of the tradition of the Lord of
Jinas, Padmasambhava,
spread and flourish in all the realms of the jinas!

As difficult as it is to utter the name of our sublime guide and teacher, out of need I beseech the omniscient lord, [336] the great and precious treasure Pema Ledrel Tsal [Drimé Özer], to heed me with his great compassion. Out of concern that the precious teachings of these myriad pith instructions, which are like refined ambrosia, might be forgotten, without citing elaborations on the path, such as sacred texts or reasonings, I have accurately written this down in accordance with the oral transmission, without mental fabrications. With the intention to benefit both myself and others, I, who bear just a vestige of being a consort, the lowliest of all disciples, Dechen Dewé Dorjé, or Kunzang Dekyong Wangmo, have written this down in an easily understandable way, a text that is praised by a prophecy of the great treasure himself. The erudite Dharma heir Tsultrim Dorjé, or Yongdrup Rikpé Dorjé, provided wonderful assistance in this composition. May this spread and flourish in all directions and at all times!

Sarva maṅgalam!

These notes were previously edited by Kyapjé Rinpoché [Drimé Özer] himself, and though he said a commentary should be written, many circumstances of time and place occurred, including the passing of Kyapjé Rinpoché himself, and the work was set aside. Then Akyé Wön Jikmé Tsultrim and my disciples suggested that the commentary could be clarified somewhat to make it easier to teach. [337] Due to this meaningful suggestion, I made additions to the text, drawing from his oral teachings that had never been received before, and somewhat clarified the text in that way.

May the Great Perfection of the Early Translation School of Padmasambhava,
the definitive meaning of the essential tradition of Düdjom Lingpa,
this profound treasure, be preserved without degeneration
until the end of saṃsāra, through both teaching and practice!

Virtue! Virtue! Virtue! *Sarva maṅgalam*!

Outline of *Garland for the Delight of the Fortunate*

Bibliography

Source Texts

Düdjom Lingpa. *Buddhahood Without Meditation: Advice for Revealing Your Own Face as the Nature of Reality, the Great Perfection. Rang bzhin rdzogs pa chen po'i rang zhal mngon du byed pa'i gdams pa ma bsgom sangs rgyas*. In vol. 16 of *Collected Works of the Emanated Great Treasures, the Secret, Profound Treasures of Düdjom Lingpa*. Thimphu, Bhutan: Lama Kuenzang Wangdue, 2004.

Sera Khandro. *The Fine Path to Liberation: An Explanation of the Stages of the Preliminary Practices for Manuals Such as "Buddhahood Without Meditation." Snang sbyang sogs khrid yig rnams kyi sngon 'gro bshad bya'i yan lag bshad pa rnam drol lam bzang*. In vol. 21 of *Collected Works of the Emanated Great Treasures, the Secret, Profound Treasures of Düdjom Lingpa*. Thimphu, Bhutan: Lama Kuenzang Wangdue, 2004.

———. *Garland for the Delight of the Fortunate: A Supremely Clear Elucidation of Words and Their Meaning, an Explication of the Oral Transmission of the Glorious Guru, as Notes on the Nature of Reality, the Great Perfection, "Buddhahood Without Meditation." Rang bzhin rdzogs pa chen po ma bsgom sangs rgyas kyi zin bris dpal ldan bla ma'i zhal rgyun nag 'gros su bkod pa tshig don rab gsal skal ldan dgyes pa'i mgul rgyan*. In vol. 21 of *Collected Works of the Emanated Great Treasures, the Secret, Profound Treasures of Düdjom Lingpa*. Thimphu, Bhutan: Lama Kuenzang Wangdue, 2004.

Citations

Dudjom Lingpa. *Buddhahood Without Meditation: A Visionary Account Known as Refining One's Perception (Nang-jang)*. Translated by Richard Barron and Susanne Fairclough. Junction City, CA: Padma Publishing, 2006.

———. *The Vajra Essence: From the Matrix of Pure Appearances and Primordial Consciousness, a Tantra on the Self-Originating Nature of Existence*. Translated by B. Alan Wallace. Alameda, CA: Mirror of Wisdom, 2004.

Dudjom Lingpa, Traktung. *A Clear Mirror: The Visionary Autobiography of a*

Tibetan Master. Translated by Chönyi Drolma. Hong Kong: Rangjung Yeshe Publications, 2011.

Dudjom Rinpoche and Dudjom Lingpa. *Sublime Dharma: A Compilation of Two Texts on the Great Perfection*. Translated by Chandra Easton and B. Alan Wallace. Ashland, OR: Vimala Publishing, 2012.

Jacoby, Sarah Hieatt. "Consorts and Revelations in Eastern Tibet: The Auto/Biographical Writings of the Treasure Revealer Sera Khandro (1892–1940)." PhD dissertation, Department of Religious Studies, University of Virginia, January 2007.

———. "The Excellent Path of Devotion: An Annotated Translation of Sera Khandro's Short Autobiography." In *Himalayan Passages: Tibetan and Newar Studies in Honor of Hubert Decleer*. Edited by Benjamin Bogin and Andrew Quintman, 163–202. Boston: Wisdom Publications, 2014.

Lama Chönam and Sangye Khandro, trans. *The Sole Essence of Clear Light: Tröma Tögal Practice, The Terma Revelations of Heruka Dudjom Lingpa and Commentary by One of His Foremost Disciples, Tülku Drimed Ödzer*. Boulder: Kama Terma Publications, 2011.

Longchen Rabjam. *The Precious Treasury of the Way of Abiding (Gnas lugs mdzod)*. Translated by Richard Barron. Junction City, CA: Padma Publishing, 1998.

Padmasambhava. *Natural Liberation: Padmasambhava's Teachings on the Six Bardos*. Commentary by Gyatrul Rinpoche. Translated by B. Alan Wallace. Boston: Wisdom Publications, 1998.

Śāntideva. *A Guide to the Bodhisattva Way of Life*. Translated by Vesna A. Wallace and B. Alan Wallace. Ithaca, NY: Snow Lion Publications, 1997.

Sera Khandro. *Love and Liberation: Autobiographical Writings of the Tibetan Buddhist Visionary*. Translated by Sarah H. Jacoby. New York: Columbia University Press, 2104.

———. *Refining Our Perception of Reality: Sera Khandro's Commentary on Dudjom Lingpa's Account of His Visionary Journey*. Translated by Ngawang Zangpo. Boston: Snow Lion Publications, 2013.

Index

About the Translator

B. Alan Wallace is president of the Santa Barbara Institute for Consciousness Studies. He trained for many years as a monk in Buddhist monasteries in India and Switzerland. He has taught Buddhist theory and practice in Europe and America since 1976 and has served as interpreter for numerous Tibetan scholars and contemplatives, including H. H. the Dalai Lama. After graduating *summa cum laude* from Amherst College, where he studied physics and the philosophy of science, he earned his MA and PhD in religious studies at Stanford University. He has edited, translated, authored, and contributed to more than forty books on Tibetan Buddhism, medicine, language, and culture, and the interface between science and religion.

Also Available by B. Alan Wallace from Wisdom Publications

Heart of the Great Perfection
Dudjom Lingpa's Visions of the Great Perfection, Vol. 1
Translated by B. Alan Wallace
Foreword by Sogyal Rinpoche

Düdjom Lingpa's visionary teachings on the Great Perfection are revealed in B. Alan Wallace's landmark translation. This volume contains four works explaining the view and practice of the Great Perfection, including *The Sharp Vajra of Conscious Awareness Tantra* and more.

Stilling the Mind
Shamatha Teachings from Dudjom Lingpa's Vajra Essence

"A much-needed, very-welcome book."—Jetsün Khandro Rinpoche

The Attention Revolution
Unlocking the Power of the Focused Mind
Foreword by Daniel Goleman

"Indispensable for anyone wanting to understand the mind. A superb, clear set of exercises that will benefit everyone."—Paul Ekman, Professor Emeritus at University of California–San Francisco

Tibetan Buddhism from the Ground Up
A Practical Approach for Modern Life

"One of the most readable, accessible, and comprehensive introductions to Tibetan Buddhism."—*Mandala*

Also Available from Wisdom Publications

The Nyingma School of Tibetan Buddhism
Its Fundamentals and History
Dudjom Rinpoche
Translated and edited by Gyurme Dorje and Matthew Kapstein

"A landmark in the history of English-language studies of Tibetan Buddhism."—*History of Religions*

Approaching the Great Perfection
Simultaneous and Gradual Methods of Dzogchen Practice in the Longchen Nyingtig
Sam van Schaik

"An important work for its breadth and attention to detail. Van Schaik's lucid explanation of the issues and technical vocabulary in the 'seminal heart', or *nyingtig*, teachings provide the reader with an essential framework for tackling the extensive primary source material found in this work."—*Buddhadharma*

Mipham's Beacon of Certainty
Illuminating the View of Dzogchen, the Great Perfection
John W. Pettit
Foreword by His Holiness Penor Rinpoche

"A riveting and wonderful work, which gives the reader a real education in some of the most compelling issues of Buddhism, especially their impact on Dzogchen."—Anne Klein, Rice University